NATURALISTIC INQUIRY

D0169071

If you don't like my book, write your own. If you don't think you can write a novel, that ought to tell you something. If you think you can, do. No excuses. If you still don't like my novel, find a book you do like. Life is too short to be miserable. If you do like my novels, I commend your good taste.

—*Rita Mae Brown,* Southern Discomfort

NATURALISTIC INQUIRY

Yvonna S. Lincoln
Egon G. Guba

SAGE PUBLICATIONS
Beverly Hills   London   New Delhi

For information address:

SAGE Publications, Inc.
275 South Beverly Drive
Beverly Hills, California 90212

SAGE Publications India Pvt. Ltd.
M-32 Market
Greater Kailash I
New Delhi 110 048 India

SAGE Publications Ltd
28 Banner Street
London EC1Y 8QE
England

Printed in the United States of America

Library of Congress Cataloging in Publication Data

Lincoln, Yvonna S.
  Naturalistic inquiry

  Bibliography: p.
  Includes index
  1. Naturalism.   I. Guba, Egon G.   II. Title.
B828.2.L56   1984   146   84-26295
ISBN 0-8039-2431-3

FIRST PRINTING

Contents

Preface

Every historical age has exhibited some characteristic way of answering the eternal questions of what there is that can be known and how one can go about knowing it. Sometimes the answer has been mystical, as in the case of the great Oriental religions. Sometimes it has been magical; the prominent anthropologist Sir James Frazier pointed out long ago the close relationship between primitive magic and modern science, in that both attempt to control the universe for the benefit of humankind. Sometimes the answer has been authoritative or revelatory, as in the case of appeals to Aristotelian pronouncements or biblical injunctions.

Today we live in the age of science. The eternal questions are best answered, it is asserted, by putting queries directly to Nature and letting Nature itself answer. This empirical approach is undoubtedly the most powerful dynamic stimulating the emergence of what we are now pleased to call the Age of Enlightenment. That this answer is right can hardly be doubted. The spectacular successes of modern physics, modern medicine, and modern space technology, but also of modern nuclear weaponry, all trace their beginnings to this shift from prescientific to scientific thinking.

But the ancient questions are not so easily stilled. Having thought them settled, we find that they reappear in new guises, not only in the very domain in which they have been so well answered, the so-called hard sciences, but also and most particularly in the "softer" sciences, that is, the human or social sciences. Cracks have begun to appear in science's magnificent edifice as new "facts" are uncovered with which the old paradigm cannot deal or explain. Normal science in the Kuhnian sense is becoming more and more difficult to sustain. Serious challenges are being mounted from the perspective of alternative paradigms that suggest new and different answers.

This book is about such a challenge. It describes an alternative paradigm that, largely through historical accident, is now traveling under the name "naturalistic." It has other aliases as well, for example: the postpositivistic, ethnographic, phenomenological, subjective, case study, qualitative, hermeneutic, humanistic. It has so many names because the persons who profess to practice it tend to take different views of what it implies, in the same way that persons who profess to be Christians may nevertheless prefer to be known as Catholic, Orthodox, Lutheran, Episcopalian, Presbyterian, Adventist, Fundamentalist, Baptist, and so on. They hold to these more specific labels in an attempt to differentiate their particular doctrines from those of others (who, needless to say, they believe have turned away from the true way). This book also takes a sectarian view; it treats "naturalism" in a particular way, and insists on certain interpretations and perspectives. But it is precisely because the matter is so involved that it is not possible to provide a simple definition of what naturalism is. Thus nowhere in the book will the reader encounter a sentence of the form, "Naturalism is defined as . . . ." Instead, a proper impression of what we mean by naturalism can be gleaned only as an overall perspective.

In an early work that attempted to apply the naturalistic perspective to the area of evaluation, one of us (Guba, 1978) cited nine different definitions of naturalism. Many of these were taken from the seminal collection of papers edited by Edwin P. Willems and Harold L. Raush and published under the title, *Naturalistic Viewpoints in Psychological Research* (1969); they well illustrated the diversity of constructions that were entertained by various proponents. We were then and remain now most influenced by the definition proposed by Willems himself:

> In behavioral research, naturalness or naturalism . . . is a function of *what the investigator does,* . . . the set of activities an investigator actually engages in while conducting his research falls somewhere in a two-dimensional descriptive space. The first dimension, which is most frequently thought of in differentiating research activities, describes the degree of the investigator's influence upon, or manipulation of, the antecedent conditions of the behavior studied, on the assumption that the degree of such influence or manipulation may vary from high to low, or from much to none. The second dimension, which is less commonly considered than the first, describes *the degree to which units are imposed by the investigator upon the behavior studied.* (Willems & Raush, 1969, p. 46)

What is salient to us is that, first, no manipulation on the part of the inquirer is implied, and, second, the inquirer imposes no a priori units on the outcome. Naturalistic investigation is what the naturalistic investigator does, and these two tenets are the prime directives.

But *why* these two directives should loom so important is very difficult to explain or to understand. It is not just a matter of the investigator's predilection, exercising his or her right of free choice, as it were. The reasons are embedded in the very assumptions on which the paradigm rests. And that is a most difficult matter to grasp. We are all so imbued with the tenets of science that we take its assumptions utterly for granted, so much so that we almost cannot comprehend the possibility that there might be other ways of thinking. And when other ways are suggested, we are inclined to shut our ears, feeling that merely to listen to them is, quite literally, a heresy.

This book proposes such a heresy. We do not argue that the ideas it contains are original with us, or that we have expressed them better than others before us. We have, however, tried to cast them into a form that might be palatable and appear reasonable to an audience of readers who have not entertained them before and who might, *quite properly,* approach them with an attitude of extreme skepticism. And we have added enough practical material so that the reader who might be persuaded of them on theoretical grounds might also be able to apply them, however tentatively. This is a book aimed at helping the reader both to understand and to do naturalistic inquiry.

However, because the book is intended as an introduction, it skirts many of the more sophisticated questions that might be asked of a new paradigm. We do not trace, by and large, the roots of the ideas that are proposed. We make no real effort to ground the writing in the philosophical and epistemological literature that is so relevant. We do not trace out the implications of the ideas for society at large. These are matters for other volumes.

This book should not be viewed as a completed product. It is more profitably seen as a snapshot in time of a set of emergent ideas. A historical comparison of our earlier papers and book will reveal that our thinking has undergone many changes, some of them dramatic. Those changes might be interpreted as demonstrating that we have rushed into print too quickly in the past—and that perhaps we have done so again—or that our ideas have been so poorly conceptualized that we must continuously revise them to avoid further embarrassment. While such allegations may be partially true, we prefer to think that these changes are the inevitable accompaniment of a burgeoning field in which new questions are being raised almost more quickly than the old can be (even partially) answered.

By way of illustration of this continuous press for change, let us cite just one example that currently is engaging our attention. We have for some time argued that inquiry is not and cannot be value free, but the full implications of that assertion have just begun to dawn on us. *If* it is true (as we surely believe) that inquiry is inevitably value determined, then any given inquiry will necessarily serve *some* value agenda. (The import of that statement is most clearly seen in the field of evaluation, which, by definition, is intended to result in some value judgment.) That of course is not a new idea, however strange it may sound to persons accustomed to thinking of science as a means of putting questions directly to Nature. Indeed, writers of two traditions have dealt with it for some time: feminists and critical theorists. A recent bibliography by Reinharz, Bombyk, and Wright (1983) under the title "Methodological Issues in Feminist Research" lists literally hundreds of books and papers bearing on this issue. Critiques from the perspective of critical theory pervade the literature as well; what has come to be known as *critical ethnography* is one offshoot. At the moment our interest is in exploring the relationships of these two traditions to an understanding of the role of values in inquiry (indeed, one of us, Lincoln, spent the fall of 1984 in the United Kingdom in order to explore this issue with British and Scottish critical theorists, who have been particularly incisive in their assessment of traditional research). While we deal with the problem of value impingements on inquiry in some detail in this book, it seems clear that our ideas are very much in evolution; it will not be surprising to *us* to find ourselves saying different (and, we hope, more sophisticated) things a year or two hence.

The book itself consists of thirteen chapters. The first seven are devoted to laying out the arguments against the conventional inquiry paradigm, which we will most often label the "positivistic," proposing an alternative paradigm, the "naturalistic," and arguing for its adoption. Chapter 1 provides an overview of the rise of positivism, the difficulties it is currently encountering, and the nature of the five axioms of the competing naturalistic paradigm, albeit it in meager detail. Chapter 2 argues the alternative paradigm's legitimacy; it answers the following questions: Granting the fact that the positivist paradigm is in trouble, why should we accept *this* paradigm as its replacement? How do we know it deserves consideration as a legitimate competitor? We rely heavily on the work of Schwartz and Ogilvy of SRI International, who have come to the conclusion that a paradigm revolution is under way in many fields that we believe parallels the inquiry paradigm revolution we are espousing. Chapters 3 through 7 deal with the five basic axioms in turn, relating to the (assumed) nature of reality, the interaction between inquirer and object of inquiry (or, in the case of human inquiry, inquirer and respondents), the possibility of generalization, the nature of explanation (the viability of the concept of causality), and the role of values. A great deal of evidence is cited from the so-called hard sciences to illustrate the fact that the paradigm shift is not simply something that characterizes human research but something that pervades inquiry of all sorts.

Chapter 8 represents a swing away from the purely theoretical and toward the practice of naturalistic inquiry. Is it the case that loyalty to one or another paradigm has implications for the methodology that an investigator employs? To put it another way, do paradigms imply methodologies? We argue in Chapter 8 that they do, and we present what we believe is a synergistic set of procedures and methods that carry out the intent of naturalistic axioms. We stress the fact that other techniques and methods are not excluded (for example, we would be the last to argue that quantitative methods should not be used), but that certain methods are more congenial to each paradigm (just as quantitative methods are the methods of choice for most positivists).

Chapters 9 through 13 are the "doing" chapters. Chapter 9 takes up the question of what it can mean to "design" a naturalistic study, in view of our insistence that the design cannot be given a priori but must emerge as the study proceeds. Is there anything that an investigator can do "up front," especially since that may be necessary to attract funding? Chapter 10 deals with implementation questions: what to do in the field (and naturalistic inquiries *always* take place in the field, that is, in natural rather than contrived settings). Chapter 11 raises the thorny issue of trustworthiness: Why should the reader of an inquiry report believe what is said there? Criteria parallel to the conventional (but inapplicable) criteria of internal validity, external validity, reliability, and objectivity are proposed, and selected means of meeting them are described. Chapter 12 discusses the means by which data are processed (analyzed), stressing the fact that in naturalistic inquiry, data processing is a continuously ongoing activity, making possible the meaningful emergence or unfolding of the design and the successive focusing of the study. Chapter 13 deals with three activities that tend to occur near the end of a naturalistic study: writing a case report (the case study is, it is argued, the reporting mode of choice for the naturalist); carrying out member checking—a trustworthiness technique to improve credibility; and auditing, another trustworthiness technique that parallels conventional checks on reliability and objectivity.

We could not close without mentioning the names of those persons whose input and collaboration have been most prized by us. Prominent in this listing must be Shulamit Reinharz, who read the full manuscript and raised many penetrating questions about it; Robert Heinich, who, as editor of *Educational Communication and Technology Journal,* stimulated the writing of two papers that forced us to come to terms with our ideas; Garrel Pottinger and Douglas Lackey, who read the chapter on causality from their perspective as philosophers of science and helped us to see a variety of problems in our formulations; Peter Schwartz and James Ogilvy, whose writing stimulated us to the realization that the naturalistic paradigm had much broader limits than we had at first imagined, and who helpfully supplied additional material for our use; Thomas Skrtic, who provided an opportunity to apply many of these ideas in a two-year study, conducted under the auspices of the University of Kansas, of the provision of services to handicapped youngsters in rural areas, and who helped us see the utility of that experience; and Dennis Palumbo, who as (then) director of the Center for Public Affairs at the University of Kansas provided both of us (at different times) the opportunity to engage in reflective thought. We are also indebted to those friends and colleagues who on occasion challenged us most directly and forced us to rethink many of our positions, notably Thomas Cook, Ernest House, Michael Quinn Patton, Robert Stake, and Daniel Stufflebeam. None of these persons can be held responsible for the ideas we express, but all of them had a hand in shaping those ideas, even when we disagree.

We also express our thanks to Mary King, who typed several of the chapters, and to Judith Meloy, who did a great deal of proofing, at the Indiana University end of the operation. We are particularly grateful to Carlene Cobb and her patient, tolerant, and sweet-tempered staff at the University of Kansas School of Education word-processing center. They have seen us through endless drafts and revisions, usually in the face of heavy work demands from other quarters. They deserve medals, if not sainthood.

Finally, we must acknowledge the indirect and anticipatory stimulation we received from the many young minds that we hope to influence. In the earlier monograph relating naturalistic inquiry to evaluation, the following quotation from Charles Darwin appeared:

> Although I am fully convinced of the truth of the views given in this volume, . . . I by no means expect to convince experienced naturalists whose minds are stocked with a multitude of facts all viewed, during a long course of years, from a point of view directly opposite to mine. . . . But I look with confidence to the future, to young and rising naturalists, who will be able to view both sides of the question with impartiality.

To those young minds that we hope to reach out and touch, we dedicate this book.

—*Yvonna S. Lincoln*
Lawrence, Kansas

—*Egon G. Guba*
Bloomington, Indiana

Acknowledgments

We gratefully acknowledge permission to quote from the following sources:

Cook and Campbell, *Quasi-Experimentation: Design and Analysis Issues for Field Settings.* Copyright 1979, Houghton Mifflin Company. Used with permission.

Webb/Campbell/Schwartz/Sechrest, *Unobtrusive Measures: Nonreactive Research in the Social Sciences.* Copyright 1966, Houghton Mifflin Company. Used with permission.

Reason/Rowan, Editors, *Human Inquiry: A Sourcebook of New Paradigm Research.* Copyright 1981, John Wiley and Sons, Ltd. Reprinted with permission of John Wiley and Sons.

Bok, *Lying: Moral Choice in Public and Private Life.* Copyright 1978, and used with permission of Pantheon Books, a Division of Random House, Inc.

Hesse, *Revolutions and Reconstructions in the Philosophy of Science.* Copyright 1980, Indiana University Press. Used with permission.

Kerlinger, *Foundations of Behavioral Research.* Copyright 1973, Holt, Rinehart and Winston, Publishers. Used with permission.

Tranel, "A lesson from the physicists," *Personnel and Guidance Journal, 59,* 1981; and Smith, "Naturalistic research," same issue and volume. Copyright AACD. Reprinted with permission. No further reproduction authorized without permission of AACD.

Carley, *Rational Techniques in Policy Analysis.* Copyright 1980, Heinemann Educational Books, London. Used with permission.

1

Postpositivism and the Naturalist Paradigm

And as we think, so do we act.

(Schwartz and Ogilvy, 1979)

PARADIGMS AND PARADIGM ERAS

The history of humankind is replete with instances of attempts to understand the world. Our curiosity has been directed at the same fundamental questions throughout time; our progress as inquirers can be charted by noting the various efforts made to deal with those questions. What is the world? How can we come to know it? How can we control it for our purposes? What is, after all, the *truth* about these matters?

The concept of truth is an elusive one. Julienne Ford, in her delightfully whimsical book, *Paradigms and Fairy Tales* (1975), asserts that the term *truth* may have four different meanings, which she symbolizes as $Truth_1$, $Truth_2$, $Truth_3$, and $Truth_4$. $Truth_4$ is the familiar *empirical* truth of the scientist; a claim in the form of hypothesis or predicate (an affirmation or denial of something) is T_4 if it is consistent with "nature" (or, in Ford's own language, "preserves the appearances."[1] $Truth_3$ is *logical* truth; a claim (hypothesis or predicate) is T_3 if it is logically or mathematically consistent with some other claim known to be true (in the T_3 sense) or ultimately with some basic belief taken to be T_1 (to which we shall return in a moment). $Truth_2$ is *ethical* truth; a claim is T_2 if the person who asserts it is acting in conformity with moral or professional standards of conduct.[2]

$Truth_1$, with which we are most concerned here, may be called *metaphysical* truth. Unlike the case of a claim's being T_2, T_3, or T_4, a claim that is said to be T_1 cannot be tested for truthfulness against some external norm such as correspondence with nature, logical deducibility, or professional standards of conduct. Metaphysical beliefs must be accepted at face value; as Aristotle knew (Reese, 1980, p. 70) and Ford affirms, basic beliefs can never be proven T_4—in conformity with nature—or False$_1$. They represent the ultimate benchmarks against which *everything else* is tested, for if there were something more fundamental against which a test might be made, then that more fundamental entity would become *the* basic belief whose truth (T$_1$) must be taken for granted.

Now certain *sets* of such basic or metaphysical beliefs are sometimes constituted into a *system of ideas* that "either give us some judgment about the nature of reality, or a reason why we must be content with knowing something less than the nature of reality, along with a method for taking hold of whatever can be known" (Reese, 1980, p. 352). We shall call such a systematic set of beliefs, together with their accompanying methods, a *paradigm*.[3]

Paradigms represent a distillation of what we *think* about the world (but cannot prove). Our actions in the world, including actions that we take as inquirers, cannot occur without reference to those paradigms: "As we think, so do we act." But, while paradigms are thus enabling, they are also constraining:

> A paradigm is a world view, a general perspective, a way of breaking down the complexity of the real world. As such, paradigms are deeply embedded in the socialization of adherents and practitioners: paradigms tell them what is important, legitimate, and reasonable. Paradigms are also normative, telling the practitioner what to do without the necessity of long existential or epistemological consideration. But it is this aspect of paradigms that constitutes both their strength and their weakness—their strength in that it makes action possible, their weakness in that the very reason for action is hidden in the unquestioned assumptions of the paradigm. (Patton, 1978, p. 203)

It is the authors' posture that inquiry, whether in the physical or social sciences, has passed through a number of "paradigm eras," periods in which certain sets of basic beliefs guided inquiry in quite different ways. We shall briefly describe these periods as prepositivist, positivist, and postpositivist, and show that each period had its own unique set of "basic beliefs" or metaphysical principles in which its adherents believed and upon which they acted. We shall take the position that the positivist posture, while discredited by vanguard thinkers in every known discipline, continues to this day to guide the efforts of practitioners of inquiry, particularly in the social or human sciences. Further, we shall argue that, since these methods are based on metaphysical principles that are dissonant with the principles guiding the vanguard development of substantive (discipline) thought, it is imperative that inquiry itself be shifted from a positivist to a postpositivist stance. *For, if a new paradigm of thought and belief is emerging, it is necessary to construct a parallel new paradigm of inquiry.*

SOME CAVEATS

In discussing the eras through which paradigms have passed, it will be easy to assume that there exists somewhere *the* paradigm that past efforts at paradigm formation have approximated more and more closely. If science could successfully converge onto that paradigm, then it could quickly tease out its consequences, test them in the empirical world, and come, finally, to "true" understanding. A study of the history of science might be very important if we are to achieve an understanding of those successive approximations; it might be asserted, as Barnes suggests, that "the subject matter of the historian of science can only be demarcated by recognizing what it is in the past that exhibits causal continuity with present science" (cited in Hesse, 1980, p. 47). But, as Hesse (1980, pp. 4-5) points out:

> The present is in this crude sense the standard of truth and rationality for the past, and gives the inductivist historian grounds for the reconstruction of past arguments according to an acceptably inductive structure, and for judging past theories as simply false and often ridiculous. *Such inductive history is of course, among its other defects, self-defeating, because if all theories are dangerous and likely to be superseded, so are the present theories in terms of which the inductivist judges the past.* (emphasis added)

We may draw from these remarks the following caveat: Since all theories and other leading ideas of scientific history have, so far, been shown to be false and unacceptable, so surely will any theories that we expound today. This insight induces a certain degree of humility in claims for the "ultimate truth" (T_1) of anything that is asserted here. This book should therefore be regarded not as an attempt to make ultimately true (and modern) pronouncements, but as an effort to mark our place along the path of understanding—a path that unfortunately is never ending. We are not setting forth a new orthodoxy; instead, we aim to make it a little more difficult to hold onto the old.

A second caveat is that theories, whether scientific or otherwise, are remarkably immune to change; hence one cannot expect an easy time of it when proposing something as radical as a paradigm revision. Theories are, to borrow a term from modern organization theory, "loosely coupled" (Weick, 1976.) There is, as Hesse (1980) suggests, a "many-to-one" relation between theoretical and practical facts; it is possible to fit many different idealizations (theoretical facts) to a single practical fact:

> Many conflicting networks may more or less fit the same facts, and which one is adopted must depend on criteria other than the facts: criteria involving simplicity, coherence with other parts of science, and so on. Quine, as is well known, has drawn this conclusion explicitly in the strong sense of claiming that any statement can be maintained true in the face of any evidence: "Any statement can be held true come what may, if we make drastic enough adjustments elsewhere in the system." (Hesse, 1980, p. 86)

Thus the loosely coupled nature of theories makes it possible for scientists to squirm mightily before giving up a theory (or a paradigm). Any conflicting fact can be accommodated by making adjustments elsewhere in the system.

Along the same lines, Wimsatt (1981, p. 134) has noted what he terms the "robustness" of prevailing theories, a robustness, he claims, that derives from the fact that portions of theory are "walled off from" (loosely coupled to) one another:

> The thing that is remarkable about scientific theories is that the inconsistencies are walled off and do not appear to affect the theory other than very locally . . . . When an inconsistency occurs, results which depend on one or more of the contradictory assumptions are infirmed. This infection is transitive; it passes to things that depend on these results, and to their logical descendants, like a string of dominos—until we reach something that has independent support. The independent support of an assumption sustains it, and the collapse propagates no further. If all deductive or inferential paths leading to a contradiction pass through robust results, the collapse is bounded within them, and the inconsistencies are walled off from the rest of the network. For each robust result, one of its modes of support is destroyed; but it has others, and therefore the collapse goes no further.

Thus the failure of a paradigm to be fully coherent, that is, entirely internally consistent,[4] can also be one of its chief defenses against challenge. As paradigms are assaulted by "facts" that do not fit, the facts can be walled off—a possibility only because the paradigm is loosely coupled. Further, even those elements of the paradigm that are most affected by the conflicting facts may be supported in independent ways—a fact that could not obtain if the paradigm were completely coherent. The result of this state of affairs is that it becomes possible for adherents of the paradigm to resist stoutly, even if at times irrationally, the efforts of others to replace it. Making it even a little more difficult to hold onto the old paradigm may itself turn out to be an enormously difficult task, not one to be taken on by the fainthearted!

THE PREPOSITIVIST ERA

Of the three "paradigm eras," the prepositivist is both the longest and the least interesting from a modern perspective; indeed, its lack of provocative acts and ideas is best illustrated by its very title— *pre*positivist. This era is simply a precursor to the more exciting period that followed. It ranges over a period of more than two millenia, roughly speaking, from the time of Aristotle (384-322 B.C.) to that of (but not including) David Hume (1711-1776). One might expect that "science" would have made enormous strides over such a long period, but it did not, largely because Aristotle (and many other prepositivists) took the stance of "passive observer" (Wolf, 1981). What there was in "physis," Aristotle argued, occurred "naturally." Attempts by humans to learn about nature were interventionist and unnatural, and so distorted what was learned. Wolf (1981, p. 22) comments:

> Aristotle believed in natural motion. Humans' interference produced discontinuous and unnatural movements. And, to Aristotle, such movements were not God's way. For example, Aristotle envisioned the idea of "force." The heavy cart being drawn along the road by the horse is an unnatural movement. That is why the horse is struggling so. That is why the motion is so jerky and uneven. The horse must exert a "force" to get the cart moving. The horse must continue to exert a "force" to keep the cart moving. As soon as the horse stops pulling, it stops exerting a "force" on the cart. Consequently, the cart comes to its natural place, which is at rest on the road.

Aristotle's mind was broad ranging enough to touch virtually every conceptual problem imaginable at his time. Not the least of these problem areas was that of logic. Aristotle contributed two principles, commonly known as the Law of Contradiction (which states that no proposition can be both true and false at the same time) and the Law of the Excluded Middle (which holds that every proposition must be either true or false), which, when applied to noninterventionist or passive observations, seemed sufficient to generate the entire gamut of scientific understandings that were needed (Mitroff and Kilmann, 1978). Wolf further observes:

> Within the world of the mind, these thoughts occurred thousands of years ago. Scientists were passive then. It would take a while before

they would attempt to reach out and touch, to try ideas and see if they worked. (p. 23)

When scientists did begin to reach out and touch, to try ideas and see if they worked, in short, when they became *active* observers, science passed into the positivist period. The movement was slow; Isaac Newton (1642-1727) is said to have commented that "if I have seen further, it is because I have stood on the shoulders of giants." But the number of giants was exceedingly small. Only a few workers had emerged who went beyond Aristotelian science, and it is useful to observe that they also came from essentially noninterventionist fields: three astronomers (Copernicus, 1473-1543; Galileo, 1564-1642; Kepler, 1571-1630) and a logician/mathematician (Descartes, 1596-1650). Further, their work did little to challenge the prevailing paradigm of inquiry, however much it may have exercised established religion. It did, however, pave the way for that challenge.

THE POSITIVIST ERA

Positivism may be defined as "a family of philosophies characterized by an extremely positive evaluation of science and scientific method" (Reese, 1980, p. 450). Indeed, its early adherents saw in this movement the potential for the reform of such diverse areas as ethics, religion, and politics, in addition to philosophy, to which field it finally became confined. As a philosophy, the movement began early in the nineteenth century, primarily in France and Germany; its most powerful advocates in the twentieth century were formed into a group known as the Vienna Circle of Logical Positivists, which included philosophers and scientists such as Gustav Bergman, Rudolf Carnap, Philipp Frank, Hans Hahn, Otto Neurath, and Moritz Schlick, the last having founded the group. Schlick held an endowed chair at the University of Vienna that had been established in the memory of Ernest Mach, an extreme advocate of operationalism,[5] whose ideas the group proposed to promulgate.

But positivism had its major impact not in reforming ethics, religion, and politics, or even philosophy, but scientific method. The concepts of positivism provided a new rationale for the doing of science that amounted to a literal paradigm revolution, although that revolution took place so slowly and was so imperfectly perceived by even the major actors caught up in it that its revolutionary character was never appreciated. If it is difficult for a fish to understand water because it has spent all of its life in it, so is it difficult for scientists—and prepositivist scientists were no exception—to understand what their basic axioms or assumptions might be and what impact those axioms and assumptions have upon everyday thinking and lifestyle.

Given this slow and little-understood change, it is not surprising that different scientists and philosophers would have somewhat different views of just what positivism implied, and on what ground it stood. That confusion continues today, as can be seen from a reading of some representative authors on the topic. For example, David Hamilton, in a paper prepared for an informal workshop at the University of Illinois in 1976, suggests that positivism began with the publication of John Stuart Mill's *A System of Logic* in 1843. Hamilton (1976, p. 2) comments on this work:

> Historically, *A System of Logic* was a powerful interpretation, formalization, and defense of the secular ideologies which had emerged alongside the political, economic, and social revolutions of the late eighteenth and early nineteenth centuries. Its twentieth century importance, however, is rather different. Mill's *Logic* offered a coherent set of principles of procedure for use in the social and natural sciences. Although subjected to considerable criticism . . . , Mill's original formulations have survived till the present day as the dominant methodological paradigm.

Hamilton summarizes Mill's assumptions as follows:

(1) The social and natural sciences have identical aims, namely, the discovery of general laws that serve for explanation and prediction.
(2) The social and natural sciences are methodologically identical.
(3) The social sciences are merely more complex than the natural sciences.
(4) Concepts can be defined by direct reference to empirical categories—"objects in the concrete."
(5) There is a uniformity of nature in time and space. Hamilton comments that this assumption, itself an induction, enabled Mill to overcome Hume's objections to logical inference and thereby invested induction with the same procedural certainty as syllogistic logic. We may note that such an argument has been found to be invalid by modern philosophers; see the discussion below about the problem of the underdetermination of theory.
(6) Laws of nature can be naturally (inductively) derived from data. Hamilton comments that Mill had little to say about theory because he held it to be isomorphic with "empirical uniformities."
(7) Large samples suppress idiosyncracies ("partial causes") and reveal "general causes" (the ultimate laws of nature).

A second example: Wolf (1981, p. 56) discusses positivism in the guise of Newtonian mechanics, which he says rested upon the following assumptions regarding the "physical and therefore mechanical world":

(1) Things move in a continuous manner. All motion, both in the large and in the small, exhibits continuity.
(2) Things move for reasons. These reasons were based upon earlier causes for motion. Therefore, all motion was determined and everything was predictable.
(3) All motion could be analyzed or broken down into its component parts. Each part played a role in the great machine called the universe, and the complexity of this machine could be understood as the simple movement of its various parts, even those parts beyond our preception.
(4) The observer observed, never disturbed. Even the errors of a clumsy observer could be accounted for by simply analyzing the observed movements of whatever he touched.

A third example: Schwartz and Ogilvy, whose work will occupy a considerable portion of our attention in Chapter 2, describe the Newtonian "world view" as holding that matter consists of very small particles that are assembled into larger and larger complexes. The essential ideas are captured by the metaphor of the billiard table.[6] The metaphor supports a deterministic physics—if we knew the masses, positions, and velocities of all the particles we could predict the future from the laws of physics. But Schwartz and Ogilvy (1979, p. 32) point out,

> Embedded within the mechanistic view of the world are three basic assumptions. The first is that there is a most fundamental level of reality (i.e., the basic building blocks) composed of the smallest particles and the complete set of forces that govern them. Once we find that fundamental level and the laws that govern it, the world laws that govern matter and energy on the very small scale must be very similar, and hopefully identical, to those that apply on the very large scale. The governing laws thus would be universal, so that we ought to be able to build a picture of planets moving about the sun out of an understanding of the particles of which matter is composed. Finally, there is the assumption that we, as observers, can be isolated from experiments and the world we are studying to produce an "objective" description.

A fourth example: Mary Hesse (1980, p. vii), a British epistemologist and historian of science, suggests that what she calls the "standard account'' of scientific explanation within an ''empirical philosophy'' depends upon a series of assumptions:

> The most important of these are the assumptions of *naive realism,* of a *universal scientific language,* and of the *correspondence theory of truth.*
>
> These three assumptions between them constitute a picture of science and the world somewhat as follows: there is an external world which can in principle be exhaustively described in scientific language. The scientist, as both observer and language-user, can capture the external facts of the world in propositions that are true if they correspond to the facts and false if they do not. Science is ideally a linguistic system in which true propositions are in one-to-one relation to facts, including facts that are not directly observed because they involve hidden entities or properties, or past events or far distant events. These hidden events are described as theories, and theories can be inferred from observations, that is, the hidden explanatory mechanism of the world can be discovered from what is open to observation. Man as scientist is regarded as standing apart from the world and able to experiment and theorize about it objectively and dispassionately.

A fifth example: Hesse (1980, pp. 170-171) also presents a statement of what are taken to be the characteristics of empirical method described by Habermas, who was presumably himself drawing upon the work of Dilthey:

> 1. In natural science experience is taken to be objective, testable, and independent of theoretical explanation. . . .
> 2. In natural science theories are artificial constructions or models, yielding explanation in the sense of a logic of hypothetico-deduction: *if* external nature were of such a kind, *then* data and experience would be as we find them. . . .
> 3. In natural science the lawlike relations asserted of experience are external, both to the objects connected and to the investigator, since they are merely correlational. . . .
> 4. The language of natural science is exact, formalizable, and literal; therefore meanings are univocal, and a problem of meaning arises only in the application of universal categories to particulars. . . .
> 5. Meanings in natural science are separate from facts.

A sixth example: Harre (1981, p.3) provides yet another formulation:

> The positivist tradition in scientific methodology has been based upon the principle that the only reliable knowledge of any field of phenomena

reduces to knowledge of particular instances of patterns of sensation. Laws are treated as probabilistic generalizations of descriptions of such patterns. The sole role of laws is to facilitate the prediction of future sensory experience. Theories are logically ordered sets of laws. In consequence theories are reduced to a logical apparatus necessary to the business of prediction. It follows that for a positivist, the task of understanding a theory is exhausted by two processes. Analysis of theoretical discourse is aimed at revealing its logical structure. The empirical content of the theory is supposed to be brought to light by identifying those logical consequences of the set of laws which purport to describe observations. There are, therefore, two sides of modern positivism: one logical and one empirical. Modern positivism is sometimes called "logical empiricism."

Harre goes on to raise the question of how it ever happens that positivism gains a foothold. He describes positivism as a kind of fallback position, a "positivist retreat" that occurs whenever there is a serious loss of confidence in current theory in some field. Scientists, he speculates, tend to take their theories and models very seriously, as representations of reality, as factual descriptions of what actually occurs. But, he goes on:

> If we are to take an imagined mechanism seriously as a possible representation of reality there ought to be some way of deciding between rival candidates for the role of best explanation. Sometimes the ingenuity of theorists produces a multitude of seemingly possible mechanisms, all capable of being imagined to produce close analogues of the empirically observed patterned regularities. But at the other extreme, it sometimes happens that the most talented and imaginative thinkers can make no headway at all in imagining any mechanism capable of simulating the behaviour of the real world in the field they are investigating. The former situation brought on a positivist reaction among astronomers in the sixteenth century, the latter among subatomic physicists in the twentieth. At the heart of the positivist reaction is a denial that theory could represent hidden realities. According to positivism a science should be taken as no more than a well-attested body of rules for predicting the future course of observation. But these "internal" historical conditions are not sufficient to account for the retreat to positivism. Historical studies clearly reveal an odd twist to this retreat. As scientists abandon the search for a deep knowledge of nature they tend to adopt a militant, even an arrogant posture, sometimes persecuting those who hope to continue on the path of scientific tradition. A kind of glorying in ignorance is displayed, like the Paduan professors who refused to look through Galileo's telescope. Positivist retreats seldom last beyond a single generation of scientists, though the damaging effect of widespread abandonment of

Good Point [margin annotation]

realism can sometimes be felt for a long time after the dominant figures have departed. (Harre, 1981, pp. 7-8)[7]

It is very clear from this sample of statements about positivism that there is no clear agreement about what either the philosophy or the method encompasses. Positivism can be reshaped, apparently, to suit the definer's purpose, and while there is certainly remarkable overlap in these statements there are also some inconsistencies and some idiosyncracies. One might venture to say that the particular form of definition offered by any commentator depends heavily upon the counterpoints he or she wishes to make. (The significance of that observation for the ways in which positivism will be interpreted later in this book should not be overlooked; we are "guilty" of the same "crime.") But it does seem to be the case that these authors do agree on one point: Positivism is passé. Harre's scathing comments noted a few paragraphs ago leave no doubt that he not only disagrees with the positivist position but believes it to be the product of small, confused minds who retreat to it because they lack any other viable alternatives. Such a harsh judgment is undoubtedly a strong overreaction, but hear some more temperate critics:

- Mary Hesse (1980, p. vii) having given it as her opinion that the three most important assumptions underlying positivism are naive realism, belief in a universal scientific language, and a correspondence theory of truth, goes on to comment, "Almost every assumption underlying this account has been subjected to damaging criticism."
- Schwartz and Ogilvy (1979, p. 32), having described what they take to be the three basic assumptions of the Newtonian world view, add that "all of these basic assumptions are now being challenged by theoretical and experimental findings."
- Wolf (1981, pp. 51-56), after describing his view of the assumptions "concerning the physical . . . world" of the Newtonian, comments, "But it would take nearly fifty years for the true [*sic*] story to be told"; with the "end of the mechanical age" coming into view because of certain unexplainable (in positivist terms) phenomena: the inability of physicists to find ether, that necessary component of wave theories of light, and their inability to deal with "the ultraviolet catastrophe," the failure of physicists to explain the colors of heated (glowing) objects.

CHALLENGES TO
AND CRITIQUES OF POSITIVISM

What is the nature of the challenges to and critiques of positivism that have brought it to its metaphoric knees? Space precludes the level of treatment that such a question deserves, but one may point to the following issues:

(1) Positivism leads to an inadequate conceptualization of what science is:

- Hesse (1980, pp. 46-47) cites the work of Barry Barnes, who

    asserts that all attempts to find demarcating criteria, that is, necessary and sufficient conditions for a belief system to be science, have failed. These failures include all verifiability and falsifiability criteria, and all specific appeals to experimentation and/or to particular kinds of inductive or theoretical inference. At best, he argues, the concept "science" must be regarded as a loose association of family resemblance characteristics involving, among other things, aversion to all forms of anthropomorphism and teleology, and consequent tendencies to secularism, impersonality, abstraction, and quantification.

    While it would be inappropriate to argue that this failure is entirely produced by adherence to positivistic principles, it is clear that the paradigm has offered no way out of the dilemma.
- Positivism thoroughly confuses two aspects of inquiry that have often been called the "context of discovery" and the "context of justification." The former deals with the genesis or origin of scientific theories and the latter with testing them. Positivism excludes the former and focuses on the latter. The process of theory conceptualization is seen as noncognitive or nonrational and hence outside the pale. But any theory, no matter how bizarre its origins, is admissible so long as it is coherent (T_3) and testable (T_4). In terms of these constraints, much of Einstein's work, for example, would be considered nonscientific by positivists, who would hardly be persuaded by or interested in Einstein's thought (*gedanken*) experiments.

It may be the case, as Cronbach (1982) seems to suggest, that verification has taken precedence over discovery within positivism because proponents of that formulation could not devise a means for coming to grips with it systematically. He comments:

"Design of experiments" has been a standard element in training for social scientists. This training has concentrated on formal tests of hypotheses—confirmatory studies—despite the fact that R. A. Fisher, the prime theorist of experimental design, demonstrated over and over again in his agricultural investigations that effective inquiry works back and forth between the heuristic and the confirmatory. But since he could offer a formal theory only for the confirmatory studies, *that part came to be taken as the whole*. (pp. ix-x; emphasis added)

- Positivism severely constrains the possible uses or purposes of science to prediction and control. Indeed, what is often called the "pragmatic criterion" of success in science is that it should lead to increasingly successful prediction and control. Such a delimitation forces out of contention other legitimate purposes, as, for example, *verstehen* or understanding, description, problem responses, status determination, and so on. It focuses on what might be called *kennenschaft* to the virtual exclusion of *wissenschaft*.

Of course, none of these reasons are sufficient to lead to discarding positivism, but they are sufficient to lead to an extreme degree of discomfort among practicing scientists who would prefer to have a more solid conceptualization to use as a touchstone.

(2) Positivism is unable to deal adequately with two crucial and interacting aspects of the theory-fact relationship:

- *The underdetermination of theory, sometimes also called the problem of induction.* In deduction, given the validity of the premises, the conclusion must be true and it is the only conclusion possible. But in induction, there are always many conclusions that can reasonably be related to certain premises. Deductions are closed but inductions are open. Thus there is always a larger number of theories that can fit observations more or less adequately. Hence there cannot be convergence, no ultimate conclusions, no certain or "true" (T_i) theory. Nor is this situation helped by the fact that there is no agreement about what a theory is (a pattern, network, nomological net, hypothetico-deduction system) or what it is for (to systematize, uncover, predict, explain).
- *The theory-ladenness of facts, that is, the apparent impossibility of having "facts" that are not themselves theory-determined.* It is, many assert, impossible to have an observational language that is not also a theoretical language. The "truth" of propositions (facts on trial) cannot be determined except in relation to a true theory, but, as we have just seen, true theories cannot be derived because of the problem of underdetermination. Hence the reasoning is entirely circular.

(3) Positivism is overly dependent on operationalism, which has itself been increasingly judged to be inadequate.

- Operationalism is simply not meaningful or satisfying; recalling the quotation from Ford (see note 5), most people are more interested in fear than in the number of fecal boluses emitted every hour.
- Operationalism is too shallow, depending as it does almost entirely on sensations for its "facts" and refusing to deal with meanings or implications.

- Operationally defined facts are just as theory-laden as are any others.
- Despite the good intentions and the best efforts of the Vienna Circle of Logical Positivists, neither they nor any of their adherents have been able to rid science of its metaphysical underpinnings.
- The strict practice of operationalism results in a meaningless splintering of the world. Since nothing exists for the operationalist except through the instruments that measure it, even such conceptually close entities as two IQ scores measured by two different IQ tests must be asserted to be different *despite* a high correlation between them.

(4) Positivism has at least two consequences that are both repugnant and unfounded:

- *Determinism,* repugnant because of its implications for human free will and unfounded because of recent findings in many fields that argue strongly against it, for example, the Heisenberg Uncertainty Principle (Chapter 4).
- *Reductionism,* repugnant because it would make all phenomena including human phenomena ultimately subject to a single set of laws, and unfounded because of recent findings in many fields including mathematics and physics that rule out the possibility in those fields, for example, Gödel's Theorem (Chapter 5).

(5) Positivism has produced research with human respondents that ignores their humanness, a fact that has not only ethical but also validity implications.

- It has emphasized *exogenous* research—that is, research in which all aspects of the research, from problem definition through instrumentation, data collection and analysis, and use of findings, have been researcher-determined—to the virtual exclusion of *endogenous* research— that is, research in which the respondents have equal rights of determination.
- It has emphasized *etic* research—that is, research carried out with an outside (objective) perspective—to the virtual exclusion of *emic* research— that is, research carried out with an inside perspective (subjective).

(6) Positivism falls short of being able to deal with emergent conceptual/empirical formulations from a variety of fields; three examples:

- Gödel's Incompleteness Theorem, which states that no axiomatic system of mathematics is able to provide information about both the completeness and consistency of that axiomatic system; or, put another way, it asserts that no theory of mathematics asserted to be complete can also be internally consistent.

- Heisenberg's Uncertainty Principle, which asserts that the position and momentum of an electron cannot *both* be determined, because the action of the observer in making either measurement inevitably alters the other.
- Bell's Theorem, which asserts that no theory compatible with quantum theory can require spatially separated events to be independent.

The consequences of these three formulations, as well as others, for the basic premises of positivism, including ontology, objectivity, and causality, are devastating.

(7) Positivism rests upon at least five assumptions that are increasingly difficult to maintain. These five assumptions capture the most salient aspects included in the various definitions of positivism that have already been reviewed,[8] and will *form the basis for the counterproposals that are the backbone of this book:*

- An ontological assumption of a single, tangible reality "out there" that can be broken apart into pieces capable of being studied independently; the whole is simply the sum of the parts.
- An epistemological assumption about the possibility of separation of the observer from the observed—the knower from the known.
- An assumption of the temporal and contextual independence of observations, so that what is true at one time and place may, under appropriate circumstances (such as sampling) also be true at another time and place.
- An assumption of linear causality; there are no effects without causes and no causes without effects.
- An axiological assumption of value freedom, that is, that the methodology guarantees that the results of an inquiry are essentially free from the influence of any value system (bias).

The consequences of these several critiques of positivism are sufficiently telling and widely appreciated that a significant number of vanguard scientists have abandoned that paradigm and moved into the postpositivist era. We shall describe next what are still clumsy and emergent efforts to carry out that move.

THE POSTPOSITIVIST ERA[9]

Positivism has been remarkably pervasive. We have noted that its precursor era does not have a name of its own but is called, simply, the prepositivist era. Similarly, the new era has not yet gained sufficient credibility or self-assurance to have assumed a name of its own; it too is called by a simple name: postpositivism. The grip of *its* precursor is still on it; it is just as difficult for the modern-day scientist of whatever stripe to throw off the shackles imposed on thinking by the positivists as it was for Galileo's inquisitors to take his telescope, and what it revealed, seriously; or for Lavoisier's fellow chemists to be able to accept oxygen without simultaneously wondering where all the phlogiston had gone. The reader who has never contemplated postpositivist ideas may be in for a surprise; indeed, a rude shock. As the aphorism goes, "Expect the unexpected."

Perhaps the *most* unexpected aspect of postpositivism is that its basic tenets are virtually the reverse of those that characterized positivism—perhaps not so surprising, after all, when one contemplates that postpositivism is as much a reaction to the failings of positivism as it is a proactive set of new formulations; reaction, too, is a form of "standing on the shoulders of giants."

An example: it will be recalled that Habermas, expanding on the ideas of Dilthey, outlined what he took to be the crucial axiomatic differences between hermeneutics and empiricism. In opposition to what he saw to be the five central aspects of positivism—objectivity, hypothetico-deductive theory, external lawlike relations, exact and formal language, and separation of facts from meaning—Habermas proposed five counterpoints, which Hesse (1980) declares have *now* come to characterize the natural sciences as well. Indeed, she asserts, the positions ascribed by Habermas to the empirical sciences, while valid at the time that he wrote, have been "almost universally discredited" (Hesse, 1980, p. 172). She goes on:

Paralleling the five points of the [Habermas] dichotomy [of natural and human sciences], we can summarize this post-empiricist account of natural science as follows:

1. In natural science data is not detachable from theory, for what count as data are determined in the light of some theoretical interpretation, and the facts themselves have to be reconstructed in the light of interpretation.

2. In natural science theories are not models externally compared in nature to a hypothetico-deductive schema, they are the way the facts themselves are seen.

3. In natural science the law-like relations asserted of experience are internal, because what we count as facts are constituted by what the theory says about their interrelations with one another.

4. The language of natural science is irreducibly metaphorical and inexact, and formalizable only at the cost of distortion of the historical dynamics of scientific development and of the imaginative reconstructions in terms of which nature is interpreted by science.

5. Meanings in natural science are determined by theory; they are understood by theoretical coherence rather than by correspondence with facts. (pp. 172-173)

Objective reality has become very relative indeed!

Another instance: Rom Harre (1981), whose scathing dismissal of positivism was quoted above, also contrasts positivism with the "new paradigm." Where positivism is concerned with surface events or appearances, the new paradigm takes a deeper look. Where positivism is atomistic, the new paradigm is structural. Where positivism establishes meaning operationally, the new paradigm establishes meaning inferentially. Where positivism sees its central purpose to be prediction, the new paradigm is concerned with understanding. Finally, where positivism is deterministic and bent on certainty, the new paradigm is probabilistic and speculative.

Most of the distinguishing features of the postpositivist paradigm have emerged from fields such as physics and chemistry, customarily denoted as the "hard sciences." But the argument for the new paradigm can be made even more persuasively when the entities being studied are human beings.[10] For such research, Heron (1981) advances six arguments in favor of the postpositivist paradigm:

(1) The argument from the nature of research behavior. Heron argues that researchers cannot define one model of behavior for themselves and a different one for their respondents. If the basic model for research behavior is that of "intelligent self-direction," then, to be consistent, the same model must be applied to the respondents.

(2) The argument from intentionality. Heron (1981, p. 23) argues for the necessity of checking with the respondents to be sure that their intentionality and the researcher's interpretation of it coincide: "When I am interpreting such basic actions [as walking, talking, looking, pointing] in terms of their more complex intentions and purposes, than I need to check against the [respondent's] version of what he was about, for a person may walk, talk, or look or point to fulfill many different higher order intentions."

(3) The argument from language. Language formation is interpreted by Heron as an archetype of inquiry itself. When human beings communicate they must agree on the rules of language they will follow. Hence the use of language contains within itself the model of cooperative inquiry. Heron (1981, pp. 26-27) asserts:

I *can* use the language to make statements about persons who have not contributed or assented to the formulation of those statements. . . . [But]

to use language in this way is to cut it off from its validating base. . . .
The result is a set of alienated statements hanging in an interpersonal
void: statements about persons not authorized by those persons. . . . My
considered view of your reality without consulting you is a very different
matter from our considered view of our reality.

(4) The argument from an extended epistemology. Heron notes that
while science as *product* takes the form of a set of propositional
statements, the *process* of scientific inquiry involves not only propositional knowledge but also *practical* knowledge (the skills, proficien-
cies, or "knacks" of doing research) and *experiential* knowledge (knowing a person or thing through sustained encounters). He notes:

> What I am arguing . . . is that empirical research on persons involves
> a subtle, developing interdependence between propositional knowledge,
> practical knowledge, and experiential knowledge. The research conclu-
> sions . . . necessarily rest on the researcher's experiential knowledge of
> the [respondents]. This knowledge of persons is most adequate as an
> empirical base when . . . researcher and [respondent] are fully present
> to each other in a relationship of reciprocal and open inquiry, and when
> each is open to construe how the other manifests as a presence in space
> and time. (p. 31)

(5) The argument from axiology. Heron argues that the truth of
a proposition depends on shared values. The data that researchers
generate, he suggests, depend upon their procedural norms, which in
turn depend upon their shared values. If the facts are about persons
other than the researchers, "they have indeterminate validity, no secure
status as truths, until we know whether those other persons assent to
and regard as their own the norms and values of the researchers"
(p. 33).

(6) The moral and political argument. Research in the conventional
sense usually exploits people, Heron asserts, for knowledge is power
that can be used against the people from whom the knowledge was
generated. The "new paradigm" avoids some of these difficulties
because

> (1) it honours the fulfillment of the respondents' need for autonomously
> acquired knowledge; (2) it protects them from becoming unwitting ac-
> cessories to knowledge-claims that may be false and may be inap-
> propriately or harmfully applied to others; (3) it protects them from
> being excluded from the formation of knowledge that purports to be
> about them and so from being managed and manipulated . . . in ways

they do not understand and so cannot assent to or dissent from. (pp. 24-35)

But just what is this new postpositivist paradigm? If we accept that its axioms or assumptions are virtually the inverse of those of positivism, we are not *definitively* helped because, as we have seen, different writers have cast the positivist assumptions in different terms; hence postpositivism's definition depends upon whose positivistic description is followed.

Of course, some scholars insist that postpositivism is nothing more than an overreaction, and that it is time for a rapproachement that realigns positivism with the relativism that characterizes postpositivism. One such writer is Donald T. Campbell, who suggests that it is time to move into a post-postpositivist era, in which positivism and postpositivism are married off and live happily ever after. In his William James Lecture #5, delivered in 1977, for example, he describes science as a *social system,* with all the usual attributes of such a system: norms, jobs, communication channels, modes of recruiting and rewarding members and keeping them loyal, and so on. He says:

> But I want to assert that among all these belief-preserving mutual admiration societies, all of which share this common human tribalism, science is also different, with different specific values, myths, rituals, and commandments, and that these different norms are related to what I presume to be science's superiority in the improving validity of the model of the physical world which it carries. . . . In spite of the theory-ladenness and noisiness of unedited experimental evidence, it does provide a major source of discipline in science. . . . The experiment is meticulously designed to put questions to "Nature Itself" in such a way that neither the questioners, nor their colleagues, nor their superiors can affect the answer. . . . In our iterative oscillation of theoretical emphases, in our continual dialectic that never achieves a stable synthesis, we are now ready for a post-post-postitivist theory of science which will integrate the epistemological relativism recently achieved with a new and more complex understanding of the role of experimental evidence and predictive confirmation in science. (cited in Brewer & Collins, 1981, pp. 15-16)

Now this whole statement moves from hidden assumptions rooted in the positivist tradition. "Theory-ladenness" and the "noisiness of unedited experimental evidence" are treated as minor technical inconveniences. The place of values in inquiry is ignored and the delusion of objectivity is maintained in claims such as that experiments can be designed meticulously enough so that no one can influence the outcome, only "Nature Itself." But what this perspective misses completely is the fact that postpositivism is not merely a perturbation, a wrinkle, a new angle that simply needs to be accommodated to make everything all right. Postpositivism is an entirely new paradigm, *not* reconcilable with the old. Rapproachements, accommodations, compromises are no more possible here than between the old astronomy and Galileo's new astronomy, between phlogiston and oxygen, between Newtonian and quantum mechanics. We are dealing with an entirely new system of ideas based on fundamentally *different*—indeed, sharply contrasting— assumptions, as the quotations from Mary Hesse, Rom Harre, and John Heron so vividly illustrate. What is needed is a transformation, not an add-on. That the world is round cannot be added to the idea that the world is flat. Nor is the notion of a paradigm transformation simply an intellectual fashion, as Pollie (1983) suggests. To make this point crystal clear, it is worth making a brief digression into the nature of axiomatic systems.

FEATURES OF AXIOMATIC SYSTEMS[11]

Axioms may be defined as the set of undemonstrated (and undemonstrable) "basic beliefs" accepted by convention or established by practice as the building blocks of some conceptual or theoretical structure or system. They are the statements that will be taken as Truth$_1$ in the sense proposed by Julienne Ford. Probably the best known and most widely experienced system of axioms is that undergirding Euclidean geometry. Euclid set himself the task of formalizing what was known about geometry (literally, the measurement of earth or surveying) at his time; essentially, that meant systematizing the rules of thumb used by land surveyors, which had never been "proved" but which everyone knew had validity. It was Euclid's powerful insight that these rules could be "proved" by showing them to be logical derivatives from some simple set of "self-evident" truths; or, to use Ford's terminology, that they could be shown to be T$_3$ by demonstrating their consistency with the basic beliefs—the self-evident truths—taken to be T$_1$. Euclid began with four such basic beliefs, which have since come to be known as the axioms of Euclidean geometry (Hofstadter, 1979):

(1) A straight line segment can be drawn joining any two points.
(2) Any straight line segment can be extended indefinitely in a straight line.

(3) Given any straight line segment, a circle can be drawn having the segment as radius and one end point as center.
(4) All right angles are congruent.

With these four axioms, Euclid was able to derive ("prove") the first 28 of the eventually much larger set of theorems (statements shown to be T_3), but the twenty-ninth proof he attempted turned out be intractable. In despair, and driven by the need to go on to other theorems, Euclid finally simply assumed it as a fifth axiom:

(5) If two lines are drawn that intersect a third in such a way that the sum of the inner angles on one side is less than two right angles, then the two lines inevitably must intersect each other on that side if extended far enough.

The more modern way to state this axiom is as follows: Given a line and a point not on that line, it is possible to construct only one line through the point that is parallel to the given line.

As compared to the first four axioms, the fifth seems strained and inelegant; Euclid was sure that eventually he would be able to find a way of proving it in terms of the first four. But his hope was not to be realized in his lifetime or, indeed, ever; two millenia of effort by mathematicians have failed to provide a proof.

It is now known that a proof in Euclid's sense is impossible, but that fact was hidden from mathematicians' minds during many centuries when assiduous efforts were made to find it. Early attempts at proof were of the form that mathematicians would call *direct,* but, these having failed, *indirect* proof was sought, one variant of which is to assume the *direct opposite* of what one wishes to show and then to demonstrate that this opposite assumption leads to absurd conclusions (theorems). In that case, the original formulation rather than its opposite can be assumed to be correct. It was exactly this approach, however, that culminated in so-called non-Euclidean geometries, for not only were the consequences of non-Euclidean (opposite to Euclidean) axioms not absurd, they were in fact of great utility. One such geometry is called Lobachevskian; this form takes as its fifth axiom, "Given a line and a point not on that line, it is possible to draw a bundle of lines through the point *all of which* are parallel to the given line." Now this axiom flies in the face of all human experience; yet it yields results of great interest, for example, to astronomers.

One of the theorems "provable" (in the sense of T_3) from the Euclidean fifth axiom is that the sum of angles in a triangle is $180°$. But the sum of angles of a Lobachevskian triangle is *not always 180°* but approaches 180° as the triangle becomes "small." An intuitive understanding of this point can be had from examining the (impossible in either geometry but useful for pedagogical purposes) triangle shown in Figure 1.1. Assuming we have a triangle with three angles of 40°, summing to 120°, it is clear that as the triangle is bisected from its 40° superior angle by a perpendicular bisector, each of the smaller triangles now has a sum of angles of 150°. Now of course all human experience argues that triangles *do* have a sum equal to 180°, but that is simply evidence for the fact that, within Lobachevskian geometry, *all earth-size triangles are small.* But astronomically sized triangles are very much larger, and astronomers find that Lobachevskian geometry provides a better "fit" to the phenomena that they investigate than does Euclidean.

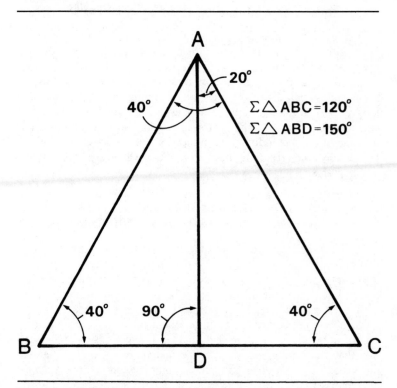

Figure 1.1:   Smaller "Lobachevskian" triangles have large sums of angels (approaching 180°).

From this digression we may deduce several crucial points:

(1) Axioms (basic beliefs) are arbitrary and may be assumed for any reason, even if only for the "sake of the game."
(2) Axioms are *not* self-evidently true, nor need they appear to be so; indeed, some axioms appear to be very bizarre on first exposure.
(3) Different axiom systems have different utilities depending on the phenomena to which they are applied. These utilities are *not* determined by the nature of the axiom system itself but by the *interaction* between the axioms and the characteristics of the area of application. Thus Euclidean geometry is fine for terrestrial spaces, but Lobachevskian geometry is preferred for interstellar spaces.
(4) A decision about which of several alternative axiom systems to use in a given case is best made by testing the "fit" between each system and the case, a process analogous to testing data for fit to assumptions before deciding on which statistic to use in analyzing them.

We are ready now to deal with the axioms of the particular postpositivist paradigm we advocate in this book, which we will term the "naturalistic paradigm." The assumptions of that paradigm are briefly outlined in the next section and are contrasted with those of the positivist paradigm; the question of testing their "fit," particularly for use in human inquiry, is delayed for extended treatment in Chapters 3 through 7. The next section will also provide a preview of some of the methodological implications of the selected paradigm for actually doing research; these implications will be explored in detail in Chapter 8.

THE AXIOMS OF
THE NATURALISTIC PARADIGM

We have made the point several times that the particular formulation of the positivistic paradigm that one adopts depends as much upon the countercase that one will propose as upon anything else; the selection of points is essentially arbitrary. This presentation is not different in that respect; we hope, however, that the reader will agree that, first, we have selected to emphasize more salient rather than more bizarre aspects of positivism, and, second, that we have not misstated the position that a committed positivist would take on these points, whatever might be said about other points. The points of contrast that we have chosen are, we believe, crucial to an understanding of the naturalistic paradigm and the ways in which it differs, contrasts, and even conflicts with the positivistic.

TABLE 1.1   Contrasting Positivist and Naturalist Axioms

Axioms About	Positivist Paradigm	Naturalist Paradigm
The nature of reality	Reality is single, tangible, and fragmentable.	Realities are multiple, constructed, and holistic.
The relationship of knower to the known	Knower and known are independent, a dualism.	Knower and known are interactive, inseparable.
The possibility of generalization	Time- and context-free generalizations (nomothetic statements) are possible.	Only time- and context-bound working hypotheses (idiographic statements) are possible.
The possibility of causal linkages	There are real causes, temporally precedent to or simultaneous with their effects.	All entities are in a state of mutual simultaneous shaping, so that it is impossible to distinguish causes from effects.
The role of values	Inquiry is value-free.	Inquiry is value-bound.

Immediately following is a formal statement of the five axioms in both their naturalistic and positivistic versions; these are also summarized in Table 1.1 for convenience. The reader should here acquaint him- or herself with the axioms and delay concerns about whether these axioms provide a better fit to the phenomena of sociobehavioral inquiry until this matter comes under close scrutiny in later chapters.

Axiom 1: The nature of reality (ontology) (expanded in Chapter 3).

- *Positivist version:* There is a single tangible reality "out there" fragmentable into independent variables and processes, any of which can be studied independently of the others; inquiry can converge onto that reality until, finally, it can be predicted and controlled.
- *Naturalist version:* There are multiple constructed realities that can be studied only holistically; inquiry into these multiple realities will inevitably diverge (each inquiry raises more questions than it answers) so that prediction and control are unlikely outcomes although some level of understanding (*verstehen*) can be achieved.

Axiom 2: The relationship of knower to known (epistemology) (expanded in Chapter 4).

- *Positivist version:* The inquirer and the object of inquiry are independent; the knower and the known constitute a discrete dualism.
- *Naturalist version:* The inquirer and the "object" of inquiry interact to influence one another; knower and known are inseparable.

Axiom 3: The possibility of generalization (expanded in Chapter 5).

- *Positivist version:* The aim of inquiry is to develop a nomothetic body of knowledge in the form of generalizations that are truth statements free from both time and context (they will hold anywhere and at any time).
- *Naturalist version:* The aim of inquiry is to develop an idiographic body of knowledge in the form of "working hypotheses" that describe the individual case.

Axiom 4: The possibility of causal linkages (expanded in Chapter 6).

- *Positivist version:* Every action can be explained as the result (effect) of a real cause that precedes the effect temporally (or is at least simultaneous with it).
- *Naturalist version:* All entities are in a state of mutual simultaneous shaping so that it is impossible to distinguish causes from effects.

Axiom 5: The role of values in inquiry (axiology) (expanded in Chapter 7).

- *Positivist version:* Inquiry is value-free and can be guaranteed to be so by virtue of the objective methodology employed.
- *Naturalist version:* Inquiry is value-bound in at least five ways, captured in the corollaries that follow:
  Corollary 1: Inquiries are influenced by *inquirer* values as expressed in the choice of a problem, evaluand, or policy option, and in the framing, bounding, and focusing of that problem, evaluand, or policy option.
  Corollary 2: Inquiry is influenced by the choice of the *paradigm* that guides the investigation into the problem.
  Corollary 3: Inquiry is influenced by the choice of the *substantive theory* utilized to guide the collection and analysis of data and in the interpretation of findings.
  Corollary 4: Inquiry is influenced by the values that inhere in the *context*.
  Corollary 5: With respect to corollaries 1 through 4 above, inquiry is either *value-resonant* (reinforcing or congruent) or *value-dissonant* (conflicting). Problem, evaluand, or policy option, paradigm, theory, *and* context must exhibit congruence (value-resonance) if the inquiry is to produce meaningful results.[12]

Following the naturalistic rather than the positivistic version of these key axioms has, as one might expect, enormous implications for the *doing* of research; these implications are very briefly sketched in the following section and will be pursued in more detail subsequently.

IMPLICATIONS FOR THE
DOING OF RESEARCH

An inquirer doing research in the style or mode of the naturalist paradigm needs more than just the five axioms listed above as guides. In this section we shall describe very briefly some of the more important implications of the paradigm for actual research operations. The importance of these modes will be more fully appreciated as we return to them in more depth in Chapter 8.

We shall describe fourteen characteristics of operational naturalistic inquiry. These characteristics can be justified in two ways: (1) by their logical dependence on the axioms that undergird the paradigm, and (2) by their coherence and interdependence. These fourteen characteristics display a synergism such that, once one is selected, the others more or less follow. Some attempt will be made in the paragraphs that follow to support these claims.

Logical Dependence upon the Axioms

Characteristic 1: Natural setting. N (the naturalist) elects to carry out research in the natural setting or context of the entity for which study is proposed because naturalistic ontology suggests that realities are wholes that cannot be understood in isolation from their contexts, nor can they be fragmented for separate study of the parts (the whole is more than the sum of the parts); because of the belief that the very act of observation influences what is seen, and so the research interaction should take place with the entity-in-context for fullest understanding; because of the belief that context is crucial in deciding whether or not a finding may have meaning in some other context as well; because of the belief in complex mutual shaping rather than linear causation, which suggests that the phenomenon must be studied in its full-scale influence (force) field; and because contextual value structures are at least partly determinative of what will be found.

Characteristic 2: Human instrument. N elects to use him- or herself as well as other humans as the primary data-gathering instruments (as opposed to paper-and-pencil or brass instruments) because it would be virtually impossible to devise a priori a nonhuman instrument with sufficient adaptability to encompass and adjust to the variety of realities that will be encountered; because of the understanding that all instruments interact with respondents and objects but that only the human instrument is capable of grasping and evaluating the meaning of that differential interaction; because the intrusion of instruments intervenes in the mutual shaping of other elements and that shaping can be appreciated and evaluated only by a human; and because all instruments are value-based and interact with local values but only the human is in a position to identify and take into account (to some extent) those resulting biases.[13]

Characteristic 3: Utilization of tacit knowledge. N argues for the legitimation of tacit (intuitive, felt) knowledge in addition to propositional knowledge (knowledge expressible in language form) because often the nuances of the multiple realities can be appreciated only in this way; because much of the interaction between investigator and respondent or object occurs at this level; and because tacit knowledge mirrors more fairly and accurately the value patterns of the investigator.

Characteristic 4: Qualitative methods. N elects qualitative methods over quantitative (although not exclusively) because they are more adaptable to dealing with multiple (and less aggregatable) realities; because such methods expose more directly the nature of the transaction between investigator and respondent (or object) and hence make easier an assessment of the extent to which the phenomenon is described in terms of (is biased by) the investigator's own posture; and because qualitative methods are more sensitive to and adaptable to the many mutually shaping influences and value patterns that may be encountered.

Characteristic 5: Purposive sampling. N is likely to eschew random or representative sampling in favor of purposive or theoretical sampling because he or she thereby increases the scope or range of data exposed (random or representative sampling is likely to suppress more deviant cases) as well as the likelihood that the full array of multiple realities will be uncovered; and because purposive sampling can be pursued in ways that will maximize the investigator's ability to devise grounded theory that takes adequate account of local conditions, local mutual shapings, and local values (for possible transferability).

Characteristic 6: Inductive data analysis. N prefers inductive (to deductive) data analysis because that process is more likely to identify the multiple realities to be found in those data; because such analysis is more likely to make the investigator-respondent (or object) interaction explicit, recognizable, and accountable; because this process is more likely to describe fully the setting and to make decisions about transferability to other settings easier; because inductive data analysis is more likely to identify the mutually shaping influences that interact; and because values can be an explicit part of the analytic structure.

Characteristic 7: Grounded theory. N prefers to have the guiding substantive theory emerge from (be grounded in) the data because *no* a priori theory could possibly encompass the multiple realities that are likely to be encountered; because believing is seeing and N wishes to enter his transactions with respondents as neutrally as possible; because a priori theory is likely to be based on a priori generalizations, which, while they may make nomothetic sense, may nevertheless provide a poor idiographic fit to the situation encountered (the fact that a woman recounts a set of gynecological symptoms to her doctor that, in 80 percent of patients, indicates cervical cancer is not sufficient reason to schedule her for surgery without examination to determine whether she might not be one of the 20 percent); because the mutual shapings found in a particular context may be explicable only in terms of the contextual elements found there; and because grounded theory is more likely to be responsive to contextual values (and not merely to investigator values).

Characteristic 8: Emergent design. N elects to allow the research design to emerge (flow, cascade, unfold) rather than to construct it preordinately (a priori) because it is inconceivable that enough could be known ahead of time about the many multiple realities to devise the design adequately; because what emerges as a function of the interaction between inquirer and phenomenon is largely unpredictable in advance; because the inquirer cannot know sufficiently well the patterns of mutual shaping that are likely to exist; and because the various value systems involved (including the inquirer's own) interact in unpredictable ways to influence the outcome.

Characteristic 9: Negotiated outcomes. N prefers to negotiate meanings and interpretations with the human sources from which the data have chiefly been drawn because it is their constructions of reality that the inquirer seeks to reconstruct; because inquiry outcomes depend upon the nature and quality of the interaction between the knower and the known, epitomized in negotiations about the meaning of data; because the specific working hypotheses that might apply in a given context are best verified and confirmed by the people who inhabit that context; because respondents are in a better position to interpret the complex mutual interactions—shapings—that enter into what is observed; and because respondents can best understand and interpret the influence of local value patterns.

Characteristic 10: Case study reporting mode. N is likely to prefer the case study reporting mode (over the scientific or technical report) because it is more adapted to a description of the multiple realities encountered at any given site: because it is adaptable to demonstrating the investigator's interaction with the site and consequent biases that may result (reflexive reporting); because it provides the basis for both individual "naturalistic generalizations" (Stake, 1980) and transferability to other sites (thick description); because it is suited to demonstrating the variety of mutually shaping influences present; and because it can picture the value positions of investigator, substantive theory, methodological paradigm, and local contextual values.

Characteristic 11: Idiographic interpretation. N is inclined to interpret data (including the drawing of conclusions) idiographically (in terms of the particulars of the case) rather than nomothetically (in terms of lawlike generalizations) because different interpretations are likely to be meaningful for different realities; and because interpretations depend so heavily for their validity on local particulars, including the particular investigator-respondent (or object) interaction, the contextual factors involved, the local mutually shaping factors influencing one another, and the local (as well as investigator) values.

Characteristic 12: Tentative application. N is likely to be tentative (hesitant) about making broad application of the findings because realities are multiple and different; because the findings are to some extent dependent upon the particular interaction between investigator and respondents (or object) that may not be duplicated elsewhere; because the extent to which the findings may be applicable elsewhere depends upon the *empirical* similarity of sending and receiving contexts; because the particular "mix" of mutually shaping influences may vary markedly from setting to setting; and because value systems, especially contextual values, may be sharply at variance from site to site.

Characteristic 13: Focus-determined boundaries. N is likely to set boundaries to the inquiry on the basis of the emergent focus (problems for research, evaluands for evaluation, and policy options for policy analysis) because that permits the multiple realities to define the focus (rather than inquirer preconceptions); because focus-setting can be more closely mediated by the investigator-focus interaction; because boundaries cannot be satisfactorily set without intimate contextual knowledge, including knowledge about the mutually shaping factors involved; and because foci have no meaning in any event in abstraction from the local investigator value systems.

Characteristic 14: Special criteria for trustworthiness. N is likely to find the conventional trustworthiness criteria (internal and external validity, reliability, and objectivity) inconsistent with the axioms and procedures of naturalistic inquiry. Hence he or she is likely to define new (but analogous) criteria and devise operational procedures for applying them. Chapter 11 is devoted to this matter; here it is worth noting that the conventional criterion of internal validity fails because it implies an isomorphism between research outcomes and a single, tangible reality onto which inquiry can converge; that the criterion of external validity fails because it is inconsistent with the basic axiom concerning generalizability; that the criterion of reliability fails because it requires absolute stability and replicability, neither of which is possible for a paradigm based on emergent design; and that the criterion of objectivity fails because the paradigm openly admits investigator-respondent (or object) interaction and the role of values. The case will later be made that there exist substitute criteria (called credibility, transferability, dependability, and confirmability) together with corresponding empirical procedures that adequately (if not absolutely) affirm the trustworthiness of naturalistic approaches.

Coherence (Mutual Reinforcement) Among the Characteristics

A second justification for claiming that the above list of fourteen characteristics is justifiable for naturalistic inquiry is the fact that they display a remarkable coherence and interdependence. One simple illustration will suffice to make the point that each may be taken as a raison d'être for the others; and that the exclusion of any one of them would seriously damage all.

In doing research from a naturalistic perspective, N is forced into the natural setting because he or she cannot specify, without an a priori theory or hypothesis, what is important to control or even to study. Until N has spent some time in the setting he or she cannot specify the focus (problem, evaluand, or policy option) in more than rudimentary form, or place boundaries on it. N could not design a contrived study (an experiment, say) because he or she would not know what to contrive. If theory is to be grounded in data, those data must first be located and analyzed inductively. Since N cannot specify the precise form of the data to be sought, he or she must fall back on an open-ended adaptive instrument: the human being, who, like the "smart bomb," can identify and wend its way to (purposefully sample) the target without having been precisely preprogrammed to strike it. Humans find certain data collection means more congenial than others; they tend toward the use of qualitative methods that "extend" human senses: seeing, hearing, and tacit "sixth-sensing" that lead one to observation, interview, documentary analysis, and the like. These methods results in insights and information about the sending context so that the extent of transferability and applicability in some other receiving context may be judged. No aggregations, no generalizations, no cause-effect statements can emerge, but only idiographic interpretations negotiated with knowledgeable respondents; hence an air of tentativeness surrounds any proposed application. Finally, the case study mode lends itself well to the full description that will be required to encompass all of these facets and make possible understanding on the part of a reader (building on his or her own tacit knowledge and making "naturalistic generalizations" possible). Judgments about the trustworthiness of such a process cannot be made with conventional criteria; criteria devised especially for and demonstrably appropriate to naturalistic inquiry are required.

AN OVERVIEW

The remainder of this volume is devoted to a fuller explication of the ideas that have been introduced so sketchily in this chapter. Chapter 2 is an effort to provide further legitimation for the naturalistic paradigm by showing its resonance with a more encompassing new "paradigm of thought and belief" that draws upon *substantive* (rather then merely methodological) vanguard ideas from a wide variety of disciplines. Chapters 3 through 7 deal in more detail with each of the five axioms—reality, knower-known interaction, generalizability, causality, and values—and make the case that the naturalistic version of these axioms provides a better fit to sociobehavioral phenomena at least, if not to all phenomena. Chapter 8 deals in more detail with the first thirteen of the fourteen characteristics listed in this chapter, and closes out the first and more theoretical part of the book.

Beginning with Chapter 9, we attempt to provide more practical guidelines for the actual *doing* of naturalistic inquiry. That chapter discusses the design of a naturalistic study (although, as the reader can guess, the term "design" will be found to have a somewhat different meaning than is conventionally the case). Chapter 10 gives directions for actually carrying through a design. Chapter 11 returns to the theme of trustworthiness techniques. Chapter 12 outlines the procedures for inductive data processing, and Chapter 13 for writing the case study and closing out the inquiry with a general member check and audit.

NOTES

1. The concept of "preservation of appearances" was common in medieval and early positivist periods.

2. The wisdom of taking T_2 on faith (as one often must) is called into question by the frequency with which it is discovered that one or another well-known scientist has "fudged" the data.

3. We are aware that this definition of *paradigm* is not that which scientists customarily use, that is, a model or pattern (as for example, a paradigm equation that illustrates the procedures for solving an entire class of equations). It is, however, consistent with the use of that term by Kuhn (1970) and others who have written in a similar vein about "paradigm revolutions."

4. A serious question can be raised whether any theory that aims at comprehensiveness can also be perfectly coherent. Gödel's Theorem in mathematics suggests that a comprehensiveness/coherence union is in principle impossible. See the excellent discussion in Hofstadter (1979).

5. We cannot resist citing a memorable paragraph from Julienne Ford (1975, p. 149), who, in describing operationism in terms of the concepts of Percy W. Bridgman, a staunch advocate, says:

> Bridgman's argument is quite simply that to be meaningful a variable must be defined in terms of the measurement operation that would be involved in detecting it in reality. This view is usually termed *operationism* (though it is sometimes referred to as operationa*l*ism) and it amounts to the methodological assertion that any variable which cannot be directly represented by a measurement operation has no place in science. Thus a hypothesis like *"Those rabbits will be afraid"* is regarded as meaningless. However, the statement, *"Those rabbits will be seen to be emitting more faecal boluses per hour than is normal for rabbits"* is perfectly meaningful as far as Bridgman and his men are concerned. Fear, then, is meaningless to the operationist but an observably increasing defecation rate does have meaning. (Notice incidentally that Cockneys seem to think that Bridgman has a point: The Cockney rarely says "Huck is afraid", instead he says "Huck is shitting himself".)

6. This same metaphor also served David Hume in his critique of the concept of causality. See Chapter 6.

7. Harre's reference to the "Paduan professors who refused to look through Galileo's telescope" is a famous instance of what might be called the "reluctant mind," the mind that refuses to accept the need for a new paradigm and that capitalizes on what we earlier termed the "loose coupling" of theory. Galileo, it will be recalled, had gotten himself into trouble with the Church (it was only in 1983 that the Church admitted having committed a major blunder in Galileo's case; *Time,* May 23, 1983, p. 58) because of his publications outlining a heliocentric universe, a formulation clearly at odds with the Church's position that the universe was geocentric. Ordered to an inquisition in 1633, he was censured and actually condemned to death, although the sentence was suspended in view of his abject recantation. But prior to the official "hearing," Galileo was visited in Padua by a group of inquisitors, composed (to the eternal shame of all academics) mainly of professors from the nearby university. According to the story, which may well be apocryphal, Galileo invited his visitors to look through his telescope at the moon and see for themselves the mountains and the craters that the marvelous instrument revealed for the first time. But his inquisitors refused to do so, arguing that whatever might be visible through the telescope would be a product not of nature but of the instrument. How consistent this position is with Aristotelian "naturalism"! Galileo's active intervention in building the telescope and viewing the moon through it were, to the inquisitors' prepositivist minds, an exact illustration of how the *active* observer could distort the "real" or "natural" order. Their posture was perhaps not so much a "glorying in ignorance," as Harre claims, but adherence to the best "scientific" principles of the time.

Another example of the fact that even the best thinkers of an era may have difficulty in throwing off the constraints imposed by the paradigm they follow can be found in the conversion of the field of chemistry from a phlogiston-based theory of combustion and calcination to an oxygen-based theory. The oxygen theory seemed to offer a better explanation of these two phenomena than did the phlogiston theory/and, indeed, offered an explanation of several other phenomena that had not been contemplated by the phlogiston theories: respiration and acidity. Chemists steeped in the phlogiston theory were accustomed to working with equations that included terms for either the absorption or emission of phlogiston. When Lavoisier provided a variety of evidence in support of the oxygen theory, many chemists were prepared to accept his formulation but stumbled over one crucial issue: What happened to the phlogiston in Lavoisier's equations? They could not understand that the very concept of phlogiston was foreign to the paradigm being offered by Lavoisier; that it did not require explanation in the new paradigm, that the construction of the new paradigm denied phlogiston's existence. For an instructive treatment of this important piece of chemical history, see McCann (1978).

8. The reader should recall at this point our earlier caveat about describing the positivist paradigm in terms that best accommodate the rebuttal or counterproposal that the critic intends to make.

9. The reader should be aware that we use the term "postpositivist" to refer to paradigms that represent genuine breaks with the positivist tradition. A substantial number of writers who refer to their own work using this phrase are, in our terms, only *neo*positivists. They have attempted to respond to criticisms of positivism by making adjustments or accommodations, not by radical revision. They represent modern-day counterparts of the "reluctant minds" that we have already encountered in our description of the "Paduan professors" or the phlogiston-oriented chemists. We shall return to this theme repeatedly throughout this book.

10. One notable difference between conventional and emergent paradigms can be detected in the terminology common to each to describe human entities being studied. Positivists tend to call them "subjects," or even "objects of inquiry," treating them as though they were equivalent to the inanimate objects encountered in physics and chemistry. We prefer to call them "respondents," a term that not only retains their humanness but reminds us of the interactive character of human inquiry.

11. The language of this and the following section follows closely Guba and Lincoln (1982).

12. This assertion is one of the most central in this book. If it were not the case that these various value aspects could be resonant or dissonant, one need not be too concerned about which paradigm was being used in any particular inquiry. But it is precisely because the foci of modern inquiry and the substantive theories used in their study may rest on assumptions that are inconsistent with those of the positivist paradigm that it is imperative to move to a paradigm that *is* resonant. The fact that the emergent substantive theories in virtually all disciplines are better supported by the naturalist paradigm will be argued in Chapter 2.

13. Hofstadter (1979) points out that adaptability and perfectability stand in a trade-off relationship to one another. The more perfect an instrument is for some specific purpose, the less adaptable it must be for other purposes. The human, while far from perfect as an instrument, is nevertheless infinitely adaptable.

2

Is the Naturalistic Paradigm the Genuine Article?

It seems well-nigh unethical at present to allow . . . case studies of this nature.

(Campbell & Stanley, 1963)

GROWING LEGITIMATION

It must be evident to the reader that accepting the naturalistic paradigm involves a good deal more than a simple accommodation in one's previous thinking. It is in fact a *revolutionary* move; revolutions, unless one is convinced beyond a shadow of a doubt of their necessity, ought to be stoutly resisted. Why should anyone accept the naturalistic paradigm as a logical successor to the positivist point of view? Positivism may have its faults; why should the mantle of legitimation fall on the shoulders of naturalism?

The answer to that question is complex; indeed, the question can be addressed at a variety of levels. At one level, it may be supposed that the entire approach should be dismissed out of hand because of the well-known objections to the "one-shot case study design" so roundly scored by Campbell and Stanley (1963, p. 177):

Such studies often involve tedious collection of specific detail, careful observation, testing, and the like, and in such instances involve the error of misplaced precision. How much more valuable the study would be if the one set of observations were reduced by half and the saved effort directed to the study in equal detail of an appropriate comparison instance. It seems well-nigh unethical at present to allow, as theses or dissertations in education, case studies of this nature.

Material in this chapter from Peter Schwartz and James Ogilvy, *The Emergent Paradigm: Changing Patterns of Thought and Belief* (Analytical Report 7, Values and Lifestyles Program), copyright 1979 by SRI International, is used by permission of SRI International (Stanford Research Institute), Menlo Park, CA 94025.

But even the strictest constructionists do not take so severe a posture today. Thus Cook and Campbell (1979, p. 96), in commenting on this same design, assert:

> Our predecessors have probably been mistaken in identifying the design we are discussing as "The One-Shot Case Study." Single-setting, one-time-period case studies as used in the social and clinical sciences occur in settings where many variables are measured as the post-test; contextual knowledge is already rich, even if impressionistic; and intelligent presumptions can be made about what this group would have been like without X. These three factors can often serve the same roles that pretest measures and control groups do more formally in more elaborate experimental designs. It may even be that in hypothesis-testing case studies, the multiple implications of the thesis for the multiple observations available generate "degrees of freedom" analogous to those coming from numbers of persons and replications in an experiment (Campbell, 1975).

The reader will have detected the carry-over of positivist presumptions in this statement. But it is less important to note that Cook and Campbell persist in the old paradigm than to see that they are now willing to admit the case study design as a *legitimate* confrere to experimentalism (although we would assert they do so on erroneous grounds—in the 1975 reference cited in the quotation, Campbell more fully develops the relationship between observational checkpoints and the positivist concept of "degrees of freedom"; the interested reader is urged to pursue that line of thought more fully).

At another level, it is of interest to note certain formal parallels between the naturalistic paradigm and scientific paradigms as defined by Mary Hesse (1980). She describes certain conditions for *models of the structure of science* that without doubt could be met equally well by the naturalistic paradigm as any other. Science, according to Hesse (1980, p. 125), is essentially a "learning machine," and she asserts that all models of it

> presuppose that the subject matter of learning is the empirical world. . . . Again, almost without exception, models of science presuppose that the learning process returns to the empirical world, which provides checks and reinforcements, and is the subject of prediction and control.

While the naturalist might demur on the last point, on the grounds that science may well have objectives other than prediction and control, the description is otherwise apt for naturalism. Moreover, Hesse goes on to describe the several stages of operation of this scientific "learning machine": receipt of empirical input, processing of that input (with some resulting loss of information), and development of certain "coherence conditions" that essentially are simplifications that make it possible for the human mind to deal with an otherwise imponderable mass of information. Surely these same characteristics hold for naturalism, although, again, we may demur to the extent of saying that the coherence conditions may well develop, for the naturalist, simultaneously with the inquiry rather than prior to it.

At yet another level, we may note that the output of naturalism often is a locally grounded theory; such theories typically take the form of *pattern* theories as that term was used by Kaplan (1964). Reason (1981, p. 186) comments on this form of theory:

> This pattern model [of explanation] is quite different from the more familiar deductive model of explanation which is used by experimentalists. First, the deductive model involves general laws which explain some phenomenon, while the pattern model involves a number of phenomena all of equal importance, then explains the connections between them. Second, the deduction of unknown parts from known parts is not possible in the pattern model. Indeed, prediction is not important in the pattern model; explanation lies in demonstrating the connections of a puzzling item with other items and the whole pattern. Third, the pattern model is rarely if ever finished, and finally, the pattern is subject to change in the course of its development as new data becomes available.

From these comments we may reasonably deduce that the kinds of theories that commonly emerge from naturalistic inquiries are of a form—pattern theories—that nevertheless is well understood and accepted by philosophers of science.

At still another level, we may inquire whether naturalism fits the definition of *disciplined* inquiry, which, some writers assert, is the most significant basis for judging whether or not an investigation should be entertained as meaningful. Cronbach and Suppes (1969, p. 16) assert that the feature that most prominently distinguishes disciplined inquiry from other forms is that it be conducted (the process) and reported (the product) in such a way that all of its aspects can be examined publicly:

> The report of a disciplined inquiry has a texture that displays the raw materials entering the argument and the logical processes by which they were compressed and rearranged to make the conclusion credible.

Mary Lee Smith (1981, p. 585) comments:

> For an inquiry to qualify as disciplined, it must be conducted and reported so that its logical argument can be carefully examined; it does not depend on surface plausibility or the eloquence, status, or authority of its author; error is avoided; evidential test and verification are valued; the dispassionate search for truth is valued over ideology. Every piece of research or evaluation, whether naturalistic, experimental, survey, or historical must meet these standards to be considered disciplined.

There is no reason to believe that naturalistic inquiry cannot meet the requirements set down by either Cronbach and Suppes or Smith; indeed, we shall argue in Chapter 11, in which we deal with trustworthiness issues, that naturalistic inquiry may meet the twin criteria of inspectable and verifiable *process* and *product* better than do conventional inquiries.

It is also useful to note that there are many precedents for doing the kind of research that we are here labeling "naturalistic." Louis M. Smith, in a 1979 review of the status of participant observation, educational ethnography, and other case studies, is able to list a total of 146 references: 27 "general studies" (4 of non-Western cultures, 5 of modern communities, 10 of formal organizations, and 8 of informal groups); 65 "observational studies of educational systems" (7 of school and community, 5 of school systems and "interorganizational" educational systems, 16 of schools, 12 of classrooms, 20 of curricula and program evaluation, and 5 of teaching careers and student teaching); 34 "methodological statements on participant field studies" (15 papers and chapters, 9 monographs and books, and 10 collections); and 20 "methodological statements on participant observation" (12 papers and chapters, 3 monographs and books, and 5 collections). The total of 146 is remarkable indeed for such a recent addition to the methodological armamentarium, particularly one whose legitimacy is held by some to be in such grave doubt!

The evidence that exists at those various levels is persuasive, but far and away the most compelling approach to the question of the naturalistic paradigm's legitimacy is conceptual. In fact, the paradigm is resonant with vanguard thinking in almost every formal discipline that exists; if one is interested in inquiry that is ongoing at the forefront of disciplines, the naturalistic paradigm is *the* paradigm of choice, the paradigm that provides the best fit to virtually all phenomena. To see that this is so, we shall first make a lengthy digression to learn something about the "new paradigm of thought and belief" that is emerging in multiple disciplines, and then undertake the question of the extent to which this new paradigm provides substantive support for the naturalistic inquiry paradigm.

THE "NEW PARADIGM" OF SCHWARTZ AND OGILVY

Peter Schwartz and James Ogilvy, two scholars with SRI International, have provided in their monograph *The Emergent Paradigm: Changing Patterns of Thought and Belief* (1979) a most remarkable analysis of the concepts that are currently emerging in a variety of disciplines and disciplinelike areas including physics, chemistry, brain theory, ecology, evolution, mathematics, philosophy, politics, psychology, linguistics, religion, consciousness, and the arts.[1] From this analysis Schwartz and Ogilvy have abstracted seven major characteristics of the "new paradigm" that are virtually diametrically opposed to those of the "dominant paradigm." The reader should note that the paradigms being addressed here are *not* inquiry paradigms, but paradigms characterizing disciplinary world views. The seven characteristics are summarized in Table 2.1. It is impossible in a short space to do justice to the richness of the Schwartz and Ogilvy development. Nevertheless, at least a rudimentary understanding of the terms of Table 2.1 is essential to the case to be made shortly: that this "new paradigm" substantially supports the naturalistic paradigm as an inquiry approach.

(1) Movement from simple to complex realities. Schwartz and Ogilvy (1979; henceforth S&O) point out that diversity and interactivity are characteristics of reality that are becoming more and more apparent. It is no longer sufficient to abstract out for intense study one or a few elements (variables?) while holding everything else "constant." To coin a phrase, most *ceteris* are not *paribus;* most other things are *not* equal. Variation is the order of all contexts. Thus, S&O assert, it is "in principle impossible to separate a thing from its interactive environment" (p. 10). Furthermore, it is no longer possible to view systems as merely the sums of their parts; as systems become more and more complex, they "develop unique properties" that cannot be accounted for or predicted from the properties of parts.

(2) Movement from hierarchic to heterarchic concepts of order. Older paradigms were based on the principle of hierarchy; there was an inherent order in nature, whether it was the political "divine right of kings," the primacy of male over female, or the chemical table of elements. "God's in his heaven and all's right with the world," as Voltaire put it. But recent discoveries have led emergent thinkers to

TABLE 2.1   Changes in Basic Beliefs—Dominant versus Emergent Paradigm

Dominant Paradigm *From:*	*Emergent Paradigm* *Toward:*
Simple	Complex
Hierarchy	Heterarchy
Mechanical	Holographic
Determinate	Indeterminate
Linearly causal	Mutually causal
Assembly	Morphogenesis
Objective	Perspective

SOURCE: Based on Schwartz and Ogilvy (1979, p. 13).

understand that *if* there are orders, many of them exist side by side; which is predominant at any moment depends on a number of interacting—and rapidly shifting—factors. Moreover, there is growing doubt that *real* orders exist *at all,* that they are imposed by human thinking rather that legitimated by the Law of Nature. S&O sum it up by saying:

> The old conception of order was hierarchical. . . . The emergent order is heterarchical. . . . Heterarchy is a shift from the rule by one to several rules by some . . . a system of mutual constraints and influence. The whole system goes not where any one interest would take it. Rather than merely a compromise or average of all the interests, there is a movement that is unpredictable and different from those of the particular component interests. (p. 13)

(3) Movement from mechanical to holographic images. This is a particularly difficult concept to grasp because it is essentially metaphoric, but it is nevertheless a powerful and pervasive notion. S&O are speaking here of the model or analogy one has in mind about the nature of the world and how that analogy or model shapes what one can think or believe about it. The predominant metaphor of the nineteenth century and much of the twentieth was the machine—not surprisingly, in view of the power of Newtonian mechanics to explain such phenomena as the orbits of the planets. The world was a wondrous machine, a clock, and God was often referred to as the Great Clockmaker. But, S&O point out, if one takes the concepts of complexity and heterarchy seriously, the machine ceases to be a very useful metaphor; they propose instead the metaphor of the hologram.

Holography is a very sophisticated imaging process, the possibility of which was first predicted mathematically; it was later produced with physical mechanisms. Its operation depends upon splitting a laser beam into two components, which are then projected at slightly different angles onto some object to be "photographed." But the "film" is no ordinary film; it records not a physical image but a pattern of interference waves produced by the two laser beam components that reach it at slightly different times. It is somewhat like making a sound recording not by grooves that correspond to actual sound patterns but by digital patterns that can be retranslated into sound when "played." Since the two laser beams "see" the object from slightly different perspectives, when they are recombined they produce interference patterns that can be recorded physically.

It turns out that holographs have an unusual property. If a normal recording or a normal film were damaged in some way—for instance, through the loss of some portion of the whole—then that same portion of information would also be lost. If a section of sound tape is cut out for 18 minutes, say, those 18 minutes are forever gone. Or if the image of a man is cropped out of a negative of a group picture, the association of that man with that group is forever destroyed. But holographs have the property that, *even if* large portions of the recorded interference patterns are lost, the remaining pieces, no matter how tiny, *will all have complete information* and will be able to reproduce the original image in its *entirety* (and in three dimensions!). Every piece of a system has complete information about the whole, in this view. As S&O suggest:

> With the holographic metaphor come several important attributes. We find that the image in the hologram is created by a *dynamic* process of interaction and differentiation. We find that the information is *distributed* throughout—that at each point information about the whole is contained in the part. In this sense, everything is interconnected like a vast network of interference patterns, having been generated by the same dynamic process and containing the whole in the part. (pp. 13-14)

Thus, while the whole is more than the sum of its parts, each part contains the whole within itself. The implications of this possibility boggle the mind!

(4) Movement from determinacy to indeterminacy. S&O point out that the believer in a mechanistic universe can also easily believe in a determinate one. In principle, if one knew the position and velocity of all of the particles in the world at any instant, then—given sufficiently complex computational equipment—one could predict the entire future state of the world.[2] But we have already seen in Chapter

1 that determinism is one of the "repugnant and unfounded" objections to positivism given credence by a variety of developments, including especially, in physics, Werner Heisenberg's Indeterminacy Principle. S&O comment:

> These simplistic notions [of in-principle determinism] were laid to rest by Heisenberg's Indeterminacy Principle, which tells us that (1) at a subatomic level the future state of a particle is in principle *not* predictable, and (2) the act of experimentation to find its state will itself determine the observed state. . . . It means that *ambiguity* about the future is a condition of nature.[3]

(5) From linear toward mutual causality. The dependence on mechanical models that are deterministic in every detail makes it almost inevitable that scientists should also have believed in a linear causality. The idea of causality, S&O aver, has gone through at least three stages: the simple push-pull model so well exemplified by the billiard ball analogy; the more elaborate probabilistic model introduced through considerations of thermodynamics, and including the idea of feedback; and the emergent model, which includes not only feedback but also *feedforward*. (See Chapter 6 for a more complete treatment of models of causality.) The latter formulation blurs the distinction between cause and effect greatly and introduces the notion of *mutual* causality—the simultaneous influencing of factors over time in such a way that it is no longer relevant to ask which caused which. S&O state:

> The new paradigm adds positive feedback, which means that the feedback signal from B affects A in a fashion such that A tends to increase B. In the simplest and most negative form that is called a vicious circle. However, when it is of mutual benefit for both A and B, then it is like symbiosis. Both A and B evolve and change together, each affecting the other in such a way as to make the distinction between cause and effect meaningless. (p.14)

(6) From assembly to morphogenesis. As the metaphor for form has been altered from mechanical to holographic, so the metaphor for change has moved from assembly toward morphogenesis. The old metaphor, S&O suggest, is the "construction project," in which separable components (now millitated against by the reality complexity hypothesis) were assembled in terms of some knowable plan or blueprint. When left to its own devices, nature resorts to entropy—the gradual disordering of itself into its most basic elements. But even a brief encounter with the world is persuasive of the proposition that

most change is not entropic; indeed higher-order forms are seen continuously to evolve from lower-order forms. S&O borrow the term "morphogenesis" from biology, in which field it has been used to "describe the evolution of galactic forms out of the primordial chaos" (p. 14). Mathematicians have also found it possible to describe this process in terms of "catastrophe theory." What is important to note is that morphogenetic change occurs dramatically and unpredictably, and operates in ways to create higher-order forms from lower. S&O comment:

> If a system is complex—composed of diverse elements that interact by mutually causal and indeterminate processes—and the system is open to external inputs, then it can change morphogenetically. A new form, unpredicted by any of its parts, can arise in such a system . . . . The requirements for morphogenesis are diversity, openness, complexity, mutual causality, and indeterminacy. When these conditions exist, we have the ingredients for qualitative change. (p. 14)

(7) From objective to perspectival views. S&O note that mental processes, instruments, and even our disciplines are not neutral. Thus objectivity is an illusion, but subjectivity in the usual sense is not the only alternative:

> We suggest that perspective is a more useful concept. Perspective connotes a view at a distance from a particular focus. Where we look from affects what we see. This means that any one focus of observation gives only a partial result; no single discipline ever gives us a complete picture. A whole picture is an image created morphogenetically from multiple perspectives. (p.15)

S&O also point out that perspectives require more than the simple accumulation of facts—*engagement* is also necessary. To know something is to become sufficiently engaged with it so that we can see it in the context of our own concerns. Multiple perspectives are needed so that we are not blinded by our own biases. Acknowledging the inescapability of perspective is very different from the attempt to gain objectivity by abstracting from all perspectives, which is the more usual approach. Finally, S&O suggest, perspective changes the very concept of reality:

> There may, indeed, be an ultimate reality. However, every time we try to discover what it is, our efforts will be partial. Thus we see a shift from the "absolute" truth discovered by the "right" method

TABLE 2.2   Basic Beliefs and Associated Principles of the New Paradigm

New Paradigm Basic Belief	Associated Principle
Complex	Real-world entities are a diverse lot of complex systems and organisms.
Heterarchic	Systems and organisms experience many simultaneous and potentially equally dominant orderings—none of which are "naturally" ordered.
Holographic	Images of systems and organisms are created by a dynamic process of interaction that is (metaphorically) similar to the holograph, the three-dimensional images of which are stored and recreated by the interference patterns of laser beams.
Indeterminate	Future states of systems and organisms are in principle unpredictable.
Mutually causal	Systems and organisms evolve and change together in such a way (with feedback and feedforward) as to make the distinction between cause and effect meaningless.
Morphogenetic	New forms of systems and organisms unpredicted (and unpredictable) from any of their parts can arise spontaneously under conditions of diversity, openness, complexity, mutual causality, and indeterminacy.
Perspectival	Mental processes, instruments, and even disciplines are not neutral.

toward a plurality of kinds of knowledge explored by a multiplicity of methods. (p. 15)

The seven basic beliefs of the "new paradigm" are summarized in Table 2.2

The reader may have noticed that these seven basic beliefs, much like the implications for doing research that were summarized in Chapter 1, have a synergistic relationship to one another—none could stand alone. Schwartz and Ogilvy have also noticed this characteristic, and, indeed, make much of it:

There is a difficulty of communication that must be noted. Describing a quality, which is itself a descriptive term, is very difficult. How do you describe blue or big when the meaningful referents are themselves changing? Thus, a shift in color from blue toward red is not too difficult, but blue toward big is almost nonsensical. Not only has there been a shift in the quality itself, but in its context as well. The meaning of the new description has changed. We will describe the shifts in quality in sequence; however, *their meaning is found in the whole pattern.* (p. 10; emphasis added)

We have made an effort to illustrate this interrelationship through the materials displayed in Tables 2.3 through 2.9 Each table deals with one of the seven basic beliefs—complexity, heterarchy, and so on—and illustrates its meaning through a series of descriptive sentences that amplify and clarify it. These descriptors are based upon the S&O monograph, although they are not, in the main, direct quotations. They have been included because, in our judgment, they represent incisive comments upon some characteristic of the belief. The reader will quickly see that many of the descriptors for any one basic belief are couched in terminology that draws upon one or more of the other six beliefs, thereby demonstrating the synergism that we claim exists. The seven basic beliefs are indeed a "matched set," with each dependent to a significant degree on the others. We may note that this interdependence itself illustrates the S&O contention that "facts" take their meaning from their context; in that sense each belief finds its meaning-imparting context in the other six. The reader will find it useful to spend some time browsing through these tables, as a way of building up his or her own propositional—and tacit—fund of information about the S&O "new" paradigm.

RELATIONSHIPS OF THE NATURALISTIC PARADIGM TO THE SCHWARTZ AND OGILVY "NEW" PARADIGM

We have been asserting that the S&O "new" paradigm, drawn from an analysis of a wide variety of *substantive* fields, supports the naturalistic paradigm, which purports to provide *methodological guidelines*. What is the basis for that assertion, and what evidence exists in favor of it?

Tables 2.3 through 2.9 summarize some of the most cogent explanatory descriptors derivable from S&O about their seven basic beliefs—the basic beliefs that undergird their "new" paradigm. Is there any relationship between these sentences and the five axioms of the naturalistic paradigm, briefly defined in Chapter 1 (and to be dealt with in Chapters 3 through 7)? We believe that there are substantial overlaps, and have summarized these in Table 2.10.

The rows of Table 2.10 represent the seven basic beliefs (terms) of the S&O new paradigm, while the columns correspond to the five axioms of the naturalistic paradigm as described in Chapter 1. The entries "primary" or "secondary" in the 35 cells of the table represent our judgment calls about the extent to which the naturalistic axiom draws support from each of the S&O terms. So, for example, in our opinion, the "multiple reality" axiom draws primary support from

TABLE 2.3   Some Explanatory Descriptors for the Basic Belief: Complexity

	Descriptor
A-1	All boundaries in actual ecosystems are arbitrary.
A-2	Systems and organisms cannot be separated from their environments because their meaning and even their existence depends upon their interactions with other systems and organisms.
A-3	Knowledge requires engagement with a system or organism in its environment, so that it can be seen in its meaning-defining context.
A-4	As systems and organisms become more complex, they develop unique properties (the whole is more than the sum of its parts).
A-5	Systems and organisms cannot be decomposed (fragmented) into individual elements (parts) because their unique systemic and organic properties transcend the elements (parts).
A-6	Each element has both the independent properties of wholes and the dependent properties of parts.
A-7	Holism is vindicated over atomism, and diversity is vindicated over homogenization (uniformity).
A-8	Meaning is not atomistic but contextual; to find meaning one needs to focus on the complex interrelationships that create a structure.
A-9	Inquiry must account for history and detail rather than permanence and generality.
A-10	Complex systems and organisms can undergo qualitative (revolutionary) as well as quantitative (incremental or evolutionary) changes.

the S&O terms "complexity" and "perspective," and secondary support from "heterarchy," "holographic," "indeterminacy," and "mutual causality." It is our judgment that "morphogenesis" makes no particular contribution to "multiple reality"; that cell is therefore blank.

Tables 2.11 through 2.15 are based on Table 2.10 and display the several S&O descriptors that we believe are most relevant. Thus Table 2.11 displays five descriptors selected from among those of Table 2.3 (complexity) that we believe best demonstrate the primary support that the axiom of multiple reality receives from that group of descriptors. Table 2.11 further displays two descriptors from Table 2.4 (heterarchy) that provide secondary support for multiple reality. The display proceeds in systematic fashion until the first column of Table 2.10, all dealing with multiple reality, is exhausted. Table 2.12 then picks up the tale for the second naturalistic axiom, knower-known relationships, and so on through the remaining tables for the remaining axioms. Again the reader is advised to spend some time browsing through these tables to determine for him or herself the nature and degree of support provided by the S&O terms for the naturalistic axioms.

Of course, the descriptors do not "speak for themselves"; the reader must supply sufficient interpretation to make the relevance of each

TABLE 2.4   Some Explanatory Descriptors for the Basic Belief:
Heterarchy

	Descriptor
B-1	The order we experience is a function of an activity of ordering performed by the mind; all apparently "real" orders are also determined by a mental ordering activity.
B-2	Different individuals tend to experience the same order because all rational creatures order experience using the same intrinsic categories— a shared paradigm.
B-3	The metaphor for the new order is the pond with its traceries of ripples rather than the edifice of concrete and steel with a place for everything and everything in its place.
B-4	"Hierarchies" are multiple and overlapping.
B-5	Which system(s) or organism(s) is (are) dominant or superior at any given time depends on the total situation and is determined by system or organism interactions.
B-6	While there may be vertical orderings at some point in time, many exist on a comparable level; centralization is giving way to decentralization.
B-7	Structures of systems and organisms operate heterarchically, creating a net of mutual constraints and influences.
B-8	Movement among systems or organisms is not mere compromise or averaging; it may be unpredictable and different from the interests or tendencies of the interacting systems or organisms.
B-9	Human action is oriented more toward pluralism than singularity (of values, political structures, and so on); it is mediated more by a heteracity of guiding principles than by a hierarchy of functions.
B-10	Facilitation rather than command becomes the primary process of guiding outcomes.
B-11	Authority derived from natural or transcendent order gives way to legitimacy granted by voluntary association.
B-12	Voluntarism and inventiveness replace necessity and conformity.

NOTE: Contrast the term "heterarchy" with "anarchy" (no order) and with "hierarchy" (order determined by a "natural" or assigned superiority).

TABLE 2.5   Some Explanatory Descriptors for the Basic Belief:
Holography

	Descriptor
C-1	Information is distributed throughout the system rather than concentrated at specific points.
C-2	At each point information about the whole is contained in the part.
C-3	Not only can the entire reality be found in the part, but the part can be found in the whole.
C-4	What is detected in *any* part must also characterize the whole (a form of generalization).
C-5	Everything is interconnected.

TABLE 2.6   Some Explanatory Descriptors for the Basic Belief:
Indeterminacy

	Descriptor
D-1	Ambiguity about the future is the condition of nature.
D-2	In complex systems and organisms, future possibilities can be known but precise outcomes cannot be predicted; that is, predictability is replaced by probability.
D-3	Not everything is possible, but among the possibilities choices do affect outcomes.
D-4	There is a reciprocal involvement between the knower and the known.
D-5	The nature of the observation process affects the results; measurements are determined by the relationship between the observer and the observed.
D-6	Study in depth usually increases uncertainty.
D-7	Planning is less a matter of prediction and control than of detecting errors (twists, shifts, unexpected developments) and responding to them.

TABLE 2.7   Some Explanatory Descriptors for the Basic Belief:
Mutual Causality

	Descriptor
E-1	Strict deterministic causality is replaced by unpredictable innovation arising morphogenetically through mutually causal interactions and fluctuations.
E-2	There is a complex of mutually interacting "causes" leading to a particular outcome.
E-3	The universe is an interconnected network, an indivisible whole.
E-4	We are part of the net; what we do affects other parts, including what we wish to study; thus any description of reality is always partial.
E-5	Evolution (change) is less mediated by the conquest (or replacement) of one variant by another than by their ability to adapt together; mutual adaptation is the basis for mutual evolution; mutual causality leads to co-evolution.
E-6	To understand a system or organism completely requires knowledge of its history, which cannot be known completely from its present condition.
E-7	In complex systems and organisms, mutual causality leads not to stability but to symbiotic ehange (positive feedback and feedforward) and evolution.
E-8	Mutual causality in complex systems and organisms tends to produce unpredictable results.
E-9	Differences grow rather than diminish.
E-10	The concept of influence replaces those of control and power.

descriptor apparent. Relevance is a judgment call, so it would not be surprising if the reader should judge some descriptors irrelevant despite their placement in the tables. It is also a judgment call whether a descriptor provides primary or secondary support for an axiom; again

TABLE 2.8   Some Explanatory Descriptors for the Basic Belief:
Morphogenesis

	Descriptor
F-1	New and different systems and organisms arise out of old through a complex process that amplifies deviation through reciprocal (mutual) causality (positive feedback and feedforward) and through interactions with the surrounding environment.
F-2	Fluctuations in a system or organism are not merely random errors or deviations from the significant average; rather, such fluctuations can be the source of a new order.
F-3	Fluctuations in a system or organism interact, affecting each other and mutually causing whole new systems and organisms to arise.
F-4	Differences produce changes.
F-5	More highly ordered systems and organisms are produced from less highly ordered, simple systems and organisms; order can arise even from disorder.
F-6	Very complex systems and organisms can arise through very dense and complex interactions rather than through the summing (assembly, aggregation) of information bits or elements.
F-7	Change is not only continuous and quantitative but discontinuous and qualitative.
F-8	Components constrain but do not determine emergent form in morphogenetic change.
F-9	There may be sharp discontinuities between scientific "truths."

the reader may differ with our judgment. It would be surprising indeed, however, if, despite some occasional disagreements, the reader should conclude that, on balance, the claim of support is unwarranted.

The reader may have noted, in scanning Tables 2.11 through 2.15, that while the S&O basic beliefs have meaning for the conduct of research in virtually every known discipline area, they seem to have special relevance for research into human behavior, research of the kind commonly labeled "social/behavioral." It is no accident that this should be the case, for as S&O themselves point out, the new paradigm is metaphorically very similar to the human organism:

> The total pattern of change is somewhat like a change in metaphor from reality as a machine toward reality as a conscious organism. Machines are mechanical and relatively simple. They are organized hierarchically from components, and they function linearly and predictably. We can stand outside them and study them.
>
> A conscious being—say, a human being—is very complex and unpredictable. People behave one way now and a different way later. When they change, they often change suddenly. They are internally inter-

TABLE 2.9   Some Explanatory Descriptions for the Basif Belief:
Perspective

	Descriptor
G-1	Where and how one looks at systems and organisms affects what will be seen; the knower's perspective is crucial in determining what is known.
G-2	What we believe about systems and organisms determines much of what we see (believing is seeing).
G-3	Any one focus or observation provides only one perspective; no discipline gives a complete picture; knowledge is at best partial.
G-4	No description, model, or theory is ever complete; what is required is a multiplicity of perspectives, each of which enriches and complements the others.
G-5	One form of knowledge or method cannot be reduced into another (an antireductionism principle).
G-6	Knowledge is protected not by abstracting from all perspectives (the claim for objectivity) but by balancing multiple perspectives to constrain bias (the claim for fairness).
G-7	Objectivity is an illusion.
G-8	All knowledge, far from being disinterested, is ultimately interested knowledge; an imperative for science is to conduct inquiry as if people really mattered.
G-9	Reality is not something that remains no matter what people think about it; reality is utterly dependent on human cognition.
G-10	Publicly shared reality is not unchanging (objective); what counts as reality shifts as shared paradigms shift.
G-11	The concept of paradigm shift (itself a kind of perspectival difference) opens the possibility of an almost limitless proliferation of research programs based on widely different assumptions.

connected, consisting of many complex subsystems. They are externally interconnected with other people and the world around them. When
people interact they affect each other. Because of this complexity of
interaction, people don't always see the same things; they have unique perspectives. In the same way, the emergent paradigm of the actual world is complex, holographic, heterarchical, indeterminate,
mutually causal, morphogenetic, and perspectival. The shift in metaphor
is from the machine to the human being. *We are like the world we
see.* (p. 15; emphasis added)

IS THE NATURALISTIC
PARADIGM LEGITIMATE?

In this chapter we have asked the question, Is the naturalistic
paradigm the genuine article? Or, to put it another way, Is it a
legitimate guide for inquiry? The answer to these questions seems to
be a resounding "Yes!"

TABLE 2.10 Support for the Naturalistic Axioms Provided by the Schwartz and Ogilvy Terms

Schwartz and Ogilvy Terms	Multiple Reality	Knower-Known Interaction	Time and Context Dependence	Mutual and Simultaneous Shaping	Value Dependence
Complexity	primary	–	primary	–	–
Heterarchy	secondary	–	secondary	secondary	secondary
Holographic	secondary	–	secondary	secondary	–
Indeterminacy	secondary	primary	primary	–	–
Mutual causality	secondary	secondary	secondary	primary	–
Morphogenesis	–	–	secondary	primary	–
Perspective	primary	primary	–	–	primary

TABLE 2.11   S&O Descriptors Supporting Axiom 1:   Reality

Descriptor

From Complexity (primary support):

A-2	Systems and organisms cannot be separated from their environments because their meaning and even their existence depends upon their interactions with other systems and organisms.
A-4	As systems and organisms become more complex, they develop unique properties (the whole is more than the sum of the parts).
A-5	Systems and organisms cannot be decomposed (fragmented) into individual elements (parts) because their unique systemic and organic properties transcend the elements (parts).
A-8	Meaning is not atomistic but contextual; to find meaning one needs to focus on the complex interrelationships that create a structure.
A-9	Inquiry must account for history and detail rather than permanence and generality.

From Hierarchy (secondary support):

B-1	The order we experience is a function of the activity of ordering performed by the mind; all apparently "real" orders are also determined by a mental ordering activity.
B-9	Human action is oriented more toward pluralism than singularity (of values, political structures, and so on); it is mediated more by a heteracity of guiding principles than by a hierarchy of functions.

From Holographic (secondary support):

C-5	Everything is interconnected.

From Indeterminacy (secondary support):

D-4	There is a reciprocal involvement between the knower and the known.

From Mutual Causality (secondary support):

E-3	The universe is an interconnected network, an indivisible whole.

From Perspective (primary support):

G-1	Where and how one looks at systems and organisms affects what will be seen; the knower's perspective is crucial in determining what is known.
G-2	What we believe about systems and organisms determines much of what we see (believing is seeing).
G-5	One form of knowledge or method cannot be reduced into another.
G-9	Reality is not something that remains no matter what people think about it; reality is utterly dependent on human cognition.

First, we were able to make a series of arguments that indicate a greater degree of acceptability for the new paradigm than might have been the case even just a few years ago. Strict constructionists of the Campbell and Cook persuasion are taking a much softer line, apparently willing to admit that there might be some utility in one-shot case studies after all. The descriptions of patterns or models of inquiry proposed by leading epistemologists contain nothing that would exclude

TABLE 2.12   S&O Descriptors Supporting Axiom 2:
Knower-Known Interaction

Descriptor

From Indeterminacy (primary support):

D-4	There is a reciprocal involvement between the knower and the known.
D-5	The nature of the observation process affects the results; measurements are determined by the relationship between the observer and the observed.

From Mutual Causality (secondary support):

E-4	We are part of the net; what we do affects other parts, including what we wish to study; thus any description of reality is always partial.

From Perspective (primary support):

G-1	Where and how one looks at systems and organisms affects what will be seen; the knower's perspective is crucial in determining what is known.
G-6	Knowledge is protected not by abstracting from all perspectives (the claim for objectivity) but by balancing multiple perspectives to constrain bias (the claim for fairness).
G-7	Objectivity is an illusion.

naturalism from consideration as one of their number. Pattern theories encompass the grounded theories that are often the output of naturalistic studies. Naturalistic inquiry clearly qualifies as disciplined, if one follows the definition of Cronbach and Suppes; indeed, naturalism may satisfy their criteria better than the conventional paradigm does. Finally, we see that there are many useful precedents for the kind of inquiry that is here labeled "naturalistic," but that is also known by such names as "ethnographic," "field study," "case study," or "participant observation."

A much more compelling argument in favor of naturalism can be made, however, by pointing out the conceptual resonance between the major axioms of naturalism and the major basic beliefs that, according to Schwartz and Ogilvy, now characterize emergent, vanguard thinking in virtually every major discipline or discipline-like area of scholarly endeavor. Their seven basic beliefs have not simply been picked out of the air; rather, they represent the analytic residue remaining after the particulars of physics, chemistry, brain theory, mathematics, and so on have been "boiled off." It is amazing that only two scholars should have sufficient intellectual power, between them, to deal with the seemingly disparate ideas that characterize these several fields, but no less amazing is the fact that all of these disparities seem to be converging on a similar set of undergirding assumptions. Moreover, these

TABLE 2.13   S&O Descriptors Supporting Axiom 3:
Time and Context Dependence

Descriptor

From Complexity (primary support):

A-2   Systems and organisms cannot be separated from their environments because their meaning and even their existence depends on their interactions with other systems and organisms.

A-3   Knowledge requires engagement with a system or organism: in its environment, so that it can be seen in its meaning-defining context.

A-9   Inquiry must account for history and detail rather than permanence and generality.

From Heterarchy (secondary support):

B-5   Which systems or organisms are dominant or superior at any given time depends on the total situation and is determined by system or organism interactions.

From Holographic (secondary support):

C-1   Information is distributed throughout the system rather than concentrated at specific points.

From Indeterminacy (primary support):

D-2   In complex systems and organisms, future possibilities can be known but precise outcomes cannot be completely known from its present condition.

From Mutual Causality (secondary support):

E-6   To understand a system or organism completely requires knowledge of its history, which cannot be completely known from its present condition.

E-8   Mutual causality in complex systems and organisms tends to produce unpredictable results.

From Morphogenesis (secondary support):

F-7   Change is not only continuous and quantitative but discontinuous and qualitative.

substantive assumptions are found to have astonishingly close correspondence with the *methodological* axioms of naturalism. If it is the case, as we shall argue later (Chapter 7), that research paradigms must be resonant at the level of assumptions with the substantive paradigms that guide inquiry if meaningful data are to emerge, it is clear that the naturalistic is the paradigm of choice in virtually every scholarly field.

Finally, it seems clear that whatever may be the state of affairs regarding paradigm fit in the so-called hard and life sciences, the naturalistic paradigm provides a better degree of fit with substantive paradigms in the areas of social/behavioral research. That case will also be made in detail in upcoming chapters, but the overall validity

TABLE 2.14   S&O Descriptors Supporting Axiom 4:
Mutual and Simultaneous Shaping

Descriptor

From Heterarchy (secondary support):

B-7   Structures of systems and organisms operate heterarchically, creating a net of mutual constraints and influences.

From Holographic (secondary support):

C-5   Everything is interconnected.

From Mutual Causality (primary support):

E-1   Strict deterministic causality is replaced by unpredictable innovation arising morphogenetically through mutually causal interactions and fluctuations.

E-2   There is a complex of mutually interacting "causes" leading to a particular outcome.

E-3   The universe is an interconnected network, an indivisible whole.

E-7   In complex systems and organisms, mutual causality leads not to stability but to symbiotic change (positive feedback and feedforward) and evolution.

From Morphogenesis (primary support):

F-1   New and different systems and organisms arise out of old through a complex process that amplifies deviation through reciprocal (mutual) causality (positive feedback and feedforward) and through interactions with the surrounding environment.

F-2   Fluctuations in a system or organism interact, affecting each other and mutually causing whole new systems and organisms to arise.

F-5   More highly ordered systems and organisms are produced from less highly ordered, simple systems and organisms; order can arise even from disorder.

F-8   Components constrain but do not determine form in morphogenetic change.

---

of the assertion can be estimated from the S&O quotation at the end of the preceding section. We *are* like the world we see, and, more important, the world we see is like us.

Practitioners of conventional social/behavioral research, which relies so heavily on statistical analysis, are well aware that every statistic rests on certain assumptions that they are required to test *before* using it. Assumptions of that sort are not, as novice students of statistics are wont to believe, things one assumes about the data; rather, they are claims that must be tested with reference to the data in order to legitimate the use of that statistic. A statistical technique that assumes treatment effect additivity, for example, or an underlying normal curve, cannot be used, legitimately, in situations in which the data are found *not* to meet the assumptions undergirding that statistic. Similarly, one

TABLE 2.15   S&O Descriptors Supporting Axiom 5:   Value Dependence

Descriptor

From Heterarchy (secondary support):

B-9   Human action is oriented more toward pluralism than singularity (of values, political structures, and so on); it is mediated more by a hetaracity of guiding principles than by a hierarchy of function.

From Perspective (primary support):

G-1   Where and how one looks at systems and organisms affects what will be seen; the knower's perspective is crucial in determining what is known.

G-2   What we believe about systems and organisms determines much of what we see (believing is seeing).

G-6   Knowledge is protected not by abstracting from all perspectives (the claim of objectivity) but by balancing multiple perspectives to constrain bias (the claim of fairness).

G-8   All knowledge, far from being disinterested, is ultimately interested knowledge; an imperative for science is to conduct inquiry as if people really mattered.

G-10   Publicly shared reality is not unchanging (objective); what counts as reality shifts as shared paradigms shift.

G-11   The concept of paradigm shift (itself a kind of perspectival difference) opens the possibility of an almost limitless proliferation of research programs based on widely different assumptions.

may argue, it is not legitimate to use an inquiry paradigm resting on assumptions that cannot be justified in the data field. And where, today, *especially* in the social/behavioral sciences, can one investigate a phenomenon about which one could assert a tangible reality, independence of the observer, stability over all time and context factors, direct and unidirectional causality, and freedom from value constructions?

In the five chapters to follow, the five axioms of the naturalistic paradigm will be addressed in detail. The brief definitions offered in Chapter 1 (so far the reader's only anchor in this conceptual sea) will be expanded and explicated. In particular, an effort will be made to show the utility of those axioms in social/behavioral science, in order to buttress as fully as possible the claim that for those sciences, the naturalistic paradigm is *the* paradigm of choice.

NOTES

1. This monograph is but a summary of a much larger collection of documents produced by the project. Unfortunately, the project is funded by a consortium of businesses and industries that hold a proprietary interest in the outcomes. Copies of the larger collection of documents are available only to sponsors or to subscribers at a $500 fee.

2. Douglas Hofstadter provides an interesting commentary on this possibility in his essay, "A Conversation with Einstein's Brain," in which he postulates the ability to put questions to Einstein—and to receive answers—even after Einstein's death! See Chapter 26 in Hofstadter and Dennett (1981).

3. Some physicists believe it to be the case that the world is actually *created* by the act of choosing. Each act of choice puts the world on a particular one of the infinite number of tracks it might have pursued—all indeterminate until choices occur. See Wolf (1981).

3

Constructed Realities

I fell asleep, and while sleeping, I dreamed that I was a butterfly. But when I awoke, I was uncertain whether I was a man
dreaming that I was a butterfly, or whether I was a butterfly
dreaming that I was a man, dreaming that I was a butterfly.

(Old Chinese Paradox)

Cognition is the most socially-conditioned activity of man, and
knowledge is the paramount social creation.

(Fleck, 1979)

Struggles with the concept of reality are as old as humankind.
Literature, poetry, plays, epic ballads, all have offered explanations
for the great questions: Who am I? What am I doing here? What is
the purpose of life? And, what is real? Their putative answers are the
subject of the world's great religions, the greatest of the world's
philosophical and moral thought, and most rock 'n' roll music. Their
expressions can be found at any point in life. They exist embedded
in everyday life, in the rash of self-help books that proliferated in the
1960s and 1970s, in serious disciplinary considerations ranging from
psychology to sociology to quantum mechanics, and, finally, in newer
constructions of formal philosophy or philosophy of science.

REALITY FOR THE
PERSON ON THE STREET

The everyday consciousness of reality and its chameleonlike quality pervade politics, the media, and literature. A story is told about
Jocko Conlan, a National League umpire, who, when trying to define
criteria for calling a given pitch a ball or strike, finally declared, "They
ain't nothin' til I calls 'em." Conlan's blatant construction of baseball
reality may be an overstatement, especially now that we have entered
the era of the instant replay, but it characterizes well a phenomenon

Material in this chapter quoted from Weston La Barre, *Culture in Context: Selected
Writings of Weston La Barre,* copyright 1980 by Weston La Barre, published by Duke
University Press, 1980, is used by permission.

that is not new. Consider, for instance, Tom Wicker's April 5, 1981, editorial on Alexander Haig shortly after the Reagan assassination attempt: "High White House officials, in their present circumstances, have little choice but to *put the best possible face on Secretary of State Haig's performance* the day President Reagan was shot" (emphasis added). Having been confronted with Haig's remarkable "performance," which was clearly unexplainable in terms of any of the rules that might be invoked under such dire circumstances, White House officials found themselves forced to engage in "face-making," face-saving, or, more succinctly, in the creation or construction of a palatable reality into which Haig might fit.

And Haig himself was not immune to the construction of quaint realities. Upon his resignation, *Newsweek* magazine speculated as to why he had seemingly not succeeded in the job he was hired to do:

> Early on, Alexander Haig's persistent verbification of nouns, expropriation of compound military-bureaucratic voguisms and caveating of almost everything back-burnered the rest of his style. Such obfuscatory phrase-turns as "posthostage-return-attitude" or "nuance-al differences" and the still elusive "epistemologicallywise" eyebrow raised U.S. and allied officials alike who could not figure out what the Secretary was elocuting. Pundits mercilessly characterized Haigspeak as "haigledygook" and "Haigravation." Informationed Haigally that a question could not be answered "the way you contexted it," Sen. John Glenn of Ohio gamely comebacked, "Will you burden-share?" And even the normally support-providing Wall Street Journal bluntly derisioned, "What language is the Secretary speaking?" ("Why Haig Quit," 1982, p. 24)

It would appear that the construction of realities must depend on some form of consensual language. Unable to agree on what that might be, the press and most everyone else gave up trying to understand reality as Haig constructed it. *Sic transit gloria* foreign policy à la Haig.

One does not have to be drawn into the malapropisms and neologisms of Haig, however, to appreciate the experience of constructed realities. In the same week—the week of October 19, 1981—both *Time* and *Newsweek* magazines reviewed Diana Trilling's book on the Jean Harris-Herman Tarnower tragedy. Consider, for the moment, the very different perspectives on the same book evinced by the reviewers. Jean Strouse (1981, p. 101), writing for *Newsweek,* condemns Trilling's treatment of Mrs. Harris:

> Trilling has no use for objectivity. She announces that she first conceived this book "in a spirit of partisanship," of "unqualified sym-

pathy" for Mrs. Harris, but later changed her mind. She here proceeds to try the headmistress all over again (isn't that double jeopar-
dy?) in a special inquiry of her own—it might be called trial by
innuendo—and she indulges in a little armchair psychoanalysis on the
side. . . . Was [Trilling] in too great a hurry to get this book out before
her competitors? Is she reaching for the mass market with her chatty
tone, . . . histrionics . . . rhetorical flourishes and attempts to sound
"with it"?

R. Z. Sheppard (1981, p. 101), writing for *Time,* on the other hand,
found the book quite admirable in several respects:

Diana Trilling is a redoubtable essayist whose clear thinking and case-
hardened prose have cut through much of the intellectual and political
lard of the past 40 years.

The betting was that Trilling, 76, would turn out the most thoughtful
account, though not the fastest or most marketable. One hesitates to
deliver a verdict before all the evidence is in, but it is unlikely that
Trilling's treatment of Tarnower's death and Harris' conviction will
be bettered.

In the best sense of the term, this set of reviews represents what
Schwartz and Ogilvy (1979) would call a move from the objective to
the perspective. Neither Trilling's book nor either of the reviewers
makes claims to objectivity; they represent perspectives, or what would
be called "multiple realities." And none of them either purports to
or seeks to represent the reality as constructed by Mrs. Jean Harris
(which none of us will probably ever know or have access to).

Even George Will, the noted and widely read conservative colum-
nist, is not above dealing with constructed realities, although he does
not title them as such. In a July 24, 1983, editorial on former Secretary
of State Henry Kissinger's alleged deviousness, Will treats the issue
of where Kissinger made mistakes in assessing public opinion:

Kissinger's liberal critics are mistaken about the world; his conservative
critics are mistaken about political realities. . . .

Critics on the left and right join in charging that pessimism or cynicism
or some other un-American trait caused him to distrust the American
public, and hence to pursue defeatist policies with devious methods.
Actually, he trusted too much in the public's readiness to maintain
the sinews of national strength amidst the atmospherics of detente.

If he was naive it was not, as conservative critics charge, about the
Soviet system. Rather, it was about public opinion, the subtlety of
which he overestimated. *A flaw in his detente policy was misplaced*

confidence in the constancy of a public condemned to live with am-
biguities. (p. 5A; emphasis added)

For Will, the central concern is whether Henry Kissinger constructed
a world view that served him well or ill, and, in Will's opinion, Kissinger misconstructed the reality of public opinion.

Other examples of daily trafficking with notions of reality are
voluminous. As with bridge or Parcheesi, once the rules of the game
are understood, one can look for examples of one's own, and find
them at every turn without venturing further than daily newspapers
or weekly news magazines. The game is sufficiently easy to play. The
everyday examples abound.

But examples exist in more rarified circles also. Efforts to come to
grips with reality can be found, for instance, in the plethora of self-
help books that has emerged. These books are sometimes referred to
as "self-administered psychology." But in the sense that they mirror
quite accurately the concerns and problems people see themselves fac-
ing, they are excellent exemplars of the stride toward alternative
lifestyles and, at some deeper level, are reflective of the emergent
paradigm in action. One such book, by Stewart Emery (1978), is particularly helpful because it confronts the issues of reality directly:

> Our individual personal reality—the way we think life is and the part
> we are to play in it—*is self-created. We put together our own per-*
> *sonal reality.* It is made up of our interpretation of our perceptions
> of the way things are and what has happened to us. We make some
> basic decisions about life when we are being born, and we add to the
> script and embellish it during our childhood. We end up with a view
> of ourselves and the world that is usually highly inaccurate, because
> our perceptions of the world at an early age are not accurate. . . . Out
> of that we put together an environment that is a perfect reflection of
> our view of the world.
>
> We write our script by the time we are about seven years old. Then
> we treat the world as if it were the back lot at Universal Studios. We
> pick out our sets and our props. We go to Wardrobe, which may be
> Sears or Macy's or Saks Fifth Avenue and choose our costumes. We
> select a location and begin filming the story of our life as we see it,
> starring US. *We literally create a reality that reflects our view of the*
> *world and who we are in relation to it.* (p. 39; emphasis added).

While Emery speaks most clearly of the problem of self-created,
or constructed, realities, others in this genre are equally forceful, if
only by indirection. Shere Hite's *The Hite Report* (1976) and *The Hite*

Report on Male Sexuality (1981), both widely read when they first appeared, are equally interesting examples of constructed realities. In Hite's books, the realities happen to be primarily those of women (in the first instance) and men (in the latter) responding to questionnaires asking for self-revelation concerning attitudes and practices of individual sexuality. Nevertheless, reading even snippets of responses lends a sense to the variety of experiences and constructions placed upon such intimate human contact.

An equally fascinating example is the recent "discovery" of the "G spot" (G for Gräfenberg, the purported discoverer of such a spot, supposedly an area of erectile tissue responsible for profound orgasms in women). Whether or not such a "spot" exists is open to question, although a recent book has emerged that argues for it forcefully (Ladas, Whipple, & Perry, 1982). What is interesting for present purposes is the *series* of realities that surround the existence of the G spot. On the one hand, there are unexplained phenomena regarding human (and especially female) sexual experience. Apparently, the G spot "explains" those previously unexplainable phenomena reasonably well. On the other hand, one wonders, in the face of hundreds of years of autopsies on human bodies—especially those of the twentieth century, which have become increasingly meticulous with the addition of more sophisticated machinery for looking at the interior of cells—why no one ever "saw" this particular "spot," or why there is conspicuous absence of mention of such curious tissue in centuries of writings and drawings of portions of the dissected human anatomy. Finally, one has to conclude, with an amused interviewee in *Time* magazine: "It's less interesting whether the Gräfenberg spot is there than that people want to search for it" (September 13, 1982).

The popular literature on Eastern religions and mysticism also provides dozens of examples of reality concerns. Readers of the now extensively reviewed (and often well-received) Carlos Castañeda (1974, 1977) books on his training by the mysterious Yaqui Indian, Don Juan, provide the reader with extensive "reality disjunctions" on virtually every page. Are we to believe that Castañeda has invented his stories, in response perhaps to some subconscious understanding of the relative new Western need to be connected once again to mystery and power? Are we to believe that Don Juan is a real person, imbued with powers sufficient to enable Castañeda to become disembodied, to fly, to "see" things that no ordinary man has seen? Are we to believe that Don Juan is a real Indian with understandings of hallucinogens native to the North American deserts, which he has used to induce the dream and waking states in Castañeda that he reflected in his writings? What *are* we to believe about these writings? One person's reality will undoubtedly be another's mystical allegory, and still another's hogwash. The realities that we are able to construct out of the writings of Castañeda undoubtedly reflect strongly the belief structure that we bring to those same writings. Those with belief structures that admit to the existence of things unseen and unknown will undoubtedly form strong attachments to the rings of "truth" there, while those who believe in nothing unseen or unknown will dismiss the tales of power as either drug-induced hallucination or creative hyperbole. It depends, as Schwartz and Ogilvy would point out, on "perspectival" creation of reality.

In an interview conducted by Sunno Bhikko (1975), Achaan Chaa, an Eastern mystic, is equally enigmatic on the nature of reality:

> Student: Are defilements such as greed or anger merely illusory, or are they real?
>
> /Chaa/: They are both. The defilements we call lust or greed or delusion—these are just an outward name, appearance. Just as we can call a bowl large, small, pretty, or whatever. This is not reality. It is the concept we create from craving. (p. 124)

This is simply another way in which reality is "constructed," in this instance by an Eastern mystic and guru. There are, of course, multiple ways in which "reality" may be constructed, and there are multiple rationales for so doing. We will return to that point later in this chapter. For the moment, it will be helpful to continue considering ways in which problems with traditional constructs of reality have plagued writers and researchers.

"REALITY" IN THE DISCIPLINES

Another group that has grappled with reality and its meaning are those persons in academic disciplines who have examined method and its implications for knowing what we believe we know. Conspicuous among the disciplines most directly involved have been the several social behavioral sciences. David Bakan, professor of psychology at York University in Ontario and past president of one division of the American Psychological Association, in an article based on a presidential division address, argued that it was high time for psychology to "kick the science habit" (Bakan, 1972). In defense of his argument, he cited the fundamental conflict of the experimentalists versus the empiricists from the 1920s and 1930s, which essentially ignored two concrete facts in the history of scientific research: first, that experimentalism is but one form of empiricism, and, second, that empiricism— or reliance on observation or experience—has been responsible for most of the scientific advances to date. In general, to give the devil his due,

> the marriage between psychology and natural science brought a critical attitude to the study of psychological phenomena, and this was an important step forward. *But the attempt to transfer other features of the natural sciences also had negative effects.* Principally, this alliance: 1) deflected psychology away from its primary subject matter—thinking, feeling, and willing; and 2) perpetuated an unwillingness to recognize the special quality of psychological phenomena that [he calls] *reflexivity.* (Bakan, 1972, p. 86-88; first emphasis added; second, in original)

But, Bakan goes on, traditional science, as it has come down to us from the natural sciences, has largely failed the enterprise of psychology: "Behaviorism's ideal of prediction and control not only fails on scientific grounds but makes the psychologist appear monstrous and contemptuous" (p. 88). But "psychology now has an opportunity to free itself from the natural-science model, *to pursue intrinsically relevant goals*" (p. 86; emphasis added), because "an authentic psychology must also concern itself with *reflexivity*: the effect of thinking, feeling and willing . . . on [true psychological processes such as thought and emotion] themselves" (p. 88). In short, Bakan's cry for psychology to eschew traditional or conventional science for a more relevant or empirical science (based, as he notes, on discovery rather than prediction and control) is a cry to focus on those things that make men and women human, the cognitive and creative processes. This focus would include the cognizing and creation that revolves about constructions of reality.

Sociology was also affected; the "paradigmatic crisis" of the early 1920s, from which sprang the "interpretive" sociologies (Pope, 1982),

> [stood] opposed to the tenets of the old positivism. None of the symbolic interactionists and ethnomethodologists believe that social science should aim to produce lawlike sets of propositions, but believe instead that social science should provide a deeper understanding of individuals, their perceptions, and *the meanings they attach to social life* (Reynolds, 1980/1981; emphasis added).

One such way of dealing with meanings attached to social life was the epistemological position described as "constructive alternativism" by George Kelly, a personal construct psychology that attempts to "do justice to the internal world of the person" (Pope, 1982). This theoretical and methodological approach "fall[s] within the 'verstehen' approach, the central spirit of which is coming to an understanding of the view of the world held by those people involved in a situation rather than adopting a 'stranger' perspective or ascribing structural function to external aspects (stimuli) of the environment" (Pope, 1982, p. 3). Kelly (1955) himself claimed that it was "presumption to assume that a person's constructions of reality were convergent with reality [*sic*] and suggested that "the open question for man is not whether reality exists or not but what he can make of it." Events or situations are theoretically open to as many constructions as there are persons engaged in them, or as many reconstructions by a single individual as imagination allows. Kelly's emphasis, as a therapeutic psychologist, was upon individual construction of individual realities, and upon the structure of the construct systems that individuals evolve for themselves, in order that meaning might be imposed on individual experiences (Pope, 1982; Kelly, 1969a, 1969b).

Schutz (1967) likewise found reality an artifact difficult to explain unless rooted in the meanings that are constructed and attached to everyday life by individuals. This phenomenological perspective, a strain of interpretive sociology, tries "to study social behavior by interpreting its subjective meaning as found in the intentions of individuals. The aim, then, is to interpret the actions of individuals in the social world and the ways in which individuals give meaning to social phenomena" (Schutz, 1967, p. 11).

Educationists, too, have not been without struggles with reality. Stake (1977), in an early *Evaluation News*[1] guest editorial entitled "Some Alternative Presumptions," took on "truth" (and therefore reality) for the evaluation community. In doing program evaluation, he commented,

> there is too great a temptation to suppose that truth is to be found in words and to suppose that intuitions are only poor facsimiles of truth. In practical matters, what is in fact true is that which is understood. . . . In any circumstance the truth might be but a single truth—but evaluators are certain not to find it. What they can find are multiple truths, multiple understandings, some contradictory to others. Evaluators should seek to resolve the contradictions and misunderstandings but *should expect that they will have to portray the multiple realities they find*" (p. 19; emphasis added).

Nor have the neo-Marxists in education remained free of the quarrel surrounding questions of what is real. They, perhaps more than any others, save the naturalists and ethnomethodologists, have concerns, not, as one would suspect, over whether or not social reality is a constructed set of meanings (which they freely grant), but over *whose* construction ought legitimately to prevail. Michael Young (1971, p. 2), for instance, suggests that "sociologists should treat as problematic the dominant legitimizing categories of educators and should view them as 'constructed realities' which are realized in particular institutional contexts" (Reynolds, 1980/1981, p. 81), because

> existing categories that for parents, teachers, children and many researchers distinguish home from school, learning from play, academic from non-academic and able or bright from dull and stupid must be conceived as socially constructed, with some in a position to impose their constructions or meanings on others.

Barton and Walker (1978, p. 274) buttress this emergent educational sociology by stressing that it views

> man [sic] as an active participant in the creation and construction of social reality. . . . The nature of school knowledge, the organization of the school, the ideologies of teachers, indeed any educational issue, all become relative—and the central task for the sociology of education becomes to reveal *what constitutes reality for the participants in a given situation, to explain how those participants came to view reality in this way.* (emphasis added).

It is with constructs of reality that we are mainly concerned, but it is of more than passing interest that neo-Marxists engaged in criticism of naturalistic or ethnomethodological approaches have come down firmly in the camp of the positivists, arguing that "naturalism . . . does not appear to be concerned with the validation and objectification of the knowledge that is produced. . . . In the focus of its work, the naturalistic perspective is concerned mostly with the 'micro' world of the school and within-school interaction, neglecting to focus on the possible material determination of this phenomenological world. Naturalism accords to the social scientist the role of passive reporter of events and member accounts rather than interpreter of the world that Marxist analysis wishes the intellectual to adopt" (Reynolds, 1980/1981, p. 87).

The Marxist critique is partly legitimate, in that focus on educational issues rarely links those issues to wider socioeconomic analysis in any meaningful fashion. Nevertheless, non-Marxists will argue, and equally legitimately, that dialectic materialism is simply another social (or economic) construct in the world of ideas, and only one of many that might be used in successful criticism of the educational enterprise. Marxists or non-Marxists have equal difficulty realizing that the business of schooling—what it is about, what it should be doing, who should be engaged in it—is itself a construction from culture to culture (and perhaps from community to community).

Jon Magoon (1977), presumably not a neo-Marxist, has commented extensively on what he calls "constructivist research," by which he means "a refocusing of educational research on another part of the schooling phenomena and consequently taking an approach to it that is called ethnographics; that is, an extensive descriptive and interpretive effort at explaining the complexity" (p. 652). Magoon has extensively documented the fact that constructivist modes have been utilized, although largely ignored, over the past fifty years, in sociology, in psychology, in education, and in philosophy. The time is now, he argues, for us to recognize such approaches as legitimate ones, and "that a significant part of the context of behavior that educational researchers observe is a structure produced by the constructions of the observed subject" (p. 655). His comprehensive listing of studies with constructivist perspectives in educational research demonstrates that researchers are utilizing such approaches and that they may be useful for needs educationists have, but fail to meet. The more traditional norm, a focus on "predictions about precise individual behavior," has blinded us to the fact that "pattern explanations are equally legitimate and useful and may be a better scientific goal approximation for many purposes" (p. 688).

Still another commentary available on the problem of creating (and maintaining) reality comes in the very powerful case study on ward attendants' perspectives in a state hospital originally published by Bogdan, Taylor, DeGrandpre, and Haynes (1974), and re-presented in Bogdan and Taylor's *Introduction to Qualitative Research Methods* (1975). The realities of ward attendants, the realities of the ward for Bogdan and Taylor, who were nonparticipant observers for nearly a year, and the perspectives of administrators of the hospital (for the severely and profoundly retarded and others) demonstrate that reality is indeed a construction. To Bogdan and Taylor, the sheer number of relatives employed at the state institution make the town "a company town"; to the ward attendants, "money . . . is the only reason" people were working there. To hospital administrators, not enough money from the state and too few trained employees left them living at the administrative, fiscal, and managerial edge, and they were clearly upset that several sociologists should be permitted to watch daily events on the wards. The seemingly endless filth ("You get used to it.... You

don't smell it anymore," says the ward attendant), the incessant large
and small cruelties, the process of consuming food turned into a savage,
hurried, and brutal survival strategy, all suggest that reality as experienced by ward attendants is not reality as experienced by residents
is not reality as experienced by sociologists and special educators interested in discovering the nature of programs at a state hospital.

Bogdan and Taylor (1975, pp. 10-11) explain:

> We have seen vivid scenes and behavior such as rocking and head-
> banging by residents interpreted in markedly disparate fashion. One
> attendant explained self-mutilation and head-banging as a direct result
> of severe mental retardation, while another claimed that a resident may
> bang his head against the wall as a response to sheer boredom and
> lack of programming. Similarly, one staff person remarked sadly,
> "These patients could really be helped if there were a program for
> them," while another praised the institution for its program: "I know
> I have the best recreation program in the country. We do everything
> for these kids." The staff's views of residents further exemplify the
> gross differences in perceptions. . . .
>
> Truth then emerges not as one objective view but rather as the com-
> posite picture of how people think about the institution and each other.
> Truth comprises the perspectives of administrators, line-level staff, pro-
> fessional workers, outsiders, volunteers, maintenance staff, residents
> and family.

Bogdan and Taylor have drawn upon this body of case study material
in order to demonstrate the uses of qualitative methods for achieving
verstehen, but in the process have demonstrated profoundly that social
reality is a construction based upon the actor's frame of reference
within the setting. Each views the state hospital as a rather different
arena, meeting needs as much (or more) for those who work there as
those who are incarcerated.

Weston La Barre, a cultural anthropologist, provides another
disciplinary viewpoint on the construction of reality from a social scientist's point of view. His particular *bête noir* was the damage done to
the concept of culture as proposed by quantitatively oriented social
scientists, but the point is equally applicable when any disciplinarian
takes elements of culture and context out of their natural setting:

> Counting does have its uses in the social sciences. But in anthropology
> cultures are molar complexes, with reticulated meanings—that infor-
> mants can tell us about best. Numbers here can only operate with etical-
> ly fragmented shards assembled from maimed wholes. The less trivial

and the more complex the data, the less legitimately available is the quantitative method. Besides, relevant quantifying can only operate on the basis of prior insight. Statistical voyagers from atoll to atoll would be mere camp followers of a masterly Malinowskian insight. The cultural statistician, curiously, cares little for insights into functioning wholes but seems principally enamored by his method. "Have method, will travel"—and from guru to guru as these kaleidoscopically change. "Empirical sociology" is already a mere branch of statistics, which is the main subject. However, we repeat, social science statistics are often useful in proving what we already know. Or think we know.

It may be impossible to show the numbers-minded why their manipulations are so unsatisfactory in the social sciences. Their statistical operations may be mathematically impeccable, and equations marvelously "sophisticated" (read, complex), but they have missed the boat. I have in mind here Whiting's elegant Rube Goldberg contraption for explaining circumcision—in such rainy *kwashiorkor*-afflicted regions as, say, the *locus classicus* deserts of the pastoral-Semitic Near East, with polygyny thrown in free. In my view, the Semites have already explained the real motive for circumcision in their abundant documents, though it depends on only a single constantly reiterated and deeply imbricated symbol, the immortal snake. If etically defined research later discovers that the wives of circumcised men have a lower incidence of cervical cancer, that is very interesting, and a triumph of etic science for us. But it is not the late-Old Stone Age motive for circumcision.

What is wrong with the quantifier is not only his locus of meaning but also his unexamined semantic predicament. Who cares about seventy percent truths anyway? This simply means that the numerical baskets are thirty percent full of irrelevant noncomparables. Some qualitatively undiscerned cobblestones have somehow gotten in with the apples and oranges. The supposed entities turn out to have been slippery words after all. They have evidently been dealing with something else, perhaps only round things. In the early days of anthropology, assuming that a field worker is manufactured through mere attendance at classes, Boas used to ask a single question of students returning from the field: "Did you find your Indians?" The question to be asked of the quantifying social scientist is, "Have you found your entities?" Are verbally defined data enough? Are words entities? (La Barre, 1980, p. 15)

Yes, Virginia, even statistics can only result in yet another constructed reality.

THE PHILOSOPHER'S VIEWPOINT

The point to the foregoing discussion is that however limited the examples (and there could be hundreds more), researchers in a variety of disciplines in the social sciences have been and are grappling with social constructivist approaches, wherein the contribution of each individual in the context to the creation of a reality is recognized. These individual realities often overlap one another, simply because many of them are an effort to deal with the same putative phenomenon, but they differ in the meanings that are attached to the phenomenon and in the sense making in which each actor engages in order to keep his or her world whole and seamless.

Yet the person on the street and social scientists are not the only persons who have come to grips with the question of reality. There are always the philosophers, before us and among us now. At some fundamental level, they have introduced arguments asserting that "reality" might exist at any one of four levels, which we will conveniently label objective reality, perceived reality, constructed reality, and created reality for the purpose of discussing them as ontological positions.

(1) Objective reality. This stance has also been called naive realism, or hypothetical realism. It asserts that there is a tangible reality, and experience with it can result in knowing it fully. Physical, temporal, and social reality all exist, and with sufficient time and reasonably good principles of investigation, inquiry can converge on those realities even though individual studies may be only approximations. Realism, the view that "the world of which we have knowledge exists independently of our knowledge of it," has, according to Skagestad (1981, pp. 77-78), explanatory power with respect to two "puzzling facts":

> One is the fact of error elimination, or, on the phenomenal level, the fact of exchanging one belief for another. There would be no point in changing beliefs only to go on changing beliefs indefinitely. This activity of changing one's beliefs can be rendered rational only as an attempt to reach a belief which will not thereafter need to be changed.

With that argument, Skagestad argues (after Peirce) that what one is, or ought to be, doing in changing beliefs is approximating "reality" (which nevertheless may remain unknown) more closely, or moving toward more perfect understanding of the reality that exists outside of ourselves and independent of the knower. The second argument advanced is

> the drift toward consensus in science; that is, the fact that independent investigators, starting from different assumptions and different

observations, tend ultimately to arrive at the same conclusion. This fact . . . is explained by the hypothesis that their different inquiries are directed toward one and the same reality. (pp. 87-88)

Skagestad himself has pointed out that these arguments for a singular reality are not without loopholes. Stability of a belief does not increase its probable validity. After all, false beliefs may "persist for ages." And occasionally, the independence of investigators may itself be suspect, or the investigators may be products of a culture that impels them to certain beliefs that follow facts.

Nevertheless, realism, and therefore reality, must be taken seriously, according to Skagestad. This particular ontological position adopts the stance that individual inquiries may be only approximations, but, sooner or later, convergence will occur. Hence the cry, "More research is needed." The whole, for naive realists, is the sum of the parts.

(2) Perceived reality. The second ontological position asserts that there is a reality, but one cannot know it fully. It can be appreciated only from particular vantage points, which some prefer to call *perceptions.* A perception (a la the blind men and the elephant) is a partial, incomplete view of something that is nevertheless real, and capable of different interpretation when seen from different viewpoints. It is partial and incomplete only because each perception yields experience of only a limited number of *parts* of the whole (the tail, the trunk, the leg, and so on).

The major differences between the position of the naive realists and the perceived realists is that the former believe and hope that reality may at some point be known to all. With a sufficient body of research into the physical, social, and temporal, reality should rise out of the mists that enshroud it and become known. The perceptual realists believe that no one person—or, indeed, a group of many persons—can know all of reality at any point in time. Reality for any individual—or group or even a discipline—is at best only a partial picture of the whole, and will continue to remain so. But both the naive (or hypothetical) realists and the perceptual realists adopt the ontological position that there *is* a reality out there, a "real" reality, if you will; the differences lie between what the two groups believe is knowable about that reality.

(3) Constructed reality. Those who see reality as a construction in the minds of individuals asserts that it is dubious whether there is a reality. If there is, we can never know it. Furthermore, no amount of inquiry can produce convergence on it. There is, in this ontological

position, always an infinite number of constructions that might be made and hence there are multiple realities. Any given construction may not be (and almost certainly is not) in a one-to-one relation to (or isomorphic with) other constructions of the same (by definition only) entity. The definition is implied by the use of some common referent term, which is nevertheless understood (or constructed) differently by different individuals (or constructors). Some examples of constructions that are given the same definition might be the following: Harvard University; the Bronx Zoo; "Ma" Bell; handicapped children; educational research; social science; good manners; a controlled experiment; the Manhattan atomic bomb project; tort; Bobby Knight, the Indiana University basketball coach; communism; the Battle of the Bulge; welfare mothers; nursing homes; alternative lifestyles; God; urban blight; juvenile delinquency; a Camperdown elm tree; the Moonies; realpolitik, as practiced by Henry Kissinger; Watergate; the Vietnam era; the middle ages; or trickle-down economics. Each of these examples means (calls to mind, suggests, elicits a response, signifies) something quite different to different individuals, although they may agree on some formal definition that constitutes a partial description of the entity.

None of those things exists in a form other than those constructed by the persons who "recognize" the term (that is, who have encountered it at least once before in some form). Nor is any of those things "really" the sum or aggregate of the individual constructions. Each is undoubtedly incomplete or erroneous to some degree. Of course, constructed realities (or constructions) are often related to, and equally often inseparable from, tangible entities. No one would argue, for instance, that Bobby Knight did not exist, or that the Battle of the Bulge never happened (although there are people who have argued, for instance, that the Holocaust never happened, but was merely a political construction to arouse worldwide sympathy for the Jews). Events, persons, objects are indeed tangible entities. The meanings and wholeness derived from or ascribed to these tangible phenomena in order to make sense of them, organize them, or reorganize a belief system, however, are *constructed realities*.

Under this ontological position, the constructed realities ought to match the tangible entities as closely as possible, not, however, in order to create a derivative or reconstructed single reality (or fulfill the criterion of objectivity), but rather to represent the multiple constructions of individuals (or fulfill the criterion of fairness).

If one were to look for a theory of truth that conformed to this particular ontological position, it would have to be a consensus theory, which asserts that observation sentences (and any correct application of general observation terms or descriptions) are those that are reinforced as such by the consensus of the community. More than mere consensus is required, however; there are external constraints that limit what can be agreed upon. Nevertheless, in general, group agreement determines truth (Hesse, 1980, p. 145).[2]

(4) Created reality. The fourth and final ontological position is that there is no reality at all. Reality is best understood as a standing wave function that is not *realized* (note the term) until some observer "pops the qwiff" (Wolf, 1981), "qwiff" being a quantum wave function. Until it is "popped," the quantum wave function (or *probable* reality) remains simply probabilistic.

Wolf's discussion of the problem of Schrödinger's cat is helpful in understanding created realities. He introduces his example with the following paragraphs:

> What do we mean when we speak of "reality"? We usually mean the world that we sense. The world out there is made up of things that we can see, hear, taste, smell and touch—real, solid, substantial objects of our everyday existence. We take it for granted that these things would exist in their same sensible form even if we were not there to observe them.
>
> Our observations simply verify an already existing reality.
>
> Yet, that isn't what quantum mechanics seems to be telling us. It appears to indicate a drastic departure from what we could call our classical mechanical heritage. Certainly this is the position of what later came to be known as the Copenhagen position or the Bohr Complementarity Principle, there is no reality until that reality is perceived. Our perceptions of reality will, consequently, appear somewhat contradictory, dualistic, and paradoxical. The instantaneous experience of the reality of Now will not appear paradoxical at all. It is only when we observers attempt to construct a history of our perceptions that reality becomes paradoxical (Wolf, 1981, p. 127).

Schrödinger's cat, named after Erwin Schrödinger, a physicist who first posed the problem of activating several realities at once, has several elements contained in the "story." The elements of the example include the following:

(1) A closed steel case containing one radioactive atom. The atom has a half-life of one hour, that is, in a large sample of such atoms half of them would remain after the passage of one hour while the other

half would have decayed. Thus, after one hour, the probability of finding the atom still in the case is .5.

(2) A photocell sensitive to emitted radiation. If the atom decays the resulting radiation trips the photocell, which in turn releases a deadly gas.

(3) A live cat is introduced into this cage at the same time that precisely one atom of radioactive element has been released in it. Question: At the end of an hour, what will we find on opening the case, a live cat or a dead cat?

Wolf points out that according to quantum mechanics, *you* control the fate of the cat if you are the one to open the cage. After one hour, there are two equally likely scenarios regarding whether the cat is alive or dead. Wolf (1981, p. 189-191) observes: "In a certain sense, the universe has become *two* universes. In one, there is a living cat and a happy you, and in the other, there is a dead cat and a sad you." If you did not reach over to open the cage and thereby disturb it (potentiate the wave function, or pop the qwiff), these two universes would go on forever, side by side, indefinitely. When you open the cage you *create* the reality that you find. Until then, there is only potential.

This position, incidentally, is quite in line with the "new" physics. Zukav, in his scientific and metaphysical treatment of the new physics, *The Dancing Wu-Li Masters* (1979, p. 28), introduces first the differences between Newtonian mechanics and quantum mechanics:

> The lesson of Newtonian physics is that the universe is governed by laws that are susceptible to rational understanding. . . .
>
> Contrary to Newtonian physics, quantum mechanics tells us that our knowledge of what governs events on the subatomic level is not nearly what we assumed it would be. It tells us that we cannot predict subatomic phenomena with any certainty. We only can predict their probabilities.
>
> Philosophically, however, the implications of quantum mechanics are psychedelic. Not only do we influence our reality, but, in some degree, we actually *create* it. Because it is the nature of things that we can know either the momentum of a particle or its position, but not both, *we must choose,* which of these two properties we want to determine. Metaphysically, this is very close to saying that we *create* certain properties because we choose to measure these properties. Said another way, it is possible that we create something that has position, for example, like a particle, because we are intent on determining position and it is impossible to determine position without having some *thing* occupy the position that we want to determine. (emphasis in original)

Zukav, working with physicists to write this book, asserts that they are asking questions that have an eerie tone for nonphysicists: *"Did we create the particles that we are experimenting with?"* He quotes Wheeler, a physicist at Princeton, who wrote:

> May the universe in some strange sense be "brought into being" by the participation of those who participate? . . . The vital act is the act of participation. "Participator" is the incontrovertible new concept given by quantum mechanics. It strikes down the term "observer" of classical theory, the man who stands safely behind the thick glass wall and watches what goes on without taking part. It can't be done, quantum mechanics says. (p. 29)

We should also note that some physicists are now postulating the existence of an infinite number of parallel universes. New parallel universes are created by each instance (of which there must be billions each second throughout the universe) of popping the qwiff, actions analogous to opening the cage containing Schrödinger's cat. This is a radical position indeed, but one now assumed by many responsible, creative, and perfectly sane scientists.

WHAT IS A REASONABLE POSTURE REGARDING REALITY?

Although we are quite drawn to ontological position 4, created reality, it is not necessary for our purposes to adopt so radical a stance (although it is a perfectly reasonable one for a contemporary physicist). Instead, we shall settle for a less extreme alternative: position 3, constructed reality. Position 4 requires a greater suspension of disbelief than does the idea of constructed reality. Certainly the notion of constructed reality is quite sophisticated in itself; it will readily handle social and behavioral realities, which are those realities addressed by the kind of inquiry in which we are basically interested.

To follow an earlier argument for a moment, the reader might note that while positions 1 and 2 adopted virtually the same posture on reality—that is, that there is a reality—and the only quarrel came in whether or not individuals might ever know it wholly, ontological positions 3 and 4 also exhibit similarity in their basic assumptions about the *nature* of reality—that is, *it doesn't exist until either* (1) it is *constructed* by an actor or (2) it is *created* by a participant.

EXAMPLES OF CONSTRUCTED REALITIES

There are a number of examples to which we could point that would provide a "feel" (the development of a tacit "mass") for the notion of constructed realities. For example, consider *labels, euphemisms, and stereotypes*. Euphemisms construct reality in ways that make it more palatable. Stereotypes construct reality so as to make it easy to deal with, and in order to create quick reference points for categorization. Labels help us sort reality easily. Consider the following quotation from an essay by Thomas Griffith, "Stuck with Labels," that appeared in *Time* magazine, April 27, 1981:

> Everyone admits the injustice, the oversimplification of labels, but the press sticks them on anything and everything nonetheless. When it doesn't invent a label itself, the press gratefully seizes on someone else's catch phrase. That's how Ronald Reagan early captured the high ground on his budget cutting. He promised not to harm the "truly needy" and to provide a "safety net" for protected groups like the aged. These soothingly imprecise phrases, so often repeated by Republican orators and in the columns, have set the tone of the budget debate.

But, Griffith goes on to say, labels can "mislead," they lack subtlety ("a button that says RIGHT TO LIFE or RIGHT TO CHOOSE leaves little space for reservations"), and they may even reverse meaning (he points out that the label "conservative" has become fashionable again).

Another example of reality construction is apparent in the *proceedings in a court of law*. The adversarial system is designed on the one hand to construct at least two realities for the jury's consideration and, on the other hand, to create a single reality from the multiple memories of witnesses (a distillation of the essence of the crime). The essence of defense is that the jury can be brought to see an alternative construction of the reality that the prosecution distills, so that the evidence absolves the defendant. The way to instill the legendary "reasonable doubt" is to spin (construct) an alternative reality.

There is a story of a famous trial lawyer who had never lost a case. In a trial in which the body had never been found, the lawyer attempted to instill doubt by saying continuously, while pointing at the courtroom door, "At any moment, the victim might come walking through that door." He thought he had won the case because each time he said that the jury would involuntarily look at the door, as if expecting that the alleged victim *would* walk through it momentarily. The doubt, he thought, had been planted. But the jury returned a verdict of guilty, because, as the foreman later explained to the stunned lawyer, "We noticed that the defendant *never* looked expectantly at the door." The moral of the story is, of course, that everyone is free to construct reality for his or her own uses, and the jury "read" the reality of the defendant quite accurately.

A third example of construction is linguistic construction, usually encapsulated best in *dictionaries*. The study of a dictionary—what words are in it and what words are not—is a useful way to determine the characteristics of a culture. Recall Orwell's *1984* and "newspeak," which did not include words for concepts such as freedom and democracy. Without such words the reality of their achievement can never come to pass.

Madison Avenue sales messages constitute a fourth example of reality construction. Virtually all advertising is directed at instilling some reconstruction that the advertiser finds useful; a macho image if one is selling powerful cars or liquor; the image of a youthful, slim, and sexy woman if the item to be hawked is cosmetics or perfume; the image of a connoisseur or *bon vivant* if one is selling theatre or concert tickets. A recent *Consumer's Report* (July 1983) has an article showing how Miller and Budweiser are selling beer as a reward (usually for hard work): "This Bud's for you!"

A fifth example, and one that is most appropriate in this work, is that of *theories*. All theories, including methodological theories, are constructions. This fact has enormous significance in relation to the problem of value-resonance, which will be considered in Chapter 7. But we know already from earlier discussions on the work of Julienne Ford (see Chapters 1 and 2) that no theory can ever be tested directly.

A final example concerns a joint U.S.-Soviet social studies project, which has been undertaken by a number of social studies curriculum developers in both countries. A newspaper article recently ran the headline,"U.S.-Soviet Textbook Project May Be Delayed" (Bloomington, Indiana *Herald-Telephone*, July 11, 1981, pp. 1,7). The article cited an interim report of this project that included some examples of the Russian response to American textbooks. In part, the article said:

Textbooks in both countries tend to glorify the accomplishments of their own nation and denigrate the contribution of others. . . .

The report lists some samples of information which the reviewers questioned. A Soviet 10th grade world history book for example reads: "The ruling circles of England, France, and the U.S.A. encouraged the aggressors (Germany, Italy, and Japan in World War II) to attack the U.S.S.R., counting on the mutual destruction of both sides in such a war and the strengthening of their own position in the post-war world." . . .

Concerning the bombing of Hiroshima and Nagasaki, the book reads: "The use of atomic weapons against Japan was not provoked by a military necessity. This inhuman act served long-term political goals;

to intimidate the nations of the world and force them to bow before the power of the U.S.A."

The Soviet author states that the fate of the Japanese was sealed by the Soviet entry into the war on August 8, 1945, and therefore the atomic weapons were not needed.

[On the other hand] the Soviet response to American textbooks contains numerous claims of bias and misinformation in the sections dealing with the Soviet Union. . . . "Major attention is devoted to Soviet foreign policy. Many textbooks do not provide the most basic information about the Soviet Union's political and socio-economic systems, its economy and culture."

The reviewers claimed that much information about the October Revolution was biased and contained factual errors and that the Bolsheviks were not given proper credit for their role in the revolution. Reviewers objected to the use of such terms as "police state," "totalitarian regime," and "undemocratic system" in describing the Soviet Union political system.

Does anyone doubt that this project will be some time in getting off the ground?

The point is that examples of such constructions exist everywhere. A person need not be a psychologist, a chemist, or a physicist in order to confront the clashes that are the daily fender-benders of reality. Weekly news magazines and local hometown newspapers abound with constructions and reconstructions of social and political reality. They are there for the looking and for the reading.

A WORD ON RATIONALISM

"Rational" is a word currently in favor. "Rationalizing" is a word the current connotation of which is somehow psychologically disparaging. "Irrational" is a word altogether too loosely applied in contemporary society. "Rational" has come to mean (as its root suggests) that sweet reason has prevailed (usually in the political decison-making arena); "rationalizing" has come to mean that someone, having committed some act to which he or she had given little overt thought, now has made up some excuse for the behavior; and "irrational" has come to mean very nearly out of one's mind. We would like to take issue with virtually every usage in common parlance today.

Rationalizing, for instance, is nothing more than sense making in the face of chaos, subconscious behavior, tacit knowledge, and outright forgetfulness. It is part and parcel of reality construction for individuals and institutions to engage in *ex post facto* reasoning to justify, explain, attribute, or make sense of behavior. As such, it is an apparently quite human characteristic that merely seeks to impose order on conflicting stimuli, disorder, and information overload. It is a word that has fallen into disrepute quite undeservedly.

Rationalism and irrationalism, however, represent a more dangerous combination, since the dualism implied by this juxtaposition asserts that if one does not see reality my way, then one is, clearly, irrational. Rejecting rationalism (on the part of others) does not mean automatic acceptance of irrationalism. Rather, it may mean acceptance of multiple rationales, or conflicting value systems, or even separate realities. The parallel is drawn to a statistical argument, that of accepting or rejecting the null hypothesis. If one rejects the null hypothesis, it does not mean that only one other alternative may be accepted. There are a variety of alternatives that may account for the rejection of the null hypothesis. Rejection of the null only means that the null hypothesis is rejected. By the same token, rejecting rationalism is not tantamount to accepting irrationalism. Between rationalism and irrationalism, there exist an infinity of rationales and realities.

NOTES

1. *Evaluation News,* although a true newsletter, was at that time published without volume numbers, and the issues appeared sporadically; thus it is not possible to give a more complete reference here.

2. There are two other theories of truth, a "correspondence" theory and a "coherence" theory. A "correspondence" theory of truth asserts that observation sentences are true if they correspond to reality (that is, exhibit isomorphism). This is a traditional positivist/instrumentalist or operationalist position associated with naive realism. A "coherence" theory asserts that an observation sentence is warrantably asserted if and only if it is provable within some given theory. Truth is coherence within a system (see Hesse, 1980, pp. 145ff.).

4

The Disturbing
and Disturbed Observer

Aristotle's thoughts would continue to play a role in Western thinking for nearly two thousand years. . . . Anytime humans intervened, they interfered. . . . It would take a while before [scientists] would attempt to reach out and touch, to try ideas to see if they worked. . . . Galileo brought before his skeptics a new way of science. It was the *doing* of science, the active participation of the observer with the observed. [Galileo did not believe] that he was disrupting nature. Instead, he was attempting to reveal the natural laws by *removing* those disruptions that keep us from seeing the truth. . . . Isaac Newton was able to bring together the concepts of passive observation and active observation. . . . Active observation was [for him] nothing more than an extension of passive observation. Instruments simply detected; they did not alter the existing world they explored. . . . But [the mysteries that challenged the Newtonian mechanical age] would start a revolution in the scientific world. The active observer would be replaced by the disturbing observer.

(Wolf, 1981, passim)

INVESTIGATOR-OBJECT DUALISM

The concept of the active observer "researching out and touching, to try ideas to see if they worked," was entirely consistent with the positivist point of view. Science was thought to be empirical, nontautological, formal, and exact. Its chief aim was instrumental control; its major criterion was that it should yield increasingly successful predictions. What could be more appropriate to such a model of science than that the scientist be pictured as objective, independent, standing on his or her own platform while manipulating the world, and arranging through methodology that the data should speak for themselves? Surely if there had been a T-shirt designed for the occasion, its logo would be a white-coated demigod walking on water! As

Wolf (1981, p. 56) suggests, for the scientist of the Newtonian mechanical age,

> the observer observed, never disturbed. Even the errors of a clumsy observer could be accounted for by simply analyzing the observed movements of whatever he touched.

It must have been a comfort to nineteenth-century scientists to believe that they could behave like bulls in china closets and still have it all come out right! And if the maintenance of a discrete distance between investigator and object sufficed to guarantee objectivity, well, the maintenance of a discreet distance would probably work equally well in human research!

The general belief in the salutary effect of separating investigator and object is based on the premise of subject-object dualism; needless to say, the investigator is the subject and the entity being studied is the object. The use of the term "dualism" is illuminating; it suggests that there is a certain "twoness" or "separateness" that characterizes investigator-investigated (knower-known) relationships. Philosophically speaking, the world has witnessed the passage of many such dualisms, for it is tempting to divide the world into neat dichotomies.[1] Some examples:

- form-substance
- medium-message
- mind-body
- good-evil
- theoretical-empirical
- analysis-synthesis
- induction-deduction
- psyche-soma
- experimentation-speculation

But on analysis, most of these dichotomies disappear. The form-substance dyad is destroyed by the mass-energy equivalence in physics. Virtually everyone is familiar with the catch phrase: The medium *is* the message. Physicians have learned to deal with psychosomatic problems. Induction and deduction can be played off through retroduction. And so on. If these pairs of terms have any utility, it is to remind us that they are thesis and antithesis, from which some synthesis, dialectically shaped, can emerge.

And so it is with subject-object, investigator-entity being investigated, knower-known, and similar dyads describing the relationship between inquirer and that being inquired into. We saw in Chapter

1 that the positivist form of the axiom describing the "inquirer-respondent relationship" is as follows:

> The inquirer and the object of inquiry are independent; the knower and the known constitute a discrete dualism.

The naturalist version, however, states:

> The inquirer and the "object" of inquiry interact to influence one another; knower and known are inseparable.

In this chapter we make the case for the latter proposition, and also present some arguments in favor of *retaining this interactivity even if it were possible, as positivists assert, to remove it by some appropriate methodological intervention* (which of course the naturalist categorically denies to be possible in the first place).

THE FIRST CHINK IN
THE POSITIVIST ARMOR: REACTIVITY

Despite some interesting evidence produced by "mind over matter" parapsychologists, investigators of *physical* phenomena have felt fairly comfortable with the positivist version of this axiom, at least at macroscopic levels. But it did not take long for investigators of *human* phenomena to come to the realization that *their* "subjects," even when out of direct contact with the investigator (as in a questionnaire situation), nevertheless reacted differentially to the research stimulus. A name was soon coined for this phenomenon—not unsurprisingly, *"reactivity."* Webb, Campbell, Schwartz, and Sechrest (1966, p. 13), in their introductory chapter to the now-classic *Unobtrusive Measurement,* define reactivity as "error from the respondent":

> The most understated risk to valid interpretation is the error produced by the respondent. Even when he is well-intentioned and cooperative, the research subject's knowledge that he is participating in a scholarly search may confound the investigator's data. Four classes of this error are discussed here: awareness of being tested, role selection, measurement as a change agent, and response sets.[2]

Awareness of being tested is often called the "guinea pig" effect. Much of the discussion found in Campbell (1957) and Campbell and Stanley (1963) relates to this "threat" to internal validity. The mere knowledge that he or she is involved in a study is sufficient to alter, possibly significantly and certainly to an unknown degree, the respondent's reaction to the investigator. Role selection has to do with the fact that the respondent may choose, in providing data, from among a variety of "selves," all of which are "true," or may exhibit a variety of behaviors, all of which are "proper." Choices may be made on bases extraneous to the investigation (and therefore "error producing"), including even, for example, the desire to cooperate as fully as possible! "Measurement as change agent" refers to the possibility that the mere act of measurement, as in a pretest, may alter ("bias") the respondent for subsequent measurement situations ("preamble" or "practice" effects). Finally, "response sets" has to do with the demonstrated fact that respondents exhibit certain typical biasing behaviors, such as their tendency to endorse rather than reject any statement and the tendency to prefer strongly stated to weakly stated statements. Famous instances of reactivity well documented in the literature include the Hawthorne effect, the Pygmalion effect, and the John Henry effect. There is little doubt that the research community is well aware of, as well as wary of, reactivity.

Responses to this "threat" to internal validity are various. One is the use of statistical and/or field controls intended to eliminate or even out the bias. As any casual reader of Campbell and Stanley (1963) is well aware, the basic techniques include the use of equivalent comparison groups (equivalent either by deliberate selection or by randomization processes) and the use of pretest-posttest comparisons (of course the use of pretests itself introduces one of the sources of reactivity). Since, however, neither of these techniques will by itself eliminate all reactivity threats, Campbell and Stanley advise their readers to resort to the Solomon Four-Group Design, in which one group receives both pretest and posttest, as well as the "treatment" (the so-called experimental group 1); a second group receives pretest and posttest but *no* treatment (control group 1); a third group receives treatment and posttest but no pretest (experimental group 2); and a fourth group receives only the posttest (control group 2). Using the Campbell and Stanley notation, the design is as follows:

$$
\begin{array}{llll}
E_1: & O_1 & X & O_2 \\
C_1: & O_1 &   & O_2 \\
E_2: &   & X & O_2 \\
C_2: &   &   & O_2
\end{array}
$$

Aside from the obvious impracticality of such a complex design (the number of instances in which its use is reported in the literature is tiny; its main virtue seems to be as an intellectual tour de force to demonstrate that, in principle, the problem *can* be solved), it is dubious whether all sources of reactivity are in fact dealt with adequately. The treatment, X, cannot be assumed to be homogeneously supplied (despite the best efforts at maintaining tight field controls), and other sources of reactivity are not accounted for. As an example, consider the fact that when X is supplied, the person administering it has characteristics—sex, ethnicity, age, and dress, for instance—that may produce reactivity in the samples. Comparing experimental group 1 with control group 1 may adequately account for the effects of pretest reactivity, say, or the effects of history (another Campbell and Stanley threat to validity), but cannot separate out reactive effects of the particular experimenter from the treatment *per se*. Of course, it is possible to compare experimental group 1 with control group 2, which effectively eliminates any such reactivity from the equation. But, unfortunately, that reintroduces the possibility of pretest reactivity. Confounding of some sort continues.

A second mode of response to the reactivity threat is that proposed by Webb et al. (1966): the use of unobtrusive measures. Such measures have been defined as signs that indicate a type of behavior or a behavior pattern *but are not meant to do so*. Put another way, unobtrusive measures are indicators left behind by an ignorant subject, unaware that what he or she took to be "innocent actions" are now to be used as data. But are such measures ethical? There are surely several points of view on *that* issue. Some observers argue that insofar as the actions producing the unobtrusive measures are *public,* they are fair game for the researcher. But while placing empty liquor bottles into one's garbage may itself be a public behavior, the action that the bottles are interpreted to represent—drinking—is not a public behavior; indeed, not even when taking place in a bar, not to mention the privacy of one's home. Webb et al. (1966, pp. v, vii) take the position that their readers will no doubt find their techniques "differentially acceptable," because they have different "moral boiling points." But leaving it to the individual researcher to resolve questions such as these on an ad hoc basis is surely irresponsible.

Finally, researchers seeking to overcome the problems of reactivity have at times resorted to out-and-out deception. Subjects are given misinformation about the purposes of the research, even to the extent of being made to believe that *they* are investigators themselves. Sometimes the fact that they are subjects of a study is kept from them entirely. One-way mirrors are in common use. The reader who doubts these allegations is invited to examine sources such as Bok (1978) and especially Diener and Crandall (1978), who cite literally hundreds of cases of lies and deception, all done in the name of seeking "truth."

All of these measures seem rather desperate in view of the fact that what they are intended to control is nothing more complex than reactivity. Now if reactivity were the only problem needing to be handled, it might not be too difficult to condone at least some of these techniques. If one were confident that, given these safeguards, reactivity would be eliminated and the investigator would be returned to the pure, objective status envisioned in the positivist paradigm, it might be worth the effort to mount elaborate designs and perhaps even to engage in a bit of skullduggery now and then. But there are even larger chinks in the positivist's armor that make the whole question of reactivity moot. The inquirers were not merely clumsy; they were in fact utterly disturbing.

THE SECOND CHINK:
INDETERMINACY

In the 1920s the science of physics, assaulted on all sides by phenomena it could not explain, was in a state of disarray. The models of the atom that had been devised by the best physicists of the time failed to provide an adequate accounting for the simultaneous wave-particle nature of radiation, including visible light. Werner Heisenberg, a young German mathematician, was inspired by a personal contact with Neils Bohr, the inventor of the last viable atomic "model" (the familiar model that pictures the atom as a miniature solar system), to apply his newly developed "operator" mathematics to some of the more intractable problems that had been encountered. The results were to stun the world. At the international Solway Conference held in 1927, Heisenberg provided proof of the proposition that it is impossible to determine both the mass and the momentum of a particle simultaneously, for measuring either one will render the other immediately and forever indeterminate. Here was the ultimate instance of observer disturbance! Tranel (1981, p. 426) comments:

> Heisenberg demonstrated his uncertainty principle by proposing, by way of an ideal or "thought" experiment, a remarkably uncomplicated mental image. At the Copenhagen Conference he asked his audience

of leading scientists from around the world to imagine someone holding a gun in his hand. With this gun the person is able to "shoot" a single electron into a dark chamber that is totally empty of all other atoms, even those of air. An observer of this process has an ideal "microscope" with which the movement of the electron through the dark chamber can be observed by directing a single photon of light onto it. (At least one photon of light is necessary or it couldn't be observed.) What happens, however, as Heisenberg explained, is that the photon, as it strikes the electron, throws it out of its predicted path of movement. "By the very act of lighting up the electron's movement, that movement would be disrupted" (Moore, 1966, p. 151). From this, the conclusion is that it is impossible both to see the electron and to measure its velocity. At best, the observer would be able to calculate from the observational data "the probability of its being in a certain approximate area" (Moore, 1966, p. 152).

This state of indeterminacy, while proposed by Heisenberg in relation to subatomic particles, turns out to be much more widely applicable and meaningful than just in that limited physical arena. We have already seen from our discussion of the Schwartz and Ogilvy "new paradigm" (Chapter 2) that indeterminacy is a characteristic of substantive theories in virtually all fields, and at all levels. As Heisenberg (1958, p. 58) himself put it, "What we observe is not nature itself, but nature exposed to our method of questioning." In the same vein, Tranel (1981, p. 427) comments:

> If in physics one cannot observe without distorting the object of observation, it seems all the more apparent that distortion must occur when both the observer and the observed are human persons about whom predictability is precluded by virtue of the uniqueness of each. Without an awareness of the distortion one might be causing by the method of observation, or even an awareness that distortion is possible, one is open to false conclusions.

Thus observation not only disturbs but it shapes! But there is a third chink in the positivist's armor. Not only is there reaction and indeterminacy, there is also *interaction,* especially when both investigator and respondent are human beings.

THE THIRD CHINK:
INTERACTION

Observation not only *disturbs* and *shapes* but is *shaped by* what is observed. Gary Zukav (1979, p. 114), in his remarkable little book that traces certain parallels between the "new" physics and Zen, comments:

> The tables have been turned. "The exact sciences" no longer study an objective reality that runs its course regardless of our interest in it or not, leaving us to fare as best we can while it goes its predetermined way. Science, at the level of subatomic events, is no longer "exact," the distinction between objective and subjective has vanished, and the portals through which the universe manifests itself are, as we once knew a long time ago, those impotent, passive witnesses to its unfolding, the "I"'s of which we, insignificant we, are examples. The Cogs in the Machine have become the Creators of the Universe.

This interaction should not seem so startling to us, should not have caught us so off guard. A little thought would have demonstrated it to be there all along. Consider even so simple a research task as making up a questionnaire to be sent to a random sample of some population about which one wishes to know some things. What could be more objective, less interactive? But consider: Immediately at the stage of conceptualizing the questionnaire, the researcher asks him or herself questions such as, "Are these respondents likely to stand still for a questionnaire that takes more than 10 minutes to fill in?" "What's their reading level?" "What's their level of sophistication?" "What can I reasonably expect them to be willing to tell about those matters?" "Will they have enough insight concerning themselves to be able to deal with these questions?" And so on. The questionnaire maker is being shaped throughout by his or her expectations of what the sample of respondents will be like, and how they are likely to react to whatever instruments he or she may finally send out.

Now consider a person receiving the questionnaire. His or her first impulse is probably to throw it away, and a fair proportion of potential respondents will do that. But some will not. *They* are likely to be asking themselves such questions as "Who is this who is asking?" "Do I owe them a favor?" "Will I reap any political benefits from responding?" "How shall I shape my response to reap the maximum benefits?" "Can any harm come to me if I answer honestly?" And so on. Thus the respondents are constantly being shaped by their perceptions and expectations about the researcher and his or her use of the data.

Imagine that some do respond, and the investigator now has their answers in hand. The questionnaires must now be "processed," put into a form in which they can be summarized, probably treated statistically and aggregated. More decisions are needed. What does one do about the comments written into the margin? What if two responses have been marked, even though the instructions were very clear that only one should be? Is one thrown out? Randomly? Through inspection and surmise of what the respondent "most probably means"? Again, the researcher is in the position of shaping the responses in ways that conform to his or her own expectations as well as surmising what the respondents are like or what they "really meant."

How much more must it be the case that investigator and respondent shape one another's behaviors and responses when they are in a face-to-face situation, as in an observation or an interview! An interview is said to be a conversation with a purpose, but it would be a rare conversation that was entirely one-sided, no matter how dominant one member of the dyad might be or how submissive the other.

In a very real sense, then, investigator and respondent together *create* the data of the research. Each influences the other, and the direction that the data gathering will take in the next moment is acutely dependent upon what data have already been collected, and in what manner. There is in the investigator-respondent dyad a transitivity, a continuous unfolding, a series of iterations. Each shapes the other and is shaped by the other.

The investigator has only a limited series of choices in dealing with this state of affairs. One is simply to ignore it; that alternative of course would be naive and no responsible investigators from prepositivists on have ever seriously considered it. A second alternative is to attempt to devise a series of methodological safeguards that will effectively eliminate its effects. That solution might work *if* all one had to deal with was reactivity (that, of course, is the belief of the positivist), but, as we have seen, the solutions that have been proposed are hardly adequate to deal with the phenomenon even at that level, not to mention the levels of indeterminacy and interactivity. A third alternative is to take the phenomenon into account as best one can (a succeeding chapter on trustworthiness techniques will have some proposals along these lines), but conceding at the outset that one's best efforts will nevertheless be inadequate.[3] A fourth alternative, and far and away the best choice, is to *capitalize* on this state of affairs by exploiting opportunities that this interaction affords. More will be said about that below.

The "mutual shaping" that both investigator and respondent(s) undergo is not unlike the "mutual causality" of Schwartz and Ogilvy (1979), a consideration to which we shall return in Chapter 6. It also affords a means for dealing with the "multiple constructions" provided by different respondents, as we noted in Chapter 3. And of course it is also greatly influenced by values of both investigator and respondents (and other values as well), as we shall demonstrate in Chapter 7. Before we turn to these matters, however, it will be useful to pursue two additional questions: (1) What justifications can one give for choosing to capitalize on interactivity rather than endeavoring to exclude it, as the positivists would do? (2) What safeguards can one mount which, while perhaps not entirely adequate, would provide at least some reassurance against the intrusion of bias? We shall deal with these problems in the next two sections.

SOME JUSTIFICATIONS FOR
INCLUDING INTERACTIONS

Interactions between investigator and respondents cannot be eliminated from the research equation even if one wishes to do so, as we have tried to show. But one can regard their presence either as an *intrusion* leading to error or as an *opportunity* to be exploited. We prefer the latter posture, and will discuss six reasons for our belief that inclusion of interaction is preferable to exclusion *even if exclusion were possible*. Several of the reasons we shall cite are applicable even in cases of research in which the entity being investigated is *not* human; all come into play when the entity being investigated *is* human.

(1) Theories and facts are not independent. Theories are underdetermined, while at the same time facts are theory-laden (Hesse, 1980). What does that mean? On the one hand, any collection of "facts" is subject to meaningful interpretation within a *variety* of possible theories; indeed, it might be asserted that the number of theories that could account for any given set of facts is always very large. This difficulty is sometimes referred to as the problem of induction; inductive proof, unlike deductive proof, cannot be *conclusive;* it can at best be *persuasive*. On the other hand, facts themselves can be construed as facts only within some theoretical framework; facts in and of themselves have no absolute meaning. Many epistemologists are now of the opinion that there can be no observational language that is theory-free. Thus one can have no facts without theory, and no conclusive theory without an infinite number of facts.

The investigator is caught between these poles; indeed, if there were no other way to demonstrate the quality of indeterminacy, this situation would by itself provide ample evidence that the inquirer can never hope to "know" anything with certainty.

But of course that does not mean that the investigator cannot pursue knowledge within some limits. Some grounds for belief will be found to be more persuasive than others. Which grounds to attend to is a matter of judgment. And it is only reasonable to assert that the investigator's judgment can be relied upon to the extent that he or she interacts with the phenomenon over time so that its etiology, including its history and its present context, can be fully understood and appreciated. If theories and facts are *not* independent, it is impossible to divest inquiry of some amount of human judgment. The investigator must determine when an appropriate balance is reached such that the "facts" support the proposed (grounded) theory and the proposed theory does not overdetermine the facts. Continuing and intensive interaction between investigator and "object" is essential to the formation of sound (even if not compelling) judgments. Efforts to achieve "objectivity," insofar as they imply establishing and maintaining distance between the investigator and "object," detract from rather than support this purpose.

(2) Purposeful sampling and emergent design are impossible to achieve without interaction. We made the point in Chapter 1 (with more to be said in Chapter 8) that naturalistic inquiry relies upon *purposeful* rather than representative sampling (Guba and Lincoln, 1981; such sampling is also referred to as "interactional," Ford, 1975; and "theoretical," Glaser and Strauss, 1967; Patton, 1980) and *emergent* rather than preordinate design (Stake, 1975). Purposeful sampling can serve a variety of purposes; Patton (1980) identifies six types: sampling *extreme or deviant cases,* when the purpose is to obtain information about unusual cases that may be particularly troublesome or enlightening; sampling *typical cases,* when the purpose is to avoid rejection of information on the grounds that it is known to arise from special or deviant cases; *maximum variation* sampling, when the purpose is to document unique variations that have emerged in adapting to different conditions; sampling *critical cases,* when the purpose is to permit maximum application of information to other cases because, if it's true of critical cases, it is also likely to be true of all other cases; sampling *politically important* or *sensitive* cases, when the purpose is to attract attention to the study; and *convenience* sampling, when the purpose is to save time, money, or effort. Clearly a thoughtful investigator is needed to identify a purpose or purposes, and interaction is needed to find those cases that match the purpose: unusual cases, typical cases, cases that display maximum variation, and so on.

Further, the very requirement of an emergent design, in which succeeding methodological steps are based upon the results of steps already taken, implies the presence of a continuously interacting and interpreting investigator. At times only simple refinements in procedure or a simple adjustment in questions to be asked may be called for, but at other times an investigator may strike out on a wholly new tack as a result of a single insight. Such matters cannot be anticipated preordinately, nor can programs be built before the fact that will make the needed adjustments automatically. When changes are not only evolutionary but also morphogenetic, a knowledgeable investigator thoroughly steeped in the details of the inquiry is needed.

(3) To move beyond "mere" objectivity requires a level of mature judgment that can be achieved only by continuous interaction. Rowan (1981) raises the questions of how researchers are to think, what logic they should bring to bear on the inquiry process, and how to move back and forth between theory and research encounters with subjects. To get a handle on these difficult matters he draws upon a proposal by Hegel that there are three levels of consciousness possible:

- A *primary level,* in which we are "one-sidedly subjective" in carrying out "naive inquiry." But, Rowan suggests, we soon learn that this approach leaves us at the mercy of our feelings, and open to manipulation by more dominant personalities. Thus we move to a second level.
- A *social level,* in which we are "one-sidedly objective," interested only in facts and what can be proved true or false. This seems to be the level at which positivists have traditionally attempted to function. But the tight control implied by this posture leads to overcontrol that prevents further development. To break out we must move to a third level.
- A *realized level,* which is "objectively subjective":

  At this level we refuse to go on suppressing our primary subjective experience, and we find ways of going down into it and rescuing material from it, which is then raised to conscious awareness. Because this material is brought up through the social level, it is better informed and educated, much stronger and less vulnerable. In the process it changes. At the primary level, feelings swept over us and overwhelmed us; at the realized level, we are able to choose and to own our feelings. At the primary level, we were at the mercy of symbolic forms, in our unchosen dreams and daydreams; at the realized level we are now able deliberately to use images and symbols in creative ways for our research purposes. At the primary level, intuition was an occasional flash of insight, often accurate but quite unbiddable; at the realized level it is our main way of thinking, enabling us continually to see the wood as well as the trees. (Rowan, 1981, p. 116)

To achieve the realized level with respect to any particular object of inquiry implies a sufficient experience with it at a tacit, subjective

Must see wood as well as the trees

level in order to use "images and symbols" in creative ways. The inquirer must *continually* see the wood as well as the trees.

(4) Human research is inherently dialectical. Dialectics is a way of thinking about human experience in terms of contradictions and conflicts. If the researcher seeks to understand human experience, he or she must be prepared to deal with such conflict and contradiction (including, as we observed earlier, a plethora of dualisms). Most important, the researcher needs to be able to see change occurring through opposition, as emerging from the interplay of oppositional forces. Three principles are involved (Rowan, 1981):

- *The interdependence of opposites.* One pole cannot exist without its opposite. Black demands white, dominance demands submission, leadership demands followership, and so on.
- *The interpenetration of opposites.* Everything contains elements of its opposite. There is some white in every black, some submissiveness in every dominant relationship, some followership in every leader. Freud's love-hate ambivalence is a classic example.
- *The unity of opposites.* Every absolute if carried to its logical extreme is found to turn into its opposite. Ultimate whiteness dazzles and blinds or blackens, the idealization of dominance results in complete submission to even higher authority, the leader simply shows the way to where the mob is headed in any event.

All these contradictions are counterintuitive and counterrational; to deal with them, the researchers must be able to pull them together in a synthesis that includes and accounts for the contradiction. The conflict can never be fully resolved; it is likely that one resolution will lead, in turn, to another contradiction, and so on. Change is thus inevitable and continuous.

Rowan (1981, p. 132) concludes:

If we apply this whole set of thoughts about dialectics to the research cycle we arrive at a whole different way of doing research from the traditional one. . . . We shall be looking for contradictions, and trying to do justice to all that is there. And at the "making sense" phase of research, instead of trying to "kill" our data by setting out a list of hypotheses and shooting each one down with a "yes" or a "no"—as if that were what human inquiry were all about—we try instead to "keep our data alive" by allowing the contradictions to emerge, and by exploring the ways the opposites are interdependent, how they interpenetrate, and how they are also a unity.

To accomplish those goals clearly requires an inquirer who is in a constant, sensitive, and dialogical relationship with other humans.

(5) Meaningful human research is impossible without the full understanding and cooperation of the respondents. In the weak sense of this assertion, we mean simply that unless respondents willingly cooperate with an investigator in uncovering "truths" about themselves, the inquirer has no hope of coming to a full understanding of the situation. In this sense, Glass (1975, p. 11) has remarked, in connection with evaluative inquiry:

> There are no techniques available to the contemporary evaluator that do not depend heavily for their validity on the cooperation of the persons being evaluated. . . . I know of no significant study which could not have been subverted by the deceit, passive resistance, or non-cooperation of an unwilling group of subjects.

But there is a stronger sense in which this statement is also true. Without seeking out cooperative and interacting relationships, the inquirer literally cannot hope to do human research at all, even research that is somewhat tainted by invalidity, as the above passage suggests. It is not just that the study is subverted; it is rendered *impossible* in any meaningful sense, for human relationships are distinguished from the kinds of relationships one observes in natural events by their *reciprocity*. Human beings are always in relationships—with one another and with the investigator as well. One cannot study people without taking these relationships into account. And of course the relationship between the investigator and other respondents, which is part of this overall web of relationships, must be authentic; it is, as Esterson (1972) points out, a *special form* of reciprocity because it includes a study of itself as part of the larger study. (The reader will want to spin out for him or herself the meaning of such reciprocal study in the light of the dialectical argument posed just above.) If the reciprocal relationship of investigator and respondents is ignored, the data that emerge are partial and distorted, their meaning largely destroyed. And of course the very existence of this reciprocal relationship depends on the willingness of the respondents to participate in it and support it.

(6) It is the quality of interaction that provides the human instrument with the possibility of fully exploiting its own natural advantages. As Hofstadter (1979, p. 75ff.) so elegantly states the case in his parable called "Contracrostipunctis," it is possible to be too perfect. In this fairy story, the Tortoise is telling his friend Achilles about their mutual

friend, Crab, who had recently purchased what was, ostensibly, the Perfect Record Player. In fact, Crab was so insufferable about asserting the unsurpassable quality of his new record player that Tortoise was at once determined to disprove the claim, by devising a record that the Perfect Record Player could not play. The solution was simple; devise a record that contained exactly those frequencies that would result in the record player vibrating itself to pieces. Crab, having mounted this record (appropriately titled, "I Cannot Be Played on Record Player I") on his player, was dismayed when the player *did* shake itself to pieces. He returned to the record shop to complain; but the salesman there, having groveled suitably, was able to persuade Crab that he had for sale an even *more* perfect record player than the first—which he promptly unloaded onto the unsuspecting Crab. Of course, Tortoise simply repeated *his* ploy. Indeed, Crab, as it turned out, was a slow learner, and went through several more iterations before he realized the futility of going on. Listen to Hofstadter's next few lines of dialogue:

> *Achilles:* Oho—I have an idea! He could easily have outwitted you, by obtaining a LOW-fidelity phonograph—one that was not capable of reproducing the sounds which would destroy it. In that way, he would avoid your trick.
>
> *Tortoise:* Surely, but that would defeat the original purpose—namely, to have a phonograph which could reproduce any sound whatsoever, even its own self-breaking sound, which is of course impossible.
>
> *Achilles:* That's true. I see the dilemma now. If any record player— say Record Player X—is sufficiently high fidelity, then when it attempts to play the song, "I Cannot Be Played on Record Player X," it will create just those vibrations which will cause it to break. . . . So it fails to be Perfect. And yet, the only way to get around that trickery, namely, for Record Player X to be of lower fidelity, even more directly ensures that it is not Perfect. It seems that every record player is vulnerable to one or another of these frailties, and hence all record players are defective.
>
> *Tortoise:* I don't see why you call them "defective." It is simply an inherent fact about record players that they can't do all you might wish them to be able to do. But if there is a defect anywhere, it is not in THEM, but in your expectation of what they should be able to do! And the Crab was just full of such unrealistic expectations. (Hofstadter, 1979, p. 77)

Humans, although admittedly low-fidelity (imperfect) instruments, nevertheless have a lot going for them; the problem is not in their imperfectability but in the unrealistically high level of expectations set for them. Although they may be imperfect, they are also infinitely adaptable, as the Perfect Record Player clearly was not. NO record will result in a low-fidelity record player shaking itself to pieces; the reproduction may not be entirely faithful, but it is at least there.

This adaptability displayed by human instruments is truly remarkable. An appropriate metaphor is that of the military's "smart bomb," the bomb that need not be programmed exactly to the target but only lofted in its general direction. Thereafter, the bomb has the ability to wend its own way to the target, dependent upon its detecting certain characteristics (such as heat) that it is capable of recognizing as being linked to the target, however ineffably. Similarly, the human instrument, while perhaps not as precisely gauged as an IQ test, for example, can sort people on intelligence *and* determine whether intelligence is an important characteristic to which to pay attention in some situation. The human instrument can duplicate virtually any other instrument people have devised, perhaps with a little less reliability or discriminatory power, but probably well enough for most purposes— and for many simultaneous purposes at that!

Moreover, the human instrument can bring to bear all of the power of its tacit knowledge. When a teacher is asked, for example, to separate out the well-behaved children from the discipline cases in a classroom, he or she does it largely on the basis of tacitly absorbed experience. He or she may be unable to tell precisely why child A belongs in the well-behaved group and Child B in the discipline group, but nevertheless can make the judgment in ways that stand up to later scrutiny.[4] Moreover, the advantage of beginning with a fund not only of propositional knowledge but also of tacit knowlege and the ability to be infinitely adaptable make the human investigator ideal in situations in which the design is emergent; the human can sense out salient factors, think of ways to follow up on them, and make continuous changes, all while actively engaged in the inquiry itself.

In order for the human instrument to use all of these abilities to the fullest extent possible, there must be frequent, continuing, and meaningful interactions between the investigator and the respondents or other objects of investigation. If this interaction were to be nullified, say, by some magical methodology that could "truly" guarantee objectivity, the trade-off would hardly be worth it. Who would claim that the gain in objectivity would be worth the loss of adaptability, insight, and knowledge base that would be involved?

There are, then, compelling reasons for conducting inquiry in ways that maximize rather than minimize the investigator's interactions. The quality of interaction must be good if an appropriate balance between factual theory-ladenness and theoretical underdetermination is to be found and maintained. Purposeful sampling and emergent designs are impossible without it. The "objectively subjective" Hegelian realized level cannot be achieved in its absence. The dialectical-dialogical nature of human research cannot be exploited adequately without it. Full respondent cooperation and understanding will not be forthcoming without it. Finally, and perhaps most important, such interaction is absolutely essential if the full power of the human instrument's capabilities is to be realized.

CAN ADEQUATE SAFEGUARDS BE MOUNTED AGAINST INVESTIGATOR BIAS?

Might it be the case, however, that for the sake of the alleged gains achieved in maintaining a high level of interaction between investigator and respondents we may be giving away more than we realize? Isn't there something to be said for objectivity? How can we even know whether we ought to trust an investigator's findings when we seem to be so willing to give methodological *carte blanche*?

These are not only reasonable but crucially important questions. We need to recognize that objectivity in its pure form is an unattainable state (it would in fact be attainable only if there were a single, tangible, reality "out there," a contingency denied in the first axiom of the naturalistic paradigm). On the other hand, one cannot therefore conclude that balance and fairness are not worth striving for, even though one may fall short of their full attainment.

Do naturalistic evaluators have some strategies for dealing with this problem? Naturalists are as aware as any inquirers of the possible sources of difficulty in using humans-as-instruments, in building upon the interaction of investigator with context/respondents as *the* source of data. Humans get tired. Humans exhibit selective perception. Humans cannot simultaneously occupy all vantage points and so they have limited perspective (in the usual sense as well as in Schwartz and Ogilvy's sense of that term). Humans "go native," as the anthropologists used to say, and they also exhibit ethnocentrism, the opposite pole (Lincoln & Guba, 1981).

We shall see in the treatment of trustworthiness (Chapter 11) that there are techniques the naturalist can employ that, while they fall short of *guaranteeing* balance and fairness, can nevertheless provide a system of useful checks and balances. Included among these techniques (all of which will be examined in detail later) are *member checks* (referring data and interpretations back to data sources for correction/verification/challenge); *debriefings by peers* (systematically talking through research experiences, findings, and decisions with noninvolved professional peers for a variety of purposes—catharsis, challenge, design of next steps, or legitimation, for example); *triangulation* (cross-checking of data and interpretations through the use of multiple data sources and/or data collection techniques, as well as different investigators); *prolonged engagement and persistent observation* (maintaining long-term, in-depth contact in relation to salient features); use of *reflexive journals* (introspective journals that display the investigator's mind processes, philosophical position, and bases of decisions about the inquiry); and the *independent audit* (a process similar to the fiscal audit, whereby an external auditor examines the inquiry to establish that the *process* was carried out in ways that fall within the bounds of good professional practice, and that the *products* are consistent with the raw data). The reader ought not to feel, therefore, that what is being traded away is too valuable to be lost for the sake of some specious claims about increasing investigator sensitivity or adaptability. In fact, as will be seen, sound ways of approaching the trustworthiness questions are available that, while not compelling (nothing within the naturalistic paradigm can be, by definition), can be quite persuasive.

NOTES

1. Indeed, one of the present authors is so accustomed to reducing everything to dichotomies, and playing off their elements against one another, that his students often refer to him as Mr. 2 × 2!

2. The use of the term "error" is instructive. Note the positivist bias. If the respondent reacts differently than he or she "normally" (in the real world?) would, an "error" is introduced into the data. The investigator's impact on the context is ignored.

3. But, the reader may object, if one takes that attitude, how can one ever *really know* anything? The naturalist, unlike the positivist, does not seek certainty, believing that such a search would be equivalent to seeking the Holy Grail. Having given up the idea of tangible reality, the naturalist is not too disturbed at the notion of limiting knowledge to possibilities.

4. We should never forget that every psychological test, no matter how sophisticated and objective it may appear, ultimately rests on this sort of human judgment for its validity.

5

The Only Generalization Is:
There Is No Generalization

> The trouble with generalizations is that they don't apply to particulars.

GENERALIZATION AS
THE AIM OF SCIENCE

We have seen that a frequently mentioned aim of science is prediction and control. But prediction and control cannot be accomplished without something on which to base predictions or formulate controlling actions. It is the role of laws, those statements that Kaplan (1964) calls "nomic" or "nomological" generalizations, to provide such a base. While such nomic generalizations have a number of defining characteristics, possibly the most important is that

> the generalization must be truly universal, *unrestricted as to time and space*. It must formulate what is always and everywhere the case, provided only that the appropriate conditions are satisfied. (Kaplan, 1964, p. 91; emphasis added)

That is to say, generalizations are assertions of *enduring* value that are *context-free*. Their value lies in their ability to modulate efforts at prediction and control.

Indeed, so convinced are many scientists that generalizations are the be-all and end-all of inquiry that they seriously question whether scientific activity aimed at something other than the establishment of generalizations is worth the effort. They assert that if one rejects the goal of achieving generalizations, all that can be left is knowledge of the particular—and they ask, "What value could there be in knowing only the unique?" But this posture ignores the fact that we are not dealing with an either/or proposition; the alternatives include more than deciding between nomic generalizations on the one hand and unique, particularized knowledge on the other. We shall spend much of this chapter exploring an intermediate position.

Generalization, it must be admitted, is an appealing concept. The dictionary defines the general as "pertaining to, affecting, or applicable to each and all of a class, kind, or order." Each and all! When a generalization has been devised, no member of that class, kind, or order can escape its pervasive influence. What could be more appropriate if the aim is prediction and control? The concept oozes determinism, and seems to place the entire world at the feet of those persons who can unlock its deepest and most pervasive generalities. How grandly these concepts fit in with political processes, too; social science can discover generalizations that make it unnecessary for lawgivers to think through the particulars of each case. Rather, generalizations will serve their purposes, and what is good for one is good for all—at least all in that class.[1]

It should not be doubted that the concept of generalization has the influence that we have ascribed to it here. Beginning with John Stuart Mill and continuing to today's postpositivists, many have subscribed to the proposition that generalization is among the most basic of scientists' goals. Hamilton (1976) has observed that among Mill's assumptions (see Chapter 1) is that the social and natural sciences have identical aims, namely, the discovery of general laws that serve for explanation and prediction, and that Mill's "ultimate major premise" was that there exists a uniformity of nature in time and space. Indeed, Mill felt that the latter premise was essential to overcome certain objections that had been raised about the inductive nature of generalization. For if the postulated uniformity did indeed characterize nature, then inductive logic was as procedurally certain as was deductive logic—a mistaken notion, but one nevertheless persuasive to Mill and many of his adherents.

Schwartz and Ogilvy (1979, p. 32) comment that among the positivists' major assumptions was that

> the laws that govern matter and energy on the small scale must be similar, and hopefully identical, to those that apply on the very large scale. The governing laws thus would be universal, so that we ought to be able to build a picture of planets moving about the sun out of an understanding of the particles of which matter is composed.

Unfortunately, that belief has turned out to have been mistaken also.

Hesse (1980) suggests that the aim of prediction and control is primary even in postpositivist thought through the adoption of what she terms the "pragmatic criterion" for science. This criterion states, simply enough, that science will be judged successful to the degree that it is able to produce "increasingly successful prediction and control of the environment" (p. 188), a statement that certainly supports the continuation of dependence on generalizability. There are of course some postpositivists, particularly naturalists, who disagree with this position.

Despite the interest in generalizability, and the almost universal appeal that the idea has for all of us, serious questions can be raised about the feasibility of this concept in its classic form. We shall first examine several of the more important of these issues, stopping thereafter to comment on a form recently proposed by Stake and others that is termed "naturalistic generalization,"[2] and finally make a counterproposal: the working hypothesis.

SOME PROBLEMS WITH THE CLASSIC CONCEPT OF GENERALIZABILITY

The classic concept of generalizability, as defined by Kaplan, suffers from a number of deficiencies, which are briefly outlined below:

(1) Dependence on the assumption of determinism. In the final analysis, there can be no generalization unless there is also determinism; if there are no fixed and reliable linkages among elements, then one cannot derive statements about those linkages (laws) that will be found to hold in "truly universal" ways.

We have seen that the Newtonian and, more broadly, the positivist metaphor for the world was the machine. Indeed, scientists did not take the machine to be simply a metaphor but believed that, in fact, the world *was* one Great Machine. Dickson (1982, p. 137) suggests the term "mechanomorphism" to denote "the belief that god is a mechanical force and that the universe is governed by natural law." Wolf (1981, p. 43) quotes the eminent French scientist, the Marquis de Laplace, as pontificating, at the turn of the nineteenth century:

> We ought, then, to regard the present state of the universe as the effect of its previous state and as the cause of the one which is to follow. Given for one instant a mind which could comprehend all the forces by which nature is animated and the respective situation of the beings who compose it—a mind sufficiently vast to submit these data to analysis—it would embrace *in the same formula* the movements of the greatest bodies of the universe and those of the lightest atom; for it, nothing would be uncertain and the future, as the past, would be present to its eyes. (emphasis added)

Wolf goes on to comment, "Perfect determinism, from a heartbreak to an empire's rise and fall, was no more than the inevitable workings of the Great Machine" (p. 43).

The existence of a "grand" formula as envisioned by Laplace was not an uncommon assumption; again, it should be stressed that this expression was taken literally and not metaphorically by its adherents. The ultimate generalization, in effect, *was* this grand formula, which has a very large number of terms, sufficiently large to embrace every particle in the universe. Any particular phenomenon was a special case; many of the "coefficients" of terms in the formula would go to zero, but what remained would describe the phenomenon perfectly. It was only the natural limits on the human mind that prevented the discovery and utilization of the formula; had Laplace known about the power that would eventually be built into computers, he probably would have nourished the hope that this formula would, sooner or later, be known.

But of course the very idea of determinism rests, as we now understand, on shifting sand. Indeed, as Schwartz and Ogilvy remind us (see Chapter 2), determinism is rapidly being replaced by indeterminism in the "new" paradigm; indeterminism is now the basic belief that determinism once was. And without the base of determinism on which to rest, the possibility of generalizability comes seriously into question. Generalizability becomes, at best, probabilistic.

(2) Dependence on inductive logic. Generalizations are not found in nature; they are active creations of the mind. Empirically, they rest upon the generalizer's experience with a limited number of particulars, not with "each and all" of the members of a "class, kind, or order." From that experience springs, as Ford (1975) suggests, an *imaginative* generalization, one that goes beyond the bounds of the particulars, making assertions that presumably apply not only to its generating particulars but to all other similar particulars.

Now the rules of *deduction* are *closed;* given certain premises, it is possible to derive conclusions that are *absolutely* true (T₃), conclusions that are compelling and binding upon the receiver. But induction is essentially an *open* process, as Reese (1980, p. 251) suggests:

> The widespread distinction between induction as an inference moving from specific facts to general conclusions, and deduction as moving from general premises to specific conclusions is no longer respectable philosophically. This distinction distinguished one kind of induction from one kind of deduction. It is much more satisfactory to think

of induction as *probable* inference and deduction as *necessary* inference. (emphasis added)

Epistemologists such as Hesse (1980) have stressed the fact that theories are underdetermined; the same arguments might well hold for the generalizations (laws) that are sometimes said to be the component elements of theories. Thus Hesse (1980, p. 187) on theory:

> Theories are logically constrained by facts, but are underdetermined by them: that is, while, to be acceptable, theories should be more or less plausibly coherent with facts, they can be neither conclusively refuted nor uniquely derived from statements of fact alone, and hence no theory in a given domain is uniquely acceptable.

That is to say, while generalizations are constrained by facts (especially if the facts are the particulars from which the generalization is induced), there is no single necessary generalization that *must* emerge to account for them. There are always (logically) multiple possible generalizations to account for any set of particulars, however extensive and inclusive they may be.

If the logical consequence of indeterminism is that generalizations can be, at best, probabilistic, the logical consequence of reliance on induction is that generalizations can be at best relativistic expressions (Hesse, 1980, p. xiv). There are no absolutes; all "truth" is relative; there are no final metacriteria. And there are certainly no absolute laws. The issue, as we shall see, is *what it is to which the "generalization" is relative.*

✓ *(3) Dependence on the assumption of freedom from time and context.* Kaplan has reminded us that nomic generalizations, at least, must be of a form that is "always and everywhere the case, provided only that the appropriate conditions are satisfied." But all of our experience tells us that there are always many "conditions, contingencies, and disjunctions" (Wiles, 1981) that must be taken into account.

It is difficult to imagine a human activity that is context-free. Your response, reader, to what is on these pages may take a variety of forms. For example, you might turn to a colleague and remark, "What nonsense this is!" If you were using these materials to instruct a class in research methods, you might wish to pose certain counterarguments, in order to appear constructive and scholarly in your critique. If you were to question the authors about their beliefs while they were on the podium of a national meeting, you might be a bit more snide and acerbic in your statements. If you were to discuss this chapter with the authors over a bottle of beer at a convenient pub, your demeanor might be very different yet. And so on. It is also likely that the view that will be taken of this analysis will be sharply different in the year 2000 (should we have the good fortune of being remembered then) from that of the present. Presumably by 2000 we will know a good deal more about the issues being uncovered tentatively here.

But the problem is much more intractable than this small example suggests. Listen to Lee J. Cronbach, as he ruminates "Beyond the Two Disciplines of Scientific Psychology" (1975, pp. 122-123):

> Generalizations decay. At one time a conclusion describes the existing situation well, at a later time it accounts for rather little variance, and ultimately it is valid *only as history*. The half-life of an empirical proposition may be great or small. The more open the system, the shorter the half-life of relations within it are likely to be.
>
> Propositions describing atoms and electrons have a long half-life, and the physical theorist can regard the processes in his world as steady. Rarely is a social or behavioral phenomenon isolated enough to have this steady-state property. Hence the explanation we live by will perhaps always remain partial, and distant from real events . . . and rather short lived. The atheoretical regularities of the actuary are even more time bound. An actuarial table describing human affairs *changes from science into history* before it can be set in type. (emphasis added)

Cronbach's analysis is a powerful one because it takes into account not only changes in sociobehavioral generalizations, which have short half-lives and might be explained on the basis that our knowledge is so rudimentary in these areas that frequent updates are necessary, but also changes in physical/chemical/biological generalizations, for example, the failure of DDT to control mosquitos as genetic transformations make them resistant to that pesticide, and the shifting of the value of the gravitational constant, so that while s will continue to equal gt^2, the actual distances covered by falling bodies will differ.

Cronbach's metaphor of the radioactive substance, constantly decaying and displaying a characteristic half-life, seems a particularly apt one. Further, his notion that all science eventually becomes history demolishes the proposition that generalizations are time-free; generalizations inevitably alter, usually radically, over time, so that, eventually, they have only historical interest.

Some critics, unwilling to give up easily on the Kaplan definition, point out that we have so far overlooked the phrase therein contained: "provided only that the appropriate conditions are satisfied." If the difficulty is that generalizations do not take adequate account of time factors and contextual conditions, they assert, there is an easy solution: Enlarge the generalization to include as many of these temporal/contextual variables as may be necessary so that the generalization *will* hold. But this proposal poses two difficulties of its own: First, it tends to move us back to the Laplacian grand equation (for surely if, in their view, we included *all* variables there could be no doubt that the generalization would hold—and there need be only one generalization!), and, second, it defeats the purpose of seeking generalizations in the first place: to facilitate prediction and control. For if the equation becomes too complex, has built into it so many spatiotemporal factors as may be necessary, then of course the mind boggles (even when computer aided) at the task, and the resources needed to set up the controls are stretched beyond all bounds. It is far easier, and more epistemologically sound, simply to give up on the idea of generalization, at least as prescribed by Kaplan. Accepting generalizations (to whatever extent they may be possible) as indeterminate, relative, and time and context bound, while not a wholly satisfying solution, is at least a feasible one.

✓ *(4) Entrapment in the nomothetic-idiographic dilemma.* The terms "nomothetic" and "idiographic" were coined by German philosopher Wilhelm Windelband to describe, on the one hand, the natural sciences (the term "nomothetic" implies "based on law"), and, on the other, the "cultural" or human sciences (the term "idiographic" implies "based on the particular individual").[3] The essential dilemma is simply this: Generalizations are nomothetic in nature, that is lawlike, but in order to use them—for purposes of prediction or control, say—the generalizations must be applied to particulars. And it is precisely at that point that their probabilistic, relative nature comes into sharpest focus.

Consider the example of the woman who comes in to see her gynecologist for her routine annual examination. In response to the physician's questions, she reports that she has suffered certain symptoms for some months. The physician's reaction is one of immediate alarm: "Madam," he says, "fully 80 percent of the women who report those symptoms have cervical cancer. I will call the hospital at once and arrange to have you admitted. Tomorrow morning at the latest we will do a complete hysterectomy on you." Aside from the fact that the woman in question might be well advised (heeding the latest bulletin from Blue Cross/Blue Shield) to seek a second opinion, she has other intelligent grounds for questioning the proposed course of action. She might well ask, "But suppose I am one of that group of 20 percent who do *not* have cancer of the cervix, despite displaying these systems?

Aren't you going to examine me to find out? Wouldn't you like to determine the particulars of this case before making a judgment that condemns me to expense, pain, and loss of productive time, when it might not be necessary at all to have this operation?'' The woman would be quite right in insisting that idiographic elements be considered rather than basing a judgment entirely on a nomothetic generalization.

If in fact there were a one-to-one relationship between particulars and generalizations—that is, that generalizations did not suffer from inductive loss in their formulation but could be counted on to be determinately and absolutely true—then this problem would not arise. But generalizations unfortunately cannot meet these stringent criteria; they are always inductively underdetermined, and they are always temporally and contextually relative.

The nomothetic-idiographic problem continues to haunt particularly the social/behavioral sciences and the helping professions. Consider the dilemma of the therapist trying to deal with an individual's problem within the context of psychiatric generalizations. Or the teacher attempting to get children to learn in a particular class by using only general pedagogical principles. Or the warden seeking to control the prisoners in a particular penitentiary on the basis of general correctional theories. That the dilemma continues to be of pervasive interest is evident from the literature; the reader may wish to consult Marceil (1977) for a recent analysis. Perhaps the professional group that has dealt best with this problem is the law, built largely on precedent cases (case law) that are powerful precisely because they take particulars into account.

✓ *(5) Entrapment in a reductionist fallacy.* Generalizations represent a special case of reductionism: attempting to reduce all phenomena of a given class to the purview of a single (or single set of) generalization(s). There are several difficulties with this posture. First, generalizations are of necessity parts of formal systems: sets of laws, theories, and the like that are directed at some phenomenological arena. Such formal systems, sometimes called formal languages, are by definition *closed* systems, that is, they are not open to the influence of any elements or factors that are not accounted for in the system. Hamilton (1979, p. 2) observes:

> As closed systems, formal languages are logically isolated from extraneous elements (e.g., undefined "variables") in the same way that laboratory experiments are empirically isolated from "field" settings. In general, . . . formal languages cannot fully comprehend natural (i.e., open) systems.

But there are more powerful grounds for reaching the conclusion that generalizations will always fall short of "full comprehension." Perhaps the most pervasive argument that can be brought to bear is Gödel's theorem, which, while developed in relation to number theory in mathematics, has wider applicability, that is, can lead one to better understanding in fields other than mathematics as well. The theorem itself, as quoted in Hofstadter (1979, p. 18) is simply this:

> All consistent axiomatic formulations of number theory include undecidable propositions.

Restated, the assertion of the theorem is that there exists no *consistent* set of statements (reduced to their most basic undergirding axioms) that can *ever hope* to deal with all propositions; some propositions will inevitably fall outside its purview (unless, of course, one wishes to take the option implied by Gödel: to start with an *inconsistent* axiomatic formulation!). That is, there can be no set of generalizations, consistent with one another, that can effectively account for all known phenomena (the Laplacian "grand equation" is at best an idle dream!).

This concept is an extremely difficult one to comprehend; it flies in the face of traditional positivist (and some postpositivist) postures so violently as to demand rejection. But perhaps a metaphoric explanation developed by Hofstadter will contribute to our appreciation of the full significance of this important theorem. Consider Figure 5.1, which is based on Figure 18 in Hofstadter's *Gödel, Escher, Bach* (1979). One can imagine a system of axioms and theorems, perhaps empirically derived, as might be the case with many generalizations. Imagine, Hofstadter suggests, that these form a kind of knowledge "tree," the branches of which reach out into the background of the "truths" that the inquirer seeks to discover. By its nature, the tree will remain connected: twigs to branches to trunk to roots. If the tree is "seen" against the skylike background of "truths," not all truths are reachable from the several branches of the tree. There are finite limits to what can be reached, given the tree's trunk and branches (analogously, the axioms and theorems); the remainder of the "truths" are unreachable *within this formulation*. Of course, other "trees" can be planted, two, three, four, or more, in the hope that all of the "unreachable truths" will be touched by some element of some tree. But that is precisely what is meant by the phrase "consistent formulation." The planting of several trees may get the job done, but there *are* several trees, not just one; and the trees, being separate entities, each with its own system of axioms, need not conform to any requirement of consistency. To bring the matter home to the level of generalizations, it is the case that

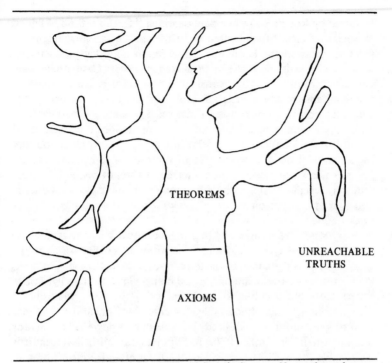

Figure 5.1: Metaphoric representation of Gödel's theorem: No consistent formulation can include all propositions.

not all generalizations that can be imagined need be consistent with one another, in fact, cannot be, if all of "reality" is to be appreciated. Any single system of generalizations, far from encompassing all elements of some phenomenon, must always fall short, to use Hamilton's phrase, of "full comprehension." This fact comes as no surprise to those who are familiar with the Schwartz and Ogilvy "new" paradigm, which asserts, as one of its major dimensions, that there are always multiple perspectives; that no one perspective can "tell the full story"; and that all perspectives aggregated do not necessarily sum to the whole of the phenomenon.

NATURALISTIC GENERALIZATION AS AN ALTERNATIVE

The concept of "naturalistic generalization," which has, on its face, an apparent relevance to the issues we have been discussing, was introduced by Robert Stake in a paper entitled "The Case Study Method in Social Inquiry," first written in 1976 as part of an assignment for the Organization for Economic Cooperation and Development and later published in *Educational Researcher* (1978). Case studies, according to Stake, are often considered nonuseful because "they are not a suitable basis for generalization" (p. 5). It seems clear that if generalization is defined in the usual sense of nomic generalization, based upon data representative of some population, the assertion of nonutility is probably correct. But, argues Stake, one must consider the situation from the perspective of the *user* of the generalization: "Case studies will often be the preferred method of research because they may be epistemologically in harmony with the reader's experience and thus to that person *a natural basis for generalization*" (p. 5; emphasis added).

Stake's posture seems to be that there are two kinds of generalizations. One kind is rationalistic, propositional, lawlike—that is the meaning we usually attach to the term in scientific discourse. The other kind is more intuitive, empirical, based on personal direct and vicarious experience—that is the meaning intended by the term "naturalistic generalization." Case studies may not contribute much if the former kind of generalization is desired, but cases are a powerful means for building the latter. Stake (1978, p. 5) points out, "I believe that it is reasonable to conclude that one of the most effective means of adding to understanding—for all readers—will be approximating through the words and illustrations of our reports the natural experience attained in ordinary personal involvements." To put it another way, if you want people to understand better than they otherwise might, provide them information in the form in which they usually experience it. They will be able, both tacitly and propositionally, to derive naturalistic generalizations that will prove to be useful extensions of their understandings.

Some of Stake's readers foundered on the issue of whether naturalistic generalizations were essentially tacit or whether they could be propositional. Were these generalizations things that were felt only "at gut level" so to speak, or could they be communicated to others in normal language? Hamilton, for example, in an unpublished seminar paper read at the University of Glasgow in 1979, understood Stake to say that naturalistic generalizations were based upon tacit knowledge, that they were the "pre-verbal, pre-cognitive product of human experience" (p. 1). He argued that there were two "contrasting accounts" of generalizations, one logical (built, he said, around concepts such as "sample" and "population") and one psychological (built around concepts such as "cognition," "abstraction," and "comprehension"). Hamilton indicated that he preferred to equate naturalistic generalization with the psychological version:

> For my part, I would like to keep to a restricted definition of naturalistic generalization. That is, it may be worthwhile to distinguish between (i) making an inside-the-head generalization, and (ii) being able to communicate the reasons for making a generalization. In short, naturalistic generalization should be located within the realm of private knowledge.
>
> Naturalistic generalizations are personal accounts of the external world which, as it were, are held in the form of non-negotiable currency. When persons wish to communicate a naturalistic generalization they must convert their holdings into a shared form of exchange. They must engage upon a key component of scientific practice—public discourse.
>
> From this perspective, naturalistic generalizations and scientific generalizations fit inside each other as "nested" concepts. They are not the same, yet they are not in opposition to each other.

Stake (1980) objected to this formulation, arguing that "the key feature is not that naturalistic generalizations cannot be shared," but "that they reside-in-mind in their natural habitat." Stake (1980, pp. 2-3) goes on:

> I responded to David Hamilton last summer, from a beach somewhere, musing as follows:
>
> > I face the water and the breeze cools my face, I am aware of a generalization that breezes blow from water to land. I am not aware of being told or having read it, though in novels and movies I have vicariously experienced incidents that verify the generalization. I have heard people remark on the coolness of the ocean breeze. But *my* generalization I believe is primarily a creation of my own experimental knowing. Even though expressed in propositional form, it is a *naturalistic generalization*.
> >
> > I wonder why breezes blow from water to land. Are people on beaches all *around* a small lake cooled by breezes blowing from the center of the lake? My experience is inadequate. My formal knowledge tells me that heat rises over land. I can recall a drawing in a book, perhaps an explanation of cumulus cloud activity. I know from personal experience and from formal learning that the water is cooler than the land (at least in months I am at the beach). Apparently it is not just heat that is rising but hot air, and faster over land than over water. So I generalize: the breeze is simply cooler air over water rushing in to replace departed air above land.

Even though I made this generalization in my own mind, it is more the creature of formal knowledge and formal reasoning, modified only slightly by (though given an important confirmation by) experiential learning. It is a formalistic generalizing.

What are we to make of all this? Hamilton and Stake, while apparently disagreeing on whether naturalistic generalization is all in the mind or whether it can be (or should be) shared publicly, nevertheless seem to agree that there are *two* kinds of generalizations: naturalistic (Stake) or psychological (Hamilton), and formalistic (Stake) or logical (Hamilton). Neither is arguing that one is a *replacement* for the other; they exist side by side, and each has its own arena of applicability.

Now it is clear that the kind of generalizations we have been talking about in this chapter tend toward the formalistic or logical (choose your term) rather than toward the naturalistic or psychological. We are not, as some of our critics contend, suggesting that the former have no utility while the latter do. While the idea of naturalistic generalization has for us a great deal of appeal (we shall return to it in Chapter 13 when we discuss case studies, for we surely agree with Stake that case studies have a great deal of utility in assisting reader understanding by inducing naturalistic generalizations), we do not believe that it is an adequate substitute or replacement for the formalistic or logical generalizations that people usually have in mind when they use the term "generalization." Yet we have, as we have tried to show in the earlier portion of this chapter, a serious problem with generalization in the nomic sense intended by Kaplan. We would replace the classic idea of generalization not with naturalistic generalization but with a new formulation proposed by Cronbach (1975): the *working hypothesis.*

THE WORKING HYPOTHESIS

We have noted that many scientists are committed to the idea of nomic generalization as the be-all and end-all of inquiry; it is these generalizations that become formulated into laws that in turn support theories from which, by hypothetico-deductive means, hypotheses are formulated that form the basis for the next round of inquiry, and so so. What could be the goal of inquiry if not the discovery of generalizable truths? What is left once generalizations are removed?

But of course the issue before us is not of the either/or variety. Between the poles of the most *general* (nomothetic) and the most *specific* (idiographic) is the broad range of the *related;* we are dealing here with a *continuum,* the two ends of which do not begin to encompass all of the possibilities that exist. The issue we pose then is simply this: If broad nomic generalizations, truly universal, unrestricted as to time and space, always and everywhere the same, are not feasible products of inquiry, are there nevertheless some ways of stating outcomes that might hold in Context B, although "discovered" in Context A? What are the bases for *transferability,* if not of generalization, from one context to another?

We believe the answer to that question is found in a concept proposed by Lee Cronbach (1975) in his classic "Beyond the Two Disciplines" paper—the *working hypothesis.* Cronbach makes a lengthy case against generalizability in the nomic sense (although he does not use that term); we have already cited a portion of this argument earlier in this chapter. He finally concludes:

> Instead of making generalization the ruling consideration in our research, I suggest that we reverse our priorities. An observer collecting data in the particular situation is in a position to appraise a practice or proposition in that setting, observing effects in context. In trying to describe and account for what happened, he will give attention to whatever variables were controlled, but he will give equally careful attention to uncontrolled conditions, to personal characteristics, and to events that occurred during treatment and measurement. As he goes from situation to situation, his first task is to describe and interpret the effect anew in each locale, perhaps taking into account factors unique to that locale or series of events.... As results accumulate, a person who seeks understanding will do his best to trace how the uncontrolled factors could have caused local departures from the modal effect. That is, generalization comes late, and the exception is taken as seriously as the rule.
>
> ... *When we give proper weight to local conditions, any generalization is a working hypothesis, not a conclusion.* (Cronbach, 1975, pp. 124-125; emphasis added).

There is much in Cronbach's language to which we would take exception. "Effects," "variables," "control," "treatment," "measurement," "modal effect," and the like are terms that have little place in the naturalistic paradigm. Nevertheless, Cronbach's ideas are powerful; they suggest that there are always factors that are unique to the locale or series of events that make it useless to try to generalize therefrom. But, he notes, inquirers *are* in a position to appreciate such factors and take them into account. And, as the inquirer moves from situation to situation, "his task is to describe and interpret the effect anew," that is, in terms of the uniqueness found in *each* new situation. Generalization comes late, Cronbach avers—and, we might echo, if at all. For, "when we give proper weight to local conditions, any generalization is a working hypothesis, not a conclusion."

Local conditions, in short, make it impossible to generalize. If there is a "true" generalization, it is that there can be no generalization. And note that the "working hypotheses" are tentative both for the situation in which they are first uncovered and for other situations; there are always differences in context from situation to situation, and even the single situation differs over time. It is said that a Chinese philosopher, upon being asked whether it is possible to cross the same river twice, replied that it is not possible to cross the same river even once! Constant flux militates against conclusions that are always and forever true; they can only be said to be true under such and such conditions and circumstances.

TRANSFERABILITY AND FITTINGNESS

How can one tell whether a working hypothesis developed in Context A might be applicable in Context B? We suggest that the answer to that question must be empirical: the degree of *transferability* is a direct function of the *similarity* between the two contexts, what we shall call *"fittingness."* Fittingness is defined as the degree of congruence between sending and receiving contexts. If Context A and Context B are "sufficiently" congruent, then working hypotheses from the sending originating context *may* be applicable in the receiving context.

Now it is one of the claimed virtues of the nomic generalization that it transends this fittingness question; one need not know *anything* about either originating and receiving contexts to know the "truth" of the generalization, assuming only that originating and receiving contexts are in some sense part of the known population of contexts and that the generalization is based upon a study of a representative sample of contexts. But working hypotheses are not that powerful; their transferability depends upon the degree of fittingness. The person who wishes to make a judgment of transferability needs information about *both* contexts to make that judgment well. Now an inquirer cannot know all the contexts to which someone may wish to transfer working hypotheses; one cannot reasonably expect him or her to indicate the range of contexts to which there might be some transferability.[4] But it is entirely reasonable to expect an inquirer to provide sufficient information about the context in which an inquiry is carried out so that anyone else interested in transferability has a base of information appropriate to the judgment. We shall call that appropriate base of information a "thick description," following the usage introduced by Geertz (1973).

What is described in the "thick description" of course depends on the focus of the inquiry, or whether it is a research, evaluation, or policy analysis inquiry, and on the salient features of the context. The description must specify everything that a reader may need to know in order to understand the findings (findings are *not* part of the thick description, although they must be interpreted in the terms of the factors thickly described); this collectivity is sometimes called the "melange of descriptors." The minimum elements to be included in this melange are described in Chapter 13.

HOLOGRAPHIC GENERALIZATION

We could not close this chapter without pointing out several implications of the Schwartz and Ogilvy "new" paradigm that may yet have enormous consequences for the whole idea of generalization. Schwartz and Ogilvy suggest that the metaphor for the world is changing from the machine to the hologram; holograms have characteristics more descriptive of the "world" as we have come to know it than does the analogue of the machine. If that is so, then one particular characteristic of holograms is of particular significance: the fact that any piece of the hologram contains in it all of the information found in the whole.

A full appreciation of this remarkable fact requires some knowledge of how the process of holography works.[5] The final product—the physical entity in which the hologram is stored—is a piece of film, not unlike that produced by any normal camera. But the image on the film is substantially different from anything produced by a Kodak or a Polaroid; it is not an image of the photographed object (that is, if the film is held to the light one will not "see" the object, even in negative form), but an image of an "interference" pattern produced by intersecting, and interacting, light waves.

The discovery of holography was actually made mathematically and not optically; indeed, the possibility of holograms was known for some years before investigators were able to establish the physical conditions needed to carry out the process. For what was needed was a perfectly "coherent" light source, that is, a light source that emitted "pure" light of a single wave length. While Dennis Gabor had worked out the underlying principles in 1947, the physical production of holograms had to await the perfection of lasers, which can emit such coherent light. The first "real" holograms could not be made until 1964.

Essentially, the hologram is produced by photographing an object using two laser beams that result from the optical splitting of a single original beam, using mirrors. Since they emanate from a single source, these two beams are perfectly coordinated insofar as the peaks and troughs of their waves are concerned. One of the beams is directed at the object to be holographed and allowed to "bounce" off it; it is then recombined with the other, unimpaired beam. But now some of the peaks and troughs in the two beams are "out of phase," because of the experience of the first beam in striking the object. "Interference" patterns of light and dark waves are formed in the interaction of these two beams, and it is these interference patterns that are actually recorded on film. Examination of the film microscopically reveals an intensely fine-grained series of light (at points of wave reinforcement) and dark (at points of wave interference) bands.

To re-create the object, a laser beam is shone through the film, and, as if by magic, the interference pattern is reconverted into an image of the original object. *Frontiers of Photography* comments:

> Since most holograms must be viewed in darkened rooms to be appreciated their effect is doubly impressive—and sometimes chilling. To a viewer who is standing in a dimly lit chamber, the holographic portrait of a man, for example, has all the stark reality of a living, breathing person, yet the substance of a photograph and the aura of a ghost. The viewer may forget that he is watching a photographic marvel and, with a shiver of recognition, think he is attending a bizarre wake in which the body has been propped up to be seen through a doorway. At that particular moment, holography may seem a breathtaking—and eerie—exercise in necromancy. (Life Library of Photography, 1972, p. 135)

While clearly not necromantic, the holographic image nevertheless possesses some rather remarkable properties:

- It reproduces the object in *three dimensions*—the image looks for all the world to be suspended in space.
- It reproduces an object the appearance of which varies *depending on the perspective of the viewer*. In one well-known demonstration, a man appears to sit at a desk with some papers before him. A magnifying glass is held in one of his hands in such a way that, from one perspective, we see one of the papers magnified in the glass. But if we move our heads slightly, the image in the magnifying glass changes too! Now we may see not the paper magnified but the watch on the man's wrist!

- It reproduces an object that, under certain circumstances, can be viewed from all sides; the observer can actually walk around it and see it front and back!

But it is not only the holographic image that has remarkable properties—the holographic process and the way in which it stores its information also has some unexpected features. Two are of special interest to us with respect to the problem of generalization:

- The information needed to produce an image from the film is stored throughout the *entire* film. When a picture is taken by normal photographic means and stored on a negative, if part of that negative is cut away, the information on that part is lost forever. But if part of a holographic film is cut away, *nothing happens!* The part that remains will produce the *whole object* just as well and as easily as if the entire film were still there. That is, complete information about the whole is stored in each and every part of the hologram, so that even the tiniest bit of the hologram is sufficient to reproduce the whole.
- The process of holography can be used to clarify an otherwise blurred image produced by normal photographic means. The reason for this remarkable capability is that even a blurred image—say a picture taken when the camera was not quite in focus—nevertheless contains *all* of the optical information that would have been contained in a clear picture. The information is simply spread out in a way that is describable mathematically; the blurring can be compensated for by the use of a holographic filter that effectively applies the mathematics in reverse. To accomplish this seeming miracle, a holographic film is produced of *any* spot in the original blurred picture, since any spot will contain all of the information related to blurring (all parts of the original are blurred in the same way). When a laser beam is passed through a transparency of the original and the holographic film, used as a filter, simultaneously, the image is converted to a more perfectly focused one. All of us are familiar with the fact that blurred images sent back by space probes can be cleared up or "enhanced"; the process by which this is done is this same holographic reverse filtering.

What are the implications of these facts? Of course, one is immediately on thin ice in attempting to reason from a metaphor, for the metaphor may be imperfect for the use to which it is put. Nevertheless, we may take some comfort from Peircian principles of abduction (retroduction) in asserting that we may come to discover

- that full information about a whole is stored in its parts, if only we knew how to get at it;

- that samples need not be representative in the usual statistical sense to render generalizations warrantable; any part or component is a "perfect" sample in the sense that it contains all of the information about the whole that one might ever hope to obtain;
- that imperfect (blurred) information from any source can be improved (clarified), if one has the appropriate filters for so doing; and
- that *both* the substantive information about an object *and* the information needed to clarify it are contained in the unclarified versions.

Of course, we are incapable of testing any of these assertions at this point in time; nevertheless they have a ring of credibility about them. Surely we can now at the very least assert that any information found in any part must be characteristic of the whole; to that extent the holographic generalization we are speculating about here is already "true."

NOTES

1. The fact that the credibility of social science has recently suffered severe setbacks among members of Congress as well as other elements of federal, state, and local governments might give one pause, if for no other reason than that one might begin to wonder whether generalization is all that it is cracked up to be!

2. We find the use of the term "naturalistic generalization" unfortunate because of the possibility of confusion with the term "naturalistic paradigm," which we ourselves use. We wish to make clear that the idea of naturalistic generalization is *not* part of our formulation of the naturalistic paradigm.

3. These terms have also been used by one of the authors to describe the two axes of human behavior in institutional settings, particularly from the perspective of an administrator (see Getzels & Guba, 1956). The spelling "idiographic" is characteristic of modern usage; Windelband used the spelling, "ideographic."

4. The problem of describing the range of the population to which the findings of a particular study might be appropriate is of course not limited to naturalistic inquiry. Indeed, the problem comes up very frequently in conventional research, particularly in the social/behavioral sciences, precisely because it is often not possible to select a sample on which to carry out a study that is representative of a defined population. Often the population cannot be delimited adequately, or, even if it can, ethical or political considerations intervene. Thus the sample is often a "convenience" sample—the sample to which the inquirer happens to have access. The question then arises, given the findings from such a convenience sample of known characteristics, what is the nature of the population to which the findings might be generalized? More than 30 years ago the eminent statistician Palmer O. Johnson provided a complete solution to this problem; unfortunately, however, the predicted parameters of the population were always so broad that sample findings could hold for populations of virtually *any* parameters!

5. An excellent, illustrated, lay treatment of holography can be found in the Life Library of Photography's *Frontiers of Photography* (1972, pp. 134-158).

6

Is Causality
a Viable Concept?

The general epistemological orientation of social science is causal. Despite our lip service to the probabilistic universe, and the long-standing admonitions of some of our science's greatest minds . . . , our closed system linear model statistics, our basic experimental research methods, our theories, and our fundamental conceptualizations of the forces that intervene in social affairs all presume a causal, deterministic universe.

(Crano, 1981)

IS CAUSALITY DEAD?

One may well ask why the history of inquiry is characterized by such an obsessional preoccupation with causality. Answers are not difficult to come by. It has long been the aim of science to achieve prediction and control, and the understanding of causes seems to many to be *the* key to their achievement. The development of interventions (an activity well favored these days) depends on the viability of the concept of causality; interventions (causes) are designed in ways that will eliminate undesirable states of affairs (effects) and/or substitute desirable ones. Further, insofar as science is deterministic, knowledge of causes and effects is central; if it could be shown that the concept of causes is deficient, the assumption of determinism would be difficult to defend. Finally, without viable causes, the hope for a nomothetic science would seem to be vain.

These reasons may explain why scientists have become enamored of the causality concept, but there are other reasons for our causality fetish that transcend the scientific. If causes are the key to prediction and control, knowledge of causes is tantamount to power. This fact may help us to understand why political figures have been willing to support scientific research, in the hope that such inquiry will produce information that can be used to good political effect. It may also explain their impatience when the inquiry does not produce immediate results.

Even more fundamental than science and politics, however, is the idea that the drive to develop causal explanations is deep-seated in the very genetic and psychic makeup of humans. Cook and Campbell (1979, p. 28), for example, describe themselves as holding a "critical-realist" perspective that is "biological evolutionary" in character:

> From the evolutionary perspective . . . humanity's *strong and stubborn psychological predispositions to infer causal relations* . . . can be seen as the product of a biological evolution of brain-mind processes, which has resulted in a psychic unity concerning causation. (emphasis added).

Similarly, Robert Oppenheimer is said to have believed that "the need to understand cause constituted the third major drive of human beings after self-preservation and the preservation of the species" (quoted in Frasher & Frasher, 1979, p. 2). Michotte (1963) builds on Piaget's idea that the concept of causality develops early in children (in two stages: phenomenalism, in which links are established without knowledge, for instance, the pebble sinks because it is white, and efficacy, in which knowledge of the effort needed to produce the effect is appreciated) to undergird his own notion that one's experience with the world leads to a belief in causality. Travers (1980, p. 32) suggests that Kant "held that cause is a way of thinking about the world *that is built into our minds. It is subjectively, and not objectively, derived*" (emphasis added). Similarly, Abel (1976, p. 2) comments:

> Kant was the first to recognize that certain alleged facts about the world are not really properties of things, but rather of the ways in which we organize our knowledge. Causality, for example, is not an inherent attribute of events, but rather provides the form for our cognitive discourse about the world; it is one of the categories of our understanding. Things cannot ever come within our experience or sensibility except insofar as they conform to those categories.

Bertrand Russell (1913) asserted that the term "cause" embodied elements of "primitive animism."

Despite the persuasive reasons for accepting the concept of causality as essential and, indeed, almost genetically determined, there are many difficulties with it. The epistemological literature abounds with criticisms of each of the formulations of causality that have been proposed, as we shall see. As a result, researchers have become increasingly wary of exhibiting unbridled enthusiasm for it—Kidder (1981, p. 229) comments, for example, that "many research students and professionals are reluctant to say 'this caused that' when they report the results of their work"—and, indeed, some researchers assert that arguments about causality amount to beating a dead horse. Thus Travers (1980, p. 32) claims:

> Discussions of causal relationships in research are pre-Newtonian. . .
>
> Modern scientists do not use the concept of cause, except during chatty moments. Current psychological literature does not use the concept of cause, and substitutes have been offered. One substitute is the idea of *functional relationship*. At least that term manages to avoid the difficulties that Newton encountered. It simply implies that variables are related in a necessary and invariant way. Thus the radii of orbits of the planets, their periodicities, and their masses are related *functionally*, and the relationships cannot be other than what they are. Only a pre-Newtonian would say that the gravitional pull of the sun *causes* the planets to stay in orbit.

The horse is thought by some to be *so* dead that all that remains is removal of the cadaver. Thus Earman (1976, p. 6) asserts that "the causation of which philosophers so fondly speak . . . lies moldering. The least we can do at this late date is to give it an honest burial."

But, as in another famous case, the reports of causality's death appear to have been greatly exaggerated. Consider the following evidence:

- Robert Ennis (1973), mounting a strong argument for the centrality of the concept of causality in educational research, deplores reluctance in the use of "explicitly causal language." He cites as examples of euphemisms such phrases as " 'brings about', 'results in', 'produced', 'contributed to', 'helped', 'effected', 'affected', and 'consequences'. Two less obvious examples are 'taught' and 'teach,' as in: Ms. Kent *taught* Frank to be honest. The most effective way to *teach* reading is to combine look-say and phonics instruction in varying patterns to fit each individual child" (p. 14).

- Myles Brand (1979), in an analysis of various approaches to causality on which we shall lean heavily below, is able to be optimistic about the future of the causality concept despite the fact that his analysis indicates serious problems with every contemporary formulation. For example, in discussing one such approach, the activity approach, he says, "Despite these criticisms [that I am able to make], I for one continue to feel the force of the intuition that causality is an anthropomorphic notion. Let me suggest an avenue of future research for this approach" (p. 260). Of another approach, the counterfactual, he says, "Much of the work on this project remains to be done, and despite my own pessimism, may well be successful" (p. 269). He ends his analysis by calling for a group effort for philosophical research on causality, saying, "I am aware of the pitfalls: . . . difficulties of group dynamics, the expenditure of time required for writing committee reports, the difficulty in funding such a project; nevertheless, in the case of causality it is a method whose benefits, I suggest, will outweigh its costs" (p. 275).

- Cook and Campbell (1979, p. 10), while acknowledging that causal epistemology is "in a productive state of chaos," nevertheless assert that their book

  is intended to help persons who conduct both basic and applied research, *who have already decided that they want a causal question answered*. . . . Although we discuss sampling and measurement issues implicated by the context surrounding causal questions, we are more concerned with the experimental designs and statistical analyses that *facilitate causal* inference. (p. 2; emphases added)

Clearly, and despite Travers's strong disclaimer, there are many inquirers who do not hide behind euphemisms or shrink from calling causality by its proper name. Causality is still with us, and it is strenuously supported and advocated by leadership figures in the field.

WHAT IS THE NATURE OF THE CONCEPT OF CAUSALITY?

We turn, then, to the following question: What is the nature of this concept of causality that is so pervasive and to which so many persons seem to be so unswervingly dedicated? And there, to coin a phrase, is the rub! Far from there being simply some minor disagreements about how the concept should be defined, as, for example, one might argue about whether the most productive way to view personality is in terms of attitudes, conscious or unconscious motivation, perception, cognition, personal organization, and the like (which are, after all, not incompatible notions), there are fundamentally different and often conflicting views about the nature of causality. Brand (1979) describes six more or less contemporary formulations (we use the term "contemporary" loosely, since the first "modern" formulation dates from the first half of the eighteenth century) that represent, first, rejections of earlier formulations, and, later, efforts to produce definitions free of the problems noted by critics in their precursors.

There are two ways to view this array of definitions, and we shall employ them both. On the one hand, we may view any particular formulation in terms of critiques mounted by epistemologists espousing other points of view. The important thing to notice about such critiques is that, while disagreeing on the definition to be given the term, these epistemologists all agree on the viability of the concept of causality. None of them wishes to throw it out, but only to devise a "better" definition. This approach can therefore be thought of as an *internal* critique; it is parallel to, metaphorically, Lutherans criticizing Catholics and Baptists criticizing them both, while, at bottom, all three groups believe in God and proceed from that fundamental premise.

On the other hand, one may view *all* formulations of causality as nonviable; asserting, in effect, that the search for a *final* definition that will prove to be useful is hopeless. This critique is *external* in form; to push the metaphor further, it is Christian cosmology being critiqued from an atheistic or agnostic point of view. Such a critique is likely not only to call for the abandonment of causality but to urge something else to replace it, something for which, ostensibly, a stronger argument can be made. We proceed with the first, internal commentary, and shall return to the second, external commentary, later.

AN INTERNAL CRITIQUE
OF THE CAUSALITY CONCEPT

By the eighteenth century, the treatment of causality had moved from Aristotle's well-known four causes (material, formal, efficient, and final)[1] to the notion that a cause is that which produces an effect. This idea is sometimes referred to as the "push-pull" or "push-from-behind" version, exemplified by the action of a billiard ball, which moves (the effect) after being struck by another moving ball (the cause).

David Hume (1711-1766) took issue with this formulation, pointing out its logical Achilles' heel: There is no *necessity* for the second ball to move when it is struck by the first. The fact that the second moves each time it *is* struck is no guarantee that it will also move on the N + 1st observation (although the series of "successful" observations might well lead to a strong inference about the *probability* of movement on the N + 1st occasion). Further, Hume asserted, no one ever "sees" a cause; the fact that C (cause) is always followed by E (effect) is not sufficient reason to assert that C is the cause of E; such an assertion is an inference, or, we might say, an imputation or attribution. Immanuel Kant, roughly a contemporary of Hume's, also noticed that causes are not "inherent attributes of events," as we have seen.

Hume proposed a reformulation that is essentially positivist in nature; virtually all modern formulation can be viewed as extensions or rejections of Hume's proposition. He suggested that three conditions must be met to warrant an inference of causality: *temporal precedence* (sometimes also referred to as the "criterion of asymmetry"), *physical contiguity,* and *constant conjunction* or *recurrent regularity.* Following Brand (1979),[2] this positivist view may be formalized as follows:

For every event C and every event E, C caused E iff:[3]

    (1) The occurrence of C began before the occurrence of E;
    (2) C occurred in the immediate geographic area of E; and
    (3) for every event similar to C that occurs, there is an event similar to E that occurs in the immediate geographic area and after it.

This Humean formulation has some serious problems. First, it does not account for simultaneous cause-effect relationships, as, for example, that Linus goes up on the teeter-totter at precisely the same instant that Lucy goes down. We may also note the impossibility of separating cause from effect in this example; does Linus go up because Lucy goes down or does Lucy go down because Linus goes up; or is there some other unidentified factor that causes both? Thus the condition of temporal precedence is met only ambiguously. Second, the formulation does not account for action at a distance, as, for example, the action of the moon in influencing tides or the action of electromagnetic fields (historically, the concept of electromagnetic fields was introduced in part to *avoid* having to accept the notion of action at a distance). So the condition of physical contiguity is also suspect. Third, the condition of recurrent regularity or constant conjunction is quickly seen to be, at best, a statistical argument, one that can neither rule out coincidences or invariant sequences (such as the fact that night always follows day) nor handle the case in which two correlated effects are both produced by another, unidentified cause. (This last set of remonstrances is so well understood that almost any beginning student of statistics will mark "True" the test item, "Correlation does not imply causation.") Finally, as Hume himself appreciated, none of these conditions can account for the fact that people often identify causes on only *one* observation of a relationship; a lengthy series of observations confirming that E always follows C is apparently not necessary to lead to the inference that C causes E. People can clearly bring some other mechanism to bear that provides, for them, a warrant for the causal inference even in the absence of the full array of information that Hume's stipulations would require.

An effort to avoid the more serious of these objections has led to the *deductive-nomological* formulation, well stated by Popper (1959, pp. 59-60) in the following illustration:

> To give a *causal explanation* of an event means to deduce a statement which describes it, using as premises of the deduction one or more *universal laws,* together with certain singular statements, the *initial conditions.* For example, we can say that we have given a causal explanation of the breaking of a certain piece of thread if we have found that the thread has a tensile strength of 1 *lb.* and that a weight of 2 *lbs.* was put on it. If we analyze this causal explanation we shall find several constituent parts. On the one hand there is the hypothesis: "Whenever a thread is loaded with a weight exceeding that which characterized the tensile strength of the thread, then it will break;" a statement which has the character of a universal law of nature. On the other hand we have singular statements (in this case two) which apply only to the specific event in question: "The weight characteristic for this thread is 1 *lb.*" and "The weight put on this thread was 2 *lbs.*"

Brand formalizes this approach as follows:

> For every event C and every event E, C caused E iff:
>
>   (1) The occurrence of E did not begin before the occurrence of C began; and
>   (2) that E occurred follows from
>   (a) a statement of the laws of nature;
>   (b) a statement of the initial conditions; and
>   (c) a statement that C occurred;
>   but not from any two of these statements.

This definition is an improvement on the Humean in at least one respect: It does not require temporal precedence of cause before effect, but permits simultaneity (statement 1). But it is by no means free of other problems. Critics suggest that this view is a tautology, for laws, to be laws, depend on causal relationships themselves. Further, not all natural laws express causal relationships—some express only concomitance, as in Boyle's Law, $PV = k$ (at constant temperature). Thus use of the nomological approach requires a priori knowledge of which statements are lawlike in form and which are not. Further, some natural laws are very loosely constructed, so that many conditions must be stated (shades of the Laplacian grand equation!) in order to use them for the purpose of making causal inferences—a circumstance that reduces one's confidence that a causal relation has in fact been captured. Even worse, this formulation no more than Hume's fails to rid one of the feeling that significant human factors not accounted for in the formal definition come into play in making causal inferences; thus experience and judgment are required to determine when a law may be applicable and whether the named conditions are sufficient. It is obvious, indeed, that humans can identify causes *without* laws altogether, as in the case of the automobile mechanic who diagnoses and cures an engine problem without recourse to the engineering principles on which it is constructed. Finally, just as Hume believed that the concept of causality might not be "real" since it is always an inference of a human observer, the nomological approach also provides a reason for bypassing causality altogether: that, since the approach can always result at least in statistical prediction, there is no need to get involved with the "messier" questions of whether causality does or does not underlie the predictability.[4]

Fascination with the question of conditions is not limited to nomologists; some epistemologists approach causality entirely from the point of view of determining the conditions necessary and sufficient to warrant a causal claim. This school of thought is frequently called the *"essentialist."* Essentialists such as John Stuart Mill and J. L. Mackie argue that a causal explanation is given when the set of conditions both necessary and sufficient for it to occur obtain. Turning again to Brand for a formal statement:

For every event C and every event E, C caused E iff:

    (1) The occurrence of E did not begin before the occurrence of C began.
    (2) The occurrence of C is necessary and sufficient for the occurrence of E (that is, without C, no E, and if C, then E).
    (3) The occurrence of C is causally prior to the occurrence of E.

The third statement should be understood to mean that if both C and E are undetermined at some point in time (as might be the case, for example, if C were itself the effect of some other cause that had not yet occurred), C must be fixed (determined) before E is. Or, to put it another way, causes and effects stand in deterministic relationships and therefore the cause must be determined before the effect can be determined.

Several serious criticisms can be made of this formulation. First, as Brand (1979) points out, the phrase "necessary and sufficient" is in set theory both symmetrical and transitive, so that C can be viewed within this definition (even if only in the trivial case) as having caused itself, thereby violating the rule of asymmetry that provided that effects cannot precede causes. Second, the third condition cited above, which is intended to overcome the causal asymmetry problem, introduces another difficulty, namely, that it places determinism in doubt (if an event is to be unfixed, there must have been some time at which the state of the world did not *require* its occurrence).

But there are other, less esoteric, difficulties. First, the approach is reductionist. Consider Blanshard's (1962, p. 452) example of deciding on the cause of malaria:

> We say that malaria is caused by the bite of the anopheles mosquito. But the bite does not in fact always produce the disease, so the cause must be not the bite, but the actual release of plasmodia into the bloodstream. But, again, malaria does not inevitably ensue, so the cause must be the attack by the plasmodia on the victim's red blood corpuscles. Malaria is still not inevitable, however, so the cause must be the loss of hemoglobin. But even this does not always produce malaria, so the cause must be that the tissues are deprived of oxygen. But this last "cause" of malaria is just what malaria is! Thus, what we do in sorting out causes and effects is to *impose an intelligible structure of discrete events upon the continuous stream of occurrence; we do it in the way that is most useful for our purposes.* (emphasis added)

Thus the search for necessary and sufficient causes leads the inquirer to more and more atomistic levels in what approaches an infinite regress. It is for this reason that essentialists are sometimes described as "micromediational"; that is, they need to deal with mediations at the finest levels because if there were even a tiny temporal gap between cause and effect, the possibility would exist that some other undetected condition had intervened that was *really* responsible for the effect.

Second, there is the matter of overdeterminism, by which is meant the possibility that there may exist multiple conditions any one (or a subset) of which may be *sufficient* to produce an effect while none alone may be *necessary*. Consider the claim, "The short circuit caused the fire." Clearly short circuits are not necessary to cause fires; fires can be caused in many ways. And even sufficiency may be in doubt. Thus the short circuit is not sufficient to start a fire in the absence of oxygen (indeed, fires cannot be caused by any means in the absence of oxygen). Thus the possibility always exists that some unrecognized factor such as oxygen is necessary, leaving the essentialist approach an indeterminate one.[5]

Finally, and for our purposes perhaps most important, the essentialist approach cannot be rid of human influences any more than can the others. To determine whether a given condition is necessary or sufficient depends upon prior knowledge and judgment (perhaps tacit knowledge), as well as the ability either to know that no other causes are present or to be able to rule them out. Such human actions go beyond the formal definitional elements. Nor should we lose sight of the significance of Abel's observation that "what we do in sorting out causes and effects is to impose an intelligible structure of discrete events upon the continuous stream of occurrence; we do it in the way that is most useful for our purposes." Thus, focusing on the role of the mosquito in the "causal chain" is useful if we intend to prevent malaria by eradicating mosquitos, but as virologists we might elect to focus on the interaction of plasmodia and hemoglobin. To paraphrase Abel, we impute or attribute causality in whatever way is most useful for our purposes, not necessarily in ways that conform to "reality." Indeed, the essentialists' reductionist approach raises a serious question of whether there is any reality at all in causal claims, for, finally, cause and effect become inseparable.

A fourth approach to the definition of causality is commonly called the "activity" or "manipulability" approach. Authorities such as Bertrand Russell, R. G. Collingwood, and Michael Scriven have chosen to focus on the everyday experience that effects are usually produced by manipulations of some kind—for instance, throwing a switch "causes" a lamp to light. Moreover, these interventions (manipulations) have human agents. Thus causal relations can be inferred from human interventions.

Brand has formalized the activity approach as follows:

For every event C and every event E, C caused E iff:

(1) The occurrence of E did not begin before the occurrence of C.
(2) There is a person P such that P used a manipulative technique (e.g., an experimental manipulation) for making C occur, and E occurred.

As we have by now come to expect, there are a number of serious objections that can be raised. First, the formulation is clearly anthropomorphic, rendering the concept of causality meaningless in the absence of human intervention, and attributing human qualities and characteristics to cause-effect relationships. However, it is worth noting the dependence of this explanation on *human* mechanisms, a theme we have commented on in other formulations and to which we shall return later. Second, from a strictly logical point of view, the idea of

P using a manipulative technique itself has causal overtones, so that the activity definition is "doubly causal"—one might say tautological. Third, while focusing on the *agency* of causality, the activity approach fails to account for the *connection* or *mechanism* between cause and effect; *why* the particular manipulation produces the effect is unexplained. Fourth, this formulation does not account for those effects, as traditionally defined, that plainly occur *without* human intervention, as, for example, the moon "causing" tides. Finally, the activity approach is no more convincing than the essentialist with respect to cases of overdeterminism, that plethora of sufficient but not necessary conditions.

A fifth approach to the definition of causality is the *counterfactual* formulation, espoused by advocates such as David Lewis and Robert Stalnaker and based on the view, originally proposed by Hume, that if the cause had not existed, the effect would not exist either. Brand formalizes this stance as follows:

> For every event C and every event E, E causally depends on C iff E would not have occurred if C had not occurred.

This formulation, similar to Mill's (1843) "method of difference," which asserts that without C there can be no E, is deficient in a number of respects. It does not deal with temporal precedence, nor with overdeterminism—a criterion that, it should be noted, begins to loom larger and larger in significance because it can be cited so often against the claims of various approaches. More directly, the relationship implied by the formal definition is much broader than mere causal dependency. Consider Kim's (1973) example: that Socrates' drinking of the hemlock, while related to Xanthippe's widowhood, can hardly be argued to have caused it. But the counterfactual, that without Socrates' drinking the poison, Xanthippe would not have been widowed, is surely true.

Mill understood that the method of difference was not enough; he urged also application of the method of agreement (if C then E) *and* the method of concomitant variation: three separate tests. But he also pointed out that affirmative findings even by all three methods was still not enough; he warned that one must also be able to affirm a *logical* relationship between C and E (that is, correlation does not imply causality; there must be some other basis than mere relationship for asserting it). Again the need for human intervention may be noted.

A final approach to the problem of defining causality in meaningful terms is labeled the *"probabilistic."* Wesley Salmon, Hans Reichenbach, and Patrick Suppes as epistemologists, as well as a whole host of statisticians, lean heavily in this direction. Nurmi (1974, p.26), not himself an advocate, states the position as follows:

> On purely intuitive grounds it appears plausible to assume that causal connections affect the conditional probabilities of events. In other words, causal factors are usually considered as statistically relevant. Particularly within the social sciences where it is widely agreed that we cannot possibly take into account all relevant causal factors affecting given phenomena, the focus on probabilities is usually viewed as necessary even if an in-principle deterministic ontology of social phenomena is assumed. In this case probabilities just express our ignorance of all the causally relevant factors.

Brand formalizes this approach as follows:

For every event C and every event E, C caused E iff:

(1) E is later than C;
(2) $P(C, E) \blacktriangleright P(E)$; and
(3) there exists no event D such that D is earlier than or simultaneous with C, and D screens off C from E.

"Screening off" means that D renders C "statistically irrelevant" to E, that is, statement 3 militates against the existence of a factor that operates on C in such a way that the probability of E is the same irrespective of the occurrence or nonoccurrence of C. An example cited by both Reichenbach and Salmon is the falling of the barometer prior to a storm. Without statement 3 the barometer's fall might be taken as the cause of the storm, but another event, the drop in *atmospheric* pressure (simultaneous, in this case, with the barometer's fall) screens off the effect, the storm, from the drop in *barometric* pressure, thereby rendering invalid the claim that the falling barometer is the cause of the storm.

This approach founders on several grounds also. First, it repeats the difficulty noted with some of the earlier formulations in requiring that causes have temporal precedence over effects. Second, it does not distinguish between causes and other conditions, such as the necessity for oxygen if the striking of a match is to cause ignition. Third, it does not deal with asymmetry; the earlier cited example of the teeter-totter cannot be handled since the probabilistic approach allows interchange of cause and effect (Linus going up and Lucy down is equivalent to Linus going down and Lucy up). Finally, the formulation defeats the basic notion of invariant accomplishment of cause and effect, that is, it essentially denies determinism (despite the claim of an "in-principle deterministic ontology"), which is, however, precisely what persons who wish to answer causal questions are most interested in (the deterministic form of causality is the strong form). Moreover, since correlation does *not* imply causation, probabilistic (statistical) indications cannot suffice in the absence of knowledge of the mechanisms involved—again, a human interpolation is required.

Nurmi (1974, p. 34) concludes that

> it can be maintained that probabilistic approaches to causality fall short of giving adequate support to causal statements, either because of their *credo* concerning the ultimately deterministic nature of causal connections in which case the analysis ends up with universal causal laws and no account can be given of improbable causal connections, or because of their unrealistic presupposition of fixed probability and analytic value if the contextual requirements can be unambiguously fulfilled. However, social causal analysis very rarely can take these requirements for granted. Furthermore, strictly speaking changes in conditional probabilities provide no evidence for causal statements *per se*. Statistical relevance may or may not be an indicator of causal connection. Only in relation to the view of causality as a lawful connection can increase in conditional probabilities be considered as a clue for further causal inquiry. And even if this view is accepted, we need to know the *modus operandi* of causal connections in order to infer causal connections from probability statements (providing the latter can be assumed to be meaningful without assumptions concerning the causal connections themselves).

WHAT CAN ONE CONCLUDE FROM THIS INTERNAL CRITIQUE?

It may be argued that mere disagreement over a formal definition of causality does not mean that the concept per se is not useful, or that there is not enough commonality to make action possible. Surely the scientific world has not been, and is not, immobilized because epistemologists cannot agree on a definition. Nevertheless, the thrust and force of this internal critique make certain conclusions reasonable if not inevitable:

(1) The concept of causality is so beleaguered and in such serious disarray that it strains credibility to continue to entertain it in any form approximating its present (poorly defined) one. Every proposed formulation has, as we have seen, serious difficulties, and some difficulties are so pervasive that they apply to almost all formulations.

Among the problems that have been identified and that continue to be intractable are these:

- The criteria of temporal precedence and asymmetry that have guided most causal epistemologists require that effects cannot be their own causes and that effects cannot precede causes; yet it seems apparent that the possibility of simultaneous causation and even backward causation must be taken seriously (consider the difficulties produced by relativistic physics, which warps time in ways not contemplated by classic epistemologists; see Mackie, 1974; Wolf, 1981).

- The criterion of recurrent regularity, a mainstay of causal epistemologists since Hume, essentially poses a statistical test that cannot rule out coincidence or invariant sequences and that is itself subject to the restriction that correlation does not imply causality.

- Some causal epistemologies appear to be tautologies, defining causality in terms of itself, as in the commonsense definition that a cause is that which produces an effect; in the nomological approach in which selection of a law from which causality may be deduced depends upon knowing a priori which laws are causal; and in the activity approach, which depends on a manipulative act carried out by a human agent and so is "doubly causal."

- Some causal approaches, notably the probabilistic, and to some extent the essentialist, actually are in the position of denying determinism as a result of the axiomatic structure they adopt, but determinism is the essence of what "in-principle" causality is all about.

- Causes seem to be hedged about with many conditions that prevent "clean" causal claims from being made, a difficulty especially troublesome to the essentialist and nomological approaches but also embarrassing for any approach that requires temporal precedence, since it is always possible that some unidentified conditions may have intervened in the time gap between cause and effect.

- Virtually no existing formulation can handle the problem of overdeterminism. There appears to be a plethora of sufficient causes for virtually any effect, but hardly anything one can identify as a necessary cause.

(2) The difficulties summarized above have implications for all scientific investigations, but especially for human, that is, social/behavioral inquiry. Consider:

- Humans are *anticipatory* beings. They may produce an "effect" in anticipation of its "cause," so that the effect may precede the cause. It is often asserted among epistemologists that "the system ought not to jump until it is kicked," but humans jump at odd times. The everyday phenomenon of the "self-fulfilling prophecy" is a case in point; an individual, fearing, let us say, that his work will be found inadequate by his superior, leading to his being fired, fails to do his work well and *is* fired. A human may in fact select from among a variety of "causes" the one that will be *allowed* to influence his or her behavior. Knowing that a game of touch football will be physically stimulating and that reading a good book will be mentally stimulating, the person chooses to be stimulated by the book and comes away with new insights and ideas. Thus the criteria of temporal precedence and asymmetry are cast into doubt.

- Human behavior may exhibit a great deal of recurrent regularity that cannot be ascribed to causes. For example, most humans tend to follow the same patterns of behavior (these are often called habits; habits are followed because they conserve energy) on arising in the morning and getting ready for the office, but it would be absurd to label any given activity in such a sequence as the cause of the next or the effect of the previous activity.

- Human phenomena seem to require even more conditional stipulations than do other kinds. We have argued in Chapter 5 that human behavior is impossible to generalize precisely because it is so intimately bound to particular times and contexts. Hence the hope that "clean" causal statements might be developed about human behavior seems to be largely vain.

- Overdeterminism seems to be the overriding condition of humans, in the sense that there is always a multitude of factors impinging on and interacting with them. To select one or a subset of these factors as *the* cause or causes of some particular human behavior is fatuous.

(3) It has been impossible to divest the concept of causality of influences depending upon human experience, judgment, and insight. Literally no formulation has been forthcoming that does not at some point depend on these matters. Consider:

- Hume (and positivists generally) denied the viability of the causality concept on the grounds that causes were always imputations made by an observer to "explain" a relationship, as, for example, that a second billiard ball moved when struck by a first. Moreover, Hume recognized the inadequacy of the recurrent regularity criterion to explain the fact that people can sometimes correctly ascribe causality after seeing only one instance of a phenomemon.

- Mill proposed three methods for assessing causation—the method of agreement, the method of difference, and the method of concomitant variation—and then went on to say that of course one must *also* be able to "affirm a logical relationship" before a causal claim was warranted. And logic exists only in people's minds, not in nature.

- Essentialists understand that human judgment is required to determine when a condition is necessary and sufficient, and to know that no other causes are present that might account for the noted effect (hence their press for micromediation).
- Nomologists agree that human judgment is necessary to decide when a law is applicable and whether the specified initial conditions are adequate to warrant a causal claim.
- The activity approach is essentially anthropomorphic and its axiomatic structure requires the intervention of a human manipulating agent.
- Abel (1976), in his book *Man Is the Measure* (we may note the appropriateness of this title to the argument being made here), has pointed out that the imputation of causes in an "imposition" of a structure selected to be "most useful for our purposes" and not because of its inherent naturalness.
- Ennis (1973) proposes the concept of "responsibility ascription" (loosely definable as "that the maker of a specific causal statement is claiming that under the existing conditions the specified cause was sufficient to bring about the effect, and that it was responsible for the effect," p. 10), but points out that "responsibility ascription involves the cause identifier in the making of value judgments" (p. 11).
- Cook and Campbell (1979, p. 30) conclude that "the concept of causality is closely linked to intentions and purposes. Most causal inferences are about attributes of the world that are particularly relevant to an active, intrusive, willful organism."

Based on these arguments, we believe that the concept of causality should be replaced (we are not ready to push, as was Bertrand Russell in 1913, for its eradication) with a formulation that takes account of the difficulties noted, has special relevance to human phenomena, and explicitly recognizes that human experience, judgment, and insight are inextricably involved. We shall discuss such a formulation later. For now, we wish to note that replacement is not the only possible course; there are others that seek to repair some of the grosser deficiencies. One of these is the "evolutionary perspective" proposed by Cook and Campbell (1979), which they dub the "critical-realist"; another approach receiving wide advocacy is to regard causality as entirely attributional.

A DIVERSION:
TWO COUNTERPROPOSALS

Cook and Campbell (1979, p. 29) describe their position as follows:

Such an evolutionary perspective, when couched in a critical-realist mode, enables us to recognize causal perceptions as "subjective" or "constructed by the mind;" but at the same time it stresses that many causal perceptions constitute assertions about the nature of the world which go beyond the immediate experience of perceivers and so have objective contents which can be right or wrong (albeit not always testable). The perspective is realist because it assumes that causal relationships exist outside of the human mind, and it is critical-realist because it assumes that these valid causal relationships cannot be perceived with total accuracy by our imperfect sensory and intellective capacities. And the perception is evolutionary, because it assumes a special survival value to knowing about causes and, in particular, manipulable causes.

We do not find this construction compelling. First, we have already seen that a concept of causality that depends on the existence of an exterior, objective world is simply not tenable. Every such formulation suffers from crippling deficiencies; morever, it has not been possible to divest even one of them of the need for human inputs that are not contemplated in its axiomatic structure. Second, we doubt on other grounds the imputation of "reality" to human behavior; the concept of a single, tangible reality onto which inquiry can converge seems to us intenable, as we have noted in Chapter 3. Third, we are unconvinced by the argument of ignorance; it seems to us at least as reasonable to suggest that we do not "perceive" causal relationships properly because they do not exist as to excuse ourselves on the grounds of "imperfect sensory and intellective capacities" (that was Laplace's problem as well, it will be recalled!). Finally, we agree that it would be very helpful to know about causes, especially manipulable causes, if they existed, in the interest of improving our chances for survival, but it will not do to wish the concept into existence simply because it would be nice to have it. "If wishes were horses, beggars would ride," and, apparently, "If wishes were causes, researchers would be able to control everything." But neither of these conditionals is likely to obtain; it seems more sensible, finally, to confront the situation boldly, to eschew the pleasure principle, and to move off into new directions.

What of the movement to transform the theory of causality into an attributional theory? It appears that as the concept of causality as "real" or "natural" loses credibility, and the influence of human judgment and experience in leading to valid causal statements becomes more and more appreciated, a tendency is emerging to describe causality as *entirely* attributional or imputational.[6] We seem to have come full circle back to Hume, who based at least part of his critique of older (to him) notions of causality on the fact that no one ever *saw* a cause but only *inferred* it from some observation that was interpreted to be an effect. Advocates of the attributional approach point out that such imputations have roots in the semantics of the situation, as, for example, in the statement, "Treatment A is effective in producing Effect X," any causal interpretation clearly depends on how Treatment A, Effect X, and the term "effective" itself are defined.

At first glance attributional formulations would seem to be complementary to the naturalist position. It is a naturalistic axiom (Chapter 3) that realities are multiple and constructed; the idea of attributed causes seems to fit well the idea of constructed realities. It is as though we had shifted from the classic, "For every effect a cause," to the counterpart, "For every constructed effect an attributed cause." Another naturalistic axiom (Chapter 4) concerns interactivity between inquirer and respondent (or object of inquiry), which also lends support to the notion that causal imputations may very well exist only in the mind of the investigator, arising because of his or her interaction with the phenomenon being studied.

But it should be noted—and this is a crucial point—that attributional formulations, while denying the *reality* of causal explanations, nevertheless continue to treat them as having *utility*. It may not be wise to treat causes and effects as if they existed "out there," attributionists seem to be saying, but it is still useful to act *as if* causes and effects existed. The concept of causality is simply a convenient way to organize the world and materially assist those who wish to predict and control ongoing events.

But we take the position that to persevere in using the concept of causality even in only that limited way is ultimately misleading. Just as scientists have had to give up "placeholder" theories such as ether (to propagate electromagnetic waves) or phlogiston (to support combustion), so, we suggest, it is time to give up the placeholder theory of causality. Indeed, if Hume and the many others since who have noted the inescapable influence of human judgment and insight in the development of causal statements are right, it is quite possible that all the causal models that have *ever* existed are simply variations on an attributional theory of causality—but simply have not been recognized as such. It is possible and credible to argue that the many criticisms that can be and have been mounted against the various earlier formulations must have been directed, even if we did not always realize it, against just those attributional theories. It does not matter, in that sense, whether causality is taken as "real" or "attributed"; the criticisms are nevertheless valid and telling. Thus, whichever position one takes, it seems clear that neither "real" nor attributional theories of causality have much utility. It is certainly time to abandon the concept of causality and to begin thinking about the world in other terms.

AN EXTERNAL CRITIQUE
OF THE CAUSALITY CONCEPT

The critique of causality mounted to this point in the chapter has taken an internal perspective, that is, it deals with the concept from the point of view of epistemologists who accept its utility (even if only in attributional form) and whose efforts are directed at improving its precision and clarity. In this section we take a different perspective: that of persons who at best doubt the utility of the concept or at worst opt to reject it outright. A metaphor helpful in understanding this contrast is to imagine believers in a diety, on the one hand, who might nevertheless argue among themselves about the precise form doctrine should take, and, on the other hand, agnostics and atheists, that is, doubters and rejecters of theism, who might nevertheless have something to offer in its place.

Rumblings are evident in a variety of fields that might influence one to entertain the agnostic/atheist view. In physics, for example, the concept of reality has been shaken severely by quantum mechanics, which suggests the nonreality of particles and replaces them with electromagnetic field interactions. But if one prohibits particles, then causal explanations also falter. If particles are replaced by energy complexes, which interact in convoluted and intricate ways, what can one say about causality? As Schwartz and Ogilvy (1979) point out, not even Einstein was successful in finding a general field theory that would *unify* data about macro- and microphenomena. Instead, his research led to a relativistic formulation in which the role of causality is very insecure.

Or consider the possibility of tachyons—particles that have speeds in excess of the speed of light. These particles exist, at the moment, only in physicists' imaginations, although there are some good reasons for taking the possibility of their existence seriously. By way of example, Wolf (1981) asks us to consider how things would appear if we were able to fly alongside a bullet that had been fired at a target. At slow speeds, the bullet would appear to progress normally toward its target, striking it sometime soon after it was fired (although we, in our parallel aircraft, would also have moved a short distance in the same direction). But if we could fly at speeds approaching that of the bullet itself, we might be able to look out the window and see the bullet in its flight path just keeping pace. If we could fly faster than the bullet, we would see the bullet flying *away* from the target and back toward its source. Or so it would appear. Wolf (1981, p. 166) observes:

> Relativity theory confirms this apparently obvious observation. But something weird would begin to take place if the bullet could be fired with a speed greater than the speed of light. Suppose the bullet hap-

pened to be moving at twice the speed of light, for example. We would notice nothing unusual about the firing if we were flying by with any speed less than half lightspeed. But the instant we reached half lightspeed, we would witness the rifle firing and the bullet hitting the target at the same time. Even weirder, as soon as we were flying by at speeds greater than half lightspeed, we would see the whole scene as if it were a film running backwards; the target would explode, sending the bullet and all of its gasses back toward the rifle where they would neatly pack themselves into the narrow rifle barrel and travel up that small, bored cylinder until all contents had repacked themselves into an undischarged round.

Since relativity successfully predicts the results of observations, we have come to trust it. Thus we would conclude that tachyons cannot exist because of the above example. This example illustrates what we would call a *causality violation*: the cause comes after the effect.

Causality violations are serious crimes in an orderly and lawful universe. Speeding faster than light will always be observed by some observers as a violation of causality. They will see events along the trail of the speeding object happening in a reverse order. Of course, not every observer will be faced with this "monkey business." If we were to observe the same violation of causality, we wouldn't think anything of it. We would simply say that *the effect was the cause and the cause was the effect.* (first emphasis in original; second, added)

It seems easier to reject the concept of causality outright than to deal with "causality violations" and situations where causes may be effects and effects causes.

Or consider Harre's (1981, p. 14) comments about the concept of causality currently entertained by physicists, which seems so remarkably different from the conventional concept as to warrant a different name:

The irony of the critical acceptance of the traditional empiricist methodology is emphasized most poignantly by the fact that the admired exemplar, physics, is based on a quite different concept of causation. Instead of a world of passive beings waiting quiescent, independent, and unchanging to receive an external stimulus to action from another moving body, physicists conceive of a world of permanently interconnected, mutually interacting centres of energy whose native activity is modulated and constrained by other such centres. The immediate cause of motion is the removal of a constraint from an active material being—for example, removal of a support from a body located in the gravitational or electromagnetic field, a body which has an active tendency to accelerate. Not even the mass of a body is a passive, independent property. According to Mach's principle, even the most

intimate power, the power to resist acceleration, is an endowment from
the system of bodies that make up the universe as a whole.

Or consider the following statement from the field of medicine made
by Harsanyi and Hutton (1981, p. 41), in their discussion of the
"Platonic disease model," which treats disease as an external entity
that "attacks healthy people more or less at random":

> The Platonic disease model worked well enough for infectious diseases,
> mainly because they were triggered by such obvious environmental in-
> fluences. But it cannot explain why some people come down with
> chronic diseases while others do not. And it is particularly useless for
> helping us understand why chronic diseases occur, for they do not
> always involve obvious external agents that are analogous to the viruses
> and bacteria of infections. Decades of research have gone into isolating
> the "causes" of cancer; viruses, radiation, and chemicals have all been
> singled out as primary suspects. But isolating a single cause has proved
> impossible; cancer seldom strikes unless a combination of factors—
> both internal and external—are present.

Critiques of causality can also be mounted at the conceptual level.
We saw (Chapter 2) the extensive arguments made by Schwartz and
Ogilvy (1979) in favor of the concept of "multiple causality" as a
replacement for the more traditional "linear causality."[7] Their
arguments are based primarily on indeterminacy as a characteristic of
the universe; thus they comment:

> The indeterminacy in nature is mirrored in the evolution of causal
> models. The simplest causal model is linear; that is, a simple action leads
> always to the same predictable result: push on a chair and it moves every
> time. Thermodynamics introduced probabilities into causality to describe
> the average behavior of whole aggregations such as a gas. Cybernetics
> gave us feedback, but with a concentration on negative feedback. That
> means that if A causes B, then B provides a feedback signal to A such
> that A changes in a way to reduce or limit the magnitude of B. A heating
> system with a thermostat functions that way. Such a system tends toward
> stability. The new paradigm adds positive feedback, which means that
> the feedback signal from B affects A in a fashion such that A tends
> to increase B. In the simplest and most negative form that is called a
> vicious circle. However, when it is of mutual benefit for both A and
> B, then it is like symbiosis. Both A and B evolve and change together,
> each affecting the other in such a way as to make the distinction be-
> tween cause and effect meaningless. (Schwartz & Ogilvy, 1979, p. 14)

The S&O concept of morphogenesis (see Chapter 2) is also relevant. If there can be morphogenetic changes—that is, changes in which new forms arise unpredicted by and unpredictable from any of the parts (or the whole) of the precursor form—we are again in the position of having to abandon simple cause-effect explanations for the change and look in other directions.

Rowan (1981) helps us to see how what he terms "ecological thinking" also militates against traditional concepts of causality, particularly in human behavior. "Human systems," he asserts, "do not work through logical sequences of cause and effect, they must be seen as interactive mutual causal systems in which causality is *circular*" (p. 127). In discussing family therapy as an example, he says:

> We must abandon the causal-mechanistic view of phenomena, which has dominated the sciences in recent times, and adopt a systemic orientation. With this new orientation, the therapist should be able to see members of the family as elements in a circle of interaction. None of the members of the circuit have unidirectional power over the whole, although the behavior of any one of the family influences the behavior of others. At the same time, it is epistemologically incorrect to consider the behavior of one individual as the *cause* of the behavior of others. This is because every member influences the others, but is in turn influenced by them. The individual acts upon the system, but is at the same time influenced by the communication he receives from it. . . . [to] continue looking at phenomena according to a causal model is a serious impediment to the understanding of the family game. (Rowan, 1981, p. 129)

These various examples seem to reinforce rather than argue against the several conclusions that we drew from the internal critique of causality. Terms such as "cause-effect reversals," "systems of constraints and endowments," "interactive combinations," "morphogenetic unpredictability," "indeterminacy," "causality violation," and the like suggest that a wholly different way of viewing relationships and interactions is required.

THE CONCEPT OF
MUTUAL SIMULTANEOUS SHAPING

Since the concept of causality has proven to be so assailable, is there any other concept that can replace it? Indeed, in view of the criticisms that have been mounted by both internal and external critics, why would one *want* to replace it? Why not simply abandon the idea altogether? We may respond to that question in two ways.

First, naturalists as well as other varieties of postpositivists retain a need for *explanation*. Within the positivist paradigm, explanation is often conceived as dependent on specifying causal links, but explanation can also mean understanding. Explanation serves to answer the question, Why? Even though naturalists tend to rely on pattern theories rather than hypothetico-deductive ones (Chapter 8) the need for understanding the *pattern* of relationships is not obviated by a rejection of causality as the major explanatory mechanism.

Second, while naturalists may eschew the kind of deterministic control that is implied and abetted by the concept of causality, they nevertheless do not give up the interest in and need for *management*. While we may not be able to produce, by our intervention, the precise outcome that we desire, we believe that it is possible to shape affairs in a desired direction, albeit with a good deal of uncertainty.

To serve these two ends—explanation and management—we need a new metaphor to replace Hume's billiard table or Laplace's "grand machine," something more in tune with contemporary insight. Some possibilities come quickly to mind; *web,* (as in web of circumstances), *net* (as in communication net), and *pattern* (as in pattern of influences). Perhaps the most powerful metaphor, however, is that interconnected mass of neurons called the brain. Within the brain every neuron is connected to every other neuron in a seemingly trackless fashion. An arm is raised, a memory is recalled, a difficult problem is solved; but who can say in what pattern of neuron firings the result was accomplished (if indeed it is the neuron *firings* that account for it)? Raise the arm again, recall the same memory, solve the same problem, and who can say whether the same neurons and the same sequence of firings were involved? Indeed, extirpate part of the brain—the part you believe to be causally involved in the particular action, if you like—and often other parts can take over to produce the movement, the recall, the problem-solving behavior. Like the hologram that contains full information about the whole in every part, so the brain can apparently use almost any of its parts to fulfill the function of any other part.

The key idea that permeates this metaphor, and that leads to a replacement concept for causality, is that of *mutual simultaneous shaping*. Everything influences everything else, in the here and now. Many elements are implicated in any given action, and each element interacts with all of the others in ways that change them all while simultaneously resulting in something that we, as outside observers, label as outcomes or effects. But the interaction *has no directionality,* no *need* to produce *that particular outcome* (indeed, the outcome may be a totally unpredictable morphogenetic change); it simply "happened" as a product of the interaction—the mutual shaping. All elements are involved as "contingently necessary" (Nurmi, 1974) in the sense that they participate in a synergistic relationship that activates them all. The resulting shaping is, moreover, "circumstances relative" (Nurmi, 1974) in that there is a plurality of shapers (overdeterminism), with each becoming meaningful in ways that depend on varying circumstances or conditions.

Given this formulation, we may attach new meanings to the terms "understanding" and "management." Understanding involves the making of *plausible* imputations that depend on one's purpose. Out of the complex of mutually interactive shapers one may select those that afford some meaningful perspective in relation to the purpose that the investigator has in mind. Recall again Blanshard's (1962, p. 452) suggestion that "what we do in sorting out causes and effects"—except that we should now read his phrase as "what we do in coming to an understanding"—is "to impose an intelligible structure of discrete events upon the continuous stream of occurrence; we do it in the way that is most useful for our purposes." Thus understanding is not a matter of *appreciating* the "real" causal links prescribed by Nature but of *imposing* a purposive structure that emerges from the *interaction* between investigator and phenomenon. This assertion should not surprise us, in view of the naturalist's second axiom; what emerges from the interaction, in accordance with the first axiom, is a *constructed* reality that is shaped in equal proportion by the investigator's purpose and the phenomenon's presentational aspect. Understanding results from an appreciation of the myriad mutual shapings that are synchronously ongoing and abstracting from that complexity a subsystem that serves the investigator's needs. Certain causality is transmuted into relative plausibility.

The concept of *management* is somewhat more difficult to elucidate. We take our cue from Harre (1981, p. 14), who, in commenting upon the concept of causation that characterizes modern physics, observes:

> Instead of a world of passive beings waiting quiescent, independent, and unchanging to receive an external stimulus from another moving body, physicists conceive of a world of permanently interconnected, mutually interacting centres of energy *whose native activity is modulated and constrained by other such centres.* (emphasis added)

We are thus asked to contemplate three ideas: *native activity, modulation,* and *constraint.*

By *native activity* we shall mean a baseline of activity or behavior against which other later activities or behaviors might be evaluated, even if only in principle. From the perspective of management we might take native activity to be that displayed (even if constantly changing) by the object or individual *prior to* management interventions. The entity will be in a continuous process of change or adjustment as various contextual factors are altered, and, incidentally, will play its role in affecting adjustments in those other factors in response to its—the entity's—adjustments.

The first aspect of management, modulation, we define as *enabling,* that is, introducing elements into a context in such a way as to make it possible for a desired adjustment or behavior to display itself. To enable is to provide the minimal elements needed for the change or adaptation; enabling may thus be thought of as the positive aspect of management. Enabling may occur without human intervention, as, for example, when a storm provides the energy that enables silt to move from river bank to ocean. But we are interested here particularly in the case in which interventions are introduced by human agents. Thus we may say that what a teacher does enables a student to learn, what a fisherman does enables the catching of fish, or what a carpenter does enables the building of a house. Of course, pupils may persist in not learning, fish are uncanny about avoiding the hook, and carpenters sometimes ruin what they are building. Thus modulation, whether by accident or intent, makes results possible *but does not guarantee them*—there are no infallible cause-effect linkages implied. Nevertheless, native activity is shaped—directed, refracted, funneled—in particular ways through enabling acts.

But enabled actions do not always occur, for constraints may exist in the context to prevent them. Thus the second aspect of management consists of *blocking* or *masking* the effects of contextual constraints so that the enabled action is not aborted. Blocking or masking may be thought of as the negative aspect of management.

We may thus assert that management is a combination of enabling and blocking/masking. Given that we wish to manage some outcome—and notice how this differs from the more common parallel, "Given that we wish to cause some effect . . ."—we have two tasks: to introduce minimum enabling elements and to block or mask the most obvious constraining forces. The issue of what those minimal enabling elements and those most obvious constraining forces are can be resolved only by a *judgment* call—human intervention is required. We will never know either enablers or constraints exactly and, even if we did, we would not have the resources needed to deal with them all. Hence there can *in principle* be no certain outcome. The focus of change is in the object or person affected, not in the manager. The object or person displays (theoretically) certain native activity, which is undergoing constant change and adjustment depending on the myriad other contextual elements by which it is surrounded, all of which are engaged in mutual shaping. All that the manager can do is provide *some* of the (known) enabling factors and block or mask *some* of the (known) constraining factors, to whatever extent resources permit. *The manager cannot directly cause any effect.* Moreover, imputations—statements of understandings—cannot be more than assertions of *plausible* relationships based on the apprehended—constructed—enablers and constraints.

There are two further complications. First, the factors that may be introduced by a manager, whether enablers or constraint blockers or maskers, pass immediately out of his or her control. Because they are injected into an ongoing and dynamic context, they themselves are caught up in the mutual shaping process and as a result change in relatively unpredictable ways. A notable example may be found in social intervention programs, which very often are found to differ dramatically in practice from what had been initially planned. Our point is that it is inevitable that this should happen, since the interventions are no more impervious to mutual shaping than is anything else. The intervention influences all of the other elements in the mix, of course, but in the process is itself changed. It may be noted in this connection that when experiments are done in laboratories, the experimenter is able to block or mask virtually everything that he or she wishes to exclude, and to introduce just those enablers that are desired. The otherwise complex milieu of the real world has been simplified to accommodate the investigator's interests. It is no wonder, then, that laboratory results are so often found to be nonreplicable in real situations.

Second, as enablers are introduced and constraints blocked or masked, *side effects* may occur that were unanticipated but that are nevertheless important. For example, the provision of funds to mount a new social program (an enabler) may interact with native activity to produce profligacy, embezzlement, or exploitation of clients as well as (or instead of) the intended helping behavior. Efforts to block out or mask the influence of socioeconomic status or ethnicity may interact to produce reverse discrimination legal suits or redneck political backlash.

Management thus involves a great deal more than the "prediction and control" promised by postivistically oriented social scientists. It is not simply a matter of learning which levers to pull or dials to twist, after which one can with certainty count on a particular effect. It is an art as much as a science, and *must be so by the nature of the beast.* But it is an art immeasurably assisted by the plausible judgment calls of experienced and sophisticated managers who have some sense of what enablers to introduce and what constraints to block or mask. But their actions can never do more than introduce—or withdraw—a number of potential mutual shapers from the much more complex mix that characterizes their constructed worlds; what emerges is the resultant of the interaction of all of those elements and is, in principle, unpredictable. Circumstances alter cases.

Thus the concept of mutual shaping that we propose involves the recognition of the following points:

- All elements in a situation are in mutual and continual interaction ("native activity")
- Each element is activated in its own way by virtue of the particular configuration of all other elements—potential shapers—that is assumed at that time and in that place.
- Judgments about which of the potential shapers may most plausibly be implicated in explaining and/or managing whatever it is that the investigator wishes to explain and/or manage is a matter both of the circumstances that exist *and* of the investigator's purpose; the investigator asks him- or herself, "What is most plausible to invoke given that purpose?"
- The peculiar web or pattern of circumstances that characterizes a given situation may never occur in just that way again, so that explanations and management actions are in a real sense unique and cannot be understood as implying either predictability or control in any given way.
- Explanations are at best "here-and-now" accounts that represent a "photographic slice of life" of a dynamic process that, in the next instant, might present a very different aspect.

This formulation of mutual shaping has, we assert, two major advantages. First, *it is consistent* with the other four axioms of naturalistic inquiry, as explicated in Chapters 3, 4, 5, and 7. Thus:

- The axiom of multiple, constructed realities is served in that the concept of mutual shaping allows for an infinite variety of situational mixes and purposeful imputations by the investigator, imputations that may, moreover, change as other constructions are uncovered and appreciated.
- The axiom of inquirer-respondent (object) interdependence is served in that the inquirer arrives at explanations through an interaction of his investigatory purposes and styles with the unique characteristics of the situation and the respondents in context.

- The axiom of limited generalizability (transferability) is served in that determinism is abandoned and neither prediction nor control is claimed to result from explanations, except at very similar times and in very similar contexts.
- The axiom of value-boundedness is served in that the values of the investigator are clearly evident in the choice of explanations (indeed, the investigator's purposes must be explicit), and contextual and respondent value-resonances are assured by virtue of the recognition of those values as part of the general shaping process.

The second advantage of the formulation of mutual shaping is that *it obviates most of the difficult epistemological problems associated with conventional causality formulations.* Thus:

- The issue of determinism disappears. It is not necessary to posit determinism or even an "in-principle deterministic ontology" while dealing with phenomena probabilistically because of "imperfect sensory or intellective capacities." The concept of mutual shapers obviates the need to label some as "causes" and others as "effects."
- The issue of temporal precedence disappears. All elements are seen to be in continuous and mutual interaction; we are no longer required to arrange incidents into a causality chain in which some elements necessarily precede others.
- The issue of overdeterminism disappears. There is no longer a plethora of sufficient but not necessary causes, only an infinite number of mutually interacting shapers. There is no need to sort these shapers into causes and noncauses, or into necessary but not sufficient or sufficient but not necessary causes.
- The requirement of recurrent regularity disappears. No statistical imputations are needed; the concept of mutual shaping does away with the requirement that some elements must inevitably be accompanied by others.
- The necessity for human judgments is not only *not* an embarrassment, but is elevated to the level of a precondition. The purposive nature of imputations is explicitly recognized.
- The conditional nature of imputations is also plainly noted. The "circumstance-relative" nature of such arguments is an intrinsic part of the formulation. The need to take account of as many conditions as one feasibly can, rather than to identify just some few that can be characterized as necessary and sufficient, is manifest.
- The tautological nature of many causality formulations is obviated.
- The need to devise explicit formulations for intervening (sufficient) mechanisms disappears.

Of course there are difficulties with the mutual shaping concept; the major one that we see is the establishment of criteria for determining when an interpretation (for some time and place) is sufficiently plausible to be persuasive. Good sociologists and anthropologists—recall de Tocqueville, Mead, Wax, Liebow, Whyte, Becker, Goffman—have made assertions, sometimes about whole cultures, that we do not find hard to accept, but there is a great difference between finding a statement persuasive and being able to say *why* it is persuasive. The development of appropriate criteria represents an intellectual task that is, at the moment, beyond us, but that, we are persuaded, will turn out to be doable.

AN EPILOGUE

We have argued in this chapter for replacing the concept of causality with that of mutual shaping. To some it may appear that the shift we are proposing is merely a semantic one. They may feel, echoing Ennis (1973), that we have done nothing more than replace explicit causal language with weak euphemisms. But we believe that our proposal goes well beyond mere semantic convenience. Two examples may suffice to make the point.

Consider the present emphasis on the development of interventions for the alleviation or elimination of a variety of educational problems: curricular relevance, motivation, proper concern for the handicapped, appropriate treatment of women and minorities, and so on. Virtually the entire basis for the hope that interventions can be identified and developed is the idea that the conditions to be changed are *effects* and that interventions can be *causes* that will produce other, more desired effects. The concept of mutual shaping makes clear that this hope is false. Interventions can be mounted, but without any assurance, *regardless of prior evaluation,* that they will in fact produce the outcomes hoped for. Indeed, all one can do is introduce yet another "shaper"—the intervention—into the mix; *how* this introduction will shape other elements in the situation, or how the intervention will itself be shaped by those elements, is a matter that can be settled only with experience over time. The intervention *may* produce the desired outcome (and it may be possible to devise some plausible explanations that will help us to understand why), but there is no a priori assurance that that will be the case.

Or consider how belief in causality itself shapes (if we may use that term) evaluation. We recently had the experience of working with a task force whose charge it was to devise ways of evaluating the effects of certain in-service teacher training workshops on the subsequent behavior of the children taught by the enrolled teachers. Imagine for a moment the causal chain implied by that charge. Workshops are planned with certain ends in mind. The plans are then put into effect, perhaps in several sites, in ways that more or less correspond to those plans, but that also deviate from them because of local exigencies. If several workshops are offered, they probably also differ in significant ways from one another as well as from the common plan. Teachers attend these workshops, each coming with a different level of commitment, interest, training, and experience. These teachers, shaped in some way by, and in turn shaping, the events of the workshop that they happen to attend, return to their schools, each in its own fiscal, social, political, cultural, and administrative environment. The conditions and circumstances of the schools constrain some elements of whatever it is the individual teacher has brought back and reinforce others; moreover, the message the returning teachers may bring (and the enthusiasm with which they bring it) may influence local decision makers in different ways, resulting in, say, greater or lesser support. Into the rooms of these teachers come the children, each with his or her own level of commitment, interest, and ability. There they are confronted by teacher actions shaped not only by all of the preceding factors but by the interactions with the children at the very moment of teaching. Finally, the children return to their neighborhoods and homes, and there they behave in ways shaped to some extent, to be sure, by what they have learned from the teacher, but by myriad other influences—such as parental expectations and peer pressures—as well.

Now consider the task: to be able to trace a causal chain whereby changes in pupil behavior can be unequivocally (deterministically) traced to events that occurred during the in-service workshop! Consider the shapings that occurred at each step in this sequence, and ask whether it is reasonable to expect evaluators to sort all of these elements out. Ask whether it is reasonable to imagine that they *can* be sorted out into neat, micromediating, cause-effect pairs! It *does* seem reasonable, however, to imagine that an evaluator, given his or her evaluative purposes, might note some new behaviors from some child, and that, by making appropriate observations and gathering appropriate interview and documentary data, he or she could begin to weave a plausible argument about the utility of the workshop in helping to shape that child's behavior. Note, by the way, that it is equally reasonable that one might devise plausible arguments about how the children's behavior might shape the workshop!

The replacement of the concept of causality with the concept of mutual shaping has, we have tried to show, powerful implications at both epistemological and practical levels. Explanations and management actions are needed and, historically, causality has provided one neat, and apparently useful, basis for providing them. But there are simply too many problems with causality to continue its use; the replacement concept of mutual shaping seems to be relatively free of these problems and, at the same time, more in tune with emergent epistemological and paradigmatic considerations.

NOTES

1. For example, the material cause of a chair is the metal, wood, and other "stuff" out of which it is made; the formal cause is the "idea" or "mental picture" of the chair held in the mind of its maker—perhaps rendered into a drawing or plan; the efficient cause is the agent, the builder, who actually constructed it together with tools; and the final cause is the purpose held in mind for the chair that led to its being built—to have something on which to sit.

2. The form of this definition and those cited in subsequent paragraphs is virtually identical to that of Brand.

3. Read "iff" as "if and only if."

4. It may be this kind of thinking that underlies the suggestion by Travers, cited earlier, that we abandon the idea of causality and replace it with the idea of "functional relation."

5. The argument of this paragraph is blunted by the fact that it fails to distinguish between concrete events and event types. A short circuit may indeed have caused a particular fire, but is neither necessary nor sufficient to cause all fires. Nevertheless the argument is frequently mounted and seems to carry some validity.

6. An extensive literature on attribution theory exists. The classic reference remains Jones et al. (1972).

7. As the reader can now appreciate, we find the Schwartz and Ogilvy usage of the term "mutual causality" unfortunate, for while their concept is very different from traditional uses of "causality," their inclusion of this term reinforces those who believe their new concept represents only a slight shift—in effect, a compromise that adjusts the older concept in response to the new insights.

7

Is Being Value-Free Valuable?

> The attempt to produce a value-neutral social science is increasingly being abandoned as at best unrealizable, and at worst self-deceptive.
>
> *(Hesse, 1980)*

WHAT ARE VALUES?

To Humpty Dumpty's assertion that when *he* used a word, it meant just what he chose it to mean, neither more nor less, Alice quite properly replied, "The question is whether you *can* make words mean so many different things." The word "value" must surely have been one of Humpty Dumpty's favorites. For example, it can be an intrinsic property of something (merit) or an extrinsic property (worth). It can be an action—to value something. It can be categorized in terms of *substance* (moral, cognitive, aesthetic, religious, political, and the like) or in terms of *function* (instrumental, technical, utilitarian, hedonic, welfare, and so on). It can have a concrete referent such as wealth or an abstract one such as piety. Reese (1980) notes that while values have been a central consideration in philosophy for millenia, it is only during the present century that the study of values has become institutionalized into a distinct philosophic specialization—axiology. Perhaps because of this very recent emergence, Reese suggests, axiology is still underdeveloped and cannot compete with other divisions of philosophy in terms of the rigor and scope of its formulations.

It is clearly beyond the scope of this volume to become embroiled in a consideration of what the "true"—or even the most useful— definition of "value" might be. We shall use the term in a less orthodox and more commonsense way than the above paragraph suggests it might be used, and this is, to denote *arbiters of preference or choice*. That is to say, a value is simply that criterion, or touchstone, or perspective that one brings into play, implicitly or explicitly, in mak-

ing choices or designating preferences. In this sense values would encompass all of the following:

- *assumptions or axioms,* as for example, the assumptions or axioms
  (T_1, basic beliefs) undergirding the conventional and naturalistic
  paradigms of inquiry, or any other conceptual system;
- *theories or hypotheses,* that is, any constructions that may be developed
  to describe or explain some phenomenon, and any logical (T_3) derivatives
  therefrom;
- *perspectives,* as, for example, the perspective that any particular discipline
  affords on some phenomenon of interest; this is, we believe, the meaning that Schwartz and Ogilvy (1979) ascribe to the term "perspective"
  as they use it, and that they warn us can never be assumed to provide
  a "complete" view (nor can the aggregate of all possible perspectives);
- *social/cultural norms,* that is, the variety of regulators of thoughts, feelings, and actions that are imposed by a society or cultural group on its
  members; and
- *personal or individual norms,* that is, the variety of regulators imposed
  by the individual on him- or herself that may reflect or differ from the
  social/cultural norms, or may go beyond them.

We pointed out in Chapter 1 that the positivist or conventional
paradigm of inquiry asserts that inquiry is value-free, that is, free from
the influence of any of the above categories; ironically, we may note,
that assertion is itself a value claim that bears investigation. On the
other hand, the naturalistic paradigm asserts that inquiry is value-
bound, specifically, that it is influenced by the values of the inquirer,
by the axioms or assumptions underlying both the substantive theory
and the methodological paradigm that undergird the inquiry, and by
the values that characterize the context in which the inquiry is carried
out. Further, the naturalist asserts, all of these sources of influence
may be in resonance (affirm, reinforce) or in dissonance with (conflict, reject) one another. We shall attempt to examine the merits of
these several claims and to determine the implications of each. Before
passing to that task, we may briefly note, however, that the various
ramifications of the term "values"—axioms, theories, perspectives,
social/cultural norms, and individual norms—are in continuous interaction (the concept of mutual simultaneous shaping) so that it is not
possible to sort out their individual influences in any actual situation.
Nor can one expect a one-to-one relationship between these terms and
the several corollaries of Axiom 5 as expressed in Chapter 1. The
former tend to describe values-in-operation, the latter values-in-impact.

CAN INQUIRY BE CONSIDERED
TO BE VALUE-FREE?

The positivist claim is that inquiry can be maintained in a value-free posture by virtue of the methodology employed. That methodology is specifically designed to isolate and remove all "subjective" elements from the inquiry situation. It is commonly believed that values are separate from facts, and that methodologies can be devised that screen out the former and focus on the latter. But a number of serious objections can be raised to that proposition, including the following:

(1) The positivist claim depends on a bifurcated view of reality, namely, that there is a "real" reality and an "apparent" reality. Facts are the arbiters of the former and values of the latter. What we have here is another example of the dualism that we have already discussed in another context (Chapter 4), a concept that we noted is largely discredited. Chapter 3 provides other reasons for doubting the existence of a "real" reality, even in the hard sciences but certainly in the social/behavioral sciences. It seems sounder to adopt the axiom of multiple, constructed realities than that of a single, tangible reality.

(2) The positivist claim depends on the separateness of observational and theoretical languages, a proposition that, we have seen, is very much in doubt (Hesse, 1980). Modern epistemologists line up heavily in favor of the proposition that "facts" are theory-laden; that it is impossible even to recognize a "fact" except within the framework of some theory. But theories are themselves constructions—some out of whole cloth—and they rest on their own axioms and assumptions, which are also values in our sense of the term. And so a simple transitivity: If theories are value-determined and facts are theory-laden, then facts must also be value-determined.

(3) There is a growing literature—much of it written by individuals whose primary allegiance remains with the conventional paradigm—that attests to the fact that inquiry cannot be value-free. A sampler of recent articles that address this point for the social sciences would include Bahm (1971), Homans (1978), Kelman (1968), Krathwohl (1980), Morgan and Smircich (1980), and Scriven (1971). These authors make the case that values are determinative of decisions about what to study, how to study it, and what interpretations to make.

(4) The history of science is replete with examples of the ways in which values influence inquiry. We shall present five here, selected to represent a wide historical band:

Galileo and astronomy. We have already referred (Chapter 1) to the case of Galileo, who, early in the seventeenth century, was censured by the Church for his proposals regarding the "new" astronomy. Much of Galileo's work depended on the use of the telescope, an instrument that he had vastly improved and put to unprecedented use. The reader will recall that it was at about this time that vanguard inquirers were moving from prepositivist to positivist presuppositions, but the values of the large majority continued to reflect the prepositivist view; they stoutly resisted emerging positivist values. Galileo, it is said, invited the Church's representatives (Paduan professors!), who had come to examine him, to view the moon through the telescope, to see for themselves what wonders it made visible. But they refused, for, in their prepositivist view, attempts by humans to study nature in any ways except passive ones were interventionist and *un*natural, and thereby distorted what was learned. The products of interventions (experiments?) could never be faithful representations of what nature was like; unnatural means cannot disclose natural laws, they believed. Accordingly, Galileo was repressed, not only because his teaching happened not to accord with that of the Church (although that lack of accord was undoubtedly important) but because it was based upon what was then viewed as an *illegitimate* paradigm of inquiry. It was their scientific values as much as their religious beliefs that prevented the inquisitors from looking through that telescope, and from accepting Galileo's account of nature as valid. Fortunately, Galileo, even though having officially recanted, continued in his studies until his death, equally certain that *his* values would eventually win out. They did, of course—until the advent of postpositivism rendered them as archaic as his positivist values had the prepositivist. If Galileo were reincarnated today, would anyone be surprised if he rejected postpositivism with the same fervor and conviction with which his inquisitors rejected positivism?

Lavoisier and oxygen. What is often called the "chemical revolution" hinges on the discovery of oxygen by Lavoisier near the middle of the eighteenth century. The history of the displacement of the phlogiston theory—the first theory to account for the phenomena of combustion and calcination (the burning of metals)—has been summarized by McCann (1978) in connection with his study of that episode as an instance of paradigm revolution. Phlogiston had been well accepted for almost half a century, but the theory had suffered from certain anomalies that led Lavoisier, among others, to an intensive program of research. McCann is especially interested in the question of how Lavoisier's proposals, which depended on a new gas that he had named "oxygen," spread throughout the chemistry community, not only in France, but in other countries as well; he names "crucial" experiments, personal contact, and authority as important influences in that diffusion. But, he notes:

> In addition to the evidence of "crucial" experiments, personal contact, and authority, there were other factors influencing conversion or resistance: nationalism (see Hufbauer on German resistance, 1971, pp. 127-131), metaphysical beliefs (see Schofield's 1970, pp. 260-262, explanation for why the materialist, Black, converted so easily while the mechanists, Priestley and Cavendish, never did), lack of convincing evidence (Schofield, 1964, p. 289 on Priestley), and the failure of either paradigm to answer all questions raised about it ("oxygen did not explain the mission of fire in combustion," Schofield, 1964, p. 289, nor did oxygen account for the similarity among metals). *Clearly, factors other than deductive logic were crucial in decisions to accept the new paradigm.* To persist in viewing confirmation in science as a purely logical operation, as many philosophers do (e.g., Hempel, 1964; Scheffler, 1967), would be to place oneself in the ironic position of claiming that a major scientific advance was based on unscientific reasoning. *It seems more accurate to conclude that non-logical elements are inherent in the scientific method.* (McCann, 1978, pp. 35-36; emphases added)

It is interesting to note in connection with McCann's discussion that he uses the word "converted," a distinctly value-oriented term. He makes the case that people are not so much *compelled* by the logic of a situation as they are *persuaded* to accept a new set of values, which then makes the conclusions fall neatly into place. The value shift is crucial; without it, rational movement cannot occur.

Darwin and Lamarck: Chance or purpose? There is undoubtedly no biologist on the face of the earth who is not convinced of the validity of the concept of evolution. But there are distinctly different points of view about how evolution is accomplished. Two polar views are the Darwinian and the Lamarckian (better, the neo-Darwinians and modern Lamarckians); the former hold that evolution occurs because of natural selection for advantage among the many mutations that are continuously occurring *by chance,* while the latter hold that evolution occurs through the inheritance of characteristics that develop *in response to environmental press.*

The late Gordon Rattray Taylor has explored this problem in his excellent little volume entitled *The Great Evolution Mystery* (1983).

His comments are illuminating in that they illustrate the role that values can play at the paradigm level. Taylor notes that Darwin himself had an open mind on the question of whether acquired characteristics could be inherited, but he notes:

> It was the neo-Darwinians, such as Haldane, Huxley, Fisher and Sewall Wright who, in the 1930s, made such an issue of the matter, backed by men like Simpson, Mayr, and Dobzhansky . . . and did so in terms so sweeping as to make a skeptic suspect that they had an uneasy conscience. For instance, Professor C. D. Darlington of Oxford called [Lamarckism] "an evil theory" and said that to inpugn Darwin's theory was "ignorance and effrontery". Harvard's professor Bernard Davis is even more categoric. "Except for those skeptics who are willing to discard rationality," he says crushingly, "Darwin's theory has now become Darwin's law." (Taylor, 1983, p. 36)

Taylor calls attention to a number of cases that provide some evidence for the Lamarckian position, chief among them being the ostrich's calluses. The ostrich, he points out, has calluses on its breast, pubis, and rump just at those points that touch the ground when the bird is sitting. It is difficult to explain this phenomenon, Taylor argues, from the neo-Darwin position, as it is equally difficult to explain a number of other similar instances such as the long legs of wading birds, the webbing in the feet of swimming birds, and the elephant's trunk. He comments:

> But while naturalists cling to the idea of inheriting acquired characteristics, which seems only common sense, geneticists reject it entirely, solely on the grounds that they know of no mechanism by which the genome could be appropriately altered by experience. Instead they ask us to believe that by pure chance, the genes needed to evoke the appropriate changes are created, or perhaps activated, and that this happens in quite a short space of time. In the case of the ostrich, they claim by pure chance genes were developed which would cause just the required calluses to develop and no others, and that those birds which acquired such genes were so much advantaged that they survived preferentially. That takes a lot of believing even if you practice— like the White Queen—believing three impossible things before breakfast. I myself can only believe it on certain days and not a few biologists have failed to manage it altogether. (p. 37)

There seems to be little doubt what Taylor's own position is in this controversy, or that his values are very much involved in taking that position. Taylor (1983, p. 38) goes on to say:

> It is easy enough to believe that selection favours modifications once they are established, and that it disfavours others. The whole question is: how do such precisely adapted modifications árise? The geneticists say: pure luck. Their opponents say: in response to a demand. The geneticists say: no one has ever demonstrated the inheritance of acquired characteristics unequivocally. But then no one has demonstrated that adaptive modifications arise *by chance*. They have been shown to arise, and to be favored by selection, but how they arise is as much a mystery as ever. Brutal treatment of the genetic material will produce abnormal and defective forms. Prolonged selection will favour the development of small modifications. But the origin of complex modifications remains a mystery. For many biologists and most laymen it is not only easier but more rational to suppose that a mechanism exists of which we are ignorant than to suppose that evolution is a matter of chance. *This is why the belief in Lamarckism has persisted so obstinately in the face of scorn and anathema.* (first emphasis in original; second, added)

The role that values play is transparent in this statement. Nor is it an accident, we would suggest, that Taylor pictures the Lamarckians as having been frequently anathemized. Anathema is a state formally visited by the Church on apostates. Darwinism was (is?) seen by many as an attack on the belief that the world is regulated by a divine plan. Replacing the deity by chance (recall Einstein's well-known comment that "God does not play at dice") is the epitome of apostasy. It is ironic that the neo-Darwinians, themselves frequent targets of the Church, should have adopted a churchly role in anathematizing the Lamarckians, who, while not ascribing the purpose they detected in nature to a divine plan, nevertheless formulated a view of evolution more acceptable to the true believer than was raw neo-Darwinism. Note too Taylor's claim that *it is more rational* to suppose the existence of an unknown mechanism than to fall in with the neo-Darwinian view. It is curious indeed to find what is essentially a value claim defended on the grounds of its imputed rationality. We doubt that the neo-Darwinians would agree with that imputation.

Pasteur and Pouchet on spontaneous generation. Mary Hesse (1980, p. 33), in discussing the assertion that conflicting scientific paradigms differ in what they assert as postulates as well as in the meaning they ascribe to them and in the criteria they use to judge them, provides a number of examples to illustrate her point that "all such differences are inexplicable by the logic of science, since they are precisely disputes about the content of that logic." One of these examples, based on a study by Farley and Geison (1974), deals with a dispute between the two French scientists Pasteur and Pouchet on the issue of spontaneous generation: the example is especially interesting because it illustrates the impact of values not only on the debate itself but on Farley and Geison's treatment of it. Hesse (1980, p. 35) says:

> Farley and Geison describe how, in the 1820s, Cuvier, the empirical scientist and political conservative, aligns himself against the postulate of spontaneous generation, which was associated with romantic *Natur-philosophie,* revolutionary politics, and philosophical materialism. By the 1860s, however, scientific legitimation had changed political sides and now favoured spontaneous generation. Now it is Darwinism that has scientific standing, and Darwinism requires spontaneous genera-tion, certainly of the separate species during the course of evolution, and perhaps originally of life itself. Darwinism is also perceived at this time to be inimical to religious order and political conservatism (in France, that meant maintenance of the Second Empire). It is Pouchet who champions Darwin and spontaneous generation, and finds himself obliged to argue their consistency with religion. Pasteur on the other hand is supported by French science, which is anti-Darwin, and he is backed by Napoleon himself. Farley and Geison recognize that up to a point the arguments on both sides of the spontaneous generation debate are validly "scientific," although Pasteur's use of experiments is sometimes questionable, and he seems to have private-ly modified his view towards acceptance of spontaneous generation as it would be required by Darwinism, without revealing this shift un-til the politically sensitive 1860s were past. The authors conclude that his behavior is consistent with the greater degree of influence from external factors than in the case of Pouchet, but they do not deny that there were scientific "facts of the matter" which came progressively to light. They also believe there are *historical* facts of the matter, for in a self-reflexive final paragraph they ask whether their own approach to the history has been influenced by their antipathy to Pasteur's social and political views, and claim that they have tried to set aside their own views and to seek objectivity critically.

It seems plain from this account that while contenders may agree on the "scientific facts" that touch upon an issue, their interpretation of those facts (which often means the way in which they develop theory) depends on nonscientific matters that may include political and social values! Apparently Farley and Geison (on their own account) are sensitive to this issue not only in respect to the positions taken by Pasteur and Pouchet (and to the shift in their positions apparently accountable in terms of the political winds), but in respect to their own analysis as well, since they identify strongly with views counter to those of Pasteur. Hesse seems surprised and unpersuaded by the final reflexive paragraph, but it is hard to imagine that it would have been preferable for Farley and Geison to withhold this information from their readers and to pretend (and perhaps even engage in self-delusion) that they, at least, could maintain objectivity even if Pasteur and Pouchet could not!

Duval, Duval, and Neely: A case of cultural preemption. Harre (1981, p. 10) provides an example of what he takes to be "the troubles infecting the naive 'experimental methodology' " that is germane to the values discussion here on several counts, as we shall see. Harre's example is drawn from a study carried out by Duval, Duval, and Neely (1979), entitled "Self-Focus, Felt Responsibility, and Helping Behavior," published in the *Journal of Personality and Social Psychology*. In this study, each of several female psychology students, after having been told a cover story to hide the true intent of the inquiry, were left alone and permitted to view themselves, apparently irrelevantly to the study, on a television monitor. Afterwards an illustrated lecture on venereal disease was displayed on the same monitor, following which the respondents were asked to fill in a questionnaire eliciting responses about their degree of willingness to contribute in various ways to remedial programs for venereal disease. Harre (1981, p. 10), a British philosopher, comments:

> There is clearly something bizarre about all this—but exactly what? Without as yet examining severally the viability of the three concepts here juxtaposed, it is clear that there is already a problematic conjunction between two conceptual systems with incompatible conceptual models. The concepts of 'self-focus' and 'helping behaviour' are drawn from a system appropriate to describing human automatisms, while 'responsibility'—felt or otherwise—belongs to the representation of some moral order. The psychology of this would require judgment, decision, conscience, and so on. It is clear that there is supposed to be a causal

relation between 'self-focus' and the onset or degree of 'helping behavior'. The effect of the insertion of 'responsibility' into this conceptual framework and of the qualification of 'helping' by 'behavior' is to propose that a form of conduct (*Handlung*) that is taken to be part of the moral order, should be subject to a putative psychological law. The idea that the moral order is part of a technology (in this case a psychological one) is a highly culturally-specific North American notion. The question of whether the North American mores which treat conduct as the behavioural output of trained automata is morally and politically acceptable, or generalizable to other cultures, is preempted by the way the 'experiment' is conceived. So we are presented with something as if it were empirical, which is heavily loaded with *unexamined* metaphysical and moral/political presuppositions.

This case illustrates several points. First, it indicates at least one way in which cultural values can intrude on an apparently value-free study, via its unexamined moral/political presuppositions. But those presuppositions also include some metaphysical ones, which go to the heart of the underlying (and unconsciously used) substantive and methodological paradigms. In this case we also detect an example of value *dissonance;* Harre makes it plain that he, at least, regards the insertion *into the same study* of concepts so dissonant as self-focus and helping behavior, on the one hand, and responsibility, on the other, as confused and problematic. Aside from the fact that it is only in North American cultural terms that these concepts can articulate, Harre seems to suggest that because they do not *really* (that is, in his value terms) articulate, the results of the study can be little more than nonsense. (North Americans may find the results meaningful, but British philosophers, at least, do not!) Thus there is more to this value business than simply the introduction of bias or of subjectivity; at stake is the absolute *scientific* meaning of the result as well. It is in large part the values of the researcher and of the reader that determine that scientific meaning, however incongruous it may appear to juxtapose the terms "values" and "scientific" in the same sentence. Nor should the reader overlook the fact that it is the present writers' naturalistic axioms that make that judgment possible, and meaningful.

There are, then, a variety of sound reasons for suggesting that, far from being value-free, inquiry is in fact affected by values of all kinds. The value-fact dualism is seriously compromised by ontological issues about the nature of reality. The apparent impossibility of separating observational and theoretical languages casts further doubt. A growing literature, much of it written by exponents of the conventional paradigm, adds up to an admission even by advocates of the influence values can have on at least such matters as problem definition and methods selection. And, finally, we see from the variety of examples offered that, whether inquirers are aware of it or not, their investigations are always value-mediated, even by such grossly nonscientific values as the political. Particularly in the arena of social/behavioral inquiry we may well conclude with Heron (1981, p. 33) that

> the "truths" researchers generate are a function of the researchers' procedural norms and underlying values. And if these "truths" purport to be about persons other than the researchers then they have indeterminate validity, no secure status as truths, until we know whether those other persons assent to and regard as their own the norms and values of the researchers. . . . the idea that science can be value-free is . . . a delusion. . . . When the subjects of a science are other persons, then the idea that the researchers' underlying value system can exclude, need not consult or consider or cooperate with the value system of the subjects, can only tend to generate alienated pseudo-truths about persons.

WHAT HAVE BEEN
THE CONSEQUENCES OF
THE VALUE-FREE CLAIM?

Despite the arguments that can be made against it, the claim of value-freedom has characterized conventional inquiry throughout its long history. And the claim has left its mark; there are a variety of undesirable consequences in evidence. It is useful to contemplate these briefly before continuing with a further analysis of value contributions as seen from a naturalistic perspective.

In an unpublished paper, Schwandt (1980) suggests that the following consequences have arisen from attempts to act "on the apparent moral obligation to remain value-free" (p. 10):

(1) The ritual of method. The efforts to preserve the value-free posture have led to insistence on using a particular methodological approach, namely, experimental method. Schwandt comments that "unfortunately, these methods have been elevated to the status of a regimen, a dogma whereby we define truth as the result of an *appropriate* inquiry methodology. . . . The value-free posture is preserved in the exercise of the ritual of method. In this instance, to act under the moral obligation to remain value-free is to conflate a particular

logic of discovery with the pursuit of truth" (p. 11). It is surely the case that a variety of methods may be useful; there is no royal road to truth.

(2) Admissible knowledge. If, in order to remain value-free, a particular method is mandated, then only those facts accessible to that method can qualify as admissible knowledge. Schwandt points out that only knowledge that can result from the "verificational, hypothesis-testing modality" is viewed as legitimate; further, types of knowledge "that do not lend themselves to expression in the current measurement parlance have been largely ignored" (p. 12). The reader will also recall the discussion of Gödel's theorem in Chapter 5 and its metaphoric representation in the tree diagram of Figure 5.1, which illustrate very clearly that there are always large areas of knowledge that are inaccessible to any approach.

(3) Coherence. A major syntactic criterion posed by positivists for the value-freedom of inquiry is that it shall be coherent, a criterion that is worked out in practice in, for example, reliability considerations. When an inquiry can be shown to have coherence it is believed to be value-free because stability indicates imperviousness to the values of the inquirer. However, Schwandt cites Polanyi as "arguing convincingly" that "coherence as the criterion of truth is only a criterion of *stability*. It may equally stabilize an erroneous or a true view of the universe. The attribution of truth to any particular stable alternative is a fiduciary act which cannot be analyzed in non-commital terms" (p. 13)

(4) The scope of moral decisions. It is commonly assumed that moral choices *follow* detached description in a study, a tendency that Schwandt describes as a "moral inversion." While conventional inquirers may agree (as we have seen) that choices among methods, theories, concepts, and the like are involved in all inquiry, and that these choices are heavily mediated by personal preferences, and while we may also note the relevance of moral decisions in research on social interventions, Schwandt asserts that "we seem slow to recognize that moral choices are likewise involved in claiming, for example, that quasi-experimental methods are 'better' methods, or that increased earnings and placement-related-to-training are 'good' measures of vocational program effectiveness" (p. 14). Our experience with nuclear weapons is all-instructive on the question of whether moral choices precede or follow scientific research and development.

(5) Normative implications of "findings." Schwandt argues that even conventional researchers implicitly recognize the value-ladenness

of their positions because they feel free to tease out normative implications of their findings in their discussion. He says:

> For example, in thumbing through a few recent issues of the *American Educational Research Journal,* it seemed quite apparent to me that moral choices are implied in these statements from the "Discussion" section of articles: *"Some practices are more effective* than others in improving race relations in segregated schools", "adverse behavioral comments had *a pervasive effect* on teacher judgments"; "these findings *showed the importance of* major field professors and academic involvement for undergraduate orientations toward scientific or scholarly careers"; *"the data showed* that high school course work, academic ability, success orientation, and educational plans *are important predictors* for women's entry into male-dominated fields" (my emphases). Ironically, these statements demonstrate an admixture of the attempt to remain value-free ("data showed", "findings showed") while espousing value-laden claims ("more effective", "pervasive effect", "important predictors"). (pp. 15-16)

(6) Forcing political decisions into a technical mode. Schwandt comments that "a particularly pernicious effect of the value-free posture in decision-making is that it encourages the forcing of political decisions about program implementation, continuation, modification, and termination into a purely technical mode" (p. 16). Further, "premature programming creates the appearance of assured and determinate control of uncertain situations through the use of linear decision-making arrangements" (p. 17). Some of the arrangements that Schwandt cites include program evaluation and review technique, critical path method, linear and goal programming, and cost-benefit effectiveness analysis. That political decision makers can, in utilizing the findings of scientific research, make decisions free from values is an absurd conclusion for anyone experienced with the political process.

(7) The search for natural laws. If data and findings are taken to be value-free, they can be imputed to nature; they have a compelling legitimacy that mere value claims can never have (for the latter are always at least arguable). It would be absurd for inquirers, recognizing the value-dependency of their work, to assert that their findings constituted exemplars of *natural* laws, for nature has no value structure. Further, as Schwandt notes:

> If value-free science means seeking predictability and control in all situations at all times (via strong knowledge claims) when we might better be seeking to understand and manage indeterminacy and openness in context-dependent situations (via weak knowledge claims), we might

well raise the question of whether science ought to be or even can be value-free. (p. 19)

To these seven consequences outlined by Schwandt, we may add an eighth:

(8) The veil of objectivity: Obscuring balance. Insofar as an inquirer may be persuaded that methodology guarantees objectivity, that is, removes all possible contamination resulting from value positions (among other things), he or she runs the risk of overlooking other possible perspectives and, therefore, of being *fair* to differing points of view. If objectivity is a useful criterion, fairness is even more so. We may recall two of the basic belief statements proposed by Schwartz and Ogilvy (see statements G-6 and G-8, Table 2.15, Chapter 2):

> G-6: Knowledge is protected not by abstracting from all perspectives (the claim of objectivity) but by balancing multiple perspectives to constrain bias (the claim of fairness).

If there is only *one* "objective" (real? true?) perspective, then, by definition, no others are worth considering. But when values *are* recognized as being involved, it is imperative that their meaning and implication be sorted out. We see this happening metaphorically in the adversarial paradigm that characterizes courts of law. No attempt is made to be "objective"; rather, each side argues its position with as much vehemence and conviction as it can. It is believed that a judge or a jury can and will achieve an "on-balance" position that is "fair" to both sides.

> G-8: All knowledge, far from being disinterested, is ultimately interested knowledge.

When knowledge is recognized as "interested," that is, value oriented, a new imperative emerges for the inquirer's guidance. Once aware of the value implications that inhere in his or her work, the inquirer is under *moral compulsion* to take account of those values. Objectivity cannot be permitted to become a veil that obscures the need for balance.

We see then that there are numerous undesirable consequences of accepting the position that inquiry can be and is value-free. It ritualizes the process of inquiry; it arbitrarily limits the range of admissible knowledge—that is, knowledge open to the inquiry process; it can give the appearance of coherence (stability) even to an erroneous view of the universe; it can delude the investigator into normative statements presumably based on "objective" data—which gives those statements a legitimacy they do not deserve and closes off reasonable argument; it can force political decisions into a technical mode that gives those political decisions a false appearance of objectivity and cloaks them in a legitimacy *they* do not deserve; it spurs the investigator on in the search for spurious natural laws whose very existence is at doubt so soon as one acknowledges the influence of values; and, finally, it militates against fairness in the name of objectivity. These are high prices to pay for the comforting self-delusion that one "stands above" all human influences! The god of science is indeed demanding when such are the rules by which one must play.

DIRECT VALUE IMPACTS

If, as the above pages argue, inquiry cannot be value-free, and if failing to recognize that fact has many undesirable consequences, it behooves the investigator, whether naturalist or otherwise (although the "otherwise" faction might have difficulty in recognizing that mandate), to take explicit account of values. Just what impact do they have? We shall respond to this question in two parts, considering first the direct (or what statisticians like to call the "main") effects and second their interactivity—resonance and dissonance. The direct impacts are the subject of this section; the resonance effects follow in the subsequent section.

We have suggested in the first four corollaries to Axiom 5 (Values) that there are four sources of impact—the values of the investigator personally, the values undergirding the substantive paradigm that guides the inquiry, the values undergirding the methodological paradigm that guides the inquiry, and the values that inhere in the cultural setting within which the inquiry is carried out.

On the first point—the *personal values* of the inquirer—we have already noted what might be called the "trivial" or "weak" impact that the investigator's values may have: selecting the problem, selecting the particular methods of data collection and analysis to be employed, guiding the interpretations to be made from the findings, and the like. We characterize this recognition as trivial or weak because it holds even for those investigators who perceive themselves as value-free, that is, "objective" in the traditional sense of the term. But when the investigator recognizes and acknowledges the part that values play, even to the point that the inquiry may be characterized as avowedly ideological, the strong sense of the impact of personal values is invoked. Consider the following statement contained in the opening pages of a dissertation recently completed by one of our students (Lather, 1983) on the subject, "Feminism, Teacher Education and Curricular Change: Counter-Hegemony and the Possibility for Oppositional Schooling":

> In the emerging tradition of self-reflective scholarship, let me make clear my own assumptions.

> I make no claims to value-free scholarship. Openly ideological in my socialist-feminism, I believe there is no end to ideology, no part of culture where ideology does not permeate. This most certainly includes the university and the production of social knowledge. This is a critical point because it reformulates the entire issue of scholarly objectivity. The ground shifts. The issue becomes the choice between empowering or impoverishing ideologies and how conscious and public one is about one's biases. Hesse terms the recognition of the pervasiveness of values and the openly emancipatory intent of a critical social science as "epistemological breaks" portending a more reflexive and, hence, valid human science. (1980: 196) The technocratic androcentrism that pervades the university is no more ideologically neutral than is my socialist-feminism. While my goal is intellectual fairness, I work within a nexus of strong value commitments which rejects the distinction between objective and subjective postures. "Disaffected from objectivity, having been its prey, but excluded from its world through relegation to subjective inwardness, women's interest lies in overthrowing the distinction itself" (Nackinnon, 1982).

A strong statement indeed, and a position that will obviously have a very high-level order of impact on the research. Clearly such a position raises serious questions about the trustworthiness of the inquiry, but that is a question for another time (see Chapter 11). What is important to note here is that the inquirer's values not only implicitly affect selected aspects of the inquiry process but may in fact be the central driving force in the work. What could a posture of value freedom mean in such a case?

Another instance of the impact of the inquirer's values on research was noted in the earlier example regarding the spontaneous generation controversy. Farley and Geison, in reviewing the case of Pasteur versus Pouchet, call their own analysis into question because, they assert, they have been influenced by their own antipathy to the position Pasteur espoused. The conventional response to this disclosure would be to reject the study as invalid; the naturalist who admits the influence of personal values finds the disclosure refreshing and no more a commentary on ultimate invalidity than would be a conventionalist's admission that a paper-and-pencil instrument had achieved something less than perfect validity. Indeed, disclosure of this information provides the reader of the research one perspective from which to judge it, a perspective that would be denied had Farley and Geison elected to "hide" their own predispositions (on the grounds of their impotence to influence the outcome) from the reader.

On the second point of impact—that of the *values undergirding the substantive theory* that guides the inquiry—we see from the earlier examples several remarkable illustrations of the "power of the paradigm," as it were. When chemists begin to take the concept of oxygen (and oxidation) seriously, the entire structure of chemistry is suddenly disjointed and the chemical revolution gets under way. When Darwinian theory fails to explain a variety of evolutionary phenomena (and the example of the ostrich's calluses is only one of literally hundreds of anomalies that neo-Darwinism finds inexplicable), Lamarckism regains a strong hold, and even those biologists who are repelled by something so patently teleological nevertheless begin to cast about for a more satisfactory formulation (recall the Schwartz and Ogilvy comments on the movement toward morphogenesis in biology). When Galileo bases new astronomy on active observation, the Church trembles and traditional science falls. Many other examples could be cited, including Euclidean and non-Euclidean geometry and relativistic and Newtonian physics, to which references have also been made earlier, and such variant formulations as psychoanalytic theory and behaviorism in psychology and bureaucratic and postbureaucratic organizational theory.

These various formulations, in each instance, point to different problems as important (Taylor, 1983, p. 165, quotes Mayr, an eminent geneticist, in commenting on the break during the 1920s between those geneticists who believed that evolution was gradual and those who felt that it occurred through abrupt mutations, as saying, "When I read what was written by both sides...I am appalled at the misunderstanding, the hostility and the intolerance of the opponents. Both sides display a feeling of superiority over their opponents 'who simply do not understand what the issues are' "); read "facts" differently depending on their own perspective; and spin out interpretations that always manage somehow to meld those facts and their own theories in absolutely unassailable ways. And of course the meld *is* unassailable precisely because, when an argument depends on value positions, there can be no final resolution; attribution of truth is indeed, as Polanyi argued (Schwandt, 1980, p. 13), a fiduciary act.

On the third point of impact—that of the *values undergirding the methodological paradigm* that guides the inquiry—well, that is, in a very real sense, what this book is all about. We have seen that there have been several major historical value shifts—we have character-ized these as the shifts from prepositivism to positivism (recall the ex-ample of Galileo and his inquisitors) and from positivism to postpositivism, or, if you will, from conventional to naturalistic paradigms (each of which is a specification of the broader rubric). We saw how in the shift from prepositivism to positivism certain basic assumptions (for example, from passive to active observer) were literal-ly turned around, and we are now arguing that in the shift from positivistic to naturalistic stances a number of new assumptions deal-ing with the nature of reality, the interaction of observer and observed, the nature of transferable working hypotheses, the phenomenon of mutual shaping, and the impact of value must be substituted for their older counterparts. If the reader remains in doubt about the validity of *that* formulation the meaning of this book will certainly be lost on him or her!

Finally, on the fourth point of impact—that of the *general cultural values* that characterize the matrix within which the inquiry is imbedded—we also have several illustrations in the examples cited earlier. It is the values of the Church that clash with those espoused by Galileo and make it politically dangerous, as well as paradigmatical-ly illegitimate, for him to argue for the new astronomy. Positions taken on the subjects of spontaneous generation or of oxygen depended in part on the country to which the investigator owed allegiance. Harre scores Duval, Duval, and Neely for failing to recognize how profoundly North American their philosophic stance is, and how they have neglected to examine their own metaphysical and moral/political presuppositions.

We may also cite our own work (Lincoln & Guba, 1981), in which we point out how an inquiry can be influenced by an overidentifica-tion of the inquirer with the cultural values that characterize a group or situation being studied, an error often referred to by anthropologists as "going native." The inverse of this situation—the inquirer who refuses to recognize that there are cultural values inherent in the group or situation that are different from his or her own—is aptly known as ethnocentrism. Either underidentification or overidentification with contextual values leads to errors; the key appears to be, as suggested by Harre, that the investigator *examine* his or her own values as well as the values of the context or situation. If the unexamined life is not worth living, the inquirer who persists in remaining ignorant of con-textual values is at best not worth listening to, and, at worst, may generate findings positively inimical to both the cause of science and the well-being of the respondents.

VALUE RESONANCE

The problem of value resonance is simply this: To the extent to which the inquirer's personal values, the axioms undergirding the guiding substantive theory, the axioms underlying the guiding methodological paradigm, and the values underlying the context are all consistent and reinforcing, inquiry can proceed meaningfully and will produce findings and interpretations that are agreeable from all perspectives. But, to the extent to which they are dissonant, inquiry proceeds only with difficulty and produces findings and interpretations that are questionable and noncredible.

Under *permissive* circumstances, it seems likely that the inquirer will select both a substantive theory and a methodological paradigm that are consistent with (reinforcing of) his or her own personal value structure. This choice is likely to be made implicitly (remembering that in most cases individuals are not conscious of their own predispositions and rarely have examined them systematically), and is more likely to focus on theoretical and methodological presuppositions than on personal and cultural ones, the latter two being even less consciously accessible than the former. But as has been apparent, throughout this chapter and previous chapters, conditions are *not* permissive; the conventional paradigm has a legitimacy and an orthodoxy that make deviation unacceptable, even unthinkable (literally, since we are all captives of our implicit values). The most pervasive dissonance is likely to occur, as a result, between *substantive theories and methodological paradigms*; as sophistication grows in a field, its theories evolve, but its methodological paradigms are not permitted the same freedom. Strict adherence to what Schwandt called "the ritual of method" is required, for "truth" is, by definition, a possible outcome *only* of the objective, value-free approach.

We can thus agree with Morgan and Smircich (1980, p. 491), who argue:

> Our basic thesis is that the case for any research method . . . cannot be considered or presented in the abstract, because the choice and adequacy of a method embodies a variety of assumptions regarding the nature of knowledge and the methods through which that knowledge can be obtained, *as well as a set of root assumptions about the nature of the phenomena to be investigated.* (emphasis added)

That is, methodological decisions involve assumptions not only about the method itself but about the *nature of the phenomenon to be investigated.* And it is essential that those implicit methodological assumptions square with the more or less explicit ones that undergird the substantive theory.

Morgan and Smircich discuss this problem somewhat further in their paper as follows:

> The quantitative methods used in the social sciences, which draw principally on the methods of the natural sciences, are appropriate for capturing a view of the social world as a concrete structure. In manipulating "data" through sophisticated quantitative approaches, such as multivariate statistical analysis, social scientists are in effect attempting to freeze the social world into structured immobility and to reduce the role of human beings to elements subject to the influence of a more or less deterministic set of forces. They are presuming that the social world lends itself to an objective form of measurement, and that the social scientist can reveal the nature of that world by examining lawful relations between elements that, for the sake of accurate definition and measurement, have to be abstracted from their context. (p. 498)

Their comments might have been made point for point from the analysis of the conventional assumptions we discussed in the early chapters of this volume. But Morgan and Smircich also describe the inverse (we would say naturalistic) view:

> Once one relaxes the ontological assumption that the world is a concrete structure, and admits that human beings, far from merely responding to the social world, may actively contribute to its creation, the dominant methods become increasingly unsatisfactory, indeed, inappropriate. For if one recognizes that the social world constitutes some form of open-ended process, any method that closes the subject of study within the confines of the laboratory, or merely contents itself with the production of narrow empirical snapshots of isolated phenomena at fixed points in time, does not do complete justice to the nature of the subject. The very nature of the phenomena under investigation challenges the utility of such methodological closure. (p. 498)

To illustrate the consequences of these dissonances we shall consider examples from two fields: reading and organizational theory.

(1) Reading. Although it is clearly an oversimplification, one might argue that the field of reading (teaching and research) has been guided by three different models or theories, which have evolved more or less consecutively. Those three might be termed "decoding" models,

"skills" models, and "whole language" or "psycholinguistic" models. Decoding depends on the acquisition of small, contingent bits of knowledge gradually assimilated to form a concept. The thought processes appropriate to reading are fragmented in this view. The skills model depends on the acquisition of a set of predetermined skills that, when learned, allow the student to read. While less fragmented than the decoding model, the skills approach still depends on acquiring a series of dissociated skills, which can be learned in virtually any order. Both decoding and skills models focus heavily on structure, and tend to regard reading as a *product,* a particular performance, to be diagnosed if faulty. Both approaches depend upon the *reaction* of the learner to the learning text.

The whole language or psycholinguistic model, more recently emergent, takes a rather different view. The focus is not on structure but on experience. Reading is seen as an extension of the language that the child already has; preexisting language and the child's natural environment are his or her main teachers. Reading is viewed by adherents of this theory as a *process,* holistic in nature, that is generated by personal experience with language and that builds upon existing language knowledge (which is, after all, well advanced by the time the child first begins to learn to read). Reading is not a reaction to a text but an *interaction* with it. The teacher does not merely make assignments and monitor them; instead, he or she constructs "meaningful and purposeful learning contexts." Reading is a "continuous and evolving process of active language learning in meaningful contexts and through purposeful experiences." This is the sort of language that is characteristic of this view, although these few samples no doubt leave one with an incomplete picture.

The question we raise is this: Which paradigm is resonant with which view, and which is dissonant? If one is guided by the decoding or skills models (both of which, although they tended to predate the whole language model, are still widely in use, because of residues of earlier teacher training and/or because the fiscal situation of many schools constrains a move to the whole language model because of the array of materials required to employ it successfully), it seems clear that the conventional inquiry model provides a good match. The very notion of "decoding" or "skills" fits well with a view of a tangible and fragmentable reality. Identifying and studying reading variables and their relationships seems quite appropriate. With structure and product as foci, research aimed at devising generalizations and cause-effect statements may not appear to be entirely aberrant. If the teacher is simply a maker of assignments and a monitor of their completion, personal interactions are kept to a minimum. In short, the value underpinning of the conventional research model is very similar to the value underpinning of the decoding or skills models.

The whole language, psycholinguistic model differs dramatically in its assumptions from either the decoding or skills models. But, the conventional inquiry paradigm has gained legitimacy as *the* way to do reading research. A disjunction with the new reading model is immediately evident. As we move to the whole language model, which views reading as a process ongoing in the learner's head in interaction with his or her environment and in view of earlier experience, we see that a research method that requires breaking phenomena down into variables and their relationships has little to recommend it. Generalization has little meaning when one is dealing with such idiosyncratic dimensions. Cause-effect relationships can hardly be sorted out when they are simultaneous and interactive.

The resulting dissonance has not gone unobserved—although perhaps it has remained unexplained. Courtney B. Cazden (1980, p. 596), writing in *Phi Delta Kappan,* observes that

> because of the nature of language itself, tests may aggravate more than they help. They will almost certainly reinforce the view that language can be developed as a set of discrete measurable subskills ready for assembly and integration at some later time. They will almost certainly aggravate the already serious imbalance between means and ends—an imbalance between too much drill on the component skills of language and literacy and too little attention to their significant use.

Note the use of the term "reinforce." The usual tests used in reading, which are products of the prevailing conventional inquiry paradigm, reinforce a view of reading that Cazden clearly rejects as no longer appropriate. Theory has moved on but method remains mired, so that in the end the theory is ill served and "imbalances" are aggravated—a severe indictment indeed.

Cazden's views are echoed and elaborated by Wolf and Tymitz (1976-1977, p. 5) in *Reading Research Quarterly:*

> In essence, we are suggesting that reading is a complex and dynamic process, and while researchers in the field would readily agree, their most commonly employed methods treat it as a static set of skills. Consider, for example, the wealth of research on subskill remediation. While there exists a reasonable amount of information on problem identification and task-structuring, we know little about the nature of how such skills become integrated into the process of reading and into

the behavioral repertoire as demonstrated in a classroom event. Whereas the field generally deserves holistic inquiry strategies, it is best characterized by focus-oriented, nonintegrative research. The problem is compounded by the fact that despite the limited knowledge regarding the dynamics and complexity of the process, a superstructure of pedagogical models has evolved which greatly influences both teacher preparation and educational practice. While most teachers do not comprehend the esoteric nature of much reading research, they frequently follow prescribed intellectual formulas, purportedly developed by some kind of systematic inquiry. Perhaps the most succinct way of phrasing the problem is that we have relied almost exclusively on *outcome* measures to study and comprehend the reading *process*.

Thus it is clear that the dissonance between substantive theory and method not only influences the particular research outcomes but legitimates "prescribed intellectual formulas" that guide practice accordingly. For teachers of reading this discussion is indeed more than polemic!

(2) Organizational theory. Organizational theory until recently has been based almost exclusively on the concept of bureaucracy as proposed by Max Weber (1947). Bureaucracies have certain characteristics, as, for example, that there is a commonly shared goal toward which all of a given bureacracy's members are committed to work; that there is a reward system consonant with that goal; that subunits of the organization are linked such that the output of one subunit serves as the input of a second, and *its* output as the input for the third, and so on; and that therefore the relative success or failure of any one subunit is a matter of concern to all. But new concepts of organization have begun to emerge that virtually negate the Weberian precepts, perhaps the best known of which is the idea of the "loosely coupled" organization proposed by Karl Weick (1976). The question then is, if one wishes to use the loosely coupled theory rather than the bureaucratic theory to guide an inquiry, does it make any difference which methodological paradigm one uses?

We may begin by asking what the points of resonance and dissonance are. Perrow (1981) suggests that while our methodological postures are resonant with the orderly, rational picture of organizations afforded by bureaucratic theory, they are quite dissonant with the picture of organizations as capable of high levels of redundancy, slack, and waste, which is what Perrow believes the concept of loose coupling implies. Research conducted with the old paradigm papers over this "micro-confusion" and converts it into "macro-order." In commenting on "the social science solution," Perrow (1981, p. 6) suggests:

> We social scientists try to eliminate disorder with rational designs. Build more prisons. Get those people off the streets. Have the administration decide what texts professors are to use and order them. Give the dean more power to fire people. Write articles with simple, orderly, elegant, and inclusive theorems or hypotheses or models: this is what the world should look like. Test the model with questionnaires that subtly create for the respondent the world we want to prove exists, what Orne calls the "demand characteristics of research instruments"— demanding the kind of behavior you wish to prove exists. Force a tight coupling between the word and the deed.
>
> We force that tight coupling by our view of what science should be. We assume that rational accounts of even so-called irrational behavior can be constructed and then confirmed by testing hypotheses generated from the accounts. But every step of the way contains self-imposed deceptions. The questions we pose to subjects assume that subjects share the world that social scientists have imagined, and in the course of this questioning we elicit responses favorable to that world conception.

Thus, if it is the case that conventional methodology has certain demand characteristics that force order and rationality, and such a methodology is used to investigate a hypothesis that celebrates disorder and irrationality, it seems clear that the hypothesis will likely be defeated *without ever having received a fair test*. We may note the irony of an "objective" methodology leading to unfair conclusions! Objectivity can indeed be an obscuring veil.

It has not escaped the notice of conventional methodologists that there exists some problem in studying the concept of loose coupling using standard research approaches. It seems clear that if the aim of inquiry is prediction and control (and if, as Hesse, 1980, suggests, the pragmatic criterion for science is continual improvement in prediction and control), then a theory such as that of loose coupling, which reeks of unpredictability, raises some difficulties. How can that be handled? The answer of at least one methodologist is to throw out the baby with the bath water—simply deny the utility of loose coupling theory as a basis for guiding inquiry. Hear Frank Lutz (1982, p. 657):

> But what seems to be implied is that, although an insufficient condition, unpredictability is still a necessary condition of a loosely coupled

> organization. *If so, the loose-coupling . . . is not a useful research model.* Predictability is a goal of, if not an essential function of, research. (emphasis added)

It seems unlikely that a better example of dissonance will ever be found!

A somewhat different solution, and one with which we are in agreement, is offered by Clark, Astuto, and Kuh (1983, p. 26) in their discussion of loose coupling as a characteristic of colleges and universities:

> Most of all we need field researchers actively tracking and recording coupling in organizations—from our myopic viewpoint especially in colleges and universities. We have no strong preferences for strategies or techniques of inquiry. Intensive descriptive reports on organizational coupling are needed. Researchers predisposed to naturalistic inquiry should have a field day.

It is not clear whether the pun in the last sentence of the preceding quotation was intended or not, but, in all events, the writers' advice seems sound. It is certainty that conventional methods can at best make only a weak contribution to the study of loose coupling (although in fairness to Clark, Astuto, and Kuh, we should note that they indicate, "Enough is known to support interesting *a priori* hypotheses which would attract individuals who prefer more conventional research methods" [p. 26]. No doubt, but will those hypotheses, recalling Perrow's caveat, prove heuristic?). The dissonance is simply too great.

EPILOGUE

The realization that values can and do influence inquiry in so many ways is more than a little anxiety-producing. There are those who, on finally being persuaded that values *do* have an influence, are inclined to despair that inquiry can have any utility, since it seemingly can yield little more than opinions. We prefer to say that it yields constructions that also have value dimensions, and such constructions are useful even if they are not absolute. We prefer a world of surprises and inconstancy; the idea that inquiry can converge on final "truth" so that, in the end, everything knowable will be known offers a dreary prospect at best. A. A. Michelson pontificated in 1894 (he was later to regret the remark) that physics had reached its zenith, and that its future would consist only of "adding a few decimal places" to results already obtained (Wolf, 1981, p. 46). Thank goodness he was so wrong!

Consideration of the role of values in inquiry leads to the question of whether being openly ideological—as naturalists perforce must be—

is not the equivalent of being blatantly ideological, that is, of using inquiry to serve one's own ends. There are two implications to that question. First, to be openly ideological seems to be preferable to being covertly ideological. One has no choice about representing *some* ideology—one cannot be alive without one. The real issue is whether one consciously takes account of it or it is left to guide one's judgment without awareness. The early work done on extrasensory phenomena at Duke University is an instructive case. Experiments resulted in high levels of statistical significance; in any other area the results would have been accepted without question. But the ruling ideology of psychology prevented the suspension of disbelief that would have been required to give the findings a fair hearing. Psychologists *knew* that within the normal epistemological paradigm the results *could not occur,* so there was no point in looking at them at all. The parallel to the Paduan professors refusing to view the moon through Galileo's telescope is startling. Apparently, out-of-hand rejection of data that do not fit the prevailing paradigm is a phenomenon of every age, not just a benighted medieval one. Surely it is better to be aware of how one's values can influence one's judgment than to deny that such an influence could be occurring at all!

Second, recognition of the ideological nature of inquiry leads inescapably to the conclusion that inquiry always—repeat, always—serves some social agenda. We recall again Heron's (1981, p. 33) remarks that, insofar as research depends upon the researcher's procedural norms and underlying values, the "truth" will

> have indeterminate validity . . . until we know whether those other persons [i.e., the subjects] assent to and regard as their own the norms and values of the researchers. . . . The idea that the researcher's underlying value system can exclude, need not consult or consider or cooperate with the value system of the subjects, can only tend to generate alienated pseudo-truths about persons.

It is for this reason that a clamor has arisen in favor of cooperative research, and not only from neo-Marxist sources. Indeed, the movement toward endogenous, emic (Chapter 1, Chapter 8) inquiry is now marked, as is well attested in the recent volume of "new paradigm"— that is, cooperative paradigm—inquiry edited by Reason and Rowan (1981).

It is time to confront the problems raised by the role of values in inquiry. It is half the battle to admit that one is sick, if one hopes for a cure. Without the admission that inquiry *is* value-bounded, there is no hope of dealing with the influence of values. At this point, *at a minimum,* we should be prepared to admit that values do play a significant part in inquiry, to do our best in each case to expose and explicate them (largely a matter of reflexivity), and, finally, to take them into account to whatever extent we can. Such a course is infinitely to be preferred to continuing in the self-delusion that methodology can and does protect one from their unwelcome incursions!

8

Doing What Comes Naturally

Saying is one thing, and doing is another.
(Montaigne, Essays)

It is one thing to say, as we did in Chapter 1, that the naturalistic paradigm has certain implications for the doing of inquiry, but it is quite another to spell out just how those implications are put into practice. In this chapter we undertake to provide an intermediate step in the transition from saying to doing. In Chapter 1, we simply listed the implications and, in very shorthand fashion, indicated in what ways the implications depended upon, or could be drawn from, the axioms of the naturalistic paradigm. In this chapter we spell out those implications in more detail, providing definition and justification. Chapters 9 through 13 will operationalize the implications and provide illustrations and applications.

WHAT IS THE FORM OF A NATURALISTIC STUDY?

As we shall see, naturalistic studies are virtually impossible to design in any definitive way before the study is actually undertaken. But naturalistic studies do have a characteristic pattern of flow or development, which is summarized in Figure 8.1. Each of the major terms displayed in the figure will be examined in subsequent sections, but, for the moment, a quick "walk through" of the figure will be helpful.

Naturalistic inquiry is always carried out, logically enough, in a natural setting, since context is so heavily implicated in meaning. Such a contextual inquiry *demands* a human instrument, one fully adaptive to the indeterminate situation that will be encountered. The human instrument builds upon his or her *tacit* knowledge as much as if not more than upon propositional knowledge, and uses methods that are appropriate to humanly implemented inquiry: interviews, observations, document analysis, unobtrusive clues, and the like. Once in the field, the inquiry takes the form of successive iterations of four elements: purposive sampling, inductive analysis of the data obtained from the

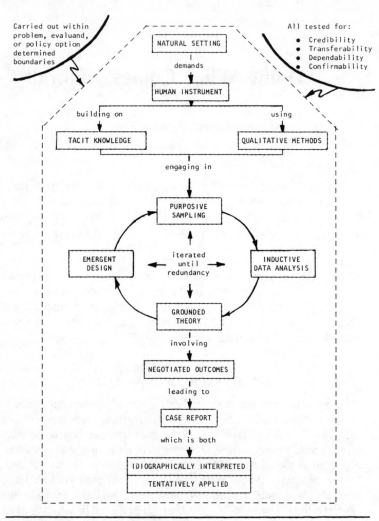

Figure 8.1:   The flow of naturalistic inquiry.

sample, development of grounded theory based on the inductive analysis, and projection of next steps in a constantly emergent design. The iterations are repeated as often as necessary until redundancy is achieved, the theory is stabilized, and the emergent design fulfilled to the extent possible in view of time and resource constraints. Throughout the inquiry, but especially near the end, the data and interpretations are continuously checked with respondents who have acted as sources, as well as with counterpart individuals; differences of opinion are negotiated until the outcomes are agreed upon or minority opinions are well understood and reflected. The information is then used to develop a case report—a case study. The case study is primarily an interpretative instrument for an idiographic construal of what was found there. It may, however, be tentatively applied to other, similar contexts, if empirical comparison of the sites seems to warrant such an extension. The entire study is bounded by the nature of the research problem, the evaluand, or the policy option being investigated (which are, however, themselves subject to revision and extension as the study proceeds). Finally, its trustworthiness is tested by four naturalistic analogues to the conventional criteria of internal and external validity, reliability, and objectivity, which are termed "credibility," "transferability," "dependability," and "confirmability," respectively. This testing begins early in the study and continues throughout, culminating in a final critical review by a panel of local respondents. Given this overview, we may undertake to consider each of the elements in greater detail.

NATURAL SETTING

When we assert that naturalistic inquiry *demands* a natural setting, we should not be understood as making a play on the word "natural," nor of espousing philosophic naturalism, nor of equating the natural with the good (often called "the naturalistic fallacy"), nor of regressing to the prepositivist (essentially Aristotelian) position that all things have their "natural" place. Nor do we wish to invoke the degree of naturalness as a justification for the naturalistic paradigm, as is often done to legitimize new theories; in psychology, for example, it is an unusual theory that does not claim to be "more natural" than its predecessors—and therefore having more inherent legitimacy.

Rather, we suggest that inquiry must be carried out in a "natural" setting because phenomena of study, whatever they may be—physical, chemical, biological, social, psychological—*take their meaning as much from their contexts as they do from themselves.* The ontological positions defined by Axioms 1 (constructed realities) and 3 (generalizations) specify that reality constructions cannot be separated from the world in which they are experienced and that any observations that might be made are inevitably time- and context-dependent. No phenomenon can be understood out of relationship to the time and context that spawned, harbored, and supported it.

The evidence that we have presented in support of those assertions has been, we hope, sufficiently persuasive that the reader is prepared to proceed on those assumptions. Yet we are tempted to offer one more illustration to seal the argument. We turn to genetics and the recent discoveries on the role DNA and RNA play in organic development. Taylor (1983, p. 183) comments:

> Molecular biologists are hypnotised by the potentialities of DNA. The invention of methods of determining the structure of DNA and RNA species quite rapidly has given their work a further impetus, and they often speak as if DNA held the *whole* secret of development. But, as we know from embryology and the transplant experiments I mentioned, *genes are only expressed when the cellular environment calls for them to be expressed.* The part of the cell outside the nucleus is essential, also, to DNA. Nuclei transplanted into cells with an unsuitable cytoplasm give up the ghost. The study of these external influences has lagged, but will certainly cause substantial modification of the picture when it goes ahead. (emphasis added)

In another place Taylor indicates further:

> Essentially, ontogeny . . . remains as mysterious as phylogeny, but one fact of general significance has emerged. The instructions emanating from the nucleus are only carried out by permission of the cytoplasm. Here I shall cite Norman McLean of Southampton University: "Selective gene activity does not itself explain differentiation." And he adds, concerning the cytoplasmic factors controlling expression, "Their identity remains a mystery." (It is amusing to recall that the great geneticist, T.H. Morgan, announced in 1926: "The cytoplasm can be ignored genetically.") (pp. 192-193)

Morgan can be excused for his ignorance, in 1926, of what future genetic studies would disclose. If he had been aware of the interaction of RNA/DNA with the external cytoplasm, no doubt he would have changed his tune. But conventional inquirers (although perhaps they too are unaware of developments such as those cited by Taylor) often insist on *not* having a natural setting; they substitute for it a completely *contrived* setting moving from *in situ* to *in vitro* environments. This requirement is laid down in the name of *control;* the laboratory represents the epitome of the controlled situation. But the very act of controlling so radically alters the environment that results obtained in the controlled setting may have meaning nowhere else except in another laboratory. (May the fact that results are so often replicated from laboratory to laboratory be laid at the feet of their contrived similarity?) We turn to an insightful comment by Urie Bronfenbrenner (1977, p. 513), an authority in developmental psychology, who asserts:

> To corrupt a contemporary metaphor, we risk being caught between a rock and a *soft* place. The rock is *rigor,* and the soft place is *relevance.* . . . The emphasis on rigor has led to experiments that are elegantly designed but often limited in scope. This limitation derives from the fact that many of these experiments involve situations that are unfamiliar, artificial, and short-lived and that call for unusual settings that are difficult to generalize to other settings. From this perspective, it can be said that much of contemporary developmental psychology is *the science of the strange behavior of children in strange situations with strange adults for the briefest possible periods of time.* (emphases in original)

It is ironic, we believe, that in their zeal to meet criteria of internal validity, conventional inquirers create (contrive) contexts that influence behavior as much as natural ones do, but produce responses that will never be found in a natural setting. Such studies may be successful in showing how respondents *may* behave (that is, in illustrating one element in the possible repertoire of behaviors, given certain enabling and blocking/masking arrangements) but almost never show how respondents *do* behave in normal situations. Within the conventional paradigm one seems to have to choose between internally or externally valid behaviors; one apparently cannot have both, except by bargaining away what would normally be described as "acceptable" levels of validity in *both* arenas. The choices appear to be high internal validity and low external validity, low internal validity and high external validity, or mediocre levels of both internal and external validity. We suggest that the naturalistic paradigm opens the possibility of having *both* high credibility and transferability (the naturalistic analogue of internal and external validity, as we shall see in a later chapter).

The mandate that a naturalistic study shall be carried out in a natural setting, far from increasing the subjectivity of the study and making it possible to engage in "sloppy" research, makes demands on the investigator in terms of time, energy, and resources that usually exceed those of a "comparable" study. The naturalistic investigator cannot confine his or her attention to a few variables of interest, ignoring the setting because it has been so carefully controlled; he or she must take account of *all* factors and influences in that context. If *any*thing may make a difference, then *every*thing must be monitored. Furthermore, the investigator must become so much a part of the context that he or she can no longer be considered a "disturbing" element (or at least the degree of disturbance must be minimized). The mere entry of the investigator, as we declare in Axiom 2, disturbs the context; the perturbations must have the opportunity to damp out. And of course some factors in the context will be more salient than others; the term of observation must be sufficiently long so that these more salient factors can, first, be identified, and then, systematically studied for a sufficient period that their influence (the way they engage in mutual shaping) can be assessed. We shall later summarize all of these requirements into two criteria termed "prolonged engagement" and "persistent observation"; more will be said about them in Chapter 11, which deals with trustworthiness issues.

THE HUMAN AS INSTRUMENT

The use of humans as instruments is not a new concept. Indeed, classical anthropology utilized virtually no other instrumentation, and much of that tradition has been maintained in modern sociology, at least the branch that continues to rely heavily on field studies. But even some of the giants of conventional inquiry have recognized that humans can provide data very nearly as reliable as that produced by "more objective" means. In the Festschrift volume honoring Donald T. Campbell (Brewer & Collins, 1981), Levine (1981, p. 173-174) describes a 1955 study by Campbell in which he "discovered that rankings of [ten submarine] crews on morale by land-based informants at the squadron headquarters correlated .9 with the crew's own rankings." He goes on to say:

Campbell concluded not only that the reports of informants were valid but also that their validity seemed to vary with their degree of access to communication with those on whom they were reporting. The informants had made no deliberate or systematic research on the relative morale of the ten submarine crews, but their judgments were almost as good as if they had. Tapping *their* knowledge was an indirect, unobtrusive, and less expensive way of getting the same information. The informants were to be seen as experts in the literal sense; that is, persons whose experience with a phenomenon reached an intensity and duration sufficient to endow their reports with a validity matched only by expensive scientific investigation. Anthropology was to be credited with inventing a method for using the indigenous knowledge of informants rather than merely duplicating it. . . . The central lesson was that stabilized interaction imposed by social roles gave the participants privileged access to certain kinds of information about each other. (p. 174)

One can only wonder what would be possible for trained investigators doing "deliberate or systematic research." Apparently what makes the data valid is "privileged access" with "sufficient intensity and duration." It is just these characteristics that we meant to catch up, in the preceding section, by the terms "prolonged engagement" and "persistent observation." If untrained (and we may presume only tangentially attentive) indigenous personnel could achieve such remarkable levels of validity (although it is interesting to note that the standard of validity invoked here is Campbell's independent "scientific" rating data; the naturalist would be more inclined to express surprise at the high correlation between Campbell's ratings and the opinions expressed by knowledgeable "insiders," and to use the latter as a measure of validity for the former!), can anyone doubt that trained investigators could achieve at least similar levels?

We should recall that Campbell's study—and its associated commentary—is based in the conventional paradigm. In such studies all elements are predetermined (the study itself recapitulates the design). Although it is surely of interest to note that the human-as-instrument functions well under conditions of *determinacy,* our interest in the human-as-instrument stems primarily from the fact that in naturalistically based studies everything is *indeterminate.* It is not as though we had a choice (as Campbell clearly had) to use one or another form of instrumentation; the naturalist has no choice *because only the human instrument has the characteristics necessary to cope with an indeterminate situation!*

In an earlier book (Guba & Lincoln, 1981), we devoted a full chapter to an exploration of the human-as-instrument in which we noted the following characteristics that uniquely qualify the human as the instrument of choice for naturalistic inquiry:

(1) Responsiveness. The human-as-instrument can sense and respond to all personal and environmental cues that exist. By virtue of that responsiveness he or she can interact with the situation to sense its dimensions and make them explicit.

(2) Adaptability. We have already noted the trade-off between perfection and adaptability. An instrument perfect for the assessment of some factor is utterly useless for assessing any other factor. But the human, imperfect as humans are, is virtually infinitely adaptable. The multipurpose human can collect information about multiple factors—and at multiple levels—simultaneously. Like a smart bomb,

the human instrument can locate and strike a target without having been preprogrammed to do so.

(3) Holistic emphasis. The world of any phenomenon and its surrounding context are " all of a piece," and the human instrument is the only one available capable of grasping all this buzzing confusion in one view.

(4) Knowledge base expansion. The human instrument is competent to function simultaneously in the domains of propositional and tacit knowledge (more of this below). As we commented in 1981, "Extending awareness of a situation beyond mere propositional knowledge to the realm of the felt, to the silent sympathies, to the unconscious wishes, and to the daily unexamined usages will lend depth and richness to our understanding of social and organizational settings" (pp. 135-136).

(5) Processual immediacy. By "processual immediacy" we mean the ability of the human instrument (and only the human instrument) to process data just as soon as they become available, to generate hypotheses on the spot, and to test those hypotheses with respondents in the very situation in which they are created.

(6) Opportunities for clarification and summarization. The human instrument has the unique capability of summarizing data on the spot and feeding them back to a respondent for clarification, correction, and amplification.

(7) Opportunity to explore atypical or idiosyncratic responses. The atypical response has no utility on an ordinary instrument; it may even have to be discarded because it cannot be coded or otherwise aggregated. The human instrument can explore such responses not only to test their validity but to achieve a higher level of understanding than might otherwise be possible.

These are formidable advantages indeed! But, of course, they are meaningless if the human instrument is not also trustworthy. Here we may make two points. First, the trustworthiness of the human instrument is assessable in much the same way as is the trustworthiness of any paper-and-pencil instrument. Second, the human instrument is as capable of refinement as any other variety. No conventional investigator expects any instrument to be perfect—certainly not when first developed, and probably not ever. Indeed, it is the experience of test-development companies (such as the Educational Testing Service) that extensive trial and revision is usually needed before an instrument can be regarded as minimally acceptable. And of course the same is true of the human instrument. One would not expect individuals to function adequately as human instruments without an extensive background of training and experience. And their performance can be improved. Luckily, human beings possess another important characteristic—the ability to learn and to profit from experience. When that learning is guided by an experienced mentor, remarkable improvements in human instrumental performance can be achieved. There is no reason to believe that humans cannot approach a level of trustworthiness similar to that of ordinary standardized tests—and for certain purposes, given some of the special characteristics enumerated above, even higher levels.

TACIT KNOWLEDGE

It is not possible to describe or explain everything that one "knows" in language form; some things must be experienced to be understood. As long ago as 1903, Moore was saying:

> My point is that "good" is a simple notion, just as "yellow" is a simple notion; that, just as you cannot, by any manner of means, explain to anyone who does not already know it, what yellow is, so you cannot explain what good is. Definitions of the kind that I was asking for, definitions which describe the real nature of the object or notion denoted by a word, and which do not merely tell us what the word is used to mean, are only possible when the object or notion in question is something complex. You can give a definiton of a horse, because a horse has many different properties and qualities, all of which you can enumerate. But when you have enumerated them all, when you have reduced a horse to his simplest terms, then you can no longer define those terms. They are simply something which you can think of or perceive, and to any one who cannot think of or perceive them, you can never, by any definition, make their nature known. (cited in Moustakas, 1981, p. 210)

Unfortunately (or, as we shall see, fortunately, from the naturalist's point of view), this inability to deal with certain concepts in language form carries over to the doing of research; it pervades that field as well. The set of understandings that, in Moore's terms, cannot be defined, is often referred to as "tacit" knowledge. Thus, Stake (1978, p. 6) comments:

> In statements fundamental to the epistemology of social inquiry, Polanyi distinguished between propositional and tacit knowledge. Propositional knowledge—the knowledge of both reason and gossip—was seen to be composed of all interpersonally shareable statements, most

of which for most people are observations of objects and events. Tacit knowledge may also dwell on objects and events, but it is knowledge gained from experience with them, experience with propositions about them, and rumination.

. . .

Tacit knowledge is all that is remembered somehow, minus that which is remembered in the form of words, symbols, or other rhetorical forms. It is that which permits us to recognize faces, to comprehend metaphors, and to "know ourselves." Tacit knowledge includes a multitude of unexpressible associations which give rise to new meanings, new ideas, and new applications of the old. Polanyi recognized that each person, novice or expert, has great stores of tacit knowledge with which to build new understandings.

Everyone has the experience of tacit knowledge and how it is used. When we speak of nonverbal cues as part of the armamentorium of unobtrusive measures, we refer to information gleaned from a situation without (often) explicit knowledge on the part of either sender or receiver that they are responding to or giving off useful information. Actors convey as much tacitly as they do through the words they speak. Dustin Hoffman, in preparing for his role in the recent hit movie *Tootsie,* in which he plays a man disguised as a woman, practiced for hundreds of hours to accomplish just the "right" gestures and movements that would characterize him as a woman rather than a man. And in its recent investigation into the Beirut massacre a special commission established by the Israeli cabinet found Defense Minister Sharon and others "indirectly" responsible for the massacre because they failed to act on their tacit knowledge. Says Roger Rosenblatt (1983, p. 39), in an essay in *Time:*

> To Sharon and others the report plainly says: You are indirectly responsible for Sabra and Shatila because you "should have felt apprehension;" you should have "take[n] the danger into account;" you "were obligated to foresee as probable" the carnage that ensued.

> But what does it actually mean when one finds somebody responsible for an act because he *should have known* what would happen? He is not imputing stupidity; the person would probably be let off the hook for merely behaving stupidly. Is he implying gross incompetence or a shallow carelessness? Perhaps, but these contentions, too, lessen the degree of culpability. No, when someone in authority is told that he ought to have anticipated a disaster, it means that the grand total of his professional experience and knowledge demanded, beyond reasonable doubt, that he behave differently than he did. Indeed, it

is also beyond reasonable doubt that he merely forgot or tossed aside all the professional experience and knowledge when he neglected to act.

Thus failure to recognize and act on one's tacit knowledge (obviously included in "the grand total of one's professional experience") has in this case been used as the basis for an adverse finding in a courtlike investigation.

But despite everyone's commonsense experience of tacit knowledge and its standing in other areas—even as prestigious as a cabinet-level inquiry—adherents of the conventional inquiry paradigm persist in ruling it out as a basis for "objective" investigations. Labeled as "merely subjective," knowledge capable of being gleaned in a situation by an investigator of appropriate background and experience is inadmissible. But there is reason to believe that such knowledge *cannot* be so arbitrarily dismissed; that tacit knowledge, like values, intrudes into *every* inquiry whether or not the investigator recognizes that fact or is willing to own it.

Heron (1981) suggests that inquiry involves *three* kinds of knowledge, which he labels "propositional," "practical," and "experiential." Science as *product*, he is willing to agree, consists of propositional, shareable statements. But science as *process* involves both practical and experiential knowledge. Practical knowledge is the knowledge of *how* to do it (the American spirit of know-how is a good example). Practical knowledge, in Heron's terms, consists of "a skill, proficiency, or knack"; and we might conclude that practical knowledge has to do with the mechanics, logistics, and techniques of mounting an inquiry. But experiential knowledge, Heron (1981, p. 27) asserts, is

> knowing an entity—person, place, thing, process—in face-to-face encounter and interaction. It is knowing a person or thing through sustained acquaintance. Empirical research, precisely because it is empirical, necessarily requires some degree of experiential knowledge of the persons or objects which the research is about. The researcher's conclusions are propositions about persons or things of which he or she has had experiential knowledge through direct encounter.

But more than that, Heron suggests, no empirical research can be carried out except through a "subtle, developing interdependence" between these three knowledge forms:

> The research conclusions, stated as propositions and laying claim to be a part of the corpus of empirical knowledge about persons, necessari-

ly rest on the researchers' experiential knowledge of the subjects of the inquiry. This knowledge of persons is most adequate as an empirical base when it involves the fullest sort of presentational construing: that is, when researcher and subject are fully present to each other in a relationship of reciprocal and open inquiry, and when each is open to construe how the other manifests as a presence in space and time. . . . So the propositional outcomes of the research depend critically on the practical and experiential components of the process of research. (p. 31)

If Heron's arguments are to be taken seriously, tacit knowledge must not only be admitted but is in fact an indispensable part of the research process; it will be influential whether its influence is recognized or not. The naturalistic paradigm acts on this insight by making the use of tacit knowledge both explicit and legitimate. Tacit knowledge becomes the base on which the human instrument builds many of the insights and hypotheses that will eventually develop (and that will be cast in propositional form). Indeed, the human instrument is the *sole* instrument that *can* build on tacit knowledge; every other instrument is perforce cast in propositional form and so is insensitive to tacit influences. Further, given the indeterminate initial form of inquiry pursued naturalistically, it is essential that the human instrument *be* permitted to use his or her tacit knowledge at full strength and in most explicit fashion. Anything else simply dulls the instrument and reduces the value of the inquiry.

Of course, the naturalistic inquirer cannot be content to leave his or her knowledge at the tacit level. That tacit knowledge must be converted to propositional knowledge so that the inquirer can both think about it explicitly and communicate it to others. Inquiry that is in the end not shareable has little utility. But requiring shareability at the end is a far cry from requiring it at the *beginning*. The latter mandate reduces the effectiveness of the instrument by such an increment as to foreclose much that might have been of value in the inquiry.

QUALITATIVE METHODS

Qualitative methods are stressed within the naturalistic paradigm not because the paradigm is antiquantitive but because qualitative methods come more easily to the human-as-instrument. The reader should particularly note the absence of an antiquantitative stance, precisely because the naturalistic and conventional paradigms are so often—mistakenly—equated with the qualitative and quantitative paradigms, respectively. Indeed, there are many opportunities for the naturalistic investigator to utilize quantitative data—probably more than are appreciated. But it is certainly true that, in practice, naturalistic investigators lean strongly on qualitative approaches.

When we assert that qualitative methods come more easily to hand when the instrument is a human being, we mean that the human-as-instrument is inclined toward methods that are extensions of normal human activities: looking, listening, speaking, reading, and the like. We believe that the human will tend, therefore, toward interviewing, observing, mining available documents and records, taking account of nonverbal cues, and interpreting inadvertent unobtrusive measures.

In our earlier work (Guba & Lincoln, 1981), we devoted several chapters to a description of available qualitative methods and presented some guidelines for their use. We organized qualitative methods into two broad categories differentiated by whether another *human* is typically present—or needed—as a source. Thus other humans are usually required for interviewing, observation, and nonverbal language situations, but they need not be present when using documents and records or assessing unobtrusive measures.

Since there is an extensive literature on these methods we will not review them again here. The interested reader is referred to the excellent references listed below, which constitute but a tiny segment of the literature available.

- *General references:* Bogdan and Taylor (1975), Bogdan and Biklen (1982), Denzin (1978), Douglas (1976), Filstead (1972), Johnson (1975), Wax (1971)
- *On interviewing:* Dexter (1970), Gorden (1980), Spradley (1979)
- *On observation:* Bogdan (1972), Jacobs (1977), McCall and Simmons (1969), Spradley (1980)
- *On nonverbal communication:* Fast (1970), Hall (1959, 1966, 1976), Harper, Wiens, and Matarazzo (1978), Mehrabian (1972)
- *On documents and records:* Anderson and Benjaminson (1976), Guba (1981b), Holsti (1969), Krippendorff (1980), Murphy (1980), Rosengren (1981), Williams (1978)
- *On unobtrusive measures:* Sechrest (1979), Webb, Campbell, Schwartz, and Sechrest (1966), Webb, Campbell, Schwartz, Sechrest, and Grove (1981)

The reader should note that most of these references are based on conventional axioms. Adjustments may have to be made to accommodate the naturalistic view.

PURPOSIVE SAMPLING

All sampling is done with some purpose in mind. Within the conventional paradigm that purpose almost always is to define a sample that is in some sense *representative* of a population to which it is desired to generalize. Even a simple random sample is representative in the sense that every element in the population has an equal chance of being chosen.

It is somewhat ironic that as the conventional inquirer strains to build confidence in his or her generalizations, sampling begins to take on a somewhat different form than the "drawing numbers from a hat" concept represented by the simple random sample—a form that approximates more and more closely what the naturalist does at the outset. Consider the concept of "population." The term identifies a group of persons, agencies, places, or other units of interest that can by definition be placed together, as, for example, the population of Chicago residents, or the population of mentally handicapped, or the population of social service agencies. But as every sampling statistician knows, inferences about populations can be made with greater and greater precision to the extent to which the population is divided into "homogeneous" (look-alike) strata: the portion of Chicago residents who live along the North Shore and earn from $75,000 to $85,000 per annum; the portion of the mentally handicapped who fall in the IQ range 60-70; the portion of social service agencies that are privately funded and serve mentally ill clients; and so on. The more homogeneous the strata can be made, the better the inferences. But of course what such stratification amounts to is the formation of subunits that are more and more alike *contextually*. The naturalist *begins* with the assumption that context is critical. He or she does not assume that there is some intermediate point at which it is efficient to cease further idiographic characterization; rather, each context is dealt with on its own terms.

If that is so, what other purposes can there be that could be served by sampling? Michael Quinn Patton (1980) suggests that, over and above random (or representative) sampling, there are six other types that serve purposes other than facilitating generalization:

- *sampling extreme or deviant cases* to obtain information about unusual cases that may be particularly troublesome or enlightening
- *sampling typical cases* to avoid rejection of information on the grounds that it is known to arise from special or deviant cases
- *maximum variation sampling* to document unique variations that have emerged in adapting to different conditions
- *sampling critical cases* to permit maximum application of information to other cases because, if the information is valid for critical cases, it is also likely to be true of all other cases

- *sampling politically important or sensitive cases* to attract attention to the study (or, sometimes, to deflect attention)
- *convenience sampling* to save time, money, or effort

In naturalistic investigations, which are tied so intimately to contextual factors, the purpose of sampling will most often be to include as much information as possible, in all of its various ramifications and constructions; hence, maximum variation sampling will usually be the sampling mode of choice. The object of the game is not to focus on the similarities that can be developed into generalizations, but to detail the many specifics that give the context its unique flavor. A second purpose is to generate the information upon which the emergent design and grounded theory can be based. As Glaser and Strauss (1967, p. 48) suggest in their discussion of "theoretical" sampling (a term more or less synonymous with our term "purposeful" sampling):

> The criteria of theoretical sampling are designed to be applied in the on-going joint collection and analysis of data associated with the generation of theory. Therefore, they are continually tailored to fit the data and are applied judiciously at the right point and moment in the analysis. The analyst can continually adjust his control of data collection to ensure the data's relevance to the impersonal criteria of his emerging theory.

The above considerations suggest that purposeful sampling has certain particular characteristics:

(1) Emergent sampling design. There can be no a priori specification of the sample; it cannot be "drawn" in advance (note how the very term "drawn" reflects a bias toward generalization-oriented random sampling).

(2) Serial selection of sample units. The purpose of maximum variation is best achieved by selecting each unit of the sample only after the previous unit has been tapped and analyzed. Each successive unit can be chosen to extend information already obtained, to obtain other information that contrasts with it, or to fill in gaps in the information obtained so far. It does not matter where the investigator begins in the sampling process (from a practical point of view, the first unit is often a gatekeeper or someone nominated by the gatekeeper), but successive units are selected in accord with the need to extend, test, and fill in information. Such successive units are most easily obtained by nominations (reputational, personal), but any means that brings the

investigator's attention to bear on heuristic new units can be employed. Techniques such as the "snowball" sampling technique have utility, as does, we would suggest, the "each one reach one" technique most often employed for Sunday school outreach activities.

(3) Continuous adjustment or "focusing" of the sample. Initially any sample unit will do as well as any other, but as insights and information accumulate and the investigator begins to develop working hypotheses about the situation, the sample may be refined to focus more particularly on those units that seem most relevant.

(4) Selection to the point of redundancy. In traditional sampling the sample size is typically designated beforehand; N is usually determined by deciding on the degree of statistical confidence one wishes to be able to place in the resulting generalizations. The size of N can be determined purely by formula, once the tolerable levels of type I and type II error are specified. In purposeful sampling the size of the sample is determined by informational considerations. If the purpose is to maximize information, then sampling is terminated when no new information is forthcoming from newly sampled units; thus *redundancy* is the primary criterion.

Naturalistic sampling is, then, very different from conventional sampling. It is based on informational, not statistical, considerations. Its purpose is to maximize information, not facilitate generalization. Its procedures are strikingly different, too, and depend on the particular ebb and flow of information as the study is carried out rather than on a priori considerations. Finally, the criterion invoked to determine when to stop sampling is informational redundancy, not a statistical confidence level.

Naturalistic inquiry is often criticized on the grounds that it cannot yield generalizations because of sampling flaws. That criticism is undoubtedly true (although trivial from the naturalist perspective). But it is equally true that conventional sampling cannot achieve the purposes for which purposive or theoretical sampling is the method of choice—"Yer puts down yer money and yer takes yer choice!"

INDUCTIVE DATA ANALYSIS

Inductive data analysis may be defined most simply as a process for "making sense" of field data. The sources of such data may be interviews, observations, documents, unobtrusive measures, nonverbal cues, or any other qualitative or quantitative information pools.

Inductive data analysis is the inverse of the usual mode of deductive data analysis used in conventional investigations. In these latter instances, data are usually defined a priori by virtue of some theory that has been brought to bear; the data are to be certain characteristics of variables, or of relationships between variables, that are specified in the theory. Conventional studies, in effect, search for empirical data that will confirm (or disconfirm) what has been deduced from the theory. When working within the naturalistic paradigm, however, the investigator typically does *not* work with either a priori theory or variables; these are expected to emerge from the inquiry. Data accumulated in the field thus must be analyzed *inductively* (that is, from specific, raw units of information to subsuming categories of information) in order to define local working hypotheses or questions that can be followed up.

Inductive data analysis bears remarkable similarities to *content analysis,* a process aimed at uncovering embedded information and making it explicit. Two essential subprocesses are involved, which may be termed, for convenience, "unitizing" and "categorizing."

Unitizing is a process of *coding,* whereby, according to Holsti (1969, p. 94) "raw data are systemically transformed and aggregated into units which permit precise description of relevant content characteristics." Krippendorf (1980, p. 57) suggests that "unitizing involves defining [information bearing] units, separating them along their boundaries, and identifying them for subsequent analysis." These units are best understood as single pieces of information that stand by themselves, that is, that are interpretable in the absence of any additonal information. A unit may be a simple sentence or an extended paragraph, but, in either case, the test of its unitary character is that if any portion of the unit were to be removed, the remainder would be seriously compromised or rendered uninterpretable. We shall describe in Chapter 12 the actual steps by which unitizing is carried out, as part of a process that we shall call the "3 × 5 card shuffle."

Categorizing is a process whereby previously unitized data are organized into categories that provide descriptive or inferential information about the context or setting from which the units were derived. The process of categorizing has been well described by Glaser and Strauss (1967) under the heading of the "constant comparative method." Essentially, the method involves sorting units into provisional categories on the basis of "look-alike" characteristics, which, in the spirit of the naturalistic paradigm, may initially be only tacitly understood. As these provisional categories begin to accumulate substantial numbers of unit cards, the analyst endeavors to write a propositional statement (a "rule") that can serve as the basis for inclusion/exclusion decisions. The rule is subject to continuous emendation as further candidates for that category are considered. In the end, however, every unit card permanently assigned to the category must be admissable under the final form of the rule. The naturalist categories are thus no less rule-defined than are the a priori categories typical of conventional inquiry. In the former case, however, the categories are defined by the collected data rather than, as in the latter case, having what will be counted as data defined by preexisting categories.

Inductive data analysis is often attacked as inadequate on several grounds. The first of these is that data are theory-laden, that is, "facts" cannot exist without a theory that defines them as facts. Hence the hope that one can collect "raw" (theory-free) data and base a theory-free analysis upon them is vain. We shall deal with this objection in the section immediately following, since it is also germane to the question of whether grounded theory is possible. But several other oft-heard objections are easily disposed of. It is said that any collection of facts can be unitized and categorized in a variety of ways; thus inductive data analysis is entirely subjective, and cannot be taken seriously. But of course theory development is equally "subjective," so that data collected under conventional rules to confirm or disconfirm a theory (via its hypotheses, as in Ford's T_4) must be equally subjective. It is said that the naturalist approach is empty-headed in that *any* data make an equally legitimate claim for attention and inclusion; seeing is believing, and the loudest and flashiest data will take precedence over others that may be equally important. That charge may be countered by noting that if "seeing is believing," it is equally true that "believing is seeing," that is, that the desire to vindicate a theory may lead one to find only those facts that support it. Naturalists prefer to think of themselves as open-minded rather than empty-headed. Finally, it is frequently asserted that given the inductive approach there can be no way to place boundaries on an inquiry—all data are equally eligible for inclusion (or exclusion). But of course all data are eligible for inclusion in a conventional inquiry as well—until it is bounded by a problem, an evaluand, or a policy option, depending on the type of inquiry being pursued. It is, as we shall see, the problem, evaluand, or policy option that provides a focus in conventional inquiry, leading to selection of a guiding substantive theory and an appropriate methodology. The naturalistic inquiry is similarly bounded.

GROUNDED THEORY

Grounded theory, that is, theory that follows from data rather than preceding them (as in conventional inquiry) is a necessary consequence of the naturalistic paradigm that posits multiple realities and makes transferability dependent on local contextual factors. No a priori theory could anticipate the many realities that the inquirer will inevitably encounter in the field, nor encompass the many factors that make a difference at the micro (local) level.

Defining grounded theory is, however, rather more complicated than appreciating the need for it:

• Glaser and Strauss (1967, p. 3), generally credited with having coined the term, indicate that a grounded theory is one that will

> fit the situation being researched, and work when put into use. By "fit" we mean that the categories must be readily (not forcibly) applicable to and indicated by the data under study; by "work" we mean that they must be meaningfully relevant to and be able to explain the behavior under study.

It is clear that the concepts of "fit" and "work" are, for these authors, essential criteria for judging whether a theory can be considered to be grounded.

• Elden (1981, p. 261), in a discussion of "participatory research," suggests that grounded theory is "local" theory:

> The project demonstrated that employees possess special expertise concerning their own work situation and its posssible improvement. Participatory research facilitated the gathering together and systematizing of isolated, individualized understanding into what I have called "local theory."

Notice that by this formulation local theory is an aggregate of local understandings that without the intervention of the researcher, would remain isolated, and, we may presume, tacit (or at least remain at the level of folklore or conventional wisdom).

• Reason (1981), in an appreciation of Paul Diesing's book *Patterns of Discovery in the Social Sciences,* describes Diesing's account of how pattern models of explanation emerge, a description that seems to fit the concept of grounded theory (as we propose to use the term) very well:

> The information that is gathered in the field situation is used by the holist to build a model which serves both to describe and explain the system. The model is built by [quoting Diesing] "connecting themes in a network or pattern" (p. 155); the connections may be of various kinds, but they are "discovered empirically rather than inferred logical-

ly" (p. 156); the result of this is an empirical account of the whole system. This account *explains* the system because it describes the kinds of relations the various parts have for each other, so that the "relations between that part and other parts serve to explain or interpret the meaning of that part" (p. 158). This type of explanation is called a *pattern model* of explanation:

> For the pattern model, objectivity consists essentially of this: that the pattern can be indefinitely filled in and extended: as we obtain more and more knowledge it continues to fall into place in this pattern, and the pattern itself has a place in a larger whole. (Kaplan, 1964, pp. 159-160) (the full quotation is drawn from Reason, 1981, pp. 185-186; the latter paragraph is a quotation within a quotation drawn from Kaplan, as noted)

Thus, grounded theory is not nomological/deductive (Ford, 1975, pp. 51ff) but patterned; it is open-ended and can be extended indefinitely; and it is discovered empirically rather than expounded a priori. However, pattern theory, like its nomological/deductive cousin, can both describe and explain a phenomenon toward which it is directed. Like conventional theory, it can also be used to predict and to generate hypotheses for test (should anyone choose to do so). Grounded theory can play the role of conventional theory for any subsequent study (one need not return to "ground zero" in each new inquiry); but conventional theory cannot legitimately claim to be based on anything more tangible than the theorist's imagination.

• Kidder (1981) describes a process called "negative case analysis" that may also be interpreted as a mode of devising grounded theory (although this approach has greater utility as a test of trustworthiness; see Chapter 11). She reviews a study carried out by Cressey (1953) dealing with the "social psychology of embezzlement" in which Cressey identified four conditions that must be present if embezzlement is to occur. He formulated an initial hypothesis that embezzlement occurred only when an individual in a position to embezzle funds could rationalize his or her actions as merely a "technical violation," and that an individual who *knew* that embezzlement was illegal would not engage in it. But he quickly found after interviewing a few convicted embezzlers that they knew very well that embezzling was illegal; hence Cressey had to shift his hypothesis to take account of these "negative cases." In fact, for a time each new round of interviews brought to his attention cases that did not fit earlier formulations, and revisions were made each time. Finally, he was able to devise a statement consistent with every case he interviewed: Embezzlers need to be in a position of financial trust, have a fiscal problem that cannot be shared with others, recognize embezzlement as a possible solution to that non-shareable problem, and be able to develop a rationalization to justify the embezzlement, such as thinking of it as a "loan." This "process of revising hypotheses with insight," as Kidder (1981, p. 241) puts it, may without much difficulty be seen as another way to conceptualize the development of grounded theory.

Whatever the form of definition may be, however, grounded theory has not escaped sharp attack by those who find it an inadequate approach to theory development. Two of the arguments deserve attention here.

First, it is said that grounded theory is inadequate because it is underdetermined—a concept we have already encountered (see Chapter 1). Underdetermination is the curse of inductive logic; while deductive logic allows for no evasions (Ford's T_3), inductive logic can be challenged on the ground that any given set of facts is always open to multiple interpretation. Thus, speaking specifically to the inadequacies, as she perceives them, of the Glaser and Strauss proposals, Ford (1975, p. 220-221) asserts:

> Certainly there are some funny bunnies who, like Glaser and Strauss, will try to seduce you into a Tiggiwinkel world of dirty smalls. These furry fellows believe unflinchingly in liberated LAUNDRY; so much so that they keep flaunting their theory-construction procedures before you. Indeed, they even attempt to lure you into that steamy backroom of the mind where they spend many sweaty hours chanting the four principal modes of John Stuart Mill's inductive methodology. . . . These strategies for theory construction are still to be found in most textbooks on sociological methodology. But you have my personal guarantee that, if you try to emulate them you will get nothing but hot and sticky. . . . So do not be bamboozled into the steam-room of routinized induction!

But the criticism of underdetermination can be leveled at *any* theory, however it may be derived. As Quine (1953) has ably argued, no theory is ever logically determined by data. Every act of theory development, whether grounded or a priori, is creative in nature, going well beyond the empirical data or conceptual imaginings that suggested it.

Second, it is argued that grounded theory is impossible to devise, because the raw data are themselves "facts" only within the framework of some other (perhaps implicit) theory; thus a theory can only discover itself. That facts are "theory-laden" seems to be well accepted among epistemologists; Hesse (1980), for example, mounts a cogent argument against the proposition that there can be separate "observational" and "theoretical" languages. But these arguments overlook the use of *tacit* knowledge; both observational and theoretical languages are themselves *propositional*. It is little wonder that when observations and theory are both cast in linguistic form—a form that necessarily imparts to them certain qualities that are artifacts of language and not necessarily of phenomena—they are found to have a relationship such that one (observation) apparently presupposes the other (theory). One could as easily (and perhaps more cogently) argue that theory presupposes facts (a position more consistent with the naturalist paradigm). Even more likely is the possibility that emerging grounded theory and the relevant "facts" presuppose one another, and develop together! But whatever may be the reader's preferred formulation of the two horns of that dilemma, it seems clear that in a naturalistic investigation tacit knowledge can and does come into play; the units of data upon which grounded theory is ultimately based may emerge because of the investigator's implicit apprehension of their importance rather than because a specific theoretical formulation brought them into focus. Admitting tacit knowledge not only widens the investigator's ability to apprehend and adjust to phenomena-in-context, it also enables the emergence of theory that could not otherwise have been articulated.

We may, finally, point to the fact that utilization of grounded theory is absolutely essential to the concept of emergent design. Theory given a priori can only be tested; the tests that may seem imperative at any given point in the development of the theory can be stipulated in advance and a design for carrying them out described in full detail. But grounded theory is both required by and contributes to the further development of an emergent design; it is as the theory is adjusted that next steps become defined and the study can continue. Grounded theory is capable of and requires continuous expansion and refinement; when the possibility for such expansion ceases the possibility for further study also ceases.

EMERGENT DESIGN

We have already noted (Chapter 1) the reasons that, within the naturalistic paradigm, designs must be emergent rather than preordinate: because meaning is determined by context to such a great extent; because the existence of multiple realities constrains the development of a design based on only one (the investigator's) construction; because what will be learned at a site is always dependent on the *interaction* between investigator and context, and the interaction is also not fully predictable; and because the nature of mutual shapings cannot be known until they are witnessed. All of these factors underscore the *indeterminacy* under which the naturalistic inquirer functions; the design must therefore be "played by ear"; it must unfold, cascade, roll, emerge.

A major distinction must be made between types of studies in which the investigator "*knows* what he or she doesn't know," and therefore can project means of finding it out, and situations in which the investigator "*does not know* what he or she doesn't know," in which case a much more open-ended approach is required. Conventional inquiry, at least in terms of its favored reconstructed logic, is *always* in the former position: nomological/deductive theory exists that leads to hypotheses to be tested or specific questions to be answered. Under these circumstances it would be ludicrous to claim that a design could not be devised beforehand and, indeed, the probability of the design's fully testing the hypotheses or answering the questions can well be judged before a single step is taken or a single dollar spent. Naturalistic inquiry is almost always in the latter position; the naturalist who claimed that he or she had a fully developed initial design would immediately be suspect. Further, many steps may need to be taken and many dollars spent before any judgment of adequacy can be made.

Of course the naturalist does not always begin empty-handed (and certainly not empty-headed!). Theory grounded in an earlier investigation may be available—but great care must be exercised to be certain that the theory is apt for the now-to-be-investigated context. The investigator may possess a great deal of tacit knowledge that is germane to the phenomena to be studied. And as the inquiry proceeds, it becomes more and more focused; salient elements begin to emerge, insights grow, and theory begins to be grounded in the data obtained. Hypotheses can be formed and questions posed. And while it would be foolish to expect a naturalist to be able to describe a design in anything more than broad-brush process strokes before the study is undertaken, it would be equally foolish *not* to expect that as the study progressed, the elements of a design would become more and more clear and explicable.

How *does* a design emerge? On site, the investigator must engage in *continuous* data analysis, so that every new act of investigation takes into account everything that has been learned so far. Inductive data analyses can be performed on a daily basis, so that insights, elements of theory, hypotheses, questions, gaps, can be identified and pursued beginning with the next day's work. If the investigation is to be carried out by more than one person, interactions can be planned (over meals, in the evenings, at special times designated for the purpose) to share knowledge and to make joint decisions on next steps. The investigator(s) may also leave the site for periods of time, to engage in common critiques under less demanding time conditions; to engage in debriefing interviews and work sessions with peers not directly involved in the study to test emerging theories and insights, check possible intrusions of bias, and solicit advice on next steps; and to engage in related searches of the literature (although care must be taken here since most of the existing literature reflects inquiry done in the conventional mode). It is essential that adequate records (an audit trail) be kept of each such action, whether in the form of file memos, minutes of longer sessions, attestations from debriefers, research syntheses, and so on. Each investigator should keep a personal journal in which his or her own methodological decisions are recorded and made available for public scrutiny. More will be said of all of these techniques in Chapter 11.

As one might expect, the concept of an emergent design poses a multitude of problems that are not faced by the conventional investigator. One set of such problems has to do with the relationships between the investigator and those to whom he or she may be accountable or upon whom he or she may be dependent: a funding agency, a dissertation committee, an in-house review agency, or simply his or her professional peers. There are many disjunctions between what a naturalist is able to stipulate before the fact and the elements that are commonly thought to be essential to a "good" design. Needless to say, virtually every specification for a good design has, historically, developed in respect to conventional inquiry; the naturalist is at a distinct disadvantage. It is clear that precise procedures cannot be specified, nor can an accurate time line be laid down. When everything "depends," only the broadest procedural guidelines can be specified at the beginning. Thus "milestone events" are unknown, as are the times at which they are likely to occur. Since most funding agencies insist that budget projections be tied to specific procedures and that accountability be reckoned in terms of providing certain "deliverables" at prespecified times, the naturalist finds it difficult to persuade any agency to support his or her work.

Another set of problems resulting from an emergent design concept affects the actual conduct of the investigation. The indeterminacy so much in evidence at the outset continues to plague the investigator—albeit with some amelioration as information begins to accumulate. There is the matter of arriving at a focus—what, finally, shall be taken as most salient to study in depth, since one cannot study everything? Sampling must be continuous, and when it must be done purposefully rather than in terms of some mechanical statistical design, a great deal more mental energy is consumed. Finding time for reflection to guide next-step decisions is also difficult; that time may have to come from that usually devoted to sleep or meals. Agreeing on an evolving decision process—with fellow investigators, debriefers, or agents to whom one is accountable—also poses difficulties. Finally, there is a delicate balance between adjusting a design to newly discovered knowledge and overreacting to "the loudest noise" or the "brightest light." All of these factors alter the conventional, almost mechanical, pursuit of a design well laid in advance to a frenzied, twisting, continuously changing endeavor. Indeed, tolerance of ambiguity may well be the most important personal characteristic the naturalistic investigator must possess.

But there is no need for panic. While naturalistic inquiry may, in these particulars, be more difficult than conventional, there are ways of coping at least minimally well with all of these problems. Subsequent chapters will provide illustrations of such coping techniques.

*   *   *

As the reader will have surmised, the steps of purposive sampling, inductive data analysis, development of grounded theory, and specification of next steps in an emergent design interact and are reiterated multiple times in the course of any particular investigation. Indeed, there is no end to an emergent design; it seems likely that any naturalistic investigation could be continued indefinitely, since it will continually dredge up new questions and insights worth pursuing. Nevertheless, at some point—typically because time or resources have expired—the study is brought to a halt. The steps outlined in subsequent sections are then taken.

NEGOTIATED OUTCOMES

By the phrase "negotiated outcomes" we mean to imply that both facts and interpretations that will ultimately find their way into the case report (below) must be subjected to scrutiny by respondents who earlier acted as sources for that information, or by other persons who are like them. Of course, not all negotiations can end in agreement, and one cannot expect an inquiry to produce findings that everyone could or would accept. But everyone does have the *right* to provide input on the subject of what are proper outcomes, and the inquirer has an *obligation* to attend to those inputs and to honor them so far as possible.

Why should the naturalistic inquirer be so concerned about what the respondents think, perhaps even to the point of altering findings in order to accommodate their views? First, it may be argued that negotiation must occur if the basic axioms of the paradigm are to be followed. If the outcome of naturalistic inquiry is a reconstruction of the multiple constructions that various respondents have made, it would seem to be obligatory that the inquirer check out that reconstruction. It is in the spirit of emic, as opposed to etic, inquiry to do so. If we take seriously the proposition that context is all important in assigning meaning to data, it is useful to carry that assigned meaning back into the context for verification. If we believe that inquiry is value-bounded, the values of the respondent must be considered. As Heron (1981, p. 33) points out:

> The truths we assert are a function of our procedural norms which in turn are a function of our shared value system. The "truths" researchers generate are a function of the researchers' procedural norms and underlying values. And if these "truths" purport to be about persons other than the researchers then they have indeterminate validity, no secure status as truths, until we know whether those other persons assent to and regard as their own the norms and values of the researchers.
>
> ... the idea that science can be value-free is ... delusion. ... When the subjects of a science are other persons, then the idea that the researchers' underlying value system can exclude, need not consult or consider or cooperate with the value system of the subjects, can only tend to generate alienated pseudo-truths about persons.

Second, to this argument that rests on the axioms we can add two others, suggested by Heron (1981), based upon the ideas of intentionality and moral/political influences. On the first point, Heron suggests that imputations of intentionality must remain imputations unless and until they are checked out with the respondents:

> When I am interpreting basic actions [such as walk, talk, look, point] in terms of their more complex intentions and purposes, then I need to check against the agent's version of what he was about, for a person may walk, talk, look or point to fulfill many different higher-order intentions. (p. 23)

On the latter point, Heron notes that conventional research usually exploits people, for knowledge is power that can be used against the very people from whom the knowledge was generated. Heron opts to work *with* respondents because:

> (1) it honours the fulfillment of their need for autonomously acquired knowlege; (2) it protects them from becoming the unwitting accessories to knowledge-claims that may be inappropriately or harmfully applied to others; (3) it protects them from being excluded from the formation of knowledge that purports to be about them and so from being managed and manipulated, both in the acquisition and in the application of the knowledge, in ways that they do not understand and so cannot assent to or dissent from. (pp. 34-35)

Third, we can argue for negotiated outcomes on the ground that such negotiation is essential if the criteria of trustworthiness are to be met adequately. We shall see that a major trustworthiness criterion is *credibility* in the eyes of the information sources, for without such credibility the findings and conclusions as a whole cannot be found credible by the consumer of the inquiry report. The justification of credibility as a trustworthiness criterion—parallel, as we shall see, to the conventional criterion of internal validity—is a complex matter, the discussion of which must be deferred to Chapter 11. Here, however, we may note that credibility is crucial and that it cannot be well-established without recourse to the data sources themselves.

As the reader may already have guessed, the negotiation of outcomes is a continuous process that goes on, formally and informally, from the very inception of the study. It occurs informally as respondents draw inferences from what the investigator does, the questions he or she asks (and doesn't ask), the cues that are pursued, the documents that are solicited, and the like. It occurs more formally at the close of every interview, when the respondent is presented a summary of what has been said for approval, correction, or extension, and during the debriefing sessions with local influence leaders at regular intervals throughout the study and particularly whenever the study team leaves the site. However, it occurs most formally at the termination of the project, when a formal review panel is constituted (Chapter 13) to critique the draft of the case report prior to its finalization. It is when and only when the study has survived these several negotiation sessions that the investigator may feel ready to produce the final version of the case.

THE CASE REPORT

Just as the scientific report appearing in journals or project reports is well suited to the conventional paradigm, so is the case report suited to the naturalistic paradigm. Definitions of a case study vary widely, ranging, for example, from Denny's (1978) formulation that a case is "an intensive or complete examination of a facet, an issue, or perhaps the events of a geographic setting over time" to such unrigorous but typical statements as that a case is "a snapshot of reality," a "slice of life," or "an episode" (Guba & Lincoln, 1981, pp. 370-371). Whatever definition one accepts, it is clear that cases are unconventional ways of reporting on inquiry. Sigmund Freud is said to have regretted that his cases read like short stories rather than technical reports—although one suspects that Freud was more concerned about the apparent loss of legitimation than with the lack of "real" scholarliness. It is certainly true that Freud's cases had an enormous impact, despite their unconventionality.

The naturalist describes three major purposes for using the case reporting mode:

(1) The case report is ideal for providing the "thick description" thought to be so essential for enabling transferability judgments. The case report is, at its best, a "portrayal" of a situation. It may read like a novel but it does so for the same reasons that novels read like novels—in order to make clear the complexities of the context and the ways these interact to form whatever it is that the case report portrays.

(2) The case report is the form most responsive to the axioms of the naturalistic paradigm. Multiple realities are difficult to communicate in scientific report form, as are the interactions of investigator and respondents (which in fact must be denied in the usual report), the values of the investigator and of the context, and the many mutual shapings that are seen to occur.

(3) The case report provides an ideal vehicle for communicating with the consumer. It provides him or her a vicarious experience of the inquiry setting. The aim of the case report is to so orient readers that if they could be magically transported to the inquiry site, they would experience a feeling of *déjà vu*—of having been there before and of being thoroughly familiar with all of its details. For the reader the case report is likely to appear grounded, holistic, and lifelike. And, perhaps most important, the case report provides the reader a means for bringing his or her own tacit knowledge to bear; if the description is sufficiently "thick," then reading it is very similar to being there and be-

ing able to sense elements too nebulous to be stated propositionally. Of course, experienced readers can build on their tacit knowledge even when reading a scientific report, but the case report surely facilitates that capability.

Unfortunately, the literature is not very helpful in transmitting knowledge of how to write a case report. Indeed, much of what is in the literature relates to cases developed for instructional purposes, for example, the Harvard business school cases. Guba and Lincoln (1981) have provided a chapter that deals with case writing, but it too is more theoretical than practical. Probably at this point in time the best way to learn to do a case is to apprentice oneself to an experienced case writer, write cases, and solicit critiques.

The writing of case reports brings its own problems. First, there is the matter of style. It is difficult to evolve a style that adequately and simultaneously serves the three purposes described above: thick description, axiomatic representation, and vicarious reader experience. The second, for example, demands a quite formal approach, whereas the latter suggests an informal—and psychological rather than logical—organization. There is the matter of deciding what to include and what to exclude; there is almost always more information than can be accommodated (some case study writers speak of "doing an information dump" in a first draft and then cleaning it up later, but the basis for the cleanup remains ambiguous). There is a special difficulty in maintaining anonymity (of the site and its inhabitants) and confidentiality (of information sources). This problem takes on ethical proportions because the persons from whom informants may need to be protected are usually themselves intimately familiar with the situation. There is the problem of maintaining an adequate audit trail—how can one demonstrate that data cited stem from local informants, observations, or documents, and not simply from the investigator's imaginings? How can one write the case so that an external reviewer (an auditor, say; see Chapter 11) can verify its contents? And finally, how can one terminate a case description without giving the impression that the phenomena continue on as described ("and they lived happily ever after")? After all, the local mutual shapings go on and on ("the beat goes on"), so that by the time the case is written and produced it is out of date. All of these are very real difficulties, as anyone who has ever attempted to write a case can attest. But none are insurmountable; Chapter 13 will provide illustrations of some ways to deal with these problems.

IDIOGRAPHIC INTERPRETATION

We have already seen in relation to the discussion of generalization (Chapter 5) that an attempt to apply lawlike generalizations to particular cases is likely to founder because of the twin problems of underdetermination and relativism. Generalizations—nomothetic statements—are always underdetermined (there is always more than one way to account for any set of data) and, when applied to the individual case, are at best probabilistic.

The naturalist is well aware of these limitations and hence rejects the notion that nomothetic statements are either possible or useful, particularly in those inquiry areas dealing with human behavior. What is found in some particular context has meaning only in the idiographic sense *for that context at that time.* And not to be overlooked is the fact that what is found depends also on the particular interactions the investigator has with elements of the site, including the values he or she brings to it.

Conventional investigators tend to reject idiographic interpretation as useless—what good does it do to know about a single site only? Of course, such evaluations are made in terms of what is taken to be science's central purpose: prediction and control (recall Hesse's [1980, p. 188] dictum that the pragmatic criterion for science is increasingly successful prediction and control). If some other purpose is postulated, as, for example, *verstehen* (understanding, or meaning experienced in situations), then the idiographic position becomes not only tenable but mandatory.

Idiographic interpretation also implies understanding in a very holistic way—another consequence of the ontological assumptions of the naturalistic position. Meaning cannot be attained for a whole simply by looking at its parts—indeed, even the aggregate of all knowledge about all parts cannot yield total knowledge. Schwartz and Ogilvy (1979) have discussed the emergent dimension of "perspective," arguing persuasively that even the accumulated wisdom of all possible disciplines cannot yield a complete picture of anything. Total immersion in a context is required to legitimate the claim that even partial understanding has been achieved. And that understanding can apply only to that context from which it was derived.

TENTATIVE APPLICATION

A further consequence of the naturalistic posture is that findings of a particular study cannot be applied in other contexts simply because they are held to be "generalizable." If there is some question whether the findings may apply even in the *same* context at some other, later time, it is surely an issue whether they apply in other, somewhat dissimilar contexts. Indeed, transferability, far from being established once and for all because certain methodological tenets, such as careful control and random sampling, have been followed, must be reassessed in each and every case in which transfer is proposed. And in order to establish transferability, similar information must be available for *both* sending and receiving contexts. That is to say, an investigator can make *no* statements about transferability for his or her findings based solely on data from the studied context alone. At best the investigator can supply only that information about the studied site that may make possible a judgment of transferability to some other site; the final judgment on that matter is, however, vested in the person seeking to make the transfer, who must be in possession of similar data for the receiving context.

It is the function of the case study, with its "thick description," to provide that essential judgmental information about the studied context. The elements to be included in the thick description have been described by Guba and Lincoln (1981), and are further discussed in Chapter 13.

                    *   *   *

The 12 characteristics that have been discussed so far might be thought of as the broad-gauged components of a naturalistic design; as should be clear by now, the particulars of the design cannot be supplied at all until the study has been under way for some time, and only incompletely supplied even when the study has been terminated. There are, however, two other elements that must be considered: although they are not part of the direct process flow, they are nevertheless crucial.

FOCUS-DETERMINED BOUNDARIES

The very openness of naturalistic inquiry and the emergent nature of its designs may give rise to the charge that what is included or excluded is entirely a matter of the investigator's subjective choices. Is it true that the naturalistic investigator has no inclusion/exclusion guidelines except those that happen to pop into his or her head serendipitously?

We challenge this view with the assertion that what guides naturalistic inquiry is the *focus* of the study, in exactly the same way that the focus guides the conventional study. By "focus" we mean one of three things, depending on the kind of inquiry that is being mounted. In the case of research, the focus is the *problem;* for evaluation, the *evaluand* (that is, the entity being evaluated); and for a policy study, the *policy option*. A discussion of these three types of foci is presented in Chapter 9.

It is our assertion that naturalistic inquiries are neither more nor less "mindless" than are conventional inquiries. What bounds the latter also bounds the former, and whatever difficulties may be faced by the naturalist (with the possible exception of the complication of a reformulated focus) will also be faced by the conventional inquirer.

TRUSTWORTHINESS

The conventional criteria for trustworthiness are internal validity, external validity, reliability, and objectivity. Now the questions *underlying* the establishment of these criteria are also appropriate to ask of naturalistic inquiry:

- How can one establish confidence in the "truth" of the findings of an inquiry for the respondents with which and the context in which the inquiry was carried out?
- How can one determine the degree to which the findings of an inquiry may have applicability in other contexts or with other respondents?
- How can one determine whether the findings of an inquiry would be consistently repeated if the inquiry were replicated with the same (or similar) respondents in the same (or similar) context?
- How can one establish the degree to which the findings of an inquiry stem from the characteristics of the respondents and the context and not from the biases, motivations, interests, and perspectives of the inquirer?

But while these *questions* are appropriate to the naturalistic paradigm, the *criteria* as formulated by conventional inquirers are not; counterpart criteria are needed. Conventional inquirers assert that they can claim internal validity for a study if its results are isomorphic with the reality they purport to describe. But when reality is assumed to be multiple and intangible, what can such a criterion mean? Conventional inquirers assert that they can claim external validity if the study is carried out under conditions of probability sampling. But when sampling is done purposively/theoretically and, indeed, when an axiom of naturalistic ontology denies the possibility of generalization as that term is usually understood, what can *that* criterion mean? Conventional inquirers feel that they can claim reliability for a study in which the results are stable and replicable, but when designs are emergent and different investigators may elect to carry out a study along different lines (even when bounded by the same problem), what are we left with? Conventional inquirers feel that they can claim objectivity for a study if there is a layer of "objective" instrumentation interposed between the inquirer and the object(s) of inquiry. But when the chief instrument is the inquirer him- or herself, does not objectivity dissolve?

In his treatment of this problem, Guba (1981a) proposes that these conventional formulations be replaced with four new terms that have a better fit with naturalistic epistemology; these he has named "credibility" (in place of internal validity), "transferability" (in place of external validity), "dependability" (in place of reliability), and "confirmability" (in place of objectivity). The full rationale for this redefinition is presented in Chapter 11; suffice it to say here that it parallels (metaphorically speaking) the conventional rationale.

Guba (1981a) has also proposed certain operational techniques that the naturalist can use to establish credibility, transferability, dependability, and confirmability. Chief among these are prolonged engagement and persistent observation, triangulation, peer debriefing, negative case analysis, and member checking, to establish credibility; thick description, to facilitate transferability; and auditing, to establish dependability and confirmability. These techniques will also be described in Chapter 11.

EPILOGUE

In this chapter we have attempted to provide an intermediate step between the extremely truncated and highly theoretical explication of the procedural implications of the naturalistic paradigm outlined in Chapter 1 and the operational statements of Chapters 9 through 13. It is important that the reader understand that the flowchart of Figure 8.1 and the treatment, in this chapter, of each of the parts shown in that figure, do not constitute an orthodoxy, an inviolable reconstructed logic, a one-way process diagram. Variations will be found in each individual study. New elements may be introduced and some of the present ones ignored. Surely the chart is not intended to represent a one-way flow; reiterations are not only possible, but encouraged, to yield some assurance that nothing important has been overlooked. Redundancy is typically eschewed in life, but in this instance it is a most useful criterion: Repeat until redundancy—and then just one more time for safety.

It is likely that at this point the reader will feel that he or she has not had very much guidance in how to *do* naturalistic inquiry—despite the jaunty title of this chapter. Naturalistic inquiry is in that sense no more natural (or easy or spontaneous) than is conventional inquiry—despite the fears of conventionalists that many inquirers will be attracted to the naturalistic paradigm because they do not have the interest, the ability, or the commitment to subject themselves to the "rigors of real research." No one promised you a rose garden; if you want to know more about horticulture, you must proceed to later chapters.

9

Designing
a Naturalistic Inquiry

> Research design is the plan, structure, and strategy of investigation conceived so as to obtain answers to research questions and to control variance. The *plan* is the overall scheme or program of the research. It includes an outline of what the investigator will do from writing the hypotheses and their operational implications to the final analysis of the data. The *structure* of the research is more specific. It is the outline, the scheme, the paradigm of the operation of the variables. When we draw diagrams that outline the variables and their relation and juxtaposition, we build structural schemes for accomplishing operational research purposes. *Strategy,* as used here, is also more specific than plan. It includes the methods to be used to gather and analyze the data. In other words, strategy implies *how* the research objectives will be reached and *how* the problems encountered in the research will be tackled.
>
> *(Kerlinger, 1973, p. 300)*

THE PARADOX OF "DESIGNING"
A NATURALISTIC INQUIRY

Kerlinger's statement illustrates the high degree of specificity that is not only deemed possible but actually taken as normative for inquiry conducted in the conventional mode. *Prior* to doing an inquiry the investigator is obliged, by this definition, to spell out the following:

- the overall plan of the study
- the hypotheses to be investigated
- the variables to be included
- the relationships expected among those variables (equivalent to stating hypotheses?)
- the methods (instruments?) for data collection
- the modes of data analysis

Indeed, the investigator is even expected to anticipate the problems that will be encountered and to indicate what will be done about them.

This definition leaves little to chance: A design is a definitive and complete statement of how the inquiry will be conducted, even those phases that may prove to be problematic. Failure to specify all of the indicated elements is a fault to be laid at the feet of the investigator; claims that ambiguities in the context or intransigencies in the phenomenon studied contributed to failure are disallowed.

Kerlinger's definition is probably narrower than it need be, even from a conventional perspective. Indeed, while he stresses (not only in this quotation but also in the paragraphs that follow it in the original) that design has the purpose not only of controlling variance but also of obtaining answers to research questions, it seems clear that his specifications are directed more to the former than to the latter. A somewhat less narrow—and more typical—set of elements usually included by conventionalists in describing design specifications is the following:

(1) The statement of a problem, an evaluand, or a policy option. While such a statement is not, strictly speaking, a part of the design, it does serve as a major criterion for judging its quality and utility and for guiding its development. If the design is usefully conceived as a statement of *means,* its appropriateness is best assessed against a statement of *ends.* Typically, the statement of problem, evaluand, or policy option includes a justification ("Why is it important to do this?") and ends with a statement of the objectives to be achieved by the inquiry.

(2) The statement of a theoretical perspective. An inquiry can almost always be carried out from any of several theoretical perspectives. To return to earlier examples, organizations can be studied using bureacratic or loosely coupled theories; reading behavior can be studied using decoding, skills, or psycholinguistic theories. From a conventional point of view, an important (but frequently overlooked) aspect of design is to select the theory that provides the most power (leverage) in relation to the problem, evaluand, or policy option, just as it is to select the statistical mode that provides the most analytic power.

(3) The statement of procedures that will be employed. It is this statement that is at the heart of the design; the quality of the design will most often be judged by the power of the procedures proposed. The statement of procedures includes specifying the following, while simultaneously showing the relationship of each element to 1 and 2 above and to one another (internal articulation):

(a) Sampling. The conventional study is most often concerned with generalizing from the sample studied to some previously defined population. Thus the design must specify sampling units (which may be multiple, as, for example, sites to be studied as well as individuals within sites). The design must provide for representative and random sampling.

(b) Instrumentation. The specification of instruments is crucial in the conventional design not only because the instruments are the means for collecting data but also because they are, simultaneously, the *operational definitions* of the variables involved. It is thus important to justify them as representing appropriate realizations of the concepts. It is also important to show that they have high validity and reliability, and, most of all, that they are objective, impervious to external human influences. If the instruments are already available, all these characteristics must be evaluated, and if the instruments are to be developed, then the developmental steps must be described and particular attention must be paid to the question of how validity, reliability, and objectivity will be brought to acceptable levels.

(c) Data-analytic procedures. In the conventional design the selection of appropriate data-analytic procedures usually comes down to the selection of a statistical test to be applied. Indeed, the concept of "experimental design" is often taken as synonymous with statistical design. However this issue may be resolved, data analytic modes are selected on a number of grounds, including *adherence of the data to the assumptions underlying the technique* (these assumptions take multiple forms: assumptions stemming from the mathematical derivation of the technique such as normality and homogeneity of variance; assumptions about the treatment, such as that the effect of the treatment shall be additive for all subjects regardless of their initial position(s) on the variables(s); and assumptions about the nature of the data themselves, such as a statistic developed for use with correlated data), and *the relative power of the technique for providing conclusive ("significant") findings.* The techniques selected must be capable of testing the hypotheses or answering the questions posed.

(4) The establishment of a time schedule. The design must fit the important events of the inquiry to a time line. Ordinarily certain "milestone events" can be identified that can be used as monitoring checkpoints to be certain that the inquiry is "on track."

(5) The designation of agents. The design specifies who it is (more often, who they are) that will implement the specified steps. Typically, vitae are attached so that interested parties can judge the appropriateness of the agents' training and experience for the tasks outlined.

(6) The projection of a budget. The design estimates the resources (time, people, funds) needed to carry out the tasks specified.

(7) The statement of the expected end product(s). In the conventional mode it is often possible to specify almost exactly what the end product will look like: a technical report for which one might be able to provide "dummy tables" in the design statement, so sure can one be about what will finally emerge. The report will be developed for a single audience (the readership of a journal, say, for a research prod-

uct; the clients or sponsors for an evaluation product; or the decision makers for a policy analysis product). It is possible and appropriate to specify a more or less precise date when the product will be available.

The reader who has followed the discussion of this book thus far will immediately appreciate the paradox that is posed if the above specifications for a design are applied to a naturalistic inquiry. The design requires precisely those things that are impossible for the naturalist to specify in advance. Consider:

- While the naturalist starts with a focus (a problem, an evaluand, or a policy option) just as does the conventionalist, the focus may very well change. If the focus determines the procedures, at least in the sense that procedures must be consistent with it, then it is quite possible that the procedures will also change.
- Theory emerges from the inquiry for the naturalist; it is not given a priori. If the methodology must be resonant with the theory, methods can be clarified only as theory emerges, and the methods may very well change in the process of theory definition.
- Sampling serves different purposes for the naturalist than for the conventionalist. The concept of "population" is foreign, as is the reason for being concerned with "population" in the first place: the desire to generalize. Naturalists sample in ways that maximize the scope and range of information obtained; hence sampling is not representative but contingent and serial—each element sampled depending on the characteristics of all the preceding elements, and no element being identified until its predecessor elements have been identified and, so far as possible, tapped.
- Instrumentation for the naturalist is not external ("objective") but internal ("subjective"). The instrument in naturalistic inquiry is not an operational definition of anything, but a sensitive homing device that sorts out salient elements and targets in on them. The instrument becomes more refined and knowledgeable in that process.
- Data analysis is open-ended and inductive for the naturalist, in contrast to the focused and deductive analysis common in conventional inquiry. Since the form of the data that will ultimately be produced by the human instrument is unknown in advance, the data cannot be specified at the beginning of the inquiry. Further, there are no a priori questions or hypotheses that can preordinately guide data-analysis decisions; these must be made as the inquiry proceeds. Since the data from a naturalistic inquiry are likely to be qualitative, statistical manipulations have little if any relevance; questions of fit to underlying assumptions and relative power are not at issue. What is at issue is the best means to "make sense" of the data in ways

that will, first, facilitate the continuing unfolding of the inquiry, and, second, lead to a maximal understanding (in the sense of *verstehen*) of the phenomenon being studied in its context.

- Timing cannot be predicted for the naturalistic inquiry as it can for the conventional. Events that cannot be described because they have yet to emerge certainly cannot be tied to a particular date. Further, one cannot tell what it is to be "on track"; the concept of "milestone events" has no prior meaning. Perhaps the only thing the naturalist can be sure of is that there will be slippage in whatever plans are made; the corollary to Murphy's Law that asserts that "things always take longer than they do" will never be better exemplified. Finally, since naturalistic inquiry always diverges rather than converges, the time span of an inquiry is not determined by a predetermined schedule but by practical considerations, such as an end to funding.

- Budgets are also virtually unspecifiable with any degree of exactness. The funder must deal with the question, What am I able or willing to spend? rather than, What will it cost to carry out these tasks? It is dubious whether the naturalist could provide a sound budget estimate stretching more than several months into the future. Of course, that fact should not be construed as providing the naturalist license to be insensitive to budget issues or profligate in resource allocation; it does imply that when tasks are as yet unknown, what it will cost to accomplish them must be equally unknown.

- Expected end products are also difficult to specify. Certainly any concept analogous to the "dummy table" will be completely foreign to the naturalist. Probably all that can be promised in advance is that "understanding will be increased," and that that increase will be noticeable to a variety of audiences, all of whom will (within practical limits) receive reports couched in their own "natural language" and building appropriately on their own prior—and tacit—knowledge.

What these considerations add up to is that the design of a naturalistic inquiry (whether research, evaluation, or policy analysis) *cannot* be given in advance; it must emerge, develop, unfold. The concept of the emerging design has already been dealt with in multiple places in this book; the considerations discussed above should make it abundantly clear (if it was not already so) why the design *must* emerge. The call for an emergent design by naturalists is not simply an effort on their part to get around the "hard thinking" that is supposed to precede an inquiry; the desire to permit events to unfold is not merely a way of rationalizing what is at bottom "sloppy inquiry." The design specifications of the conventional paradigm form a procrustean bed of such a nature as to make it impossible for the naturalist to lie in it—not only uncomfortably, *but at all.*

WHAT CAN IT MEAN,
THEN, TO DESIGN A
NATURALISTIC INQUIRY?

It does not follow, however, that because not *all* of the elements of the design can be prespecified in a naturalistic inquiry, *none* of them can. And it is also the case that the nature of naturalistic inquiry calls forth certain elements not included in conventional design that must nevertheless be considered. Design in the naturalistic sense, as we shall see, means planning for certain broad contingencies without, however, indicating exactly what will be done in relation to each.

The outline of elements that follows should not (it should be obvious) be construed in any linear fashion. Clearly one cannot talk about all elements at once; some must be presented before others. But that should not mean that those elements presented first have inviolable priority, nor should the possibility of continuous recycling be overlooked (feedback and feedforward). What is intended to be implied by this list is that all of its elements must somehow be dealt with by the naturalist contemplating an inquiry. The elements represent, it might be supposed, broad bins or pigeonholes that will be filled out as the inquiry progresses. And what goes into any one bin is determined as much by what goes in the others as by any intrinsic characteristics of its own. Given these caveats, we proceed to list the elements of a naturalistic design as follows:

(1) Determining a focus for the inquiry. No inquiry, regardless of which paradigm may guide it, can be conducted in the absence of a focus. We have made the point that the nature of this focus depends upon the kind of inquiry involved, whether research, evaluation, or policy analysis. We have previously termed the foci appropriate to these three inquiry modes "problems," "evaluands," and "policy options," respectively.

A problem is more than a mere question; it is certainly different from an objective. In another context (Guba & Lincoln, 1981, p. 88) we have suggested that a problem is a state of affairs "resulting from the interaction of two or more factors . . . that yields (1) a perplexing or enigmatic state (a conceptual problem); (2) a conflict that renders the choice from among alternative courses of action moot (an action problem); or (3) an undesirable consequence (a value problem)." The interacting factors may be concepts, empirical data, experiences, or any other elements that, when placed alongside one another, signal some basic difficulty, something that is not understood or explained at that time. The purpose of a research inquiry is to "resolve" the problem in the sense of accumulating sufficient knowledge to lead to understanding or explanation, a kind of dialetical process that plays off the thetical and antithetical propositions that form the problem into some kind of synthesis.

An evaluand is a thing-to-be-evaluated—that is, a program, organization, performance, material, facility, or the like, the value of which is to be determined. As we have noted elsewhere, value has two aspects (Guba & Lincoln, 1981): *merit,* or intrinsic value, bound to the evaluand wherever it may be (as, for example, a curriculum may be meritorious because it is up-to-date, internally well articulated, and simply written), and *worth,* or extrinsic value, independent of the evaluand to the extent that it is determined as much by the context of use as by any characteristics of the evaluand itself (as, for example, a curriculum may have a different degree of worth in a suburban school as contrasted to an inner-city school). Further, evaluations can be *formative,* that is, directed toward refinements or improvements in the evaluand, or *summative,* that is, directed toward an assessment of its overall impact. Thus the focus of an evaluation is determined by naming an evaluand, specifying whether it is its merit or worth (or both) that the evaluation is intended to establish, and indicating whether the intent of the evaluation is formative or summative.

A policy option is a proposed or existing policy the utility of which is to be determined. Utility depends in part on the extent to which the policy meets some need (caution—needs are value-determined; Guba & Lincoln, 1982) and in part on its operational, fiscal, and political viability. Further, policies may exist as policies-in-intention, policies-in-implementation (see, for example Lipsky's discussion of street level bureaucrats, 1980) or policies-in-experience, that is, policies as construed by the client group (Guba, 1984). Thus the focus of a policy analysis is determined by naming an option, specifying its apparent type (intention, implementation, or experience), and indicating whether the analysis is to deal with operational, fiscal, or political viability (or any two or all three).

Determining the focus of an inquiry serves two major purposes. First, such focusing establishes the *boundaries* for a study; it defines the terrain, as it were, that is to be considered the proper territory of the inquiry. If the research problem deals with an apparent contradiction offered to a certain already-grounded theory by a new "fact," the territories defined by other theories are not germane. If the evaluand is a new treatment for dealing with alcoholism, the worth of which is to be summatively determined with alcoholics who have not been susceptible to other approaches, then one need not examine weekly sessions of Alcoholics Anonymous attended mostly by persons already well along toward being "cured." If the policy option is a soil conservation policy to be examined at its intentional level, then one need not deal with water conservation districts. Second, such focusing effectively determines *inclusion-exclusion criteria* for new information that comes to light. The naturalist, even with inquiry boundaries quite firmly in mind, is likely, because earlier stages of an inquiry are conducted with wider sweeps of the data-collection net, to dredge up much information that, while interesting, is not exactly relevant. Focusing helps the naturalist to make the decision to retain or discard information.

It cannot be overemphasized, however, that boundaries are not cast in concrete; they can be altered and, in the typical naturalistic inquiry, will be. Initial research problem statements may be found to be inadequate or inappropriate. So, for example, Shulamit Reinharz (1979) had proposed to examine friendship patterns among adolescent patients in a mental hospital, but she found, when she arrived, that "friendship pairs" were arbitrarily defined by hospital authorities. The "normal " dynamics of friendship obviously would not be found in such a setting. A student of one of the authors (Shapiro, 1982) was interested in the apparent disjunction between the advice given to college students in "how to study" books about where to study (same quiet place, desk turned to wall to eliminate distractions, adequate preparation to obviate task-evasive behavior such as sharpening pencils, and the like) and the behavior of college students as she was able to observe it as a staff member of a university's study center. It took but a few interviews before it was clear to her that the issue of where to study could not be tackled until she had a better understanding of what students understood studying to be (doing class assignments, cramming for an examination, "psyching out" the professor, doing term papers or laboratory work, and so on). The focus of her inquiry shifted quickly from the former to the latter.

Evaluands are no more stable than are research problems. What is to be evaluated shows remarkable capabilities for metamorphosis. Surely what is written down in proposal format is rarely closely related to what is implemented. The late Malcolm Provus, for example, when appointed to head a new division of evaluation within the Pittsburgh Public Schools shortly after the passage of the Elementary and Secondary Education Act of 1965, was unable to find *any* of the dozens of projects funded under that act in operation; the Discrepancy Evaluation Model that he subsequently developed to guide his division had as its first step *defining* the evaluand—and that often while project activities were purportedly under way (personal communication). Further, it is well known that evaluands do not remain constant over time; what is done in the name of a new curriculum today is different from what will be done next week or next month, as experience and insight grow but also as boredom and recidivism set in (for example, because the Hawthorne effect diminishes).

Nor are policy options impervious to sudden and disjunctive alterations. Indeed, the distinctions among policy-in-intention, policy-in-implementation, and policy-in-experience are themselves illustrative of the illusive nature of policies. Particularly because of their susceptibility to political pressure, policies may be modified on a daily basis: Former Interior Secretary James Watt's sale of public coal-bearing lands under the existing policies of the Department of the Interior is challenged and summarily curtailed; the federal government's inclination to provide free cheese to the poor is undercut by the remark that "cheese is for rats." Indeed, the very act of policy analysis may produce early findings that result in an immediate change in the form of the proposed policy; later findings are directed not to the original but to the revised version.

Whether an inquiry can be characterized as research, evaluation, or policy analysis, the focus of the inquiry can and probably will change. Conventional inquirers regard such changes as absolutely destructive of their inquiry designs ("you will confound the variances hopelessly"); the naturalist expects such changes and anticipates that the emergent design will be colored by them. Far from being destructive, they are constructive, for these changes signal movement to a more sophisticated and insightful level of inquiry. Thus the naturalist begins inquiry with a particular focus in mind (however tenuous) but has no qualms about altering that focus as new information makes it relevant to do so. The initial design statement will reflect that intention.

(2) Determining fit of paradigm to focus. Paradigms rest, as we have shown, upon sets of basic beliefs called axioms, and we have seen that, in the case of geometry, which geometry will be selected depends upon the arena of application. Thus Euclidean geometry provides a perfectly adequate fit to terrestrial geodetics, while Lobachevskian geometry gives a better fit to astronomical. While no adequate methodology exists at this time for "testing" for fit, the investigator should pose to him- or herself the following questions, based on the naturalistic axiom system:

- Is the phenomenon represented by a multiplicity of complex constructions? If one is a chemist investigating the reaction of sodium hydroxide (NaOH) and hydrochloric acid (HCl) in a test tube, for all practical purposes one can assume that there is a single construction (and a simple one at that) with which all chemists would agree: the interaction will yield simple salt (NaCl) and water (H_2O). But if one is a social psychologist investigating group behavior, it seems better to assume the existence of multiple social realities as constructed by the several participants (not to mention yet another such reality constructed by the investigator him- or herself).

- What is the degree of investigator-phenomenon interaction, and what degree of indeterminacy will that interaction introduce into the investigation? Again, the chemist need not be overly concerned (at least at the macroscopic level) that his or her persence outside the test tube will influence very much what goes on inside, or that he or she will be somehow influenced. But the social psychologist by his or her very presence may influence the behavior of members of an observed group, and, especially if the investigator happens to be in the role of participant-observer, may influence the investigator's behavior in dramatic ways.

- What is the degree of context dependence? The chemist is likely to find the same sort of reaction between NaOH and HCl whether the test tube is in the laboratory, in a kitchen, or on top of Mt. St. Helens during an eruption. But the social psychologist cannot easily draw general conclusions from the behavior of a particular group; we need to have a great deal more information, such as the nature of the group, its apparent purpose, its assigned task (if any), the intentionality of its members, the relationship the investigator has to it (for example, whether he is seen as an "insider" or an "outsider"), the rewards or punishments that may be connected to particular forms of group behavior, and so on.

- Is it reasonable to ascribe conventional causal connections to the phenomenal elements observed? If someone were to assert that the production of NaCl and H_2O is caused by the interaction of caustic soda and acid, no one would seriously challenge the assertion (that is, even though that "causal" state is an ascription that could not be demonstrated in empirical terms). But if someone where to assert that an observed group failed to accomplish its assigned task *because* one of its members engaged in truculent, abortive behavior, that assertion would be open to serious challenge indeed. Yes, but what about the fact that the group was warned that its time was running out? What about the diversion introduced by the fact that the observer was asked to explain his or her role? What about the fact that the task was just barely within the competence of the group members to carry out? And so on. All these and many other factors interacted in mutually shaping ways that led, at some arbitrary point in time, to the judgment that the group had failed. But no single cause or simple combination of single causes is sufficient to explain that outcome.

• To what extent are values likely to be crucial to the outcome? Surely it matters little what the chemist's values happen to be as he or she observes the test-tube reaction, but it would matter a great deal to the social psychologist what the values were of the members of the observed group, what other values inhered in the context in which the group was being studied (if we are discussing a naturalistic study we would clearly be dealing with a "natural" group in its "real-world" context), and it would certainly matter what particular theory of group behavior (in turn based on certain assumptions) was brought to bear.

In short, if the investigator's situation is more like the chemist's than like the social psychologist's in the examples cited above, the use of the conventional paradigm may be appropriate, but to the extent that the reverse is true (and we would argue that to be the case in virtually all social/behavioral inquiry), the naturalistic paradigm is the paradigm of choice. The initial design should reflect consideration of these questions.

There are several other, more practical considerations that should also be taken into account while considering the "fit" question. First, is the phenomenon something about which respondents are not likely to be forthcoming? This situation is quite likely to occur in evaluation or policy analysis situations, in which respondents may feel that they have something to lose by being candid. Douglas (1976, p. 55) has described the "conflict" paradigm of research, "based on the assumption that profound conflicts of interests, values, feelings and actions pervade social life. . . . Instead of trusting people and expecting trust in return, one suspects others and expects others to suspect him. Conflict is the reality of life; suspicion is the guiding principle."

While Douglas's comments surely represents an extreme position, there can be no doubt that conflicts between investigator and respondent do occur, and, when they do, they color the findings of an inquiry. While the conventional paradigm recognizes the possibility of such conflicts, its mode of dealing with them usually involves deceiving the subjects about the "true" purposes of the inquiry (although that is relatively difficult to do if the inquiry is an evaluation or policy analysis). The naturalistic paradigm is of course no less beset by conflicts than is the conventional, but, because of its characteristics—including prolonged engagement, persistent observation, and triangulation (including triangulation with nonverbal cues and unobtrusive measures)—it is in a better position to uncover and appreciate the half-truths or falsehoods that respondents supply. When there is reason to suspect that deception, lies, or fronts may characterize an inquiry scene, the naturalistic paradigm seems better able to deal with these than is the conventional. Again, the initial design statement should demonstrate that this issue has been assessed.

There is also the question of the constraints that may be placed on the investigator by a variety of significant others. Various audiences involved in an evaluation may not be equally interested in being publicly targeted; they may feel, for example, that it is more expedient to keep a low profile than to seek a fair adjudication of their concerns. Requests for proposals (RFPs) released by funding agencies may in effect specify a paradigm even without meaning to do so. For example, numbers of RFPs recently released by federal agencies call for naturalistic, qualitative, or ethnographic studies, but then, in specifying the "scope of work," introduce conditions that could be met only within the conventional paradigm, such as a priori description of the sample; provision of instruments to be used in order to secure OMB clearance; specification of a tight time line with well-identified milestone events; and the like. Dissertation committees or peer review panels may impose requirements in the name of "standards" that force the inquirer into an undesirable stance. When such external constraints are imposed, it is up to the naturalistically inclined investigator to decide whether the problem (or evaluand or policy option) can be dealt with acceptably within those constraints; if that is not the case, ethics demand that the investigator not proceed. It is clearly *not* appropriate to just "take the money and run," that is, agree to such constraints for the sake of gaining authorization (and funding) to proceed, but, once those are in hand, to proceed to do something else.

(3) Determining the "fit" of the inquiry paradigm to the substantive theory selected to guide the inquiry. This step is taken to account for the value-resonance problem described in Chapter 7. If the theory is to emerge from (be grounded in) the inquiry at hand, this step can be passed over, for the theory that emerges will be consistent (necessarily) with the methodological paradigm that produced it. But if the theory is given a priori—either because it was previously grounded in a similar or related study or because it was accepted for other reasons, such as representing discipline state of the art or sponsor insistence—then it is important to assess the degree of fit between paradigm and substantive theory. We have previously suggested in Chapter 7 that the use of the conventional methodological paradigm to investigate phenomena conceptualized in theoretical terms that fit naturalistic assumptions may result in nonsense findings, and it may also be the case that phenomena conceptualized in terms that fit conventional assumptions are poorly

studied using the naturalistic paradigm. In either case we have, metaphorically speaking, Lutherans seeking to understand Catholic dogma in Lutheran terms (or vice versa); we would be quite sympathetic to the charge that such comparisons are unfair. Again, the naturalist must determine the degree of such fit and decide, in marginal cases, whether the degree of misfit is serious enough to invalidate the findings. The initial design statement should reflect such an assessment.

Of course the major difficulty in making such a comparison is that often the assumptions upon which the substantive theory is based are neither immediately apparent nor easily discovered. If we take seriously the work of Schwartz and Ogilvy (1979) cited in Chapter 2, the several disciplines are converging onto a new substantive paradigm that, while having different ramifications in different fields, is common to all at the level of axioms. When that development has been fully realized the problem of fit or paradigm to substantive theory will have been eliminated. Meanwhile, inquiries (whether research, evaluation, or policy analysis) are proceeding in terms of *older* assumptions that it is the responsibility of the naturalist to lay bare so that comparisons may be made and fit determined. Simply to apply the naturalistic paradigm willy-nilly is neither responsible nor ethical.

(4) Determining where and from whom data will be collected. Ford (1975) has pointed out that the intent of most sampling processes is to arrive at a "quantitative isomorph" of the population to which sample results are to be generalized. But in practice, she notes, the population is almost never possible to define or designate; one must then fall back on a "qualitative isomorph" as is achieved, for example, by snowball sampling. In this form of sampling one identifies, in whatever way one can, a few members of the phenomenal group one wishes to study. These members are used to identify others, and they in turn others. Unless the group is very large one soon comes to the point at which efforts to net additional members cannot be justified in terms of the additional outlay of energy and resources; this point may be thought of as a point of redundancy.

We have already reviewed (Chapter 8) a variety of purposive samples identified by Patton (1980): extreme or deviant cases, typical cases, maximum variation cases, critical cases, politically important or sensitive cases, and convenient cases; and concluded that for the naturalistic approach, maximum variation sampling is most useful. The sample is to be selected in ways that will provide the broadest range of information possible. Thus what is meant by a qualitative isomorph in this case is a qualitative *informational* isomorph, that is, a sample that is expanded until redundancy with respect to information is reached, at which point sampling is terminated. That sample may be large or small, but it is sufficient when the amount of new information provided per unit of added resource expenditure has reached the point of diminishing returns (that is, it would not be profitable to add even one more sample element).

Given this background, there are a number of considerations that must enter into planning a sample. They are identical regardless of what the sampled elements may happen to be, for example, whether they are field sites, individuals at field sites, documents, or any other sources of information. These considerations are as follows:

- *Providing for identification of initial elements.* Plans must be laid for identifying at least the initial elements of what will be the final sample. These initial elements can be nominated by gatekeepers, knowledgeable informants, or experts (the latter is most likely when the sample elements are not individuals but documents, sites, or other nonhuman ones). An initial design ought to discuss how the gatekeepers, experts, or informants will be identified and how the task will be presented to them (for example, asking experts to name sample characteristics likely to be important and then nominating sample elements that fit those characteristics).
- *Providing for orderly emergence of the sample.* This is best accomplished through the serial selection of elements, that is, no element is selected until all previous elements have been selected *and* tapped for information. Each successive element is chosen so as to complement the earlier units, in accord with the need to extend, test, or fill in earlier information.
- *Providing for the continuous refinement or focusing of the sample.* While, initially, any element is as good as any other, as the inquiry progresses and the problem (evaluand, policy option) becomes more finely tuned, successive sample elements may be selected in increasingly relevant ways. As the more salient aspects of the situation are identified and inquiry focuses more sharply on these, sample elements are chosen more and more to be in line with these aspects and less and less simply to be different from earlier elements.
- *Providing for termination.* As the sample unfolds, new information will become progressively scarcer, not only because the total pool of information is in any event limited, but also because the inquiry as a whole is achieving a sharper and sharper focus, thus rendering a good deal of information initially believed to be important relatively irrelevant. Some attention needs to be given to this task early on. It is likely that, in sharp contrast to the usual situation in conventional inquiry, sampling can be terminated after a rather small number of elements has been included; for example, in interviewing members of some particular group (respondents in research, or stakeholders in evaluation and policy

analysis), it is usual to find that a dozen or so interviews, if properly selected, will exhaust most available information; to include as many as twenty will surely reach well beyond the point of redundancy.

None of the above tasks can be developed fully—certainly not completed—prior to beginning the inquiry. Nevertheless, one might like to see, in a provisional plan, some discussion of each of these matters to illustrate that the investigator is aware of them, and has some plans for dealing with them.

(5) Determining successive phases of the inquiry. In contrast to the conventional inquirer, who usually approaches a study "knowing what is not known," the naturalist adopts the posture of "not knowing what is not known." Hence the study goes through several phases in order, first, to get some handle on what *is* salient (that is, what one needs to find out about); second, to find out about it; and third, to check the findings in accordance with trustworthiness procedures and gaining closure. These three phases may be described in more detail as follows.

Phase 1 might be termed the "orientation and overview" phase. While the investigator(s) may have gleaned a good deal of knowledge about a situation through the study of documents made available before a site visit (documents such as project proposals, progress reports, annual reports, newsletters, board minutes, and evaluation reports), the initial approach to respondents is made in a very open-ended way. Questions are largely of the "grand tour" type (Spradley, 1979), and seem to say to respondents, "Tell me what you think I ought to know about you (or this place, or your job, or this program, or your clients, and so on)." The object of this first phase is to obtain sufficient information to get some handle on what is important enough to follow up in detail. This phase may, depending on the nature and complexity of the focus (problem, evaluand, policy option) and the number of investigators involved (one, a team), may take from a few days to many months.

Phase 2 may be termed the phase of "focused exploration." Sufficient time must be allowed between Phases 1 and 2 for Phase 1 data to be analyzed (see below) and for more structured protocols (interview, observation) to be built accordingly. Then, during Phase 2, these protocols are used to obtain information in depth about those elements determined to be salient. The sample used as informants during this phase is selected as described in the preceding section but with one additional stipulation: They should be competent to deal with the areas of information identified as important in Phase 1.

Phase 3 may be termed the "member check" phase. Time must be allowed between Phases 2 and 3 to analyze the information from Phase 2 and to write (or otherwise develop) a report, most likely a case study. During Phase 3 the provisional report (case) is taken back to the site and subjected to the scrutiny of the persons who provided information (or counterpart persons). The task is to obtain confirmation that the report has captured the data as constructed by the informants, or to correct, amend, or extend it, that is, to establish the credibility of the case. After Phase 3, the report is cast into its final form.

Of course there are significant overlaps among these phases. First of all, as soon as even one interview has been obtained in Phase 1, or some other informational source has been tapped (say, an observation of a classroom), data analysis begins and some initial very provisional insights and hypotheses are formed. These can be pursued as subsequent informants or sources are tapped during Phase 1. During Phase 2, even though more structured approaches are being used, new informants or sources, that is, informants or sources that had not previously been tapped in Phase 1, are also provided the opportunity (best done at the beginning of the contact) to provide "stream of consciousness" inputs. The development of a report following Phase 2 may uncover certain informational gaps that can be filled during Phase 3, even though Phase 3 is not primarily an information-collection phase. The member checks characteristic of Phase 3 may also be made during the other phases, for example, by summarizing for each respondent the apparent content of an interview and soliciting agreement (including correction and expansion), or by checking information from one respondent with another.

During the initial planning period, while it is not possible for the naturalistic inquirer to specify what will be done during each phase (since that is always contingent on what has gone before), it is important to recognize the existence of these phases, to plan for them, and so far as possible to attach a provisional time line (determined more by practical considerations, such as funding period, than anything else).

(6) Determining instrumentation. The instrument of choice in naturalistic inquiry is the human, for reasons that have been reviewed in prior chapters. We shall see that other forms of instrumentation may be used in later phases of an inquiry, but the human is the initial and continuing mainstay.

It is most useful in all forms of inquiry, whether research, evaluation, or policy analysis, to organize the human instrumentation into teams. Even if the inquiry is of sufficiently small scope so that one person might conceivably carry it out, the advantages of using teams are so overwhelming that teams ought always to be used (perhaps excepting cases where resources simply cannot be stretched or reallocated over several part-time investigators). Teams have at least the following advantages (Guba & Lincoln, 1981):

- Teams can accommodate multiple roles, for example, formal functions such as data collection, data analysis, reporting, auditing, and the like; and also informal functions, such as "quarterback," "sociability expert" (the expert at gaining entrée), "bagman" (the grantsperson), and other similar roles (Douglas, 1976).
- Teams can represent a variety of value perspectives; it may even be possible to put together a team that, by virtue of prior experience, can appreciate if not share the values of significant stake-holding audiences, for example, a former teacher when groups of teachers are involved in the inquiry.
- Teams can represent multiple disciplines; so, for example, a team might include persons who had been trained in different fields such as education, psychology, and sociology.
- Teams can pursue multiple strategies; so, for example, if it emerges during an inquiry that it might be useful for a part of the team to engage in the cooperative paradigm while others engage in the conflict paradigm (Douglas, 1976), such a strategic redeployment is possible; it could under no circumstances be possible for a single investigator.
- Teams can reflect both substantive and methodological expertise, and, in the latter connection, specialized skills such as interviewing, observation, document analysis, and the like.
- Teams can be organized so as to provide for internal checks on rigor—mutual debriefings, triangulating concepts and insights developed by other team components, and even, on some occasions, carrying out parallel studies in order to provide a dependability (reliability) check.
- Teams can provide mutual support in the highly ambiguous and anxiety-producing context of the typical naturalistic study.

The initial design of the naturalistic inquiry should therefore devote some attention to the manner in which the inquiry team may be composed, given the particular contextual circumstances and study requirements, in order to accrue the above-listed benefits to an optimal degree (there will always be some trade-offs that will have to be made). The designer should also be aware of two problems and suggest some means for coping with them. These are, first, the need to provide for adequate coordination among team members (because the design is emergent, team members need to share insights and be kept up-to-date on design decisions virtually on a day-to-day basis), and, second, the need to arrange for defusing the inevitable conflicts that emerge when groups of persons work on an ambiguous problem in a team fashion. Awareness of the possibility is half the battle; arranging for mechanisms such as systematic team meetings to discharge feelings or outside reviews that provide external anchor points for team members is the other half.

Once team members have been selected and the inquiry is about to get under way, it is essential that some time be devoted to *training* the members who will serve in field roles to their tasks. Three activities can be pursued that will materially assist the members to carry out their assignments as instruments effectively and efficiently. First, the team needs to suffer a "crash course" in the culture and language of the field site. If no team member has had any experience in such a context, it may be useful to bring in an informant who can provide it vicariously. Second, the team members should practice their assignments under supervision, including such activities as role playing, post facto analysis of video- or audiotapes made during such practice sessions, and critique of such artifacts as field notes or document analyses. Finally, the team members may wish to extend their practice in more realistic ways with "surrogate" respondents—persons (or other sources) like those who will be tapped but not including sources from the actual sites that will be studied later. The initial planning for the naturalistic study should include some attention to how these prior training activities will be mounted; how, in effect, the human instruments will be trained to acceptable performance levels.

When the inquiry is actually under way, the human instruments may be improved in competence beyond their initial status. The kinds of activities carried out during the training period may now be extended to actual respondents and sources. Team members may review one another's field notes and interpretations, if possible, under the supervision of the team leader or some other team member or outside consultant designed to lead such in-service training. If video- or audiotapes of actual interviews or observations are available, these may also be reviewed, not only by the team member initially collecting them, but by all team members, who would find in such common stimulus materials the opportunity to check their own constructions in relation to those of the other members. While the press for standardization is not nearly as heavy in naturalistic inquiry as in conventional, it is nevertheless the case that checking one's own patterns of work leads to insights and improvements that might not otherwise emerge.

It is our firm conviction that if serious attention is paid to the human instrument, he or she can be as effectively improved as any other kind of instrument. No one expects a paper-and-pencil test to be perfect on its first draft; a great deal of pilot testing and screening may be necessary to find valid items, the length of the test may be increased to improve reliability, and so on. In like manner, the human instrument may be "rough" at first, but improvement is possible. As we noted in our earlier writing (Guba & Lincoln, 1981, p. 145):

> Makers of paper-and-pencil instruments may not intuitively see how the human instrument can be refashioned and refined. And yet they will readily admit that fine sopranos can, with good training, be transformed into breathtaking coloraturas; that persons who know relatively little about wine or painting or sculpture can, with practice, be turned into connoisseurs; and retraining can produce surprising results. We think that the same can happen with human beings as data collection instruments.

While it is our contention that the human instrument is perfectly adequate for *all* phases of a naturalistic inquiry, it may nevertheless be the case that other forms of instrumentation may also play a role. If we have seemingly railed against nonhuman instruments it is not because there is some inherent problem with their form or conception, but because they are typically not grounded. Thus there is no hope that such instruments can expose anything not built into them by the instrument maker, and what he or she puts in cannot be determined in any other way than on the basis of a priori theory or personal predilection. Such instruments simply cannot reflect the constructions of the respondents, but only of the instrument maker.

But if the human instrument has been used extensively in earlier stages of the inquiry, so that an instrument can be constructed that is grounded in the data that the human instrument has produced, then these objections disappear. There are many reasons such an instrument might have utility: to provide an easy way to obtain member checks from a fairly large sample of respondents (in which case the instrument is properly seen as an information-verifying rather than an information-generating device); to satisfy the needs of sponsors or clients for data from a "representative" group (remembering that most clients and sponsors will work from the conventional axioms and hence tend to find "purely naturalistic" findings noncredible); and to make possible a transformation of data from qualitative to quantitative formats, exposing them to the not inconsiderable advantage of statistical analysis and computer manipulation. Questionnaires, survey instruments, attitude tests, and all the usual armamentarium of instruments may be used, *provided* they are grounded.

The initial design of a naturalistic study should therefore attend to the following matters regarding determination of instrumentation:

- inquiry team composition
- initial training
- further training and refinement while the study is in progress
- conditions under which more "usual" types of instruments might be developed in later phases of the study given adequate grounding
- types of additional instruments that might usefully be developed, insofar as that can be foretold given the circumstances of an emergent design

(7) Planning data collection and recording modes. The human instrument operating in an indeterminate situation (not knowing what is not known) falls back on techniques such as interview, observation, unobtrusive measures, document and record analysis, and nonverbal cues. It is likely that the very first contacts with a site will involve interviewing; typically not enough will be known in advance to schedule observations, identify most useful documentary sources, and so on. And not enough will be known to formulate a structured interview protocol. Yet it is clear that most if not all of these techniques will be utilized sooner or later, and that all of these activities will become more and more structured as time passes. The initial design ought to display an awareness of these facts and to make provision for the kinds of data-collection activities that will likely occupy the team at different stages of the inquiry. All may initially interview (one or more may begin with document analysis should such be available prior to initial entry into the field), but later tasks will become more specialized, and it will be time to take advantage of the special skills that individual team members may possess.

Data recording modes will vary along two dimensions: fidelity and structure. By "fidelity" is meant the ability of the investigator later to reproduce exactly the data as they become evident to him or her in the field; clearly the greatest fidelity can be obtained using audio or video recordings (although one should not overlook the fact that these devices record only what the investigator chooses to record). Less fidelity is obtained through the use of field notes, but they have a number of advantages over high-fidelity recordings to warrant their use. First, they are simply not as threatening to a respondent as is a recording, the authenticity of which cannot later be denied. Second, the process of taking notes keeps the investigator alert and responsive. Third, field notes are not subject to the technical difficulties that beset recording, such as running out of tape at the crucial moment or having the batteries fail. Fourth, field notes provide ready access to the investigator who may wish to return to an earlier point and refresh both his or her own and the respondent's memory of what was said or seen; finding the right spot on the tape for this purpose is a difficult task. Finally, the use of field notes permits the investigator to record his or her own thoughts, whether an insight that has occurred that should be followed up or simply a comment on the disjunction between the respondent's verbal and nonverbal behavior. Indeed, the advantages of field notes over recordings seems to us so great that we do not recommend recording except for unusual reasons, as, for example, legal protection or the collection of materials for later use in in-service training exercises or for referential adequacy purposes (see Chapter 11).

Data recording varies in structure in direct proportion to the structure that it is possible to introduce into data-collection modes. Initially, since the situation is fraught with indeterminacy and questions must be very general (say, of the grand tour type), notes are not likely to be focused. Later, however, as interviews and observations become more structured, it is possible to construct more detailed and specific interview and observational protocols, which may require a good deal less writing and a good deal more checking off of prestructured responses.

The initial design for a naturalistic study should thus consider both the degree of fidelity and the degree of structure that will be useful and viable at each stage of the inquiry, and plan accordingly.

(8) Planning data analysis procedures. Not very much can be said about data analysis in advance of the study. It is clear that most analyses will be carried out in an open-ended way, following the steps to be outlined in Chapter 12, usually called the "constant comparative method" (Glaser & Strauss, 1967). Instruments developed during later portions of the study, as described in section 6 above, may have specific data analysis modes incorporated as an integral part, but since these instruments remain unknown at the outset, so must the analysis modes.

What is important to recognize is that data analysis is not an inclusive phase that can be marked out as occurring at some singular time during the inquiry (for instance, following data collection and preceding report writing). Data analysis must begin with the very first data collection, in order to facilitate the emergent design, grounding of theory, and emergent structure of later data collection phases. The design statement should indicate familiarity with this fact and should make provision for the convolution of data collection and analysis throughout all phases.

(9) Planning the logistics. The logistical considerations can be grouped conveniently, for a naturalistic study, into five categories: prior logistical considerations for the project as a whole; the logistics of field excursions *prior* to going into the field; the logistics of field excursions *while in* the field; the logistics of activities *following on* field excursions; and the logistics of closure and termination. We may consider each in turn.

(a) Prior logistical considerations for the project as a whole. The initial design statement should attend to several factors. First it needs to designate the *agents* who will implement the inquiry. Normally there will be multiple agents who will form an inquiry team. The nature of this team should be determined in light of such factors as the representation of a variety of disciplinary points of view, different inquiry skills, and the degree of acceptability of agents to respondents. The agents should clearly have the requisite professional and technical skills but also be acceptable as persons, for example, their integrity should be beyond question, and their values should not openly challenge or conflict with the values of respondents (one does not wear a three-piece suit to interview street-corner gang members). Proposed agents should be justifiable on all these counts.

Second, the design statement needs to deal with the problem of schedule. It is clear that specific events, and especially "milestone" events, cannot be foretold, but the realities of the world demand that some attention be paid to timing, for such reasons as undertaking or terminating contracts with personnel, adhering to the schedule that governs the phenomenon being investigated (for example, the school year), avoiding periods of peak activity to which respondents might be subject, and so on. Field contacts need to be arranged in advance, and busy people need to be met when and where it has been specified to do so. The design must at a minimum accommodate itself to the period designated for the study (the time at which funding will terminate, or the evaluation data will be needed to service a decision, or the policy analysis data will be needed to meet legislative calendars), and ought to specify the timing for at least the three major phases (orientation and overview, focused exploration, and member check).

The design statement should also display a recognition of significant time-related events (such as holidays) that will influence the study, and show how they will be taken into account.

Third, the design statement must deal with the budget. The most usual mode of budget projection is to cost out the activities that will be undertaken, aggregating those costs (within some time line) into a total. The emergent nature of the naturalistic design militates against such an approach. What can be specified, however, are the global categories of cost: the salaries and benefits of agents who will be involved, overhead costs on facilities and equipment, travel and maintenance costs of field activities, and the like. While these expenditures cannot be justified one to one against activities, they can at least be accounted for by reference to the overall phases and the level of expenditures that experience indicates usually occurs.

Fourth, the design statement should make some provision for an overseeing or policy board (which may at times be limited to the function of advice). Such a board serves a number of purposes: It projects a certain image and provides a certain level of legitimation for the study—a service not to be underestimated when the study is undertaken in the as-yet not quite legitimated naturalistic mode; it serves as a mechanism of critique—"keeping the inquirers honest"; and it is often a source of new ideas or perspectives that helps the study team see the woods as well as the trees. Special attention should be paid in the initial design statement to the question of what kinds of individuals could best serve these functions—and to propose a board composition accordingly. It should also be noted that the existence of a board made up of members of unquestionable integrity will also serve to build confidence in the credibility of the ultimate findings.

Fifth, the design statement should attend to the matter of arranging for peer debriefing (Chapter 11). We will see that peer debriefing is an effective way of shoring up credibility, providing methodological guidance, and serving as a cathartic outlet. But the peer debriefers ought to be persons of special characteristics; the design should reflect the fact that this problem was given serious attention and should propose particular persons—or kinds of persons—who could best discharge the reviewer responsibility.

Finally, the initial design statement should reflect arrangements for an external audit (Chapters 11 and 13). This most important step in providing evidence of dependability and confirmability must be well thought through, including the issue of whether to involve the auditor early in the study or only after it has been essentially completed. The requirements of the audit trial should be met, and the proposed design statement should lay out how this trial will be established and maintained. Particular persons—or kinds of persons—who can serve the audit function should be identified.

(b) The logistics of field excursions prior to going into the field. Again, a variety of considerations must be taken into account as plans are laid for an actual field excursion. The logistical needs can be estimated in the original design statement, but their full explication must await the period immediately preceding the actual excursion. First, a selection must be made from among the pool of available agents to carry out this particular excursion. It is probably useful to designate for each site that will be involved a team leader who will visit that site on each excursion, and other members who will rotate in order to provide multiple "eyes" for each site. The team leader should be that person who will ultimately draft the case report for that site. Second, arrangements must be made for travel to and at the site, and for housing while there. The logistics of air travel, including the problems attendant on finding the cheapest fares, can be complicated and sufficient time must be allowed to get that task accomplished. Budget can be seriously affected if wrong decisions are made. Third, a local liaison person must be identified who can handle local scheduling arrangements, including rearrangements that may be required by unforeseen contingencies—the sudden illness of a respondent, road closing because of bad weather, and so on. Finally, a field kit must be prepared that contains everything that the inquirers are likely to need in the field, ranging from local maps and lists of names, addresses, and phone numbers to mundane items such as 3 × 5 cards and rubber bands. Throughout this period close contact must be maintained with the liaison and other key locals to be certain that all arrangements are confirmed and consummated.

(c) The logistics of field excursions while in the field. While these logistics can be partially foreseen and attended to in the initial design statement, they are most likely to be arranged during the visit itself under the guidance of the team leader. Specifically, the leader will need, first, to provide for team interactions. Since methodological decisions will emerge as the inquiry progresses, and since later data collection activities are in part guided by what has already been unearthed, it is imperative that team members communicate on a regular and frequent basis so that all may be kept abreast of developments. Relatively informal communication can occur at meals: Assignments and activities for the day can be reviewed at breakfast; new insights can be shared at lunch, the happy hour, or dinner (the happy hour is especially important as a time for team members to engage in mutual support

and catharsis). More formal activities can be carried out in the evening, including some provisional and partial data analysis (unitizing and categorizing), discussions of current status, and projection of next steps.

The team leader will also need to monitor or stimulate certain other activities. These include arranging for adaptations to unforeseen circumstances or exploitation of unexpected informational opportunities (for example, discovering that a historical file exists that can shed light on how the phenomenon being studied evolved into its present form), making sure that team members keep their journals up-to-date (making journal entries each evening prior to the team interaction session also serves the purpose of preparing each participant to provide input to other team members), and carrying out and sharing preliminary data analyses, which focus later data collection steps. The team leader also has the responsibility for assembling all materials (those brought to the site as well as others collected during the excursion) for return to the home base.

(d) The logistics of activities following field excursions. Certain activities necessarily follow each excursion into the field, and time and resources must be allocated for their accomplishment. First, each team member will individually carry through the unitizing and categorizing steps outlined in Chapters 8 and 12, following which they will jointly aggregate and fold together the several category systems that have evolved. If one or more additional excursions are to occur, the team (including any replacement team members) will need to plan for them, including another round of previsit logistical planning as in b above, and development of more focused instrumentation, such as specific interview protocols. Peer debriefing typically takes place during this period, although, if the periods on site are lengthy (say, more than several weeks), such debriefing may also take place during the excursions. If formal debriefers have not been designated, team members who did not participate in the actual site visit may perform that function.

Following on one or more site visits, preliminary drafts of the report (most likely, a case study) must be developed that will be carried back during the final excursion for member checking. This activity, which is usually the responsibility of the team leader, may involve several months of intense effort (see Chapter 13) and require support from other team members and from clerical personnel (the draft may most usefully be prepared by word processor to make subsequent changes easy). Since this activity is likely to be very taxing, it is essential that provisions be made for the psychological support of the individual engaged in it. Frequent opportunities should be provided for the writer to test approaches and ideas on other site team members as well as other project staff, to reduce anxiety and provide reassurance that the writer is on the right track (or put him or her back on the right track if necessary). The writing of a case is, unfortunately, much more art than science, at least at this point in time. Most case study writers will not have adequate benchmarks against which to judge the quality of their work. It is important, therefore, that all personnel involved join to share the risks and shape the product.

(e) The logistics of closure and termination. A series of activities serves to close out the naturalistic inquiry. First, the draft of the case must be submitted to a review committee at the site for member checking for credibility. The review committee must be established, given adequate time to review the report, and provided instructions as to how to proceed. It is necessary to develop special consent forms so that the opinions expressed by members of this committee may later be referenced and, if necessary, quoted. Second, the team leader and one or more other project staff members proceed to the site, first, to convene and receive reactions from the review committee, and, second, to solicit information needed to fill in data gaps that have been discovered through the process of writing the case. Additional update information may be acquired about developments at the site since the time of the last field excursion, and decisions will have to be made whether to redraft portions of the case as required by the new data or simply to add an epilogue informing the reader but not attempting to do systematic revision; in that case the effective date of the case is the date of the last regular excursion. The field team returns to the home base with all reactions and added information in tow, and proceeds to cast the case into its final form. Decisions will have to be made at this point about how to handle dissenting opinions—whether to take them at face value, disregard them as biased, handle them via a "minority report," or accommodate them through adjustments and emendations.

When the case has reached this final stage, it is time to carry through the auditing procedures. Depending on earlier decisions, the auditor may have been involved all through the process, which provides the advantage of intimate familiarity but runs the risk of cooptation (as it might be perceived by an external audience). Or the auditor may become involved only at this final point, which has the advantage of high credibility but requires a fairly intensive orientation for the auditor, which may be expensive in terms of both team and auditor time. It is not unreasonable, however, to suggest that even a naive auditor might be able to discharge the audit functions even for a complex inquiry in a week to ten days.

Finally, arrangements must be made for the production and distribution of the inquiry reports—which may take the form of case studies, formal technical reports, or both. Naturalistic inquiries are likely to produce reports rather longer than those typically encountered (if for no other reason than the need to provide thick description), so that more time and materials are required than usual. It may also be desirable to extract from the longer report papers or other publication products; more than the usual amount of effort may be required because fitting this unusual inquiry form into formats typically required by journals and monograph or book publishers poses many difficulties.

We see, then, that a multitude of logistical considerations must be taken into account in designing the naturalistic study, and that only a few can be completely specified in the original design statement. But it is essential that such a statement at least display familiarity with the problems that can arise, and suggest how they may be dealt with when they do. And whatever else the design may say, it must make allowances for the time that will be required to handle the various logistical problems; a safe formula is to estimate the time and then triple it. Things always take much, much longer than they do.

(10) Planning for trustworthiness. Just as the conventional investigator must attend to the question of how internal and external validity, reliability, and objectivity will be provided for in the design, so must the naturalistic inquirer arrange for credibility, transferability, dependability, and confirmability. These counterpart terms were briefly defined in Chapter 8; techniques appropriate to each will be described in Chapter 11. The initial design statement must display a familiarity with their requirements, and must indicate the provisions that will be made to achieve them. Questions such as these must be addressed:

- How extensive will field contacts be in order to satisfy the requirement of prolonged engagement?
- How will the shift be managed from an open-ended "I don't know what I don't know" posture to a relatively more focused approach that can be characterized as persistent observation of salient elements?
- How will triangulation be incorporated? By sources? By methods? By multiple investigators?
- How will arrangements be made for peer debriefing? Who will serve as debriefers?

- What provisions will be made to carry out negative case analysis, to subject emerging hypotheses to continuous test and to refine them until they are fully explanatory of observed phenomena?
- What referential adequacy materials will be collected? How will they be achieved? When and by whom will they be utilized?
- How will member checks be provided for during a given field excursion? From one excursion to the next? In the final member check of the draft case study?
- How will thick description be provided for? What information will be collected that can later be synthesized into such a description?
- How will an audit trail be laid for a final dependability/confirmability audit? Who (or what kind of person) will be commissioned to do the audit?

The initial design statement should discuss each of these matters and propose some course of action, however provisional and subject to change, that is responsive to them. The techniques discussed in Chapter 11 may be incorporated as seems desirable.

SUMMARY

Designing a naturalistic study means something very different from the traditional notion of "design"—which as often as not meant the specification of a *statistical* design with its attendant field conditions and controls. Most of the requirements normally laid down for a design statement cannot be met by naturalists because the naturalistic inquiry is largely emergent. But while it may be impossible to provide specifics, it is clear that there are certain questions the naturalist must bear in mind and address, at least provisionally, from the earliest stages of conception and planning on: specifying a focus (research problem, evaluand, or policy option); determining the degree of fit between the focus as stated and inquiry paradigms that can be brought to bear on it; determining the fit between the selected inquiry paradigm and the substantive theory that will be employed; determining where and from whom data will be collected; determining the nature and scope of successive project phases (orientation and overview, focused exploration, and member check and closure); determining instrumentation; determining data analysis procedures; planning logistics (for the project as a whole, prior to an actual field excursion, during a field excursion, as follow-up to a field excursion, and for closure and termination); and planning for trustworthiness. Much can be said about the form if not the particulars of each of these activities.

The reader is again warned not to interpret the "steps" outlined in this chapter either as linear or immutable. Indeed, the focus of the naturalist should forever be on adaptation and accommodation. Review, recycling, and change must be central postures. The design, in the final analysis, does truly emerge; moreover, next steps are not merely added to past ones—often, the past steps must be retraced in new dress. There is continuous feedback and feedforward. The next four chapters will attempt to show how all that is done.

10

Implementing
the Naturalistic Inquiry

It is not enough to do good; one must do it the right way.
(John Viscount Morley)

SOME PRESUMPTIONS

It is useful to recall certain presumptions that undergird the implementation of a naturalistic inquiry. First, naturalistic inquiry is defined not at the level of *method* but at the level of *paradigm*. It is not crucial that naturalistic inquiry be carried out using qualitative methods exclusively, or at all (although mounting a naturalistic inquiry by purely quantitative means stretches the imagination). Conversely, it is quite possible to carry out a conventional inquiry using qualitative methods exclusively (although to do so would seem incredible to some). But the inquirer who does not adopt, however provisionally, the *axioms* of the naturalistic paradigm cannot be said to be *doing* naturalistic inquiry.

Second, the doing of naturalistic inquiry presumes, except under very unusual circumstances, heavy reliance on the human as instrument. We have made the point several times that the human instrument has certain special properties—chief among them being virtually infinite adaptability—that recommend the use of this form of instrumentation above all others (Chapter 8). It is also the case that human instruments can be developed and continuously refined. This chapter presumes that humans will be the major form of data collection device and that anyone committing him- or herself to this form of inquiry will have acquired, and will continue to hone, the skills needed in order to operate as an effective instrument.

Third, we shall presume that prior to implementation, the inquirer has made a serious effort to develop an initial design statement of the sort described in Chapter 9. The heavy emphasis that we have placed on the emergent nature of design should not be interpreted as a license to engage in undisciplined and haphazard "poking around." While it is certainly true that many elements of what will finally be seen as the "design" cannot be foretold (the future is in principle unpredictable), it does not follow that *nothing* can be foretold. The outline of Chapter 9 suggests those things to which the inquirer can and should attend before getting the study under way—a *springboard* that assures "getting off on the right track" and a *benchmark* against which later changes and developments can be assessed.

Finally, we shall presume that the inquirer has made every effort to become thoroughly acquainted with the field sites in which the study is to take place. Indeed, William Corsaro (1980) has strongly recommended the use of what he terms "prior ethnography": becoming a participant observer in a situation for a lengthy period of time before the study is actually undertaken. Such prior ethnography not only helps to diminish the obtrusiveness of the investigator but also provides a baseline of cultural accommodation and informational orientation that will be invaluable in increasing both the effectiveness and the efficiency of the formal work. It prepares the inquirer's mind for what will come later and so serves to sensitize and hone the human instrument. We may presume that had Margaret Mead engaged in such prior enthnography, she would not have been subject to many of the criticisms recently leveled against her work in Samoa by Derek Freeman (1983; see also Chapter 11). Of course, time and resources will not always permit prior ethnography, but its utility is so great that we recommend it to anyone seriously interested in doing naturalistic inquiry.

The importance of these presumptions cannot be overstated. Note that we are imposing three mandatory requirements and one optional (though highly desirable) requirement on anyone who wishes to label his or her work as naturalistic, in the sense of our definition of that term:

- That the inquirer adopt the stance suggested by the axioms of the naturalistic paradigm. These axioms form a synergistic set, and must be adopted as a set. Mix-and-match strategies are not allowed, nor are accommodations or compromises. We do not require the investigator to *commit* him- or herself to these axioms as a set of personal basic beliefs; we do require that the inquiry be carried out in ways that are consistent with them. (mandatory)

- That the inquirer commit him- or herself to the development of a level of skill appropriate to a human instrument and sufficiently high to ward off criticism on the grounds of instrumental inadequacy. (mandatory)
- That the inquirer devise an acceptable initial design statement that attends to those elements described in Chapter 9. (mandatory)
- That the inquirer engage in prior ethnography to provide both a springboard and a benchmark for the more formal study to follow. (optional, but highly desirable)

IMPLEMENTATION ELEMENTS
REQUIRING EARLY ATTENTION

Four items will require the naturalistic inquirer's early attention: making initial contact and gaining entrée to the site; negotiating consent; building and maintaining trust; and identifying and using informants. We consider each in turn (although note that in practice all four activities go on more or less simultaneously).

Making initial contact and gaining entrée. The tasks of contacting appropriate individuals at the inquiry site and of gaining entrée have both formal and informal aspects. These aspects may, moreover, take varying form depending on whether the inquiry is research, evaluation, or policy analysis. In the case of evaluation or policy analysis, the inquiry is *commissioned* by some person or body that has the authority to do so, that is, official gatekeepers such as the superintendent of schools, the director of a hospital, the board of trustees of a company, or a legislative body. The commission provides the inquirer with de facto access, but that fact does not ensure cooperation at other levels. Access provided by the school board, for example, by no means guarantees that the superintendent or other central office personnel, principals, teachers, parents, or other individuals or groups will automatically provide whatever the inquirer asks of them. Contact must also be made with unofficial gatekeepers, who, while perhaps lacking authority, may nevertheless be empowered by the influence they wield.

The researcher confronts a more difficult task, for an initial commission is nearly always lacking (although some applied research is sponsored by local authorities). Further, while evaluation and policy analysis are almost always carried out with respect to some particular organization or other well-defined group, research often is not; consider for example Spradley's (1979) work with skid row alcoholics, Douglas's (1976) study of nude beaches and massage parlors, and Humphreys's (1975) investigation of homosexual activity in public rest rooms. Clearly the problems of making contact and gaining entrée are multiplied many times in the research situation.

The keys to access are almost always in the hands of multiple gatekeepers, both formal and informal. In most cases those gatekeepers, before giving assent, will want to be informed about the inquiry in ways that will permit them to assess the costs and the risks that it will pose, both for themselves and for the groups to which they control access. In another context (Guba & Lincoln, 1981, pp. 295ff.) we have suggested that in the case of evaluation, two cost/risk principles are of paramount importance, and it is probably the case that these same principles also operate in the case of policy analysis and research. These principles are as follows:

- *Evaluation (or research or policy analysis) is almost always disruptive of the prevailing political balance.*
- *Evaluation (or research or policy analysis) is almost always dysfunctional to human performance.*

It seems only reasonable and fair that the inquirer should have decided to proceed with an inquiry only *after* having reached the judgment that the benefits accruing from doing an evaluation (or carrying out a research study or doing a policy analysis) will exceed the losses engendered by the political disruption and the personal dysfunctionality. The gatekeeper is interested in exactly those *same* considerations. Why should I (or we) sponsor your inquiry? What's in it for us? In what ways will you use the information that you will collect? How will you protect us against possible harm?

Typically, gatekeepers will seek to strike bargains with the investigator. The *quid pro quo* for each side must be spelled out. When the gatekeeper is in a formal position of authority, those bargains may be incorporated in a contract or a letter or agreement; informal gatekeepers may be content with *entre nous* understandings. But the inquirer must be quite clear that the latter are no less binding than the former, and that such understandings require scrupulous adherence if the investigator is to remain within the bounds of ethical practice.

It should be evident that the inquirer must deal with multiple gatekeepers, each time having to repeat the tasks of persuasion and striking a bargain. Of course, if the inquirer can point to agreements that have already been struck with the other formal or informal gatekeepers (not necessarily gatekeepers superordinate to the one currently being dealt with), the process will be expedited. But it is nevertheless the case that each gatekeeper will require (and deserves to have) his or her day in court, in order to reach an independent understanding.

Negotiating consent. Even though all of the relevant gatekeepers may have given their consent, ethical practice, whether in research, evaluation, or policy studies, demands fully informed consent from each of the respondents from whom (or about whom) data will be sought. There may be instances in which such consent is provided de facto, in that the respondent has previously given blanket consent to an organization or agency (a hospital, say, or a school records office) to make data available for legitimate inquiry purposes; in such cases a second approach by the inquirer *may* not be necessary. In most instances, however, fully informed consent must be obtained formally, attested by the respondent's signature on a form appropriate to the purpose.

The phrase "fully informed" means precisely that; insofar as the inquirer is able to predict the risks that may be involved, he or she is obliged to do so. Rationalizing that the respondent need not be informed ahead of time because he or she will be debriefed later may be a convenient fiction for the inquirer, but often such post facto debriefing may not be sufficient to undo the damage that has been done by an earlier deception. Moreover, since the design of a naturalistic study is emergent, so that it may not be possible to foretell all the risks involved when the respondent is first approached for consent, the respondent must have the option of withdrawing from the study at any later time without prejudice.

Inquirers should prepare a form in advance of any contact with a respondent, which, at a minimum, should contain the following information:

(1) The name, address, and telephone number of the person and/or agency seeking the consent. Sufficient information should be provided so that the respondent will be able to make an unambiguous identification and will know from whom and where he or she can seek recourse.

(2) A statement of the purpose of the inquiry, which, while necessarily brief, should be sufficient to convey to the respondent what his or her role will be and how information collected from him or her will be used.

(3) Specific information regarding consent and participation, as follows:

(a) Intent to maintain confidentiality and anonymity (unless that is specifically to be waived).
(b) Measures to be taken to prevent raw or processed data from being linked with a specific informant (as, for example, coding of all items, with the key to the code being maintained separately).

(c) Measures to be taken to limit access to the data, even in coded form, on a need-to-know basis.

(d) Notice that anonymity cannot be absolutely guaranteed since inquiry records have no privileged status under the law and can be subpoenaed should a case emerge (an unlikely outcome).

(e) Reservation by the respondent of the right to withdraw from the study at any time, without justifying that action, and of the right to have all data returned to him or her (following the principle that ownership of the data resides and continues to reside in the data provider).

(f) Specification of the particular steps that a respondent should take should he or she decide to wthdraw.

(g) Notice that participation is entirely voluntary unless the respondent has already agreed as part of a prior contract to participate in legitimate studies.

(4) A sign-off space for the participant in which he or she acknowledges having read and agreed to the previous stipulations as a condition of signing. A space for the date should also be provided.

It should be noted that agreeing to participate is not equivalent to agreeing to be quoted (with or without attribution). Quoting individuals exposes them to special risks because other locals may, because of their special knowledge, be able to identify the respondent even when attribution does not occur. If it is the intent of the investigator to quote respondents, the consent form should provide for a second sign-off in which such consent is specifically given, and in which it is stipulated whether that added consent applies with or without attribution.

A copy of the signed consent form should be provided to the respondent so that the conditions of agreement are continuously available to him or her.

The negotiation of consent is important in any inquiry for both legal and ethical reasons, but it is especially important when the inquiry is guided by the naturalistic paradigm. First, most contact in such a study will occur between a *human* instrument and the several respondents, a circumstance that makes it more likely that the respondent will feel threatened. It is much more difficult to relate intimate information to another human being than to a questionnaire, say. Second, because the human instrument is open-ended and adaptable, it may be the case that sensitive information not entirely relevant to the inquiry is revealed, leaving both respondent and inquirer in an ethical dilemma. Third, the results of a naturalistic inquiry are likely to be presented in case study form, in which individuals are not likely to be aggregated in a table with a large number of other anonymous respondents, but may be portrayed as individuals (even if not named). Other persons familiar with the site will find it relatively easy to ferret out the identity of any given respondent and to retaliate if they believe that they have been harmed by the respondent's testimony. Thus to the legal and moral reasons for seeking consent we may add the special sensitivity of the naturalistic approach.

Building and maintaining trust. It has always been recognized that building and maintaining trust is an important task for the field inquirer. While no one would argue that the existence of trust will automatically lead to credible data, the inverse seems indubitable. Respondents are much more likely to be both candid and forthcoming if they respect the inquirer and believe in his or her integrity.

Johnson (1975) has noted that in the conventional literature of sociology and anthropology, it is presumed that trust is, in effect, a kind of commodity for which one can barter. Once the inquirer has the trust of his or her informants, it is apparently believed, the study will proceed smoothly. Perhaps the only points of contention that existed in the classical literature, Johnson asserts, had to do with how trust is *achieved,* not with whether it can or cannot be continuously drawn upon once established. So, for example, he cites the *exchange theory* of trust, which asserts that trust results from a reciprocal exchange between inquirer and respondent (giving and receiving a *quid pro quo*); an *individual-morality* theory of trust, which asserts that trust depends upon building up a "good guy" image; the *adoption-of-a-membership* theory, which asserts that trust accrues to persons willing to commit themselves to the behavioral mores of the group; and the *psychological-need* theory, which asserts that trust is built only in those cases in which the respondents can see the inquiry as fulfilling some personal need.

Johnson suggests that each of these theories has a certain ring of plausibility, but none of them views the establishment of trust as a *developmental task* that must begin at the very first contact and continue unabated throughout the term of the inquiry. Thus, he concludes:

> The relationship of trust is a *developmental process* to some extent biographically *specific* in nature. . . . It no longer seems plausible to think in terms of developing trust as a specifiable set of procedural operations. Rather, two or more persons engaged in a common course of social action may develop a sense of trust between them. It is a reality necessarily fluid and changing, always subject to reinterpretation. (Johnson, 1975, p. 94; emphasis in original)

The development of trust, then, is something to which the naturalistic inquirer must attend from the very inception of the inquiry. In a very real sense the ultimate credibility of the outcomes depends upon the extent to which trust has been established. But trust is *biographically specific,* that is, it is a relationship existing between two persons on a one-to-one basis; thus the naturalistic inquirer will have to attend to the development of trust with *each* respondent. Further, the building of trust is a *developmental task;* trust is not something that suddenly appears after certain matters have been accomplished ("a specifiable set of procedural operations"), but something to be worked on day to day. Moreover, trust is not established once and for all; it is fragile, and even trust that has been a long time building can be destroyed overnight in the face of an ill-advised action. The question, "What have you done for me lately?" is one that the naturalist should constantly keep in mind, for it will certainly be in the forefront of the respondents' thinking.

Despite the inquirer's best efforts to build trust, some respondents will not be freely forthcoming. While they may for reasons of their own agree to participate, they will do so only reluctantly. Under such circumstances the inquirer may be well advised to adopt what Douglas (1976) has termed the "conflict" or "investigative" paradigm (a use of the term "paradigm" that should not be confused with its use elsewhere in this volume). He notes:

> The investigative paradigm is based on the assumption that profound conflicts of interest, values, feelings and actions pervade social life. It is taken for granted that many of the people one deals with, perhaps all people to some extent, have good reason to hide from others what they are doing and even lie to them. Instead of trusting people and expecting trust in return, one suspects others and expects others to suspect him. Conflict is the reality of life; suspicion is the guiding principle. (Douglas, 1976, p. 55)

While this statement is perhaps more dramatic than need be, it does have a ring of truth to it, as most experienced fieldworkers can attest. If there is reason to believe that the conditions described by Douglas exist, one may wish to utilize some of the techniques outlined elsewhere in his book. Other useful techniques are described by Guba (1981b), who has drawn on the field of investigative journalism as a metaphor for evaluation. In particular, the techniques of tracking, the key interview, and circling, shuffling, and filling described by him may have special applicability.

Identifying and using informants. The naturalist can short-circuit many of the problems posed by gatekeepers, social and cultural differences, and trust building through the selective use of informants. The reader should note that the term is "inform*ant,*" not "inform*er*"; informers should be devoutly avoided because they will almost certainly have an axe to grind that does not mesh with the naturalist's purposes and/or that falls outside the pale of ethical inquiry. As a result the information they provide will likely be distorted, and could even be deliberate misinformation. The informer who seeks personal revenge for some real or imagined wrong, the marginal man who is a misfit or outcast, the nonconformist who, precisely because of his or her tendency to nonconformity, is not likely to be able to project an appropriate image of the local scene, may all do more harm than good.

Nevertheless, informants can be useful and should be cultivated. The useful informant is one who is a legitimate, committed, and accepted member within the local context, but who is, at the same time, willing to act as a member of the inquiry team, even if only informally. By virtue of their positions within the context, such informants can provide the inquiry team with an "inside" view of the norms, attitudes, constructions, processes, and culture that characterize the local setting. Such information is especially useful to the inquirer who has not been able to practice prior ethnography, but who needs to be immersed in the local context as thoroughly and quickly as possible.

The identification of persons able and willing to act as informants is not a straightforward task that can be laid out in stepwise fashion. In some cases informants will volunteer; then the inquirer is well advised, first, to investigate thoroughly their motives for volunteering, and, second, to test information supplied by them until satisfied that it is reliable (in the commonsense meaning of that term). In other cases the inquirer will identify potential informants while carrying out inquiry activities. So, for example, an unusually insightful and forthcoming interview respondent may be recruited. In still other cases local gatekeepers may be willing to identify someone able to act in such a role (and, by identifying him or her, legitimate their own cooperation). Then the inquirer must first satisfy him- or herself that the informant is not a "double agent," serving primarily the gatekeeper's agenda.

Yet again, informants identified and recruited early in the inquiry may assist in the recruitment of others. The identification of informants is thus largely opportunistic; the inquirer must be constantly on the alert for such opportunities and must be prepared to exploit them when they do occur.

UNFOLDING THE DESIGN

The reader should note that the heading for this section does *not* read, "Operationalizing the Design," as it might if we were describing conventional inquiry. For in that case, the design is a blueprint that must be followed more or less literally. For the naturalist, however, the term "design" designates nothing more than a broad plan relating to certain contingencies that will probably arise, but the precise nature of those contingencies is unpredictable. It is anticipated that the design will change as those contingencies are realized (that is, made real or constructed by the inquirer interacting with the circumstances that have evolved). Moreover, subsequently realized contingencies may suggest, or even mandate, that earlier steps be recapitulated. The final appearance of an inquiry is thus shaped by a large number of interactions (including feedback and feedforward) unfolding over time.

In Chapter 9 we described a number of elements that should be considered in developing an initial (and open-ended) design statement. A consideration of "unfolding the design" may usefully be based on those same elements.

Determining a focus for the inquiry. An initial definition of a focus (problem, evaluand, policy option) will have been offered in the original design statement. But it is anticipated that the initial focus will change. How can those changes be monitored (as they may be shaped by contextual circumstances) or documented (as they may be introduced by specific actions of the inquirer)?

We noted in Chapter 9 that changes occur because of interactions with contextual circumstances. The research problem may change because it is found, once in the field, that things are not as they were imagined to be. The evaluand may change because of local adaptations or personal predilections of agents. The policy option may change because the policy-in-implementation turns out to be somewhat different than the policy-in-intention. It is essential that the inquirer stay abreast of such changes and note why they occur (but not in simple linear causality terms). Several techniques are helpful toward this end.

First, the inquirer should establish a schedule for regular monitoring that will disclose shifts as they occur. Second, the inquirer may wish to arrange for exception reports—reports from agents or informants that call attention to shifts from normal, prescribed, or expected activity. Third, the inquirer may wish to include checks on the focus as part of the normal member-checking process, carried out both during and at the end of the inquiry period (see Chapters 11 and 13). The changes that are documented should be included as part of the final report—usually a case study (Chapter 13).

Changes may also occur because of deliberate actions on the part of the inquirer. As salient elements in a context are identified through prolonged engagement, relevance criteria are altered; some things considered important initially are now set aside, and some new things are taken up. Only those elements considered more salient are now pursued. That pursuit in turn may lead to the inclusion of new classes of respondents, who, because of the particular constructions that they can bring to bear, further alter the focus. All such considerations may in turn produce a shift in the methodologies employed. The inquirer can document such changes, first, by testing them with one or more peer debriefers (Chapter 11), who may provide summaries of the debriefing sessions for the record, and by making entries in a methodological journal (see below) that becomes part of the documentation or audit trial for the project.

Thus inquiry foci are expected to change, and the naturalist documents those changes in the methodological journals and other records kept for the project.

Determining the fit of the paradigm to the focus. The issue of fit will have been addressed in the initial design statement. We saw in Chapter 9 that to make that determination, the inquirer would assess the focus (problem, evaluand, policy option) in terms of its relation to the naturalistic axioms, as well as to some other considerations, such as the degree of cooperation that might be expected from respondents, and the constraints that might be placed on the inquirer by respondents or sponsors. We have tried to make the case throughout this book that for virtually all instances of sociobehavioral inquiry, the naturalistic paradigm is the paradigm of choice; thus we would expect that there would be little difficulty in making the "fit" assessment at the outset and little need to reassess or change later. Nevertheless, it may be useful for the inquirer actively to consider the possibility, especially should it be the case that because of imposed constraints, he or she was initially forced to work within the conventional paradigm. A brief glance at most RFPs issued by government agencies and other funders will quickly convince the skeptic that this circumstance is not at all unusual. In such cases the inquirer may wish to provide informal reports on emergent findings in an effort to persuade the constraining groups to alter their positions.

Determining the fit of the inquiry paradigm to the substantive theory selected. Naturalists will not find this assessment much of a problem, because they will typically either ground the theory in the site data themselves or utilize a theory that has been previously grounded in a similar site. If some other a priori theory is used (a practice frowned upon by naturalists), an initial assessment of fit will have been made when the initial design statement was developed. In all cases it seems unlikely that at some later time in the inquiry it will be determined that the degree of fit is no longer close enough to warrant continuing. Nevertheless, the inquirer ought to keep this possibility in mind and be prepared to confront the eventuality in those few instances in which it may occur.

Determining where and from whom data will be collected. Essentially this step in unfolding the design is concerned with sampling— but in the purposive sense defined in Chapters 8 and 9. Of course it is essential that the inquiry focus be provisionally defined, in order to have some sense of where an appropriate sample might be located. Assuming that such is the case, the naturalistic inquirer will then simply recap steps nominally laid out in the initial design.

As a first concern, the inquirer will need to identify some *types* of sites likely to yield the information that the focus calls for. There are typically two sources helpful to the inquirer in this identification: the existing literature and experienced and knowledgeable experts. It is important to remember that the literature is very likely to reflect only conventional inquiry, and that the experts may themselves take a traditional view; the naturalist must avoid being trapped into thinking in the same conventional terms.

As an instance of how types of sites might be identified, we may consider the experience of the Special Education in Rural America (SERA) project recently completed at the University of Kansas under the sponsorship of the National Institute of Education (Skrtic, Guba, & Knowlton, 1985). The project was aimed at studying services delivered to handicapped youngsters in the context of Public Law 94-142 (the Education for All Handicapped Children Act) in rural areas of the United States. At the outset, members of the project staff review-ed the available literature on such services, and a wide variety of variables was found to have been included. A preliminary list of these variables was drawn up for presentation to the project's national ad-visory board; the list contained items such as the degree of ruralness (as defined by a variety of geographic and demographic indicators); degree of similarity between covering state legislation and the federal law; the structure and history of existing organizations for service delivery in these areas; and state legislation defining mandatory and permissive service delivery organizations and activities. The advisory panel considered this list but did not find it especially useful in designating criteria for site selection, although it did fuel a great deal of discussion.

The expertise of the panel was itself utilized in a different way. It was known from the preliminary design statement that a major prod-uct of the study was to be a series of case studies, one for each of the sites that might finally be included. In the spirit of naturalistic in-quiry, no effort was to be made to generalize across all sites; rather, it was hoped that readers who wanted to apply findings in their own contexts might look for the cases that were most similar to their own situations. The issue was to determine the characteristics on which similarity might most usefully be judged. In an effort to deal with that question, the members of the panel agreed to carry out two mental exercises. First, each would imagine that he or she was the director or chief administrator of a service delivery unit that was in principle similar to those the project had undertaken to study. Further, each would imagine that he or she had in hand completed case studies for each of the sites. The question to be posed was this: On the basis of what information would they decide which of the case studies to read, as probably being most relevant to them? The second exercise required the panelists to shift roles; they were now to imagine that they were some other possible consumer of the reports, for example, a local school superintendent whose district was served by a service delivery unit, a psychologist working within such a unit, an itinerant teacher, or some other similarly related role. Again, on what basis might one select a case as most relevant?

Each of the national panel members completed these tasks in-dependently and submitted his or her (nonuniform) statement to the project staff. The staff studied these inputs, as well as the original list of factors that had emerged from the literature review. They also took into account practical factors relating to the study as it had been funded. As a result, eight global criteria were finally identified as most salient:

(1) The geographic section of the country. It seems clear that readers would not identify well with a case drawn from some very different section of the country. Moreover, national politics demanded that, since the study was funded at the federal level, the study draw from as many different constituencies as possible.

(2) The type of service agency provided under state law. These types were at least threefold: a decentralized state department of education, a specially created intermediate district, or a locally formed and controlled cross-district cooperative.

(3) The legal/fiscal structure provided by state law and practice. Control could be tight or loose; cooperation could be mandated or made permissive; service agencies could be well funded or poorly funded.

(4) Access to the state. Formal gatekeepers in a state, such as the state superintendent of public instruction or the state director of special education, and state-level influentials, such as the director of the state teachers association or an opinion-leading superintendent of schools, could effectively act to open or close the state to any inquiry.

(5) The "ruralness" of the area being served. Ruralness is almost impossible to define in any consistent way; nevertheless, it seemed clear that the study had to be confined to areas that, on the basis of population sparcity, isolation, and size, could qualify in most people's minds as "rural."

(6) Demographics of the service unit. Such features as wealth, ethnic characteristics, sophistication of the local population, and types of occupation (agricultural pursuits) seemed important to take into account.

(7) Funding of the service unit. Both the amount of funding and the channels by which it found its way to the service agency (direct allocation by the state of P. L. 94-142 "flow-through" funds, local appropriations, local tuition, additional taxing authority, and the like) were important.

(8) Access to the service agency and to the local school districts it served. Again, gatekeepers had to be taken into account.

Several comments are in order about this list. First, several of these criteria—specifically, the two access items (state and local) and the national geographic distribution—are essentially screens through which any site candidates needed to be passed. Having already selected a site in the southeast part of the country, for example, effectively precluded adding another in that area. Any site to which it seemed likely that state- or local-level gatekeepers might block access were effectively dismissed. Second, in several cases the criteria could not be well defined operationally; one had to depend on a holistic and tacit "feel" for what they meant. Thus one cannot define ruralness with exactness or service unit demographics with precision; yet a person familiar with a particular site might comment quite intelligently and meaningfully on that site's ruralness and demography. Finally, there is no systematic way in which this list could be used to *generate* the sites that should be included. It is impossible to obtain the information needed to classify all possible sites on these criteria if only on logistical grounds (overlooking the fact that some cannot be defined accurately in any event). Virtually all these criteria are relative; for example, one cannot simply classify sites as either accessible or nonaccessible, rural or nonrural. Thus meanings shade infinitely into one another so that there are no clear representational types (as the conventional paradigm would have us seek). Judgment calls are necessarily involved.

The project staff turned once more to its national panel, as well as to other nationally knowledgeable "experts," to make those calls. When the list had been more or less established, lengthy telephone conversations were held with a large number of informants, in which they were acquainted with the intended selection criteria and asked to nominate sites that they believed fit the criteria in one or another pattern. Very often these informants would begin by naming "interesting" sites, which they would then describe in terms of the selection factors. As a result of these telephone conversations, upwards of forty sites were nominated that could be considered.

The conventional approach at this point might have involved classifying each of the nominees in some way on the eight selection criteria, and then selecting from among them in some representational way so as to match every level of each factor with every level of the others. But such an approach would generate a number of categories well in excess of the number of nominated sites (even a dichotomous characterization of each factor would lead to $2^8 = 256$ possibilities). Moreover, the staff appreciated the fact that these selection factors were just those that seemed important on a priori grounds; once the study was under way, it might well be the case that other factors of even greater apparent importance would emerge. Hence no effort was made to identify the entire sample of sites at once; rather, an initial site was selected from among the nominees purely on the grounds of convenience: one close to the project's headquarters, so that repeated visits could be made while techniques were being perfected, and the project budget could afford to have *all* project staff visit this site at least once in order to gain a common experience for training and further development.

Once this site had been selected, contact was made and entrée arranged as outlined above. Initial interview respondents were selected from personnel rosters and on the basis of nominations by gatekeepers. Once the team was on site, additional respondents were identified by "ripple" or "snowball" techniques. It happens that for this project, site visits were artifically limited to three days each; in more usual circumstances, information would be collected until one or more of the following conditions obtained: exhaustion of sources, emergence of saturation as demonstrated by redundancy, emergence of regularities in the data (a "feeling of integration"), and overextension (excessive dross, a "feeling of irrelevance") (Guba, 1978).

Finally, once a site had been selected and at least some data collected from it, then and only then was it reasonable to select a second site. To satisfy the purpose (as defined by Patton, 1980) of maximum variation sampling, the second site was selected to be as different as possible from the first, not only on those a priori criteria used to set up a pool of nominees, but on others that emerged from the first site and that had now taken on importance. Successive sites were serially selected in similar fashion.

It should again be stressed that sites were *not* selected as representative of some population. They were selected to be maximally contrastive and thereby to provide as much *different* information as possible. In contrast, when the aim of inquiry is generalization, attention will be given to *similarities* across sites. The case of SERA demonstrates the difficulty that would be encountered if one wished to define a "population" of rural special education service delivery agencies from which a "representative" sample could be drawn that could then be studied for the sake of arriving at generalizations. Such a population could be defined only in the most arbitrary way. Further, drawing a representative sample would be logistically impossible even if one thought it desirable. And it seems clear that the several sites were characterized much more by their differences than their similarities; genuine understanding can come only from seeing each case in its own context.

Determining successive phases of the inquiry. It was suggested in Chapter 9 that naturalistic inquiries may conveniently be divided into three phases: orientation and overview, focused exploration, and member checks and closure. The intent of these phases is clear: the first, to provide, through prolonged engagement and open-ended approaches ("I don't know what I don't know"), some sense of what the context and situations are like, and to get a fix on what is most salient; the second, to provide, through persistent observation and more focused approaches ("I know what I don't know"), in-depth information about those salient elements (as well as to continue unearthing new saliencies); and the third, to provide an opportunity for local verification of the credibility of the study both overall and in respect to particulars.

In the case of the SERA project, these three phases were formalized in three successive sites visits; the first two were several months apart to allow for intervening data analysis, and about six months elapsed between visits 2 and 3 to allow for the writing of a case study draft (which would serve as the basis for the member check). In the more usual situation, these phases may shade into one another, with considerable recycling and reiteration. The concept of phases is intended less to demarcate different time periods than different *intents*; the inquirer moves from one to the next when he or she feels "ready" to do so. In situations in which the inquirer will be at a site for a fairly long and continuous period, the shift from one phase to another may not be formally noted, except perhaps in a debriefing interview or in a methodological journal. Nevertheless, the naturalistic inquirer ought to give active thought to the transition.

The move from the first to the second phase parallels the distinction that is often made in conventional inquiry between the so-called contexts of discovery and of verification. We have noted that conventional inquirers tend to define inquiry in such a way that only activities relating to justification are admitted to the domain of "science." But it should be clear that within the naturalist paradigm *both* domains are eligible for inclusion as *disciplined* inquiry (if not science, redefined). Without the first, the second would be impossible. The naturalist approach also makes it clear that the discovery phase need not be simply a flight of fancy or a creative imagining; what is taken to be salient depends upon intensive fieldwork that is, in its way, as disciplined as any verification effort.

Using human instrumentation. While more conventional paper-and-pencil or brass instrumentation may be used in naturalistic inquiry (particularly in later phases, once a theory has been grounded), the preponderantly used instrument is the human being. The initial design statement will have considered the qualifications and training needed to carry out this function; during the implementation phase these earlier considerations will be put into effect.

Collecting and recording data. This aspect of naturalistic inquiry will be discussed at considerable length in the following section of this chapter. Suffice it to say at this point that it is during the period of data collection and recording (together with initial data analysis) that most design changes will emerge, leading to recycling or extensions of previous steps. The naturalistic inquirer must be especially careful, therefore, to pay attention to what is emerging from the process. Unlike conventional inquirers, who can be passive during this phase (it is only when all the data are finally in that analysis begins), naturalistic inquirers are particularly active and responsive.

Doing data analysis. So complex is this topic that an entire chapter (Chapter 12) will be devoted to it.

Planning the logistics. The treatment in Chapter 9 relating to logistical considerations to be taken into account in the initial design statement calls attention to most of the matters of importance that will need to be considered. Indeed, logistics is one of the few elements that can be foretold with some accuracy in a naturalistic study, although even here the details may vary as phases are short-circuited, extended, or totally rearranged. Nevertheless, any reasonably prudent management procedure is probably adequate to handle this matter, which requires no special elaboration here.

Planning for trustworthiness. Dealing with trustworthiness is a matter of such importance that it is dealt with in a separate chapter. Naturalistic inquiry seems to be especially assailable on the grounds of being "sloppy" or "loosey-goosey," and it is imperative that inquirers working from this paradigm take measures while in the field to increase the probability of a judgment of trustworthiness as well as to test it directly. The theory and means for doing so are examined in Chapter 11.

DATA COLLECTION TECHNIQUES

While it is the case that the major and sometimes only data collection instrument utilized in naturalistic inquiry is the inquirer him- or herself, the *sources* that instrument utilizes may be both human and nonhuman. Human sources are tapped by interviews and observations, and by noting nonverbal cues that are transmitted while those interviews or observations are under way. Nonhuman sources include documents and records, as well as the unobtrusive informational residue (conventionally called unobtrusive "measures") left behind by humans in their everyday activities that provides useful insights about them.

In a previous volume (Guba & Lincoln, 1981), we have discussed these techniques in some detail; it may, however, be useful to summarize the most salient points here, as well as to add a few new comments.

Data Collection from Human Sources

Interviewing. An interview, as Dexter (1970) has suggested, is a conversation with a purpose. The purposes for doing an interview include, among others, obtaining *here-and-now constructions* of persons, events, activities, organizations, feelings, motivations, claims, concerns, and other entities; *reconstructions* of such entities as experienced in the past; *projections* of such entities as they are expected to be experienced in the future; verification, emendation, and extension of information (constructions, reconstructions, or projections) obtained from other sources, human and nonhuman (*triangulation*); and verification, emendation, and extension of constructions developed by the inquirer (*member checking*). Interviews can be categorized further by their degree of *structure,* their *degree of overtness,* and the *quality of the relationship* between interviewer and respondent.

The degree of structure may be categorized (for all practical purposes) as either structured or unstructured. The former type is often referred to as a "focused" interview, and the latter as a "depth," "clinical," "elite," "specialized," or "exploratory" interview. As we comment in *Effective Evaluation:*

> In the structured interview, the problem is defined by the researcher before the interview. The questions have been formulated ahead of time, and the respondent is expected to answer in terms of the interviewer's framework and definition of the problem. The unstructured or specialized interview varies considerably from this mode. In an unstructured interview, the format is non-standardized, and the interviewer does not seek normative responses. Rather, the problem of interest is expected to arise from the respondent's reaction to the broad issue raised by the inquirer. As Dexter (1970, p. 3) defines this form of interviewing, it involves: stressing the interviewee's definition of the situation; encouraging the interviewee to structure the account of the situation; and letting the interviewee introduce to a considerable extent his notions of what he regards as relevant, instead of relying upon the investigator's notion of relevance. Thus, unlike a structured, focused, or standardized interview, the unstructured or "elite" inter-

view is concerned with the unique, the idiosyncratic, and the wholly individual viewpoint. (Guba & Lincoln, 1981, pp. 155-156)

To put it another way, the structured interview is the mode of choice when the interviewer *knows what he or she does not know* and can therefore frame appropriate questions to find it out, while the unstructured interview is the mode of choice when the interviewer *does not know what he or she doesn't know* and must therefore rely on the respondent to tell him or her. In the structured interview the questions are in the hands of the interviewer and the response rests with the interviewee; in the unstructured interview *both* questions and answers are provided by the respondent ("Tell me the questions I ought to be asking and then answer them for me").

The degree of overtness/covertness ranges along a continuum, at one end of which the respondent is completely unaware that he or she is being interviewed (whether structured or unstructured) and at the other end of which the respondent is fully and completely informed not only of the fact that an interview is taking place but of the purpose of that interview and how the resulting information will be used. Ethical practice requires that the interview by fully overt; if covertness seems to be required in order to ensure "honest" or "nonreactive" responses, other ways should be found to obtain the needed information, or the search for that information should be abandoned altogether.

The quality of the relationship between the interviewer and respondent can be characterized in several ways. Massarik (1981), for example, provides a typology that includes the *hostile* interview (the interviewer is the "enemy" and the relationship is "combat"); the *limited survey* interview (the interviewer is an "automaton," that is, simply a data recorder with whom the respondent has no human interaction; that is often the situation in structured interviews, particularly if the items are relatively closed-ended); the *rapport* interview (the interviewer is "a human-being-in-a-role"); the *asymmetrical-trust* interview (the interviewer is a "sage" and the respondent is a "petitioner"); the *depth* interview (interviewer and respondent are "peers"); and the *phenomenal* interview (both interviewer and respondent are "caring companions" with a commitment to "empathic search").

The interview as utilized in naturalistic inquiry may serve any of the purposes listed above; it is usually unstructured, although at later stages of the inquiry (particularly for triangulation or member-checking purposes) more structured forms may be found; it is almost always fully overt and rarely drifts far from that standard for ethical reasons;

and it is usually a depth interview (in Massarik's sense) in that interviewer and respondent may view one another as peers.

Carrying out an interview involves certain steps that, while not necessarily to be followed in linear fashion, nevertheless must be accounted for at some point in the process—and often more than once as recycling and reiteration occur:

(1) Deciding on whom to interview. This step is accomplished through the activities noted earlier in this chapter under the heading "Determining where and from whom data will be collected." The material on negotiating fully informed consent and on identifying and using informants is also relevant to this task.

(2) Preparing for the interview. This step involves doing one's homework in relation to the respondent (the more elite the respondent, in the sense of that term as used by Dexter, 1970, the more important it is that the interviewer be as fully informed about the respondent as possible); practicing the interview with an appropriate role "stand-in"; deciding on an appropriate sequence of questions (even when the interview is unstructured; see below); and deciding on the interviewer's own role, dress, level of formality, and the like. Confirmation with the respondent of the time and place of the interview is also wise.

(3) Initial moves. Although the respondent has undoubtedly been briefed with respect to the nature and purpose of the interview as part of the informed consent procedure, it is wise to recall these details at the outset. The respondent should be given an opportunity to "warm up" by being asked some "grand tour" questions (Spradley, 1979; for example, "What's a typical day like around here?" "How did you happen to get into this line of work?") that give the respondent practice in talking to the interviewer in a relaxed atmosphere while at the same time providing valuable information about how the respondent construes the general characteristics of the context. The respondent can also be given an opportunity to "organize his or her head" by being asked other general questions leading up to the matters that the interviewer wants discussed in detail later.

(4) Pacing the interview and keeping it productive. Questions become more and more specific as the interview moves along and as the interviewer begins to sense what is salient about the information this respondent can provide. It is important to keep an easy rhythm and, as much as possible, to keep the "talk turn" with the respondent (the interviewer rarely learns anything when he or she is talking). Maintenance of flexibility so that the interviewer can follow up promising leads or

return to earlier points that seem to require fuller development is essential. The skilled interviewer is adept in the use of probes—directed cues for more or extended information. Probes may take the form of silence (respondents abhor an auditory vacuum, but it must be clear that the "talk turn" is with the respondent); "pumps"—sounds such as "uh-huh" or "umm" or encouraging waves of the hand; simple calls for more ("Could you tell me more about that?"); calls for examples; calls for reactions to the interviewer's reformulations of what was said ("Do I understand you to say that . . ."; or "If I understand you correctly, you seem to be saying that . . ."), or simply questions specifically formulated by the interviewer to embellish or extend something the respondent has said.

(5) Terminating the interview and gaining closure. When the interview has ceased to be productive (the information is redundant; both interviewer and respondent display fatigue; the response seems to be guarded; and the like) it is time to terminate. At this point the interviewer should summarize and "play back" for the respondent what he or she believes has been said ("I believe the major points you have made are X, Y, and Z; does that sound right to you?"). This process has several advantages for the interviewer. First, it invites the respondent to react to—member check—the validity of the constructions the interviewer had made. Second, it often induces the respondent to add new materials of which he or she is reminded on hearing the summary. Finally, it puts the respondent on record, so he or she is less likely to deny the information later (of course absolute denials are impossible if statements have been recorded and if the informed consent form has provided for quotation; the only out then is for the respondent to exercise his or her rights of withdrawal).

Courtesy demands that the interviewer thank the respondent for his or her cooperation. The interviewer may also wish to provide additional opportunities for communication "should anything else of interest occur to the respondent," and may in fact arrange for additional interviews if it is clear that there is more ground to be covered. As a final courtesy the interviewer should follow up with a formal letter of thanks, particularly if the respondent is an "elite" subject in Dexter's (1970) sense.

Data derived from an interview can be recorded in any of several ways. Most obviously, a tape recorder can be utilized, a mode that has many advantages, such as providing an unimpeachable data source; assuring completeness; providing the opportunity to review as often as necessary to assure that full understanding has been achieved; providing the opportunity for later review for nonverbal cues such as significant pauses, raised voices, or emotional outbursts; and providing material for joint interviewer training and reliability checks. But these impressive advantages are, in our judgment, more than offset by respondent distrust (the fact that the recording does provide an accurate and unimpeachable record is often more than sufficient to constrain open and candid responses). Nor should one overlook the possibility of mechanical failure, an all too common occurrence as tape runs out or batteries discharge.

If data are not tape-recorded, one must fall back on handwritten notes taken during the interview itself. Taking notes can be disadvantageous: One cannot record everything; rapid handwriting is often later undecipherable; the respondent slows his or her tempo to permit the interviewer to keep up and may lose a train of thought or simply run out of time. But the advantages of handwritten notes are impressive: Taking them forces the interviewer to attend carefully to what is being said; the interviewer can interpolate questions or comments (including notations about nonverbal cues) onto the paper without the respondent's awareness, the notes can easily be flagged for important items to which the interviewer wishes to return later; the interviewer need not rely on his or her memory to compose the all-important summary that should be provided at the end of the interview. On balance, we recommend that interviews not be tape-recorded unless there are legal or training reasons for doing so; the advantages of handwritten notes are sufficiently marked to make that the mode of choice.

Immediately following the interview, the interviewer should get the notes in order for subsequent analysis. If the interview has been taped, that process may involve rough-draft transcripts that must be edited by the interviewer (to account for transcriber error) and then typed into final form—a not inconsiderable task that not only consumes human energy but interpolates a considerable time interval between obtaining data and being able to work with them. It is difficult to imagine, for example, how tape recordings of one day's interviews could be used effectively to help shape the next day's interview questions. Indeed, the time interval may be so substantial (several weeks may not be uncommon) that the interview is no longer fresh in the interviewer's mind, thereby considerably reducing his or her ability to process the data. If the interview has been hand recorded, the interviewer should as soon as possible (immediately after the interview, if that can be arranged) review the notes and enlarge them from memory. The notes that were taken jog the memory of the interviewer so that other items not noted when they occurred are recalled; we have known interviewers sufficiently skilled to be able in this retrospective fashion to reconstruct an interview almost as though it had actually been recorded. The interviewer can also mark his or her own comments ("O.C.") or questions ("O.Q.") or hypotheses ("O.H.") so that they will not later be taken to be respondent comments.

During this reconstruction the interviewer may begin the data analysis, at least to the extent that the next day's work can be refashioned on the basis of today's insights. The modes of utilizing and categorizing data described in Chapter 12 can be applied in rudimentary form after each interview as the first step in what will ultimately be a more formal data analysis.

Finally, the information obtained from any interview—and, as the study proceeds, from the accumulated interviews—should be subjected to triangulation and further member checking. Specific data items can be verified with other respondents or from other sources such as observation or document analysis (see below). The emerging categories (which may represent hypotheses in research, concerns in responsive evaluations, assessments in policy studies, and many, many other kinds of data) can be member checked in succeeding interviews ("I've talked to a number of teachers like you and they seem to be saying X; does that sound right to you?").

Observation. A major advantage of the interview is that it permits the respondent to move back and forth in time—to reconstruct the past, interpret the present, and predict the future, all without leaving a comfortable armchair. A major advantage of direct observation, on the other hand, is that it provides here-and-now experience in depth. Indeed, as we observe in *Effective Evaluation:*

> The basic methodological arguments for observation, then, may be summarized as these: observation . . . maximizes the inquirer's ability to grasp motives, beliefs, concerns, interests, unconscious behaviors, customs, and the like; observation . . . allows the inquirer to see the world as his subjects see it, to live in their time frames, to capture the phenomenon in and on its own terms, and to grasp the culture in its own natural, ongoing environment; observation . . . provides the inquirer with access to the emotional reactions of the group introspectively—that is, in a real sense it permits the observer to use *himself* as a data source; and observation . . . allows the observer to build on tacit knowledge, both his own and that of members of the group. (Guba & Lincoln, 1981, p. 193)

Observation is a powerful tool indeed.

As in the case of the interview, observations can be classified in multiple ways. First, the observer may act in either a participant or a nonparticipant mode; in the former instance, the observer has but one role to play, that of observer, but in the latter he or she must play two roles simultaneously, that of observer *and* that of a legitimate and committed member of the group. It is difficult to act as a participant-observer, if only for logistical reasons; that role may best be relegated to an informant who has historically been a part of the local context. Observation may be overt or covert ("under cover"), but ethics demand that covertness be eschewed except in very exceptional circumstances (the claim that it takes an "insider" to get the "real" data is not ethically compelling). And observation can take place in "natural" as opposed to "contrived" settings. In some sense this dichotomy parallels the "structured-unstructured" dichotomy of the interview, and the natural setting is preferred to the contrived for the same reasons that the unstructured interview is preferred to the structured. In most instances the inquirer is not sufficiently sure about what it is that he or she does not know to manipulate a setting to advantage. Contrivance of a setting is also contrary to the principle that phenomena take their meanings from their contexts as much as from any individual characteristics they possess; a contrived context is not only artificial (militating against external validity, to put it in conventional terms), but literally alters the phenomenon being studied in fundamental ways.

The selection of observational situations is guided by principles similar to those guiding selection of inquiry sites and interview respondents—purposive sampling intended to maximize the scope of the information obtained. Contrastive settings selected serially meet that purpose best. And while the observation is rarely as intensive or personalized as is the one-on-one interview, appropriate steps for clearing with gatekeepers, gaining fully informed consent, and maintaining courtesy are mandatory.

Observational data may be recorded in modes paralleling those available to the interviewer. For example, film or videotape recording may be used to get a complete record of what was seen and heard. Observations should no more preclude what is heard than interviews should preclude what is seen—for instance, nonverbal cues. But the use of such devices is fraught with the same disadvantages as those in tape-recording of interviews; indeed, the disadvantages may be exacerbated, because the observer may wish to record his or her own comments during the observation and these comments may be overheard and acted upon by the observed. But should the observer limit him- or herself to other forms of recording than film or videotape, a variety of modes are nevertheless available, including the following:

- running notes, straightforwardly anecdotal or organized into categories at the time that they are taken
- field experience logs or diaries, similar to field notes but usually written at some time after the actual observation
- notes on thematic units, which have been defined ahead of time, as, for example, the units specified by a grounded theory
- chronologs, running accounts of behavior organized along a fairly rigid time line (e.g., recording each separate behavioral episode and noting the time at which it occurred, or making a notation at some arbitrary temporal interval, say, every two minutes)
- context maps, that is, maps, sketches, or diagrams of the context within which the observation occurs, such as a classroom; movement of observed persons can be recorded on such maps as well
- entries according to some taxonomic or categoric system, as, for example, taxonomies or categories that have been provisionally constructed from earlier interview or observational notes
- sociometrics, relation diagrams that depict various types of interactions (e.g., who plays with whom) or relationships (e.g., who names whom as best friend)
- debriefing questionnaires, intended not for the respondents but for the observer, typically used after the observer leaves the scene, to remind him or her of major categories of information that should be noted
- debriefing sessions, with other inquiry team members, also for the sake of drawing out from the observer what has been seen and heard
- rating scales and checklists, although these forms are more usually associated with conventional inquiry since they assume a priori knowledge of what is useful to observe (the items must be specified in advance)

Observations, like interviews, are likely to take different forms at different stages of the inquiry. Early on, the observation may be very unstructured, a stage of defocusing or immersion (Douglas, 1976) in order to permit the observer to expand his or her tacit knowledge and to develop some sense of what is seminal or salient. Later, the observations may become more focused as insights and information grow.

It is useful, as it was with interview data, to interpolate periods of preliminary data analysis between periods of observation. For all practical purposes, field notes from observations can be treated similarly to field notes taken during interviews; they can be fleshed out (or transcribed, if recorded) and analyzed for preliminary units and categories of information. Those preliminary categories can be checked, expanded, and related during subsequent observations. It may also be useful to check these emerging data with some respondents for credibility; the informants that the inquiry team may have gathered about it may be pressed into service for this purpose.

Nonverbal cues. Nonverbal communication is sometimes defined as the exchange of information through nonlinguistic signs: gestures, which are more or less conscious, and body language, more or less unconscious, both fall within this definition. Students of this burgeoning field (see Birdwhistell, 1970; Hall, 1966; Mehrabian, 1972; Gorden, 1980; Wolfgang, 1977; Longstreet, 1978) have defined several branches, including *kinesics* (body movement), *proxemics* (spatial relationships), *synchrony* (rhythmic relationships of sender and receiver), *chronemics* (use of time as in pacing, probing, and pausing), *paralinguistics* (volume, voice quality, accent, and inflectional patterns, for example), and *haptics* (touching). Fortunately, there is little need for the inquirer to be more than casually familiar with these types (and their many ramifications), for what is important is less the information that such nonverbal cues communicate than the apparent disjunctions between such nonverbal behaviors and what is being communicated verbally. The observer, and even more so the interviewer, has little time to attend to and record all nonverbal manifestations, but the inquirer in either role can note instances in which nonverbal behavior conflicts with verbal behavior, giving the lie to it or at the very least raising questions about candor and completeness. The interviewer or observer who notes such disjunctions can pursue them (preferably not at the time they occur) in order to probe more deeply into the information then provided or noticed. And of course such questionable information can be subjected to more strenuous triangulation or other confirmatory efforts. Nonverbal cues are thus best used in a supplementary fashion to flag items of information that require more detailed attention later.

Data Collection from Nonhuman Sources

Documents and records. Documents and records are singularly useful sources of information, although they have often been ignored, particularly in basic research and in evaluation. But there are many reasons that they should be more consistently tapped. They are, first of all, almost always *available,* on a low-cost (mostly investigator time) or free basis. Second, they are a *stable* source of information, both in the sense that they may accurately reflect situations that occurred at some time in the past and that they can be analyzed and reanalyzed without undergoing changes in the interim. Third, they are a *rich* source of information, contextually relevant and grounded in the contexts they represent. Their richness includes the fact that they appear in the natural language of that setting. Fourth, they are often *legally unassailable,* representing, especially in the case of records, formal statements that satisfy some accountability requirement. Finally, they are, unlike human respondents, nonreactive—although the reader should not fail to note that what emanates from a documentary or records analysis still represents a kind of interaction, that between the sources and the analyzing investigator.

The terms "document" and "record" are often used interchangeably, as the dictionary will verify. For our purposes, however, we have elected to define them in somewhat different ways, because (in the terms of our definition) documents and records represent different purposes or intentionalities and because the modes of analyses for these two source types are different. Thus we shall use the term "record" to mean any written or recorded statement prepared by or for an individual or organization for the purpose of *attesting to an event* or *providing an accounting.* Examples of records would thus include airline schedules, audit reports, tax forms, government directories, birth certificates, school grade files for pupils, and minutes of meetings. The term "document" is used to denote any written or recorded material *other than a record* that was not prepared specifically in response to a request from the inquirer (such as a test or a set of interview notes). Examples of documents include letters, diaries, speeches, newspaper editorials, case studies, television scripts, photographs, medical histories, epitaphs, and suicide notes.

The complexity of the analysis of documents is exacerbated by the fact that there are so many different typologies into which documents can be sorted, all of which have relevance for analysis. In our earlier book (Guba & Lincoln, 1981, p. 229) we note:

> Documents can be sorted into various typologies. The most obvious category is the source of the document. Another very useful distinction is that between "primary" and "secondary" documents, the latter falling into the class of what would be called "hearsay" in a court of law. A secondary document is one that was not generated from firsthand experience of a particular situation or event but from other sources. Other useful dichotomies for sorting documents include those of "solicited" versus "unsolicited"; "comprehensive" versus "limited"; "edited" versus "complete" or "unedited"; and "anonymous" ver-

sus "signed" or "attributable" (Bogdan and Taylor, 1975, p. 96). To these we would add also another distinction, that between "spontaneous" and "intentional" (as in a letter to an editor). . . .

The very number of these typologies makes the whole matter of documentary classification very complex. If we used the six dichotomies suggested above, we could arrive at 2^6 or 64 categories. Further, these 64 categories could each be further subdivided in terms of the apparent motivation of the writer. If, for example, it were decided to use a simple 5-category motivational system—explication, support, self-justification, moral duty, and self-aggrandizement—we could enlarge our taxonomy to 64 × 5 or 320 categories.

It is plain that these dichotomies are, from a practical perspective, more usefully viewed as criteria than as classification modes—ways of signaling the inquirer about the relative trustworthiness of any particular documents.

The analytic process itself varies depending upon both whether the analytic categories are specified a priori and whether the documents to be analyzed are similar (for example, a series of annual reports or five-year plans) or different. The naturalistic inquirer will rarely enjoy the luxury of an a priori taxonomy, but when it occurs the analytic modes are well spelled out in such standard content analysis source works as Holsti (1969), Krippendorff (1980), and Rosengren (1981). If the documents are dissimilar, an especially useful approach is the case aggregation method outlined by Lucas (1974a, 1974b). An extended illustration of the latter is given in Guba and Lincoln (1981). When the taxonomy is to emerge in (be grounded in) the data themselves, the method of constant comparison outlined by Glaser and Strauss (1967) is applicable. Since this is the method that will be used most often by naturalists, it is described in detail in Chapter 12.

The analysis of records is a somewhat different matter. As a first principle, the inquirer should begin on the assumption that if an event happened, some record of it exists (especially in today's heavily documented society). To put it another way, every human action "leaves tracks." The second relevant principle is that if one "knows how the world works," one can imagine the tracks that *must* have been left by the action. A third principle is that, if one knows one's way around the world of records, one knows where to look for the tracks. Possibly the most useful metaphor for the "tracking" inquirer is that of the investigative journalist, a metaphor that has been explored in detail by Guba (1981b), who provides several examples of applications.

Like any other technique, the use of documents and records poses certain problems. Historically, documents have been attacked (Allport,

1942) as possibly unrepresentative, as lacking in objectivity, as of unknown validity, and as possibly deliberately deceiving (or self-deceptive). But these objections are not as serious as might at first be imagined, especially for the naturalist. Representativeness and objectivity are a great deal more important within the conventional paradigm. The possibility of deception, whether of self or of others, exists in any data source, and must always be considered. As for validity, even the conventional paradigm offers some methods for testing it: checking the credibility or honesty of the writer on other grounds (often called the *ad hominem* test), testing the plausibility of the document against other known "facts" (a kind of triangulation), and checking the document for internal consistency and coherence. There thus seem to be no insurmountable barriers to the use of documents.

Records also suffer from deficiencies. Obviously records can be in error, whether unintentionally, as in a transcription error, or intentionally, as in lowering one's age or reducing one's income for personal reasons. Records are kept according to some system, moreover, and when that system changes, records must be reinterpreted. So, for example, a dramatic decrease in the crime of breaking and entering may simply reflect the fact that the police department has decided on a different, more restrictive definition. Finally there is the problem of "official statistics," manipulation of the record to the advantage of the recorder. Johnson (1973, 1975) provides a variety of examples, such as the case of the social worker who artifically pads the number of "official" cases, including many that require nothing more than a five-minute phone call once a week, in order to provide adequate time for the "real" cases that may require extensive interaction with a client.

Many documents and records are by law open to public inspection, under the federal Freedom of Information Act and parallel state statutes. Others are specifically prohibited to the public, for reasons such as national security or the individual's right to privacy. Many others—probably most—fall into an undefined gray area. Gaining access to them (and, indeed, even to those legally open to public inspection) is often a difficult matter and may pose many ethical problems. But in any inquiry there are certain to be many documents and records that are easily available; to ignore them is to eschew a most valuable source of information.

Unobtrusive informational residues. Unobtrusive informational residue is information that accumulates without intent on the part of either the investigator or the respondent(s) to whom the information applies. It is often, and we believe erroneously, described as an unobtrusive *measure*. When Campbell and Stanley (1963) published their well-known work on true and quasi-designs, it was seen that one of the major threats, perhaps the major threat, to the internal validity of a quasi-design was the *reactivity* induced in respondents (subjects) such as the guinea-pig effect, the role-selection effect, sensitization by a pretest, response sets, and the like. Eugene Webb, a (then) colleague of Campbell's at Northwestern University, took the lead in developing techniques for obtaining data that would circumvent this reactivity; he and three coauthors, Richard D. Schwartz, Lee Sechrest, and Campbell himself, published the now-classic work *Unobtrusive Measures* (recently updated by the original authors and J. B. Grove, 1981). But very few of the examples that these authors give can literally be interpreted as *measures;* they are most often traces or residues that the inquirer can interpret to advantage.

Webb et al. describe five classes of such "measures" including physical traces (accretion and erosion measures), archival records, private records, simple observations, and contrived observations. The latter four categories are treated by us at other points (the last is by definition eliminated in the naturalistic paradigm). What we wish to concentrate on are physical traces that can be collected in the absence of the respondent who provided them (unlike observations or nonverbal cues, for example). Examples of such traces include shortcuts across lawns as indicators of preferred traffic patterns, foreign-language signs as indicators of the degree of integration of a neighborhood, worn and smudged condition of books as indicators of their use, number of discarded liquor bottles as indicators of the level of alcoholism in an apartment complex, number of cigarettes in an ashtray as an indicator of nervous tension, amount of paperwork that accumulates in the "in" basket as an indicator of work load, number of books in a personal library as an indicator of humaneness, presence of bulletin board displays in a schoolroom as an indicator of the teacher's concern with children's creativity, and many others.

Unobtrusive residues have many strengths to recommend their use. They often have face validity; they are simple and direct and, usually, noninterventional; they are stable; independent of language; and, most important in terms of the original intent of Webb and his colleagues, they are nonreactive. But of course they also suffer certain weaknesses, including the fact that they are sometimes heavily inferential; they are found in bits and pieces that are difficult to aggregate or to interpret holistically; they are serendipitous—indeed, one of the major difficulties that continues to plague their advocates is the impossibility of systematically generating a measure to fit a particular investigative situation ("finding just the right measure"); and they cannot be directly manipulated (a circumstance especially difficult for the conventional inquirer). Moreover, it is difficult to establish their trustworthiness in either conventional or naturalistic terms (see Chapter 11).

Nevertheless, unobtrusive residues are there for the taking, and it is wasteful indeed not to exploit them.

BUILDING TRUSTWORTHINESS

Chapter 11 describes in detail the steps that can be taken to demonstrate the trustworthiness of a naturalistic inquiry. But it is essential that certain measures be employed *during* the implementation of the inquiry that either increase the probability that a judgment of trustworthiness will eventually be achieved or that provide the data that will subsequently be needed to reach that judgment.

(1) Maintaining field journals. Investigators will accumulate a great deal of information in the form of field notes useful for subsequent analysis, whether resulting from interviews or observations. But in addition, the naturalistic inquirer will wish to keep at least three other forms of notes, preferably in a journal format. These include, first, a *log of day-to-day activities,* kept individually by inquiry team members, which may read much like a calendar of appointments. Each entry should include the date and time of day. The second is a *personal log*—a kind of diary, also kept individually, that includes several different kinds of entries: reflexive and introspective notations about the state of one's mind in relation to what is happening in the field (developing constructions, commentary on the perceived influence of one's own biases, expectations about what will heppen next, and the like); a record of hypotheses and questions that will be useful to follow up and/or to discuss with one's fellow inquirers; and a cathartic section in which one can vent one's frustrations and anxieties. Wax (1971), Spradley (1979), and Reinharz (1979) provide interesting commentary on this form of log. Third, at least one member of the team should keep a *methodological log* in which are recorded all methodological decisions made in accordance with the emergent design. The interested reader is referred to Lincoln (1981) for a further discussion of logs.

(2) Mounting safeguards. It is possible to institute certain practices that, while not guaranteeing trustworthiness, increase the probability

that it can be achieved. Safeguards should be mounted against the following (Guba, 1978):

- Distortions arising from the inquirer's presence at the site, both to minimize respondent reactivity and to provide sufficient opportunity for the inquirer to test his or her own conceptions and expectations. Prolonged engagement on site coupled with close monitoring of responses is a recommended practice.
- Distortions arising from the inquirer's involvement with the respondents. It is necessary to build trust and rapport with respondents while simultaneously guarding against "going native," that is, overrapport (Lincoln & Guba, 1981).
- Distortions arising from bias on the part of either the inquirer(s) or the respondents. "Such distortions may arise from wrong first impressions, slavish adherence to hypotheses formed earlier, or role-status differentials. Subjects may introduce distortion for similar reasons, or simply out of a desire to be as 'helpful' as possible" (Guba, 1978, p. 62). The best hedge against such distortions is an awareness that they may intrude and strenuous efforts to identify and correct them when they do occur.
- Distortions arising from the manner in which data-gathering techniques are employed. This is a type of distortion that can plague any inquiry by whatever paradigm, because it is produced by inadequate attention to detail. Careful checking of data codes, continuous scrutiny of data for internal and external consistency, triangulation, and continuous assessment of respondent credibility are important steps to take as countermeasures.

Whatever steps are taken for the sake of mounting safeguards should be carefully documented in the methodological log for the study.

(3) Arranging for on-site team interactions. We have already noted the need for continuous team interaction to provide input into the emergent design and to guarantee that all members of the team will be apprised on how the study is to proceed. These interactions are also important for the sake of trustworthiness, however, for communication breakdowns will lead to independent and unrelated unfoldings that cannot contribute to an orderly, systematic inquiry. Careful attention should be given, therefore, to facilitating both informal (for example, over meals and at the "cocktail hour") and formal (for example, at evening work sessions) interactions and to provide time and resources to accomplish them.

(4) Triangulating. Triangulation of data is crucially important in naturalistic studies. As the study unfolds and particular pieces of information come to light, steps should be taken to validate each against at least one other source (for example, a second interview) and/or a second method (for example, an observation in addition to an interview). No single item of information (unless coming from an elite and unimpeachable source) should ever be given serious consideration unless it can be triangulated.

(5) Gathering referential adequacy materials. The meaning of this phrase will become clear in Chapter 11; it involves the collection of material—additional interviews, observations, and documents, for example—that will not be used in the immediate data analysis but will be archived for use only after the study is essentially completed. At that point these materials may be used to test whether the constructions that have emerged are adequate to account for them as well. During the study steps must be taken to obtain such materials, earmark them for archiving, and secure them against use before the end of the project.

(6) Doing debriefing. The concept of the debriefer is also explicated in Chapter 11; the debriefer is essentially a noninvolved professional peer with whom the inquirer(s) can have a no-holds-barred conversation at periodic intervals. The purposes of the debriefing are multiple: to ask the difficult questions that the inquirer might otherwise avoid ("to keep the inquirer honest"), to explore methodological next steps with someone who has no axe to grind, and to provide a sympathetic listening point for personal catharsis. During implementation the inquirers must arrange for and carry out such debriefings, and develop a record (with entries from both the debriefer and the inquirers) that can be consulted later.

(7) Developing and maintaining an audit trail. The audit may be the single most important trustworthiness technique available to the naturalist; it will be fully explicated in Chapter 11. Using methods analogous to those of the fiscal auditor, the inquiry auditor carefully examines both the process and the product of the inquiry, in order to arrive at certain trustworthiness judgments and provide certain attestations. Just as a fiscal audit cannot be carried out in the absence of an audit trail—fiscal records—so the inquiry audit poses requirements for records as well. It is imperative that such records be maintained during the inquiry; otherwise there will be no possibility

of an audit later. A detailed listing of audit trail requirements is shown in Appendix A; the process itself is discussed in Chapter 11.

SOME IMPLEMENTATION PROBLEMS

Implementation of a naturalistic inquiry is no less problem plagued than any other form, and many of the problems are similar. Some are more or less unique to the naturalistic format, and the naturalistic inquirer needs to be aware of them before the fact. These include the following:

(1) Managing paradigm/contract disjunctions. Most inquiries, whether research, evaluation, or policy analysis, are carried out under the terms of a contract with a funding agency or under the aegis of some individual or group that has power to support or reject the work. So, for example, many investigations are responsive to a request for proposals or to the program requirements of a federal or state agency or private foundation. Graduate students are accountable to their advisory committees. The difficulty is that in general these other agencies or groups are neither fully informed about what it means to do naturalistic inquiry nor sympathetic to its aims and methods. The scope of work statement in a grant or contract proposal or the dissertation outline provided for the guidance of the graduate student are thus likely to be cast in conventional terms, as, for example, the a priori design requirements as described in Chapter 9, including designation of the sample, instrumentation, time schedule, milestone events, data analysis procedures, and perhaps even dummy tables.

What the naturalistic inquirer does in answer to these requirements is likely to be, in every sense, unreal; a proposal is written in the spirit of compliance rather than of responsiveness. Once implemented, this "compliance" design will require continuing renegotiation; eventually that renegotiation will induce resistance from the program or contracts officer, the dissertation committee, or whatever other sanctioning body may be involved. Finally, in desperation, the inquirer is likely to adopt a "safe" course to avoid further problems, perhaps even the threat of a shutdown. But adoption of such a course effectively bars further development of the inquiry; the design can no longer unfold. It is this stultification of creativity that is the final and most repugnant price accompanying the disjunctions between "normal" (in the Kuhnian sense) and emergent inquiry.

There is little that can be done about this problem unless and until sanctioning agencies come to recognize the legitimacy of the naturalistic approach and are prepared to support this new paradigm of inquiry with a new paradigm of sanction. It is not that naturalists seek freedom from accountability; rather, they seek a new form of accountability that is resonant with their basic belief system in the same way that present forms of accountability are resonant with conventional basic beliefs. That development is not likely to occur soon, however, and in the meantime those inquirers with a naturalistic bent must be prepared for misunderstandings, constant renegotiation, and the need to resist premature closure.

(2) Problems of design. There are a number of aspects of naturalistic design that pose special implementation problems. First, the need to engage in purposive sampling requires that the investigator relinquish some decision making to other persons in the situation—a loss of control about which the naturalist may feel more or less uncomfortable. The naturalist must feel confident that his dependence will not be exploited in behalf of a massive cover-up—a conspiracy to see to it that he is exposed only to "dependable" sources of information. Loss of autonomy is accompanied by a corresponding increase in anxiety; the naturalist must be prepared to live with that fact of life.

Further, because the design is emergent, time management becomes a problem. The schedule always, *always*, slips. The naturalist must be psychologically prepared to accept this additional degree of control loss. Two somewhat tongue-in-cheek principles are worth recalling: (1) Things always take longer than they do; and (2) while the first 90 percent of the project work will take 90 percent of the project time, the other 10 percent of the work will take the *other* 90 percent of the time. It will also be difficult to provide the time needed for reflection and decision making, activities urgently required if the design is to unfold properly. In conventional inquiry there is a distinct hiatus between planning a study and carrying it out; in naturalistic inquiry these two activities go on more or less cyclically. Planning time must be found while the project is itself unfolding, often in ways and at a rate beyond the inquirer's control.

Finally, it is difficult to find an appropriate balance between settling on an appropriate focus for a study while resisting, on the one hand, premature closure, and, on the other, changes that ought *not* to be made. It takes time to sort out the salient factors in a situation and zero in on them. There is an enormous press to get that "preliminary" job done so that the "real" inquiry can get under way. But tolerance of ambiguity is a rare characteristic and patience an infrequent virtue. Resisting premature closure becomes daily more difficult; yet it is essential that it be resisted so long as possible if the study is to be maximully useful. The press for closure may also stimulate the inquirer to shortcut in other ways, for example, generalizing from one site to another rather than duplicating the full inquiry at each site, or placing too much reliance on the literature rather than teasing out the idiosyncratic qualities that characterize a given context. The naturalist is thus caught on the horns of a dilemma; its resolution requires rare patience and insightful assessment.

(3) Managing problems in the field. There are a number of difficulties that typically rise up to plague the naturalist once in the field. These include, first of all, the matter of gaining entrée, which is, as we have already observed, a political matter that requires delicate handling at every level. Building and maintaining trust is a normal concomitant. It must be developed and renewed more or less constantly. Then there are the logistical problems. Everything one does in the field uses up time and resources. Travel to and around the site, weather difficulties, an extremely talkative interview respondent, accidents, fouled-up airline reservations, missed wake-up calls, all add to the confusion.

Problems of data recording and initial analysis of data also pose difficulties. Tape recorders fail to work. Handwritten notes later turn out to be illegible. There is not enough time to do even an initial analysis overnight, yet guidance is needed for tomorrow's interviews. Documents pile up that cannot be sorted, let alone read.

And of course there are the personal reactions that always accompany fieldwork, the feelings of loneliness, anxiety, fatigue, inadequacy. In the final analysis, even though you are part of a team, it's all up to you; you are the human instrument that will or will not make sense of what's "out there." There is no good way to release one's pent up emotions, no easy way to achieve catharsis. There are things to do every waking hour—and that's most of the 24 that are available.

No one has yet devised a foolproof way of dealing with these field problems. That they will be encountered is certain; that they should not be permitted to take you by surprise is only prudent. An awareness of the possibilities, careful planning to prevent them (although even the best plans will inevitably prove inadequate), and a resigned acceptance are useful antidotes to being overwhelmed. So is the knowledge that even the best naturalists confront these difficulties daily; it is not a reflection on the inquirer's competence that they occur, but evidence of the normal state of things.

SUMMARY

Implementing a naturalistic inquiry is not an easy task. It is more complex than implementing a conventional inquiry, for, in the latter case, one has a more or less complete design to follow that has virtually all of the contingencies spelled out. In naturalistic inquiry, planning and implementation go hand in hand, and usually the plans cannot be completed in time for the next operational steps that must be taken.

Implementation starts with the development of the initial design statement as described in Chapter 9. But before that design can be mounted, certain preliminary steps require attention: making initial contact and gaining entrée, negotiating consent, building and maintaining trust, and identifying and using informants. Moreover, each of these preliminary steps will be repeated multiple times during the inquiry itself, whenever a new gatekeeper is encountered, a new organizational level is to be tapped, new respondents are to be involved, and so on.

Shortly after the preliminary steps have been taken, the naturalist begins to unfold the design. The various elements of the design that can be spelled out in advance are put into place, but beyond that point, the subsequent unfolding is only nominally under the investigator's control. Continuous reassesssment, recycling, and reiteration are required. It is normal for the investigator to feel, at this point, that he or she has more balls in the air than can possibly be controlled, and some will undoubtedly fall.

Data collection is carried out with multiple techniques, some utilizing human sources directly, and some using nonhuman sources, that is, sources that are at least at one remove from a human being. The former include interview, observation, and utilization of nonverbal cues, and the latter documents, records, and unobtrusive residues. Whatever the source may be, however, it is the human instrument that is the primary mode of collecting the information.

All the while the naturalist must be concerned with trustworthiness. In the final analysis, the study is for naught if its trustworthiness is questionable. Activities such as maintaining field journals, mounting safeguards against common distortions, arranging for on-site team interactions, triangulating data, gathering referential adequacy materials, doing debriefings, and developing and maintaining an audit trail are all directed either to increasing the probability that trustworthiness will result or to making it possible to assess the degree of trustworthiness after the fact.

Finally, the implementer of the naturalistic study must deal with several inevitable problems: managing problem/contract disjunctions, dealing with aspects of unfolding design, and managing field problems. The naturalist's lot is not an easy one. To suggest that persons engage in naturalistic inquiry because it is so much easier and less rigorous than conventional inquiry is to betray ignorance of what is actually involved.

11

Establishing Trustworthiness

How can I trust thee? Let me count the ways . . .
(with apologies to Elizabeth Barrett Browning)

THE ASSAILABILITY OF
NATURALISTIC STUDIES

Probably no anthropologist is better known than Margaret Mead; her *Coming of Age in Samoa* is familiar to every literate American. The recent publication, therefore, of Derek Freeman's *Margaret Mead and Samoa: The Making and Unmaking of an Anthropological Myth* produced more than a ripple of surprised reaction. Could his charges that Mead was "astronomically wrong" about Samoa be true? Was it the case, as Freeman claims, that Mead had failed to acquire even a rudimentary acquaintance with Samoan culture before concentrating prematurely on her specialty, adolescent girls, thereby grossly mistaking the meaning of the observations she made? Was it true that Mead had come to her conclusions because she imposed, albeit unknowingly, her own ideology, emphasizing the "nurture" side of the "nature-nurture" controversy because that was what her mentor, Franz Boas, expected her to find? And finally, isn't the fact that Freeman, himself an experienced Samoan researcher, could arrive at such gross disagreements with Mead more than ample evidence of the untrustworthiness of such uncontrolled findings, irrespective of whether his judgments are right or wrong?

The naturalistic inquirer soon becomes accustomed to hearing charges that naturalistic studies are undisciplined; that he or she is guilty of "sloppy" research, engaging in "merely subjective" observations, responding indiscriminately to the "loudest bangs or brightest lights." Rigor, it is asserted, is not the hallmark of naturalism. Is the naturalist inevitably defenseless against such charges? Worse, are they true? It is the purpose of this chapter to deny those allegations, and to provide means both for shoring up and for demonstrating the trustworthiness of inquiry guided by the naturalistic paradigm.

WHAT IS TRUSTWORTHINESS?

The basic issue in relation to trustworthiness is simple: How can an inquirer persuade his or her audiences (including self) that the findings of an inquiry are worth paying attention to, worth taking account of? What arguments can be mounted, what criteria invoked, what questions asked, that would be persuasive on this issue?

Conventionally, inquirers have found it useful to pose four questions to themselves:

(1) *"Truth value":* How can one establish confidence in the "truth" of the findings of a particular inquiry for the subjects (respondents) with which and the context in which the inquiry was carried out?

(2) *Applicability:* How can one determine the extent to which the findings of a particular inquiry have applicability in other contexts or with other subjects (respondents)?

(3) *Consistency:* How can one determine whether the findings of an inquiry would be repeated if the inquiry were replicated with the same (or similar) subjects (respondents) in the same (or similar) context?

(4) *Neutrality:* How can one establish the degree to which the findings of an inquiry are determined by the subjects (respondents) and conditions of the inquiry and not by the biases, motivations, interests, or perspectives of the inquirer?

Within the conventional paradigm, the criteria that have evolved in response to these questions are termed "internal validity," "external validity," "reliability," and "objectivity."

Internal validity may be defined in conventional terms as the extent to which variations in an outcome (dependent) variable can be attributed to controlled variation in an independent variable. A causal connection between independent and dependent variables is usually assumed. Thus Cook and Campbell (1979, p. 37) define internal validity as "the approximate validity [the best available approximation of the truth or falsity of a statement] with which we infer that a relationship between two variables is causal or that the absence of a relationship implies the absence of a cause." Since a variety of factors (plausible rival hypotheses) may influence the outcome, the purpose of design is either to control or to randomize those factors. Data analysis consists of testing the outcome variance against the variance of the randomized factors (error).

Campbell and Stanley (1963) suggest that there are eight "threats" to the internal validity of a study: *history*—the specific external events occurring between the first and second measurement other than the experimental variable(s); *maturation*—processes operating within the respondents as a function of the passage of time per se; *testing*—the effects of taking a test upon the scores of a second testing; *instrumentation*—changes in the calibration of a measurement instrument or changes in the observers or scores used; *statistical regression*—tendencies for movement toward the mean when comparison groups have been selected on the basis of initial extreme scores or positions; *differential selection*—effects of comparing essentially noncomparable groups; *experimental mortality*—the effects of differential loss of respondents from comparison groups, rendering them noncomparable; and *selection—maturation interaction*—an effect that in certain designs may be mistaken for the effect of the experimental variable. The rival hypotheses represented in these eight threats must be invalidated if a study is to have internal validity.

External validity may be defined, as do Cook and Campbell (1979, p. 37), as "the approximate validity with which we infer that the presumed causal relationship can be generalized to and across alternate measures of the cause and effect and across different types of persons, settings, and times." It is the purpose of randomized sampling from a given, defined population to make this criterion achievable. If a sample is selected in accordance with the rule that every element of the population has a known probability (not necessarily equal) of being included in the sample, then it is possible to assert, within given confidence limits, that the findings from the sample will hold for (be generalizable to) the population. It should be noted that the criteria of internal and external validity are placed in a trade-off situation by their definition. If, for the sake of control (internal validity), strenuous laboratory conditions are imposed, then the results are not generalizable to any contexts except those that approximate the original laboratory.

LeCompte and Goetz (1982) point out that, just as there are identifiable threats to internal validity, so are there to external validity. They identify four: *selection effects*—the fact that constructs being tested are specific to a single group, or that the inquirer mistakenly selects groups to study for which the constructs do not obtain; *setting effects*—the fact that results may be a function of the context under investigation; *history effects*—the fact that unique historical experiences may militate against comparisons; and *construct effects*— the fact that constructs studied may be peculiar to the studied group.

Reliability is typically held to be, in the words of Kerlinger (1973, p. 422), synonymous with "dependability, stability, consistency, predictability, accuracy." Having described a "reliable man" as one whose behavior is consistant, dependable, and predictable, Kerlinger (1973, p. 443) goes on to say,

> So it is with psychological and educational measurements: they are more or less variable from occasion to occasion. They are stable and relatively predictable or they are unstable and relatively unpredictable; they are consistent or not consistent. If they are reliable, we can depend on them. If they are unreliable, we cannot depend on them.

It must be reasonable, as Ford (1975, p. 324) suggests, "to assume that each repetition of the application of the same, or supposedly equivalent, instruments to the same units will yield similar measurements."

Reliability is not prized for its own sake but as a precondition for validity; an unreliable measure cannot be valid, a fact illustrated by the well-known mental test theorem that the validity of a test cannot exceed the square root of its reliability (Gulliksen, 1950). Reliability is usually tested by replication (Ford's "repetition"), as, for example, the odd-even correlation of test items, or the test-retest or parallel-forms correlation. Reliability is threatened by any careless act in the measurement or assessment process, by instrumental decay, by assessments that are insufficiently long (or intense), by ambiguities of various sorts, and a host of other factors.

Objectivity is usually played off against subjectivity. In what Scriven (1971, p. 95) refers to as the "quantitative" contrast between these two, a contrast that is the one usually intended by conventionalists,

> "subjective" refers to what concerns or occurs to the *individual* subject and his experiences, qualities, and dispositions, while "objective" refers to what a *number* of subjects or judges experience—in short, to phenomena in the public domain.

In this sense, the usual criterion for objectivity is intersubjective agreement; if multiple observers can agree on a phenomenon their collective judgment can be said to be objective. Another conventional approach to the problem of establishing objectivity is through methodology; to use methods that by their character render the study beyond contamination by human foibles. Such a methodology is the experiment, as Campbell has observed:

> The experiment is meticulously designed to put questions to "Nature Itself" in such a way that neither the questions, not their colleagues, nor their superiors can affect the answer. (cited in Brewer & Collins, 1981, pp. 15-16)

Objectivity is threatened, then, by using imperfect methodologies that make it possible for inquirer values to refract the "natural" data—putting questions not directly to "Nature Itself" but through an intervening medium that "bends" the response; by engaging in inquiry with an openly ideological purpose; or by relying exclusively on the data provided by a single observer.

*   *   *

It should be evident that these formulations of criteria intended to respond to the four basic questions are themselves dependent for their meaning on the conventional axioms, such as naive realism and linear causality. We shall have more to say about that later, but for the moment the point to be made is that criteria defined from one perspective may not be appropriate for judging actions taken from another perspective, just as, for example, it is not appropriate to judge Catholic dogma as wrong from the perspective of say, Lutheran presuppositions.

Gareth Morgan (1983a) has made the same point in relation to his management of the project reported in the recent volume, *Beyond Method*. He set himself the task of presenting a variety of research perspectives (each written by an author committed to it) to illustrate the point that each has its own assumptions and provides a separate option for an investigator to consider. But as the project developed unforeseen issues began to emerge:

> For example, there was the question as to how the reader could come to some conclusion regarding the contrary nature, significance, and claims of the different perspectives. Using the work of Gödel (1962) as a metaphor for framing this issue, I realized that there was a major problem here: There was no obvious point of reference outside the system of thought represented in the volume from which the different perspectives could be described and evaluated. As Gödel has shown in relation to mathematics, there is a fallacy in the idea that the propositions of a system can be proved, disproved, or evaluated

on the basis of axioms within that system. Translated into terms relevant to the present project, this means that it is not possible to judge the validity or contribution of different research perspectives in terms of the ground assumptions of any one set of perspectives, since the process is self-justifying. Hence the attempts in much social science debate to judge the utility of different research strategies in terms of universal criteria based on the importance of generalizability, predictability and control, explanation of variance, meaningful understanding, or whatever *are inevitably flawed: These criteria inevitably favor research strategies consistent with the assumptions that generate such criteria as meaningful guidelines for the evaluation of research.* It is simply inadequate to attempt to justify a particular style of research in terms of assumptions that give rise to that style of research. . . . Different research perspectives make different kinds of knowledge claims, and the criteria as to what counts as significant knowledge vary from one to another. (Morgan, 1983a, pp. 14-15; emphasis added)

Or, in the vernacular of the streets, "different strokes for different folks." Different basic beliefs lead to different knowledge claims and different criteria.

THE CRITERIA APPROPRIATE
TO THE NATURALISTIC PARADIGM

Just what is it that makes the conventional criteria inappropriate to the naturalistic paradigm? If they are inappropriate, what shall we substitute in their place? There is no question that the naturalist is at least as concerned with trustworthiness as is the conventional inquirer. We say "at least" because it is precisely on the point of trustworthiness that the naturalistic investigator is most often attacked, as we tried to show in the opening paragraphs of this chapter. It therefore becomes of utmost importance that (1) the inappropriateness of the conventional criteria be well demonstrated, and (2) acceptable alternative criteria be proposed and their use defended. We may consider the four criterion areas one at a time.

(1) "Truth value." On the assumption of a single, tangible reality that an investigation is intended to unearth and display, the ultimate test of internal validity for the conventional inquirer is the extent to which the findings of an inquiry display an isomorphism (a one-to-one relationship) with that reality. But the determination of such isomorphism is *in principle* impossible, for, in order to make it, the inquirer would need to know the nature of that ultimate tangible reality

a priori. But it is precisely the nature of that reality that is at issue; if one already "knew" it there would be no need to mount an inquiry to determine it.

The conventional inquirer must therefore fall back on a less compelling test; thus the statement by Cook and Campbell cited earlier that internal validity is the "approximate validity with which we infer that a relationship between two variables is causal." The game is played by *postulating* a relationship and then *testing* it against nature (thereby preserving the naive realist posture)—putting the question to "Nature Itself." The hypothesis cannot of course be *proved* (the underdetermination problem) but it can be *falsified* (Popper, 1959).

In order to provide some (persuasive if not compelling) evidence in favor of the claim that the hypothesis is true, it is necessary to eliminate the possibility that plausible rival hypotheses could be at work. "True" experimental designs (in the sense of Campbell & Stanley, 1963) are "true" precisely because they (putatively) unambiguously rule out all such plausible rivals. But, as Campbell and Stanley note, it is not often possible to mount such "true" designs in practice. Perforce one falls back on "quasi-experimental" designs that, while better than mere guesswork, may yield inauthentic results because they are exposed to the "threats" of certain common plausible rivals: history, maturation, and the other factors reviewed briefly above. "True" designs depend for their authenticity on the ability of the investigator to mount suitable controls and/or to randomize; quasi-designs are "imperfect" in one or more ways related to control or randomization.

To score naturalistic inquiry as nontrustworthy on the grounds that controls and/or randomization were not effected is to miss the point that, at bottom, those techniques are appropriate *only insofar as one can buy into the assumption of naive realism*. If that assumption is rejected or altered, then the rational argument summarized above is cut off at the root. When naive realism is replaced by the assumption of multiple constructed realities, there is no ultimate benchmark to which one can turn for justification—whether in principle or by a technical adjustment via the falsification principle. "Reality" is now a multiple set of mental constructions. But, we may note, those constructions are made by humans; their constructions are in their minds, and they are, in the main, accessible to the humans who make them (excepting, let us say, repressed constructions—but even those may become accessible via hypnotism or psychoanalysis). The test of isomorphism, in principle impossible to apply within the conventional paradigm, becomes *the method of choice* for the naturalist. In order to demonstrate "truth value," the naturalist must show that he or she has *represented those multiple constructions adequately,* that is, that the *reconstructions* (for the findings and interpretations are also constructions, it should never be forgotten) that have been arrived at via the inquiry are *credible to the constructors of the original multiple realities.*

The operational word is *credible.* The implementation of the credibility criterion—the naturalist's substitute for the conventionalist's internal validity—becomes a twofold task: first, to carry out the inquiry in such a way that the probability that the findings will be found to be credible is enhanced and, second, to demonstrate the credibility of the findings by having them approved by the constructors of the multiple realities being studied. We shall in a subsequent section suggest techniques for accomplishing these goals.

We may note, finally, that even if Campbell and Stanley's criteria were to be taken seriously by the naturalist (and we are not arguing that they should be), naturalistic designs would probably score at least as well as the typical quasi-experimental design. Recall that it is Campbell and Stanley's point that *all eight* factors are potential "threats" to quasi-designs; is that also the case with naturalistic designs? Some of the threats can be read as equally applicable to both types; thus differential selection, differential mortality, history, and testing would affect both kinds of outcomes in about the same way. Score: 0-0. One of the threats is probably more likely in naturalistic studies— instrumentation, since changes can and do occur in human instruments and probably to a greater extent than is typical of paper-and-pencil or brass instruments. Score: quasi-designs 1, naturalistic designs 0. But one of these threats—statistical regression—does not apply at all unless quantitative methods are used, and their use is relatively rare in naturalistic studies. Score: quasi-designs 1, naturalistic designs 1. Finally, naturalistic approaches seem particularly useful in *overcoming* two of the threats—maturation and maturation/selection interaction— because naturalistic studies usually involve long-term and continuing interactions with respondents and hence facilitate the assessment of such effects. Final score: quasi-designs 1, naturalistic designs 3. The claim that naturalistic approaches score at least as well as conventional ones on Campbell and Stanley's criteria does not seem to be exaggerated.

(2) Applicability. The criterion of external validity has proved to be troublesome within the conventional framework, for, as we have already suggested, it is in a trade-off situation with internal validity.

The very controls instituted to ensure internal validity militate against clean generalizations. In the final analysis, results that are acquired in that epitome of the controlled situation—the laboratory—are discovered to be applicable only in other laboratores. In that connection we have already cited Urie Bronfenbrenner (1977) on the field of developmental psychology (Chapter 8).

For the naturalist, however, the difficulty with the concept of external validity is not simply that its achievement conflicts with the achievement of internal validity, but that it is based on a conventional axiom that is rejected by the naturalist paradigm. Indeed, naturalists make the opposite assumption: that at best only working hypotheses may be abstracted, the *transferability* of which is an empirical matter, depending on the degree of similarity between sending and receiving contexts. In the classic paradigm all that is necessary to ensure transferability is to know something with high internal validity about Sample A, and to know that A is representative of the population to which the generalization is to apply. The generalization will apply to *all* contexts within that same population.

The naturalist rejects this formulation on several grounds. First, as we saw in Chapter 8, the concept of "population" is itself suspect. As every sampling statistician knows, inferences about populations can be made with greater and greater precision to the extent to which the population is divided into homogeneous strata. But of course such stratification amounts to the formation of subunits that are more and more contextually alike. If one wishes to know, under those circumstances, whether something found out about a stratum of Chicago residents also applies (is generalizable to), say, a stratum of New York residents, the two strata will have to be compared on those factors that define them. That is to say, in order to be sure (within some confidence limits) of one's inference, one will need to know about *both* sending and receiving contexts. We move then from a question of generalizability to a question of *transferability*. Transferability inferences cannot be made by an investigator who knows *only* the sending context.

The condition of representativeness is absolutely basic to the conventional axiom of generalizability. And that axiom in turn seems to depend upon the axiom of naive realism. If there are to be generalizations that are, in Kaplan's sense (see Chapter 5), nomic and nomological, that is, time and context free, there must be some basic rules of nature that govern situations under all circumstances. These basic rules cannot be mere inventions of the mind (constructions); they must be "real," characteristics of Nature Itself, out there waiting to be discovered. Again the naturalist finds him- or herself in a fundamental propositional disagreement.

It should be clear from the above that if there is to be transferability, the burden of proof lies less with the original investigator than with the person seeking to make an application elsewhere. The original inquirer cannot know the sites to which transferability might be sought, but the appliers can and do. The best advice to give to anyone seeking to make a transfer is to accumulate *empirical* evidence about contextual similarity; the responsibility of the original investigator ends in providing sufficient descriptive data to make such similarity judgments possible. Even if the applier believes on the basis of the empirical evidence that sending and receiving contexts are sufficiently similar to allow one to entertain the possibility of transfer, he or she is nevertheless well advised to carry out a small verifying study to be certain.

Finally, we may note, as in the case of internal validity, naturalistic studies seem to be at least as impervious to the "threats" to external validity as are conventional ones. We noted earlier that LeCompte and Goetz (1982) have specified four threats. Selection effects are threats if the constructs being tested are specific to a single group, but this is precisely what the naturalist believes obtains in every instance unless there is evidence to the contrary, that is, evidence that would show that another group is sufficiently similar to warrant ignoring this possibility. Setting effects are threats because the results may be a function of the context under investigation. But the naturalist sees this state of affairs not as a threat but as the normal circumstance confronting investigators. History effects are threats because unique historical experiences may militate against comparisons. The naturalist expects that to happen. Construct effects are threats because the constructs studies may be peculiar to the studied group. Of course, says the naturalist. The naturalist sees these four states of affairs not as threats but as affirmations of the greater validity of the naturalist axioms. The axioms take these matters into account; they are seen not as effects that undermine external validity but as factors that have to be accounted for in making judgments of transferability.

(3) Consistency. As we have seen, the key concepts undergirding the conventional definition of reliability are those of stability, consistency, and predictability. Within conventional studies reliability is typically demonstrated by replication—if two or more repetitions of essentially similar inquiry processes under essentially similar conditions

yield essentially similar findings, the reliability of the inquiry is indisputably established.

But replicability depends, again, upon an assumption of naive realism. There must be something tangible and unchanging "out there" that can serve as a benchmark if the idea of replication is to make sense. If the thing "out there" is ephemeral and changing, noted instabilities cannot be simply charged off to the inquiry procedure; they are at least as much a function of what is being studied as of the process of studying. The quotation from Ford (1975) that requires that the repetitions be applied "to the same units" is telling; it is precisely that condition that can never be met, just as one can never cross the *same* stream twice (if it is indeed possible to cross the *same* stream even once!). Replicability in the traditional sense can be determined only within a given framework—and that framework is itself a construction, not an inevitable and unchanging part of "reality."

The naturalist is willing to concede what might be called "instrumental" unreliability. Conventional theory tells us about unreliabilities of paper-and-pencil or brass instruments, and surely the human instrument displays its equivalents. Humans do become careless; there is "instrumental decay" such as fatigue; the human mind is tentative and groping and it makes mistakes. But the naturalist is not willing to have charged off to his or her "unreliability" changes that occur because of changes in the entity being studied (a construction, remember) or because of changes in the emergent design as insights grow and working hypotheses appear.

The naturalist sees reliability as part of a larger set of factors that are associated with observed changes. In order to demonstrate what may be taken as a substitute criterion for reliability—*dependability*—the naturalist seeks means for taking into account both factors of instability *and* factors of phenomenal or design induced change. It can be argued that this naturalist view is broader than the conventional, since it accounts for everything that is normally included in the concept of reliability plus some additional factors. We shall return later to the question of how this can be accomplished operationally.

(4) Neutrality. The conventional concept of objectivity may be viewed from three perspectives:

(a) Objectivity exists when there is an isomorphism between the data of a study and reality—when the questions are put to "Nature Itself" and it is "Nature Itself" that answers. One might term this the ontological definition, based on a correspondence notion, and it founders, as must by now be evident, on the naive realist axiom. In all events it would never be possible to test objectivity if it were defined in this way.

(b) Objectivity exists when an appropriate methodology is employed that maintains an adequate distance between observer and observed. One might term this the "epistemological" definition, based on the notion that it is possible for an observer to be neither disturbing nor disturbed (a kind of naive positivism), and it founders on the axiom of subject-object dualism.

(c) Objectivity exists when inquiry is value-free. One might term this the "axiological" definition, based on the notion that is possible to allow Nature to "speak for itself" without impact from the values of the inquirer or any of his or her cohorts. It founders on the axiom of value-dependence.

As we have seen, and as Scriven (1971) points out, the typical criterion that is invoked to judge objectivity is that of intersubjective agreement. What a number of individuals experience is objective and what a single individual experiences is subjective; Scriven refers to this as the "quantitative" sense of objectivity. But, he argues, there is also a qualitative sense in which the subjective/objective distinction may be made. In this sense,

> there is a reference to the *quality* of the testimony or the report or the (putative) evidence, and so I call this the "qualitative" sense. Here, "subjective" means unreliable, biased or probably biased, a matter of opinion, and "objective" means reliable, factual, confirmable or confirmed, and so forth. (Scriven, 1971, pp. 95-96; emphasis in original)

Now the naturalist much prefers this second, qualitative (in Scriven's sense) definition of objectivity. This definition removes the emphasis from the investigator (it is no longer his or her objectivity that is at stake) and places it where, as it seems to the naturalist, it ought more logically to be: on the data themselves. The issue is no longer the investigator's characteristics but the characteristics of the data: Are they or are they not *confirmable?* The naturalist prefers this concept to that of objectivity; again, techniques for assessing confirmability will be discussed below.

The four terms "credibility," "transferability," "dependability," and "confirmability" are, then, the naturalist's equivalents for the conventional terms "internal validity," "external validity," "reliability," and "objectivity." These terms are introduced not simply to add to naturalism's mystique or to provide it with its fair share of arcane concepts, but to make clear the inappropriateness of the conventional terms when applied to naturalism and to provide alternatives that stand in a more logical and derivative relation to the naturalistic axioms. If it is true, as Gareth Morgan asserts, that different paradigms make different knowledge claims, with the result that criteria for what counts as significant knowledge vary from paradigm to paradigm, then it is essential that the naturalistic paradigm be graced with its own, more appropriate set. We offer these four for consideration.

HOW CAN THE NATURALIST MEET THESE TRUSTWORTHINESS CRITERIA?

We turn now to a consideration of means whereby the naturalist's alternative trustworthiness criteria may be operationalized, dealing with each in turn.

Credibility

We shall suggest five major techniques: activities that make it more likely that credible findings and interpretations will be produced (prolonged engagement, persistent observation, and triangulation); an activity that provides an external check on the inquiry process (peer debriefing); an activity aimed at refining working hypotheses as more and more information becomes available (negative case analysis); an activity that makes possible checking preliminary findings and interpretations against archived "raw data" (referential adequacy); and an activity providing for the direct test of findings and interpretations with the human sources from which they have come—the constructors of the multiple realities being studied (member checking).

(1) Activities increasing the probability that credible findings will be produced. There are three such activities: prolonged engagement, persistent observation, and triangulation. The first, *prolonged engagement,* is the investment of sufficient time to achieve certain purposes: learning the "culture," testing for misinformation introduced by distortions either of the self or of the respondents, and building trust. We saw in the opening paragraphs of this chapter that a major criticism leveled by Freeman (1983) against Margaret Mead was that she spent virtually no time learning about Samoan culture before she focused intensively on the special area she had carved out for herself: adolescent girls. But the meaning of adolescence presumably cannot be appreciated except in terms of larger cultural parameters. Similarly, one

might suggest, it is not possible to understand *any* phenomenon without reference to the context in which it is embedded; indeed, Schwartz and Ogilvy (1979) argue that objects and behaviors take not only their meaning but their very existence from their contexts. It is imperative, therefore, that the naturalist spend enough time in becoming oriented to the situation, "soaking in the culture through his or her pores," to be certain that the context is thoroughly appreciated and understood. Just how long is that? The answer to that question is of course relative to the context's scope and sophistication, but at a minimum it must be: "Long enough to be able to survive without challenge while existing in that culture."

Prolonged engagement also requires that the investigator be involved with a site sufficiently long to detect and take account of distortions that might otherwise creep into the data. First and foremost the investigator must deal with personal distortions. The mere fact of being "a stranger in a strange land" draws undue attention to the inquirer, with its attendant overreaction. It seems likely that unless the inquirer began as an accepted member of the group or agency being studied, distortions can never be overcome; Philip Jackson (1968) points out that in his yearlong study of a California classroom—one in which he sat virtually every day—even his sneezes continued to draw attention until the end of the year, although no one attended to the sneezes of any of the "regular" members of the class. But the investigator also introduces distortions based on his or her own a priori values and constructions. No one enters a site in a mindless fashion; there are always prior formulations, as attested to by the fact that it is always possible to write out ahead of time what one expects to find there. Fortunately this possibility also provides the basis for a test: If the investigator produces field notes and makes interpretations that are continuously predictable from the original formulation, then that investigator has either not spent enough time on site or has persisted against all logic in his or her ethnocentric posture.

There are also distortions introduced by the respondents. Many of these are *unintended;* so, for example, Bilmes (1975) describes a series of sources of "misinformation," including *perceptual distortions and selective perception* (Bilmes admittedly operates from a correspondence view of reality, so the naturalist would want to take this category with a grain of salt); *retrospective distortion and selectivity; misconstruction of investigator's questions*—and hence of the answers given to them; and *situated motives,* such as wanting to please the investigator, saying normatively appropriate things, or simply not being motivated to address the investigator's concern fully. But some distortions are *in-*

tended to deceive or confuse; Douglas (1976) is particularly articulate about the lies, fronts, and deceptions that may be practiced by informants. Indeed, he argues that the cooperative posture that characterizes most inquiry is a case of misplaced confidence; that everyone has something to hide; and that investigators are well advised to adopt an investigative posture. Whether one wishes to be as cynical as Douglas must remain an open question, but there are surely times and places in which the techniques he suggests are useful. During the period of prolonged engagement the investigator must decide whether he or she has risen above his or her own preconceptions, whether misinformation has been forthcoming and whether that misinformation is deliberate or unintended, and what posture to take to combat that problem.

Finally, the period of prolonged engagement is intended to provide the investigator an opportunity to build trust. Now, building trust, as Johnson (1975) has eloquently pointed out, is not a matter of applying techniques that guarantee it. Moreover, trust is not a matter of the personal characteristics of the investigator: a "nice guy" to whom respondents will instinctively confide their innermost secrets. Rather, it is a *developmental* process to be engaged in daily: to demonstrate to the respondents that their confidences will not be used against them; that pledges of anonymity will be honored; that hidden agendas, whether those of the investigator or of other local figures to whom the investigator may be beholden, are not being served; that the interests of the respondents will be honored as much as those of the investigator; and that the respondents will have input into, and actually influence, the inquiry process. Building trust is a time-consuming process; moreover, trust can be destroyed in an instant and then take even more time to rebuild. Prolonged engagement is a must if adequate trust and rapport are to emerge.

Before leaving the topic of prolonged engagement, we wish to add a caveat against the danger of what anthropologists have sometimes referred to as "going native." Lincoln and Guba (1981, p. 4) describe this phenomenon as follows:

> When an anthropologist has become so like the group he is studying that he ceases to consider himself a part of the profession—or ceases to consider either his cultural or professional subgroup as his dominant reference group—he is contributing to the research and begins a "performance-understanding" role (Kolaja, 1956, p. 161) within the studied group. Paul, in a discussion of this problem, named Frank Cushing as an example of an anthropologist who simply refused to continue publishing the results of his field studies. Identification with

the "natives," or co-optation, as a persistent problem of inquirer identification, has been a part of the "warnings and advice" given to new
participant observers for several decades. Gold (1969) suggests that going native is almost always the result of naivete, and happens as an
unfortunate accident. In the process of attempting to gain *Verstehen,*
he asserts, ". . . the field worker may overidentify with the informant
and start to lose his research perspective by 'going native'" (p. 36).
Moreover, "prolonged direct participation entails the risk that the
researcher will lose his *detached wonder* and fail to discover certain
phenomena that the relatively uninvolved researcher would discover"
(p. 63-64, latter italics added).

It seems clear that any tendencies to "go native" will be abetted
by prolonged engagement. The longer the investigator is in the field,
the more accepted he or she becomes, the more appreciative of local
culture, the greater the likelihood that professional judgments will be
influenced. There are no techniques that will provide a guarantee
against such influence either unconsciously or consciously; awareness
is, however, a great step toward prevention.

The technique of *persistent observation* adds the dimension of
salience to what might otherwise appear to be little more than a
mindless immersion. If the purpose of prolonged engagement is to
render the inquirer open to the multiple influences—the mutual shapers
and contextual factors—that impinge upon the phenomenon being
studied, the purpose of persistent observation is to identify those
characteristics and elements in the situation that are most relevant to
the problem or issue being pursued and focusing on them in detail.
If prolonged engagement provides scope, persistent observation provides depth.

The inquirer must sooner or later come to terms with what Eisner
(1975) has termed the "pervasive qualities" involved—those things that
really count. That focusing also implies sorting out irrelevancies—the
things that do *not* count. But rather than taking the view that the
atypical is de facto also the "intrinsically uninteresting," the naturalist
must be able to recognize when the atypical may have importance.
These goals require that the naturalist continuously engage in tentative
labeling of what are taken as salient factors and then exploring them
in detail, to the point where either the initial assessment is seen to be
erroneous, or the factors are understood in a nonsuperficial way. To
satisfy this criterion of trustworthiness, the naturalist must be able to
describe in detail just how this process of tentative identification and
detailed exploration was carried out.

Persistent observation also has its pitfall, paralleling that of "going native" in relation to prolonged engagement. In this case the danger is that of premature closure. Pressed by demands of clients or funders, and perhaps subject to the intolerance of ambiguity so characteristic of the human species, the naturalistic inquirer may come to a focus too soon—as in the case of Margaret Mead (if Freeman's charge is to be credited). This problem is especially serious in those situations in which lies, fronts, or other deceptions are being practiced, for early closure makes it especially easy to bring off such deceits. The proper practice of persistent observation calls for an aura of skepticism surrounding an intention to come to those terms called for by the situation.

The technique of *triangulation* is the third mode of improving the probability that findings and interpretations will be found credible. It seems likely that the term "triangulation" had its origins in the metaphor of *radio* triangulation, that is, determining the point of origin of a radio broadcast by using directional antennas set up at the two ends of a known baseline. By measuring the angle at which each of the antennas receives the most powerful signal, a triangle can be erected and solved, using simple geometry, to pinpoint the source at the vertex of the triangle opposite the baseline.

Denzin (1978) has suggested that four different modes of triangulation exist: the use of multiple and different *sources, methods, investigators,* and *theories.* The first of these, sources, is what people seem to mean most often when they speak of triangulation. One often encounters phrases such as, "No report was credited unless it could be verified by another person," or "The information forthcoming in interviews was discounted unless it could be checked in the available documents." These expressions suggest that "multiple sources" may imply *multiple* copies of one *type* of source (such as interview respondents) or *different* sources of the *same* information (for example, verifying an interview respondent's recollections about what happened at a board meeting by consulting the official minutes of that meeting [but note that if the minutes do not support the recollections, all one can infer is that *one* of the sources is probably in error]). Diesing (1972, pp. 147-148) supplies yet another possible meaning with respect to sources in his discussion of *contextual validation:*

> Contextual validation takes two main forms. First, the validity of a piece of evidence can be assessed by comparing it with other kinds of evidence on the same point. Each kind . . . has its own characteristic

ambiguities and shortcomings, which are unlikely to coincide with those of another kind. . . .

The second kind of contextual validation is to evaluate a source of evidence by collecting other kinds of evidence about the source . . . to locate the characteristic pattern of distortion in a source.

The first kind of contextual validation seems to be similar to Denzin's use, the second seems to be a new form in which the source itself is called into question. The presumption seems to be that if one can establish a particular *pattern* of distortion (false or biased premises, for example), then one is in a position to *correct* the information forthcoming from that source, including that which cannot be verified elsewhere.

The use of different *methods* for triangulation also has a distinguished history. Webb et al. (1966, p. 3) conclude that while triangulation by methods may be difficult, it is very much worth doing, because it makes data believable:

> Once a proposition has been confirmed by two or more measurement processes, the uncertainty of its interpretation is greatly reduced. The most persuasive evidence comes through a triangulation of measurement processes. If a proposition can survive the onslaught of a series of imperfect measures, with all their irrelevant error, confidence should be placed in it.

The unobtrusive measures proposed in their classic volume are, among other things, intended to provide for such triangulation. They also make the point that different quasi-designs, while each subject to one or more of the Campbell-Stanley "threats," may be used in tandem—a kind of triangulation—so that the imperfections of one are cancelled out by the strengths of another. It is as though a fisherman were to use multiple nets, each of which had a complement of holes, but placed together so that the holes in one net were covered by intact portions of other nets.

The concept of triangulation by different methods thus can imply either different data collection modes (interview, questionnaire, observation, testing) or different designs. The latter concept makes sense only within the conventional paradigm, however, for if the design is emergent, as in a naturalistic study, it would not be possible in advance to patch together multiple designs that had the property of warding off threats to which they might individually be exposed. The naturalist thus falls back on different modes of data collection, using any that come logically to hand but depending most on qualitative methods.

The use of different *investigators,* a concept perfectly feasible for the conventionalist, runs into some problems in the naturalistic context. If the design is emergent, and its form depends ultimately on the particular interaction that the investigator has with the phenomena (Axiom 2), then one could not expect corroboration of one investigator by another. The problem is identical to that of expecting replicability for the sake of establishing reliability. However, the naturalitst sees it as perfectly possible to use multiple investigators as part of a team, with provisions being made for sufficient intrateam communication to keep all members moving together. The fact that any one team member is kept more or less "honest" by other team members adds to the probability that findings will be found to be credible.

Finally, the use of multiple *theories* for the sake of triangulation is a formulation that the naturalist cannot accept. What can it mean that certain facts can be consistent with two or more theories? In what sense can it be the case that facts can be given more weight if they are consistent with multiple theories? We have noted repeatedly the likelihood that facts are, in the first instance, theory-determined; they do not have an existence independent of the theory within whose framework they achieve coherence. If a given fact is "confirmable" within two theories, that finding may be more a function of the similarity of the theories than of the empirical meaningfulness of the fact. Further, theories can be interrelated; many "facts" within Newtonian theory are also facts within relativity theory, for example, because, in one sense, Newtonian theory can be taken as a "special case" of relativity theory. But the fact is no more believable because it has meaning within both these theories than if it had meaning in only one of them. The use of multiple theories as a triangulation technique seems to us to be both epistemologically unsound and empirically empty.

In summary, we believe it to be the case that the probability that findings (and interpretations based upon them) will be found to be more credible if the inquirer is able to demonstrate a prolonged period of engagement (to learn the context, to minimize distortions, and to build trust), to provide evidence of persistent observation (for the sake of identifying and assessing salient factors and crucial atypical happenings), and to triangulate, by using different sources, different methods, and sometimes multiple investigators, the data that are collected. At the same time the naturalist must guard against overrapport (going native) and premature closure, and take care that modes of triangulation inconsistent with naturalist axioms are not employed.

(2) Peer debriefing. This is the second of the techniques useful in establishing credibility. It is a process of exposing oneself to a disinterested peer in a manner paralleling an analytic session and for the purpose of exploring aspects of the inquiry that might otherwise remain only implicit within the inquirer's mind.

Multiple purposes are served by such a debriefing. First, and from the point of view of credibility, foremost, the process helps keep the inquirer "honest," exposing him or her to searching questions by an experienced protagonist doing his or her best to play the devil's advocate. The inquirer's biases are probed, meanings explored, the basis for interpretations clarified. All questions are in order during a debriefing, whether they pertain to substantive, methodological, legal, ethical, or any other relevant matters. The task of the debriefer is to be sure that the investigator is as fully aware of his or her posture and process as possible (remembering that while it is not possible to divest oneself of values, it is at least possible to be aware of the role they play).

Second, the debriefing provides an initial and searching opportunity to test working hypotheses that may be emerging in the inquirer's mind. Hypotheses that may seem perfectly reasonable to an isolated investigator desperate for *some* kind of closure may appear otherwise in the view of a disinterested debriefer. If the inquirer cannot defend the direction in which his or her mind is taking him or her to a questioner, he or she may very well wish to reconsider that position.

Third, the debriefing provides the opportunity to develop and initially test next steps in the emerging methodological design. Indeed, it is a function of the debriefer to push the inquirer on such steps, perhaps even suggesting some or asking whether certain ones have been considered.

Finally, debriefing sessions provide the inquirer an opportunity for catharsis, thereby clearing the mind of emotions and feelings that may be clouding good judgment or preventing emergence of sensible next steps. Naturalistic inquiry is a lonely business, as the literature well attests (see, for example, Reinharz, 1979; Wax, 1971; Zigarmi & Zigarmi, 1978). The debriefer who listens sympathetically to these feelings, defuses as many as possible, and assists the inquirer to devise coping strategies makes an important contribution to the quality of the study.

There is no formula to prescribe how a debriefing session should be conducted, any more than one can give a prescription for a psychoanalytic interview. It is clear that the debriefer must be someone who is in every sense the inquirer's peer, someone who knows a great deal about both the substantive area of the inquiry and the methodological issues. The debriefer should be neither junior—lest his or her inputs are disregarded—nor senior—lest his or her inputs be considered as mandates, or lest the inquirer "hold back" for fear of being judged incompetent. The debriefer should not be someone in an authority relationship to the inquirer (a matter of particular note in the case of a doctoral study, which should avoid using members of the research committee as debriefers). The debriefer should be someone prepared to take the role seriously, playing the devil's advocate even when it becomes apparent that to do so produces pain for the inquirer. Both inquirer and debriefer should keep written records of each encounter, partly for the sake of the audit trail (see below), and partly for reference by the inquirer as he or she later seeks to establish just why the inquiry emerged as it did.

Debriefing has several dangers. The inquirer may come to feel that his or her progress, or judgments, or insights, are not what they should be, and therefore may suffer diminished enthusiasm and energy. A careful and empathic debriefer can do much to avoid giving that impression. There is the distinct possibility that the inquirer may be influenced by the debriefer to a greater extent than should be the case—a tendency especially likely if the debriefer operates too directly from a conventional framework and is too demanding in terms of conventional criteria. Naturalists are, it should be recalled, the methodological out-group; it is they and not the conventionalists who must prove the utility of their approach. Too much criticism can be damaging in the extreme. Yet, despite these dangers, debriefing is a useful—if sobering—experience to which to subject oneself; its utility, when properly engaged, is unquestionable.

(3) Negative case analysis. A most useful discussion of this technique has been provided recently by Kidder (1981), who sees it as analogous, for qualitative data, to statistical tests for quantitative data. The reader should be forewarned, however, that Kidder takes an avowedly conventional posture; one might regard her work as one of those attempts at striking a compromise between the "qualitative and quantitative paradigms." Nevertheless her treatment is instructive, and we shall draw heavily upon it.

Negative case analysis may be regarded as a "process of revising hypotheses with hindsight." The object of the game is continuously to refine a hypothesis until it *accounts for all known cases without exception.* Hypotheses take the form, "All members of Class X have characteristics A, B, and C." So, for example, the hypothesis might be, "All learning disabled children will exhibit poor performance in school, a 'spiked profile' of intellectual competencies (high in reading and social studies, say, but low in mathematics and science), and poor personal/social adjustment.'' Or, "All bureaucratic organizations exhibit subunit agreement on a common overall goal, perform complementary subunit functions (the output of one becomes the input of the next, and so on; commonly called "tight coupling"), and shared reward systems.'' These hypotheses are tested and refined so that, ultimately, the pattern exhibited in Table 11.1 is obtained, that is, all members of the class do share the characteristics named in the final version of the hypothesis.

Kidder cites as an example a study reported by Cressey (1953) on embezzlement. Five different versions of a hypothesis about the characteristics of embezzlers were formulated at various stages of the study, with each revision coming after certain findings inconsistent with earlier versions were obtained. Kidder (1981, p. 241) observes:

> Cressey formulated and revised his hypothesis five times before he arrived at his conclusion about the cases of embezzlement. Each time he formulated a new hypothesis, he checked it against not only new interviews but also all of his previously recorded interviews and observations. This ex post facto procedure is a necessary practice. . . . [it] forms the basis for analytic induction and negative case analysis. Negative case analysis requires that the researcher look for disconfirming data in both past and future observations. A single negative case is enough to require the investigator to revise a hypothesis. When there are no more negative cases, the researcher stops revising the hypothesis and says with confidence, "This caused that."

Leaving aside the quarrel we may have with the causal interpretation that Kidder implies is possible with negative case analysis, we may nevertheless find the Cressey example instructive. The first of the five

TABLE 11.1   Ideal Configuration After Negative Case Analysis

| Characteristics | Hypothetical Class | |
	Member %	Nonmember %
Present	100	0
Absent	0	100

hypotheses devised by him—and the data that required revision—took roughly the following form:

> Embezzlement occurs when someone "has learned in connection with the business or profession in which he is employed that some forms of trust violations are merely technical violations and are not really 'illegal' or 'wrong.'" (Conversely, if this definition has not been learned, violations do not occur.)

Cressey had to abandon this formulation as soon as interviews with incarcerated embezzlers made it plain that they knew all along that embezzling was illegal. Thus the second formulation:

> Embezzlement occurs when the incumbent of a position of trust "defines a need for extra funds or extended use of property as an 'emergency' which cannot be met by legal means."

This formulation had to be rejected when some interview respondents indicated that they had taken money without being confronted by an emergency; others said that they had at other times been confronted by emergencies and had *not* taken money. Hence the third formulation:

> Embezzlement occurs when persons in positions of trust "conceive of themselves as having incurred financial obligations which are . . . non-socially sanctionable and which . . . must be satisfied by private means."

Cressey checked this formulation against both previous and subsequent interviews and found instances in which nothing existed that could be considered a financial obligation—a past debt for which the person felt responsible—and he found other instances in which nonsanctionable obligations had existed without embezzlement. Thus the fourth version:

> Embezzlement occurs not only for the reasons cited in the third hypothesis, but also "because of present discordance between the embezzler's income and expenditures as well."

This revision did account for some previously unaccountable types, but again negative instances were formed in which the conditions existed but embezzlement had not occurred. Finally, the fifth version:

> "Trusted persons become trust violators when they conceive of themselves as having a financial problem which is nonshareable, are aware that this problem can be secretly resolved by violation of the posi-

tion of financial trust, and are able to apply to their own conduct in that situation verbalizations which enable them to adjust their conception of themselves as users of the entrusted funds or property."

Kidder (1981, p. 243) comments:

Cressey tested this hypothesis against all the data he had gathered, against two hundred cases of embezzlement collected by another researcher, and against additional interviews that he conducted in another penitentiary. He found no negative cases.

Thus negative case analysis eliminates all "outliers" and all exceptions by continually revising the hypothesis at issue until the "fit" is perfect. Kidder (1981, p. 244) suggests that negative case analysis is to qualitative research as statistical analysis is to quantitative:

Both are means to handle error variance. Qualitative research uses "errors" to revise the hypothesis; quantitative analysis uses error variance to test the hypothesis, demonstrating how large the treatment effects are compared to the error variance.

Of course, as Kidder also notes, proponents of the conventional statistical approach take exception to negative case analysis because it seems to build upon chance variations in the data at hand. But she rejects this criticism and endeavors to show the parallelism that exists between statistical analysis and negative case analysis. Whether she succeeds in that attempt is not a particular issue here; what is important to note is that the technique of negative case analysis does provide a useful means to make data more credible by reducing the number of exceptional cases to zero.

But perhaps the insistence on *zero* exceptions may be too rigid a criterion. Indeed, on its face it seems almost impossible to satisfy in actual studies (the contention that Cressey found *no* exceptions in all his own data, not to mention hundreds of other cases developed by a colleague, is a little hard to believe). In situations where one might expect lies, fronts, and other deliberate or unconscious deceptions (as in the case of self-delusions), some of the cases ought to *appear* to be exceptions even when the hypothesis is valid simply because the false elements cannot always be fully penetrated. Yet, if a hypothesis could be formulated that fit some reasonable number of cases—even as low, say, as 60 percent—there would seem to be substantial evidence of its acceptability. After all, has anyone ever produced a perfect statistical finding, significant at the .000 level? The naturalistic inquirer who would cite such evidence would have piled up a convincing argument in favor of credibility.

(4) Referential adequacy. The concept of referential adequacy was first proposed by Eisner (1975), who suggested it as a means for establishing the adequacy of critiques written for evaluation purposes under the connoisseurship model. Videotape recordings and cinematography, he asserted, provide the means for "capturing and holding episodes of classroom life" that could later be examined at leisure and compared to the critiques that had been developed from all of the data collected. The recorded materials provide a kind of benchmark against which later data analyses and interpretations (the critiques) could be tested for adequacy.

But there is no need to confine such referential tests solely to electronically recorded data segments. Indeed, it seems likely that many investigators will lack the resources if not the expertise to utilize such high-tech devices as video recorders or movie cameras. Further, the collection of information by such means is highly obtrusive. But the concept can still be utilized if the investigator will earmark a portion of the data to be archived—not included in whatever data analysis may be planned—and then recalled when tentative findings have been reached. Aside from the obvious value of such materials for demonstrating that different analysts can reach similar conclusions given whatever data categories have emerged—a matter of reliability—they can also be used to test the validity of the conclusions. Skeptics not associated with the inquiry can use such materials to satisfy themselves that the findings and interpretations are meaningful by testing them directly and personally against the archived and still "raw" data. A more compelling demonstration can hardly be imagined.

Of course, there are drawbacks to the referential adequacy approach. First and foremost, the investigator will have to surrender some of his or her hard-won raw data to the archives, agreeing not to use those materials to further the purposes of the inquiry per se but reserving them exclusively for this adequacy test. Inquirers may be reluctant to give up appreciable portions of data for what may seem to them at best a tangential purpose. Further, it is likely that conventional critics will not accept these materials unless they can be shown to be representative—in the classical sense of the term. Since naturalists do not sample with representativeness in mind, they may be hard put to meet such a criterion, and may feel (rightly) that it is not an appropriate requirement to lay on them. Naturalists using the referential materials are likely to want to "peel the onion" to a different layer, demonstrating less interest in the original analyst's findings than in developing their own. For all these reasons the referential adequacy approach does not recommend itself well to the more practical-minded or resource poor. Nevertheless, when resources and inclinations permit, the storage of some portion of the raw data in archives for later recall and comparison provides a rare opportunity for demonstrating the credibility of naturalistic data.

(5) Member checks. The member check, whereby data, analytic categories, interpretations, and conclusions are tested with members of those stakeholding groups from whom the data were originally collected, is the most crucial technique for establishing credibility. If the investigator is to be able to purport that his or her reconstructions are recognizable to audience members as adequate representations of their own (and multiple) realities, it is essential that they be given the opportunity to react to them.

Member checking is both informal and formal, and it occurs continuously. Many opportunities for member checks arise daily in the course of the investigation. A summary of an interview can be "played back" to the person who provided it for reaction; the output of one interview can be "played" for another respondent who can be asked to comment; insights gleaned from one group can be tested with another. Such immediate and informal checking serves a number of purposes:

- It provides the opportunity to assess intentionality—what it is that the respondent *intended* by acting in a certain way or providing certain information.
- It gives the respondent an immediate opportunity to correct errors of fact and challenge what are perceived to be wrong interpretations.
- It provides the respondent the opportunity to volunteer additional information; indeed, the act of "playing back" may stimulate the respondent to recall additional things that were not mentioned the first time around.
- It puts the respondent on record as having said certain things and having agreed to the correctness of the investigator's recording of them, thereby making it more difficult later for the respondent to claim misunderstanding or investigator error.
- It provides an opportunity to summarize—the first step along the way to data analysis.
- It provides the respondent an opportunity to give an assessment of overall adequacy in addition to confirming individual data points.

However, more formal checking is necessary if a claim to credibility is to be entertained meaningfully. For this purpose the investigator may wish to arrange a session, perhaps lasting an entire day or even several days, to which are invited knowledgeable individuals from each of the several interested source groups. Copies of the inquiry report may be furnished to such a member-check panel in advance for study and written commentary, while at the session itself, representatives of different groups may wish to air their disagreements with the investigator, or with one another. Clearly the investigator is not bound to honor all of the criticisms that are mounted, but he or she is bound to hear them and weigh their meaningfulness.

Of course problems emerge with the member-checking process. Most obviously, the groups brought together for the review may be in an adversarial position. The issue may turn out to be less one of the adequacy of the reconstructions than of their fairness. Checkers may be able to agree that reconstructions are fair even if they are not in total agreement with them. Care must be exercised that in an attempt to be fair the investigator does not simply reconstruct an "average" or "typical" position, which is not only in conflict with the naturalistic position on generalizability but which at bottom represents *no one's* reality.

Moreover, member checks can be misleading if all of the members share some common myth or front, or conspire to mislead or cover up. We have already noted that the naive investigator may be taken in through conspiratorial agreements about what he or she should or should not "discover" (Douglas's 1976 treatment about the several levels of fallback fronts utilized by massage parlor girls is instructive). Should he or she be so taken in, it is an easy next step for the member checks to affirm the validity of what has been "found." Unless one has reason to doubt the integrity of informants, however, the member check is probably a reasonably valid way to establish the meaningfulness of the findings and interpretations. The investigator who has received the agreement of the respondent groups on the credibility of his or her work has established a strong beachhead toward convincing readers and critics of the authenticity of the work.

The reader should be careful not to confuse the concept of member checking with that of triangulation. Superficially these two techniques appear identical, but there is a crucial difference. Triangulation is a process carried out with respect to *data*—a datum or item of information derived from one source (or by one method or by one investigator) should be checked against other sources (or by other methods or investigators). Member checking is a process carried out with respect to *constructions.* Of course, constructions may be found to be noncredible because they are based on erroneous data, but the careful investigator will have precluded that possibility by virtue of assiduous earlier triangulation. Member checking is directed at a judgment of overall credibility, while triangulation is directed at a judgment of the accuracy of specific data items.

Transferability

The establishment of transferability by the naturalist is very different from the establishment of external validity by the conventionalist. Indeed, the former is, in a strict sense, impossible. For while the conventionalist expects (and is expected) to make relatively precise statements about external validity (expressed, for example, in the form of statistical confidence limits), the naturalist can only set out working hypotheses together with a description of the time and context in which they were found to hold. Whether they hold in some other context, or even in the same context at some other time, is an empirical issue, the resolution of which depends upon the degree of similarity between sending and receiving (or earlier and later) contexts. Thus the naturalist cannot specify the external validity of an inquiry; he or she can provide only the thick description necessary to enable someone interested in making a transfer to reach a conclusion about whether transfer can be contemplated as a possibility.

The question of what constitutes "proper" thick description is, at this stage in the development of naturalist theory, still not completely resolved. Clearly, not just any descriptive data will do, but the criteria that separate relevant from irrelevant descriptors are still largely undefined. One primitive attempt to define them is detailed in Chapter 13. The reader may regard that statement as a specification of the *minimum* elements needed. The naturalist inquirer is also responsible for providing the widest possible range of information for inclusion in the thick description; for that reason (among others) he or she will wish to engage in purposeful sampling (described in Chapter 9).

It is, in summary, *not* the naturalist's task to provide an *index* of transferability; it *is* his or her responsibility to provide the *data base* that makes transferability judgments possible on the part of potential appliers.

Dependability

In an earlier paper (Guba, 1981a) one of the authors made a number of arguments useful in shoring up dependability claims:

(1) Since there can be no validity without reliability (and thus no credibility without dependability), a demonstration of the former is sufficient to establish the latter. If it is possible using the techniques

outlined in relation to credibility to show that a study has that quality, it ought not to be necessary to demonstrate dependability separately. But while this argument has merit, it is also very weak. It may serve to establish dependability in practice, but does not deal with it in principle. A strong solution must deal with dependability directly.

(2) A more direct technique might be characterized as "overlap methods." In effect, overlap methods represent the kind of triangulation urged by Webb et al. (1966) and reviewed in relation to credibility. But, as noted by Guba, triangulation is typically undertaken to establish validity, not reliability, although, by Argument 1 above, demonstration of the former is equivalent to demonstration of the latter. The "overlap methods" are simply one way of carrying out Argument 1 and not a separate approach.

(3) A third technique suggested by Guba is the method of "stepwise replication," a process that builds on the classic notion of replication in the conventional literature as *the* means of establishing reliability. The approach, somewhat analogous to the "split-half" mode of determining test reliability, requires an inquiry team of at least two persons, and preferably multiple persons, who can be divided into two inquiry teams. These teams deal with data sources separately and, in effect, conduct their inquiries independently. But there is the rub. Such an approach is quite possible within the conventional paradigm, in which a detailed research design that both teams could follow independently with no difficulty is laid out in advance. But the naturalistic design is emergent; it is precisely because the two teams could, for reasons independent of the instability problem, diverge onto two quite different lines of inquiry that stepwise replication is a dubious procedure. Guba recognized this problem and proposed to deal with it by making extraordinary provision for communication: on a daily basis, at milestone points, and whenever either of the teams saw a need for deviating from an originally chosen path (that is, a need to change the design). While such an approach may be feasible (although no doubt many conventionalists would argue that such arrangements utterly destroy the condition of independent inquiry), it is very cumbersome. Since other modes exist for establishing dependability, there seems to be little point in pursuing such a problematic alternative. It is therefore not recommended by us at this time.

(4) A fourth technique proposed by Guba is that of the inquiry audit, based metaphorically on the fiscal audit. Essentially, an auditor called in to authenticate the accounts of a business or industry is expected to perform two tasks. First, he or she examines the *process* by which the accounts were kept, to satisfy stakeholders that they are not the victims of what is sometimes called "creative accounting." The

concern here is not with the possibility of error or fraud, but with the fairness of the representation of the company's fiscal position. Accounting modes that would, for example, make the company appear to be more successful than it was, perhaps in the hope of attracting additional investors, are fair game for the auditor, who is expected to "blow the whistle" should such practices be detected.

The second task of the auditor is to examine the product—the records—from the point of view of their accuracy. Two steps are involved. First, the auditor needs to satisfy him- or herself that every entry in the account ledgers can be justified. So, for example, the auditor may send a letter to various involved parties asking them to confirm that the status of their account is thus and so, or that they did bill the company so many dollars for certain services on such-and-such date. In addition, the auditor may sample entries in the journal to ascertain whether they are supported by corroborative documents. So, for example, if an entry shows that a certain sum was paid to a salesman to reimburse expenses, the auditor may wish to see the voucher and its attached airline, hotel, car rental, meals, and other receipts. Second, the auditor reviews the amounts so as to be able to "verify the bottom line."

When the auditor has performed both these tasks to the standards required, he or she provides an attestation, for example, "Price, Waterhouse and Company have examined the books of the General Electric Company and find them to be in good order . . . ." In providing such an attestation the auditor certifies that both the process of accounting and the product—the account ledgers—fall within acceptable professional, legal, and ethical limits.

The two tasks of the inquiry auditor may be taken metaphorically as very similar to the tasks of a fiscal auditor. The former is *also* expected to examine the *process* of the inquiry, and in determining its acceptability the auditor attests to the *dependability* of the inquiry. The inquiry auditor also examines the *product*—the data, findings, interpretations, and recommendations—and attests that it is supported by data and is internally coherent so that the "bottom line" may be accepted. This latter process establishes the *confirmability* of the inquiry. Thus a single audit, properly managed, can be used to determine dependability and confirmability simultaneously. A fuller explication of the audit process is undertaken below.

Confirmability

The major technique for establishing confirmability is, as indicated above, the confirmability audit. Two other techniques (triangulation and the keeping of a reflexive journal) suggested by Guba (1981) for confirmability will be seen to dovetail with the audit process and hence are no longer discussed independently.

The major credit for the operationalization of the auditing concept must go to Edward S. Halpern, who in 1983 completed his dissertation at Indiana University on that topic. The major useful residues of that study are twofold: (1) a specification of the items that should be included in the audit trail—the trail of materials assembled for the use of the auditor, metaphorically analogous to fiscal accounts; and (2) an algorithm for the audit process itself. These two documents are included as Appendices A and B; they will be explicated here briefly.

(1) The audit trail. An inquiry audit cannot be conducted without a residue of records stemming from the inquiry, just as a fiscal audit cannot be conducted without a residue of records from the business transactions involved. Halpern suggests six classes of such raw records, which are outlined briefly below (see Appendix A for a fuller description). It may be noted in passing that the inquirer who keeps such records, suitably coded according to Halpern's notational system, will have greatly eased his or her own reporting problem. The inquirers who engaged Halpern to audit their studies were uniform in reporting that the discipline imposed on them by the need to provide an audit trail had innumerable payoffs in helping to systematize, relate, cross-reference, and attach priorities to data that might otherwise have remained undifferentiated until the writing task was undertaken. Thus there is utility in collecting information in accordance with audit requirements irrespective of whether an audit is intended and irrespective of which inquiry paradigm is being followed.

The six Halpern audit trail categories are these:

(1) *raw data,* including electronically recorded materials such as videotapes and stenomask recordings; written field notes, unobtrusive measures such as documents and records and physical traces; and survey results
(2) *data reduction and analysis products,* including write-ups of field notes, summaries such as condensed notes, unitized information (as on 3 × 5 cards), and quantitative summaries; and theoretical notes, including working hypotheses, concepts, and hunches
(3) *data reconstruction and synthesis products,* including structure of categories (themes, definitions, and relationships); findings and conclusions (interpretations and inferences); and a final report, with connections to the existing literature and an integration of concepts, relationships, and interpretations
(4) *process notes,* including methodological notes (procedures, designs, strategies, rationale); trustworthiness notes (relating to credibility, dependability, and confirmability); and audit trail notes

(5) *materials relating to intentions and dispositions,* including the inquiry proposal; personal notes (reflexive notes and motivations); and expectations (predictions and intentions)

(6) *instrument development information,* including pilot forms and preliminary schedules; observation formats; and surveys

Each of these categories is further subdivided by Halpern to provide illustrations of the kinds of evidence that might be useful for each category. Halpern's table is intended to be inclusive of all forms of inquiry and of the full range of information that might be available. Thus not all of this information would be placed before the auditor in any one situation. It is unlikely, for example, that a naturalistic study would produce much audit trail material in Category 6 (instrument development information). Probably no study would produce extensive files of *both* electronically recorded data and field notes; the inquirer relying on field notes would not be inclined also to audio- or video-record. Thus the actual task confronting the auditor may be much more manageable in practice than a casual inspection of Appendix A might suggest.

(2) The audit process. The Halpern algorithm is divided into five stages: preentry; determination of auditability; formal agreement; determination of trustworthiness (dependability and confirmability, and a secondary check on credibility); and closure. The reader should note that Appendix B provides, for each stage and its substages, a listing of tasks that should be carried out by the auditee and the auditor, guiding questions to help the auditor reach conclusions, and cross-references for the audit trail categories that must be consulted at each point.

Two considerations should be borne in mind in perusing Appendix B and in reading the following audit process description. First, the algorithm should be understood as a *reconstructed* logic, not a *logic-in-use* (Kaplan, 1964). While the stages and substages are described in a rational order, it is not the case that the sequence is inviolable; in an actual situation some of the steps may be interchanged and others may be omitted entirely. Further, there may be reiterations if circumstances require. Thus it is not order but the scope of coverage that is important. Second, the reader should note that the algorithm is based on the assumption that the auditor is called in at the very beginning of the study and thus can prescribe the nature of the audit trail as well as other helpful details. But just as evaluators are often not called in until the program they are to evaluate is well along in its development and implementation (*the* most common complaint of the evaluator is,

"If only they had called me in sooner . . . "), so auditors may not be consulted until the study is virtually complete. Indeed, there may be some utility in waiting until the end to avoid the possibility that the auditor might be coopted. After all, fiscal auditors are not consulted until after the accounts are closed; would one believe Price Waterhouse if they had been working with the General Electric accountants all year, advising them on what to do? Thus the reader should understand that (probably major) adjustments will need to be made in the algorithm depending on just when the auditor is initially contacted. If the auditor is not brought in until after the study is completed, it simply means that many of the steps of Appendix B will have to be carried out retrospectively. The danger in retrospective auditing is, of course, that deficiencies cannot be repaired; if, for example, the auditee has kept an inadequate audit trail, it may not be possible to carry out an audit at all. Problems of that sort ought to occur infrequently, however, particularly as auditees become more sophisticated about auditing requirements. There is no danger, for example, that a fiscal accountant will ever fail to keep the records that an auditor will require, for the fiscal auditor's needs are well understood and codified. One may confidently expect that an equivalent status will be reached in inquiry auditing before too long.

We turn now to a description of Halpern's five stages:

(1) Preentry. This phase is characterized by a series of interactions between auditor and auditee that result in a decision to continue, continue conditionally, or discontinue the proposed audit. Having determined that an audit might be desirable and useful, the auditee selects a potential auditor (the nature of persons suitable to be auditors is discussed below). An agreement is reached to have further conversation, in preparation for which the auditee prepares an outline indicating the kinds of audit trail materials that he or she will be able to collect and the format in which they will be made available. In their initial conversation, the auditee explains this record-keeping system to the proposed auditor, and describes the nature of the proposed study (as well as can be done in prospect). Finally, auditor and auditee discuss the three alternatives and decide to continue, continue conditionally, or discontinue their relationship. If the decision is to continue conditionally, the conditions are spelled out for the record, and the proposed audit trail is revised as necessary.

(2) Determination of auditability. This stage begins at whatever point the auditor and auditee have previously agreed should be the entry point; this may be after some specified time period or at some milestone event (if the auditor is to be involved during the course of the study),

or at the end of the inquiry (if the auditor is to perform ex post facto). The auditor's first task is to become thoroughly familar with the study: the problem (or evaluand or policy option) investigated (and how it may have changed with time), the paradigmatic and methodological approaches taken, the nature of the guiding substantive theory (and whether it is grounded or given a priori), and the findings and conclusions. The auditee's task is to arrange relevant materials in some convenient and easily accessible form, and to remain available for consultation as needed.

Next, the auditor must familiarize him- or herself with the audit trail as it has actually materialized. Presumably the trail will follow the structure and format previously agreed upon. The auditor in particular must become familiar with the linkage system that ties audit trail materials to actual events and outcomes. So, for example, if a datum is reported in a case study, the auditor must know how to trace that datum back to its original sources in interview and observation records, documents, videotapes, or whatever.

Finally, the auditor must make a determination of the study's auditability; in effect, this determination signals continuation or termination of the process. The auditor must be satisfied that the audit trail is *complete* (that is, that all of the elements in Appendix A are available or otherwise accounted for); that the trail is *comprehensible* (that is, that it can be understood and followed); that it is *useful* (that is, it is arranged in ways that make cross-referencing, indexing, organization, and the like evident); and that it is *linked* (that is, that the audit trail is systematically related to the methodological approaches, both in their initial and unfolded form). Following this determination the auditor and auditee engage in further negotiation, which may result, as in the preentry stage, in a decision to continue, continue conditionally, or discontinue the process. A decision to continue conditionally implies, of course, the auditee's ability to fulfill the conditions. A decision to continue if revisions are made in the audit trail may not be feasible, for example, if the auditor has not been consulted until after the study's completion, at which time it may not be possible to reconstruct missing items (it should be noted that even if reconstructions are possible, those reconstructions cannot be accorded the same weight as constructions made at the original time and place).

(3) Formal agreement. Assuming that a decision has been made in Stage 2 above to continue in some form, it is now appropriate to reach formal written agreement on what is to be accomplished by the audit. The agreement "locks in" the auditor; beyond this point there cannot

(ethically or legally) be a withdrawal. The contract reached should do the following: establishing the *time limit* for the audit; determine the audit's *goals* (dependability, or confirmability, or both, with possibly a secondary check on credibility); specify the *roles* to be played by both auditor and auditee (along the lines of the tasks specified in the algorithm); arrange the *logistics* of the audit (time, place, support facilities, and so on); determine the product *outcomes* (reports, presentations, and the like); determine the *format* (a possible format for an auditor's report is discussed below); and identify *renegotiation criteria* (what to do in the event that the auditee finds the auditor's report faulty or erroneous, or if either party is impelled to alter the terms of the formal agreement in some way).

(4) Determination of trustworthiness. This stage is concerned with reaching assessments of confirmability, dependability, and, as an optional feature, providing an external check on steps taken in relation to credibility. The reader will note that the algorithm as displayed in Appendix B calls for the confirmability check to precede the dependability check, an order that reverses that which has characterized the discussion so far. The order is not, however, critical.

The assessment of *confirmability* itself involves several substeps. The auditor's first concern will be to ascertain whether the findings are grounded in the data, a matter easily determined if appropriate audit trail linkages have been established. A sampling of findings (it is suggested that findings that appear, on their face, to be most bizarre or unusual be among those sampled) is traced back, via the audit trail, to the raw data—interview notes, document entries, and the like— upon which they are based. Next, the auditor will wish to reach a judgment about whether inferences based on the data are logical, looking carefully at analytic techniques used, appropriateness of category labels, quality of interpretations, and the possibility of equally attractive alternatives. The auditor should then turn his or her attention to the utility of the category structure: its clarity, explanatory power, and fit to the data. The auditor will wish to make an assessment of the degree and incidence of inquirer bias (a clear judgment call), taking into account preponderance of inquirer terminology (as contrasted to grounded terminology), overimposition of a priori theoretical concepts (believing is seeing), and presence or absence of introspections. Finally, the auditor will assess the auditee's "accommodation strategies": the efforts made by the auditee during the inquiry to ensure confirmability (for example, triangulation), the extent to which negative evidence was taken into account, and the accommodation of negative examples (which should have been mostly eliminated through negative case analysis). Upon successful completion of these steps the auditor will be able to reach an overall decision about the study's confirmability—the extent to which the data and interpretations of the study are grounded in events rather than the inquirer's personal constructions.

The assessment of *dependability* likewise involves a number of steps. First, the auditor is concerned with the appropriateness of inquiry decisions and methodological shifts: Are these identified, explicated, and supported? Inquirer bias is again reviewed to determine the extent to which the inquirer resisted early closure (early closure suggests too much dependence on the inquirer's own a priori constructs), the extent to which all data have been accounted for and all reasonable areas explored, the extent to which decisions about the conduct of the inquiry may have been overly influenced by practical matters such as arbitrary sponsor deadlines or client interests, and the extent to which the inquirer endeavored to find negative as well as positive data. Instances that suggest the inquirer may have been coopted are noted, as well as those in which premature judgments may have been reached. The possibility that the study may have been influenced by Pygmalion and Hawthorne effects is assessed, and the level of sophistication of the inquirer is taken into account. Sampling decisions and triangulation processes are again briefly reviewed. Finally, the overall design (as it emerged) is evaluated, and possible intrusion of instabilities noted. These several steps lead the auditor to a final overall assessment of dependability.

While it was not contemplated in early formulations of the audit process, Halpern found the auditor to have considerable leverage on the question of whether *credibility* had been appropriately dealt with in a study. Thus the algorithm contains an optional section (Step 10) in which the auditor can pursue that question. Essentially, this step requires the auditor to review the study from the point of view of techniques for credibility that have already been discussed—such as triangulation, peer debriefing, and member checks. To Halpern's list we would also add collection of referential adequacy materials and the application of negative case analysis.

(5) Closure. When the auditor has completed all of the tasks outlined in the Halpern algorithm, two steps remain: feedback and renegotiation, and the writing of a final report, which might more appropriately be called a "letter of attestation." In respect to the former, the auditor is obliged to review his or her findings with the auditee, for several purposes. The auditee has the right to know that all steps have been concluded in accordance with the previously negotiated agreement. If there have been errors of omission those can be called to the attention of the auditor, who should move to carry them out. Fur-

ther, the auditee has the right to hear the findings and to register concurrence or exceptions. If exceptions are noted, there may be further
negotiations between auditor and auditee to resolve them, for example, by carrying out some additional checks, reviewing work process
steps, and the like. In the final analysis, if the auditor and auditee
disagree, the auditor has the right to present the findings as he or she
sees them, and the auditee has the right to append an exception report
for the record.

In all events, the auditor must prepare a letter of attestation. While
each case probably should be treated on its own merits, it seems likely
that such a letter might be prepared according to the following outline:

(1) The charge: to determine (dependability) (confirmability) (both depend-
    ability and confirmability) (dependability, confirmability, and to review
    credibility measures).
(2) Theoretical basis for the audit (on the assumption that the typical
    reader may not be familiar with the concept).
    (a) Brief discussion of the methaphor of fiscal auditor.
    (b) Referencing of selected references (e.g., Guba & Lincoln, 1981;
        Halpern, 1983).
(3) Specification of particular goals of this audit: What are the particular
    questions that were agreed upon in the formal contract?
(4) Discussion of procedures used. Brief review of the Halpern algorithm
    (if used; if not, the actual procedures should be outlined). Additional
    steps or omitted steps should be described.
(5) Findings. Steps 8, 9, and 10 of the algorithm should be used as a
    guide for this presentation, as appropriate. Exceptions should be clearly
    explicated, together with the evidence in their support.
(6) Overall attestation, in conformity with 1 (the charge) above.
(7) Signature of auditor, together with typed name and professional af-
    filiation (for identification only).
(8) A brief vita for the auditor (one or two paragraphs) that establishes
    the auditor's credentials to carry out audits.

It would not be surprising if the reader were to be overwhelmed
by the apparent complexity of the auditing task, as imaged either by
the preceding brief description or by the more detailed Halpern
algorithm in Appendix B. In a real case, however, the steps are not
so difficult to carry out as might be imagined. The question frequently comes up about the length of time it takes to do an audit; the way
the question is asked suggests that is must be an overly long period.
Related to that question is that of the resources (usually the fee involved) for having an audit carried out. It does not seem unreasonable
to suggest that even for a complex project, a week to ten days will

be sufficient, including a day or so to browse through some initial orientational materials, three to five days to carry out the audit itself, and several additional days to prepare the report (much of which can be already available in the form of "boilerplate," once one or two audits have been done). The required resources may be no more than a typical fee for that amount of time, plus travel expenses to the site at which the audit is to be done. Some of our students have arranged "round-robin audits" for their dissertations, forming a pool from which each individual may draw someone to perform his or her audit (of course audits are not exchanged one-on-one; the possibilities for bias would be too great), and in return performing an audit for someone else.

The auditor should see him- or herself as acting on behalf of the general readership of the inquiry report, a readership that may not have the time or inclination (or the accessibility to the data) to undertake a detailed assessment of trustworthiness. If, as Cronbach and Suppes (1969) suggest, *disciplined* inquiry is inquiry that is open to inspection and verification, the role of the auditor is to make the inspection and verification on behalf of the reader and to attest to having done so. The role of inquiry auditors is thus exactly parallel to that of fiscal auditors, who, on behalf of a stakeholding group that may not be sufficiently sophisticated to read account statements themselves or may not be able to travel to the place at which such statements and their supporting documents are kept, examines the statements and attests to their accuracy and fairness.

The auditor must possess some rather special characteristics. Clearly he or she must be sufficiently sophisticated to act in such a role. Probably sophistication is most needed in the methodological arena, but knowledge of the substantive arena should not be minimized. The auditor must be someone who has sufficient experience to be trustworthy, whose judgments can be accepted as valid, and who is a disinterested party. At the same time, the auditor must be sufficiently close in peer status to the auditee that one does not dominate the other; the auditor can easily be overwhelmed by a more senior, widely published well-known auditee if he or she does not hold similar credentials and, conversely, the auditee may be overly responsive to criticisms and findings from someone who is clearly senior to him or her. The hope for an appropriate exchange and negotiation rests on roughly similar bases of power.

Finally, in the event that an auditor is involved early in the study, he or she must take great care not to be coopted. Early entry may imply a *formative* role, analogous to the role of formative evaluator. The latter's task is to produce information that will help to refine or improve whatever is being evaluated, but if the formative evaluator's recommendations are accepted, he or she will, on the next data gathering round, be collecting data on something that is partly the product of his or her own interventions. Disinterestedness is thus immediately called into question. Evaluators have not produced a solution to this conflict, and there is little reason to suppose that auditors will fare any better. But the auditor must be aware of this possibility, and professional ethics demands that he or she assess the likelihood of cooptation before agreeing to produce a final attestation. If that likelihood is more than trivial, a second previously uninvolved auditor should be employed.

* * *

The techniques discussed in the preceding pages apply specifically to the establishment of credibility, transferability, dependability, and confirmability. One final technique should be mentioned that has broad-ranging application to all four areas and provides a base for a number of judgment calls the auditor must make, for example, extent to which the inquirer's biases influenced the outcomes. That technique is the reflexive journal, a kind of diary in which the investigator on a daily basis, or as needed, records a variety of information about *self* (hence the term "reflexive") and *method*. With respect to the self, the reflexive journal might be thought of as providing the same kind of data about the *human* instrument that is often provided about the paper-and-pencil or brass instruments used in conventional studies. With respect to method, the journal provides information about methodological decisions made and the reasons for making them— information also of great import to the auditor. While much thought remains to be given to the nature of such a journal, it would appear reasonable to suggest that it consist of separate parts that include the following: (1) the *daily schedule and logistics* of the study; (2) a *personal diary* that provides the opportunity for catharsis, for reflection upon what is happening in terms of one's own values and interests, and for speculation about growing insights; and (3) a *methodological log* in which methodological decisions and accompanying rationales are recorded. Entries should be made on a daily basis in the daily schedule and personal diary, and as needed in the methodological log. Useful suggestions for how to develop and manage such a journal are found in Lincoln (1981), Reinharz (1979), and Spradley (1979).

The several techniques that have been described in relation to trustworthiness are summarized in Table 11.2 for easy reference.

SOME OTHER CONSIDERATIONS

A few final comments are in order to close out the discussion of trustworthiness.

First, the reader should note particularly that trustworthiness is a matter of concern to the *consumer* of inquirer reports. It is that person who might wish to use a research paper, act on the basis of an evaluation or formulate policy on the basis of a policy analysis who must be convinced that the study is worthy of confidence. Thus the four criteria of credibility, transferability, dependability, and confirmability must be met to generate that confidence.

Now a particular problem, which the reader may already have noticed, emerges in relation to the criterion of credibility. Almost at once the question arises, Credibility for whom? Some of the techniques suggested in relation to credibility, and particularly the member check, imply that the "whom" is that set of respondents who have acted as data sources (or their counterparts). Since *they* provided the constructions of which the investigator's findings and interpretations are reconstructions, it is *they* who must find reconstructions credible. And of course without their concurrence no outside observer would find the study credible either. But *it is the consumer* who is ultimately the "whom." The source respondents must attest to the credibility of the reconstructions, but our interest, in this chapter, is mainly that

TABLE 11.2   Summary of Techniques for Establishing Trustworthiness

Criterion Area		Technique
Credibility	(1)	activities in the field that increase the probability of high credibility
		(a) prolonged engagement
		(b) persistent observation
		(c) triangulation (sources, methods, and investigators)
	(2)	peer debriefing
	(3)	negative case analysis
	(4)	referential adequacy
	(5)	member checks (in process and terminal)
Transferability	(6)	thick description
Dependability	(7a)	the dependability audit, including the audit trail
Confirmability	(7b)	the confirmability audit, including the audit trail
All of the above	(8)	the reflexive journal

those attestations be useful to the consumer in assessing credibility from his or her perspective. Credibility is a trustworthiness criterion that is satisfied when source respondents agree to honor the reconstructions; that fact should also satisfy the consumer.

Second, we wish to call attention to the fact that naturalistic criteria of trustworthiness are open-ended; they can never be satisfied to such an extent that the trustworthiness of the inquiry could be labeled as unassailable. This fact stands in marked contrast to that of conventional inquiry. There it is putatively possible to arrange things so that one can address questions to "Nature Itself" and have Nature's direct and unaltered reply. The conventional inquirer who can demonstrate that he or she has randomized or controlled all confounding variables, selected a probability sample that is representative of a defined population, replicated the study (or those parts of it that are concerned with instruments), and secured intersubjective agreement can claim absolute trustworthiness—the inquiry is, within that closed system, utterly unassailable. One is *compelled* to accept its trustworthiness. But naturalistic inquiry operates as an *open* system; no amount of member checking, triangulation, persistent observation, auditing, or whatever can ever compel; it can at best *persuade*.

That this is so implies that the naturalistic inquirer operates under certain risks from which the conventional inquirer is shielded. There is no possibility that the naturalist can present a design (even ignoring its emergent character) that will absolutely persuade the skeptic that the results of the study will be worth attending to. Naturalistic studies simply cannot be warranted in the same way as are conventional studies. Persons asked to support or fund naturalistic inquiries or to stake future actions (and perhaps reputations) on outcomes may therefore be much more reluctant than they otherwise might be. As a result, they may make unusual and even unreasonable demands on the naturalist to which he or she cannot, of course, respond. A response of "Whoever promised you a rose garden?" is not usually accepted with good grace. The naturalist must, in the final analysis, come to terms with this aura of skepticism and doubt, or follow Harry Truman's famous dictum, "If you can't stand the heat, get out of the kitchen!"

Third, it must be clear to the reader (who surely must have been asking over and over, "Yes, but just how do I *do* these things???") that there is still a major gulf between the theoretical definitions of the trustworthiness criteria and the means of operationalizing them. It is one thing to suggest that triangulation is needed, for example, and quite something else to say how much, or what type, of triangulation will suffice to establish a minimally acceptable level of trustworthiness. It is one thing to specify a dependability audit and quite another to specify the precise processes that constitute an adequate audit (although the Halpern algorithm has provided a giant step for humankind in that direction). It seems likely that the development of operational means and decision rules for these various criteria and the techniques related to them will be an empirical matter; only through efforts to apply the criteria will the field come to an understanding of what decision rules make sense. What we have here is a situation roughly parallel to asking, "Is a reliability of .65 sufficient to establish the adequacy of a paper-and-pencil test?" or, "Is a return rate of 46 percent to a questionnaire adequate?" These questions can be answered only through experience.

Fourth, the proposed criteria, like their counterparts in conventional inquiry, have utility at several stages in the inquiry process. They can be used to assist a priori judgments in the case of proposals—to a funder, a sponsor, a dissertation committee, or similar group. The proposal can clearly indicate what the proposer expects to do to satisfy each of the criteria, and to provide at least some examples of how those proposals might be carried out. They can be used to assist the inquirer to monitor the inquiry while it is under way—to guide the field activities and to impose checks to be certain that the proposed procedures are in fact being followed. Finally, they can be used to make ex post facto judgments about reports or case studies as a prelude to a decision to publish or otherwise use them. Journal referees, dissertation committee members, members of academic promotion and tenure committees, and members of other bodies called on to make judgments can use the criteria for that purpose. That possibility in turn implies that the inquirer must make available in the report information relating to the criteria—in the same way that one might expect the conventional inquirer to report on his or her sampling procedures, data-analytic techniques, reliability coefficients, and the like.

Finally, we wish to enter a small plea against the constitution of a neo-orthodoxy in the use of these criteria. One of the difficulties in advocating a new paradigm is that the old is so entrenched that it becomes no longer simply *a* way but *the* way; it is converted into an orthodoxy. Kaplan (1964) has called the conceptualizations that inquirers produce about the ways in which they do inquiry "reconstructed logics." At best reconstructed logics are afterthoughts—rationalizations—that describe what the inquirer *believes* was done; most often they do not adequately describe what was *actually* done (what Kaplan terms "logic-in-use"). Reconstructed logics have many good uses: to train the novice, to facilitate communication among practitioners, to provide checkpoints against which even the veteran inquirer can be tested. But—and most emphatically—they are *not* prescriptions of how inquiry *must* be done. When reconstructed logics are allowed to become orthodoxies, inquirers are reduced to becoming true believers (Hoffer, 1951), a posture hardly consonant with the open position (seeking truth wherever it leads) that is typically espoused. It is dubious whether "perfect" criteria will ever emerge; until then, humility in asserting that a "new and truer (more natural?) path to knowledge" has been found will be wise.

12

Processing
Naturalistically Obtained Data

> Data is the substance of things hoped for, the evidence of things
> not seen.
>
> *(with apologies to King James)*

Within the naturalistic paradigm (and in updated versions of the
conventional paradigm as well) data are not viewed as given by nature
but as stemming from an interaction between the inquirer and the data
sources (human and nonhuman). Data are, so to speak, the *constructions* offered by or in the sources; data analysis leads to a *reconstruction* of those constructions. Dictionaries tend to define the term
"datum" as a "given"; indeed, the very word "datum" is the neuter
past participle of the Latin verb *dare,* meaning to give. But the earlier
chapters of this volume have made it plain that "facts"—the "givens"
of nature—cannot be assumed to be independent of the inquirer's
values or of the theoretical language (in the sense that that term is used
by Hesse, 1980) he or she brings to bear. Kaplan (1964, p. 385)
observes:

> Data come to us only in answer to questions, and it is we who decide
> not only whether to ask but also how the question is to be put. Every
> question is a little like the wife-beating one—it has its own presup-
> positions. It must be formulated in a language with a determinate
> vocabulary and structure, the contemporary equivalent of Kant's forms
> and categories of the knowing mind; and it follows upon determinate
> assumptions and hypotheses, on which the answer is to bear. How
> we put the question reflects our values, on the one hand, and on the
> other hand helps to determine the answer we get. If, as Kant said,
> the mind is the lawgiver to nature, it also has a share in the facts,
> for these are not independent of the laws in terms of which we inter-
> pret and acknowledge their factuality. Data are the product of a pro-
> cess of interpretation, and though there is some sense in which the
> materials for this process are "given" it is only the product which
> has scientific status and function. In a word, data have meaning, and

this word "meaning", like its cognates "significance" and "import", includes a reference to values.

Similarly, the values and the "natural language" of the respondent—the local or cultural language within which constructions are made and meanings are represented—also impinge upon the data, shaping them as surely as do those of the investigator.

The process of data analysis, then, is essentially a synthetic one, in which the constructions that have emerged (been shaped by) inquirer-source interactions are reconstructed into meaningful wholes. Data analysis is thus not a matter of data *reduction,* as is frequently claimed, but of *induction.*

DIMENSIONS AND TECHNIQUES OF DATA PROCESSING

The data of naturalistic inquiry—the observational and interview notes accumulated in the field, documents and records, unobtrusive traces, and the like—demand a form of processing very similar to that which has traditionally characterized ethnographic inquiry. Goetz and LeCompte (1981) have described five "selected" ethnographic analytic strategies, which they array along four somewhat overlapping dimensions. We first consider the dimensions and then review the strategies.

The first dimension proposed by Goetz and LeCompte is *deduction-induction.* Deductive analysis (and we may note that this is the form that most frequently characterizes conventional inquiry) begins with theoretically based hypotheses and confirms or falsifies them by reference to some body of empirical data—that is, determines their "T_4 truth," to use Ford's (1975) term. The data to be sought are defined a priori by the hypotheses to be tested, deduced from them as the hypotheses themselves were deduced from prior theory. Inductive analysis, on the other hand, begins not with theories or hypotheses but with the data themselves, from which theoretical categories and relational propositions may be arrived at by inductive reasoning processes.

The second dimension is *generation-verification.* Verificatory inquiry attempts to verify or falsify propositions or hypotheses that have been arrived at elsewhere, while generative inquiry attempts to discover constructs (which may lead to propositions or hypotheses) using the data themselves as a point of departure. Goetz and LeCompte suggest that generative inquiry is most often served by inductive analysis and verificatory inquiry by deductive analysis, although they do note that there are exceptions, as, for example, when generative inquiry is nevertheless informed by some a priori theory (as might be the case for the naturalist who uses an earlier grounded theory in pursuing a second inquiry).

The third dimension is *construction-enumeration.* Constructive analysis is a process of abstraction whereby units of analysis are derived from the "stream of behavior." In enumerative analysis previously defined units are "subjected to systematic counting or enumeration."

The fourth dimension is *subjective-objective.* Goetz and LeCompte (1981, p. 54) assert:

> Ethnographers who infer cultural and behavioral patterns as viewed from the perspective of the group under investigation must use strategies to elicit and analyze subjective data. . . . The goal is *to reconstruct the categories used by subjects to conceptualize their own experiences and world view.* This contrasts with an objective approach, *which applies conceptual categories and explanatory relationships, readily visible to external observers,* to the analysis of unique populations. (emphasis added)

It is not the subjectivity or objectivity of the inquirer that is at stake here, but the manner in which conceptual categories are arrived at, whether in the respondents' own terms or in terms brought to the inquiry by the investigator.

It should be clear from the earlier discussion in this volume that the naturalist would characterize his or her own inquiry as inductive, generative, constructive, and subjective. And, indeed, Goetz and LeCompte (1981, p. 54) themselves point out that

> traditional ethnographic case studies focus on description and explanation; their goal is to reconstruct and classify reality in order to integrate data into a set of theoretical constructs. Such work is typically *inductive, generative, and constructive.* . . . Similar . . . is research that elicits from subjects their own interpretation of reality. (emphasis added)

The latter feature is, of course, the major characteristic of *subjective* inquiry as defined by these authors.

Goetz and LeCompte go on to describe five "selected" (representative?) analytic techniques that, they suggest, may be arrayed along these four dimensions. We may imagine a continuum, the two ends of which are defined, respectively, as inductive-generative-constructive-subjective and deductive-verificatory-enumerative-objective. Nearest the former (more naturalistic) pole is the technique of *analytic induction,* described by Goetz and LeCompte (1981, p. 57) as follows:

> This strategy involves scanning the data for categories of phenomena and for relationships among such categories, developing working typologies and hypotheses upon an examination of initial cases, then modifying and refining them on the basis of subsequent cases.... Negative instances, or phenomena that do not fit the initial function, are consciously sought to expand, adapt, or restrict the original construct. In its most extreme application, analytic induction is intended to provide universal rather than probabilistic explanation; that is, all cases are to be explained, not merely some distribution of cases.

This description sounds very much like the negative case analysis technique that we have already outlined (Chapter 11). The statement fits very well what we shall recommend, although we may take some exception to the assertion that analytic induction is necessarily intended, even in the case of "most extreme application," to provide "universal" explanation, on the grounds that such an objective is in conflict with the naturalistic axiom on generalizability.

A second strategy, also tending toward the inductive-generative-constructive-subjective end of the Goetz-LeCompte continuum, but not to such an extreme, they assert, as "pure" analytic induction, is the method of constant comparison advocated by Glaser and Strauss (1967). Goetz and LeCompte (1981, p. 58) comment that

> this strategy combines inductive category coding with a simultaneous comparison of all social incidents observed. As social phenomena are recorded and classified, they also are compared across categories. Thus, the discovery of relationships, that is, hypothesis generation, begins with the analysis of initial observations, undergoes continuous refinement throughout the data collection and analysis process, and continuously feeds back into the process of category coding. As events are constantly compared with previous events, new typological dimensions, as well as new relationships, may be discovered.

Clearly the method of constant comparison provides an excellent fit with our earlier account of continuous and simultaneous collection *and* processing of data.

The remaining three strategies described by Goetz and LeCompte are probably more typical of conventional than of naturalistic studies.

The first of these, intermediate on the Goetz-LeCompte continuum, is *typological analysis*. The necessary typologies are devised on some external basis (for example, an a priori theory) and are then applied to new sets of data. The problem of data processing thus becomes, from the naturalist's point of view, relatively trivial, involving nothing more than the aggregation of (probably qualitative) information within the given categories. Of course the naturalist might well use naturalistically derived typologies, but would tend to regard such usage as peripheral to the central naturalistic data processing problem—the development of typologies and their relationships and their subsequent extension and refinement.

The second of the three remaining categories (the fourth in the Goetz-LeCompte list) is *enumerative systems*. The only apparent difference between this strategy and the previous one is that enumerative systems are quantitative, in the sense that they require frequency counts. Again the naturalist would find such data processing peripheral to his or her main interests, although not, of course, useless.

The final strategy, located at the deductive-verificatory-enumerative-objective end of the Goetz-LeCompte continuum, is that of *standardized observational protocols*. They suggest that this strategy is erroneously labeled as ethnographic, but it is one that is nevertheless widely used. Data analysis is in effect accomplished before the fact; all that remains is to code the field data (often collecting and coding of data are carried out simultaneously) into the predetermined categories. This strategy differs from the two preceding ones mainly in that the protocol is *standardized*. While it is not unheard of for the naturalist to use such protocols, it is a relatively rare case.

Our conclusion, then, is that naturalistic data processing falls toward the inductive-generative-constructive-subjective end of the Goetz-LaCompte continuum, and that the processing strategies of analytic induction and constant comparison are most appropriate. Our emphasis will be on the latter, partly because it is less extreme, partly because it makes explicit the continuous and simultaneous nature of data collection and processing, and partly because its procedures have been well explicated by Glaser and Strauss (1967).

NATURALISTIC DATA PROCESSING
AND CONVENTIONAL CONTENT ANALYSIS

Before we turn to a detailed consideration of the constant comparative method, it may be useful to consider briefly the relationship of naturalistic data processing to conventional content-analytic methods. A recent author, Rosengren (1981, p. 34), describes the field of content analysis as follows:

> In general, content analysis applies empirical and statistical methods to textual material. Content analysis particularly consists of a division of the text into units of meaning and a quantification of these units according to certain rules. An early content analyst, Berelson, defines content analysis as a method for objective, systematic, and quantitative description of the manifest content of a text. Holsti modifies this definition: content analysis is an objective, systematic, and general description of the manifest content of a text. Objectivity means that every stage in the research process must be based on explicitly formulated rules and procedures. The content of the text is to be emphasized, and the values and beliefs of the researcher must not influence the result of the examination. Some kind of reliability test can be undertaken, so that another researcher can obtain the same result from the same rules and data.

Holsti (1969) himself suggests that there are five major characteristics of modern content analysis. First, it is a process that is "carried out on the basis of explicitly formulated rules and procedures" (p. 3). While unstated, a major premise of this assertion is that the rules and procedures be formulated *before* the analysis is undertaken. As we shall see, the naturalist conforms to the spirit of this requirement but insists that the rules need not be finally formulated until the end of the inquiry.

Second, Holsti contends, content analysis is a systematic process. He defines the systematic nature of inquiry as conforming to "certain general canons of category construction" so that "the inclusion or exclusion of content is done accordingly to consistently applied rules" (p. 4). This systematicity requirement, the naturalist asserts, can be well met even under conditions of ex post facto rule development, *provided* (and it is a crucial provision) that in the end all of the data have been processed according to the same final version of the rules.

Third, Holsti indicates, content analysis is a process that aims for generality, by which he seems to mean that the results of the analysis should have "theoretical relevance," that is, should permit generalization from the analyzed text to some theoretical model. Since the naturalist typically operates without the latter and has, in any event, little interest in generalizability, this requirement is rejected within the naturalist paradigm.

Fourth, Holsti suggests that content analysis deals in manifest content. But this requirement is objectionable on several counts. First, as Krippendorff (1980, p 22) goes to great lengths to point out, content analysis is often guided by an interest in the "symbolic meaning" of texts. But such an interest has multiple implications for the analytic process, including, and perhaps most important from a naturalistic perspective, the necessity for taking context into account. Thus, Krippendorff (1980, p. 23) notes:

> Messages and symbolic communications generally are about phenomena other than those directly observed. The vicarious nature of symbolic communication is what forces a receiver to make specific inferences from sensory data to portions of his empirical environment. This empirical environment is what we refer to as the context of the data.

It is not only to the receiver that context is important; it is also crucial to the analyst (data processor). Furthermore, the inferences from data to environment may not be propositional; they may be tacit. Again the importance of creative human involvement in data processing becomes apparent.

Finally, Holsti points out that content analysis has typically been viewed as a quantitative technique. But, as we point out in our earlier book:

> Arguments against such a strictly quantitative interpretation . . . can be made, including these: (1) the frequency of assertion is not necessarily related to the importance of that assertion . . . , (2) more meaningful inferences can occasionally be drawn from qualitative than quantitative methods; and (3) emphasis on quantification of symbols and precision often comes at the cost of problem significance. (Guba & Lincoln, 1981, p. 242)

On the last point, Holsti (1969, p. 12) quotes statistician John Tukey as asserting, "Far better an approximate answer to the *right* question, which is often vague, than an *exact* answer to the wrong question, which can always be made precise. Data analysis must progress by approximate answers, at best, since its knowledge of what the problem really is will at best be approximate."

We see then that the naturalistic data processor, while feeling a certain kinship with the conventional content analyst, departs from "doctrine" in several important ways, including the timing of rule formulation, need for a priori guiding theory (and deduced categories), utility of generalizable findings, and rejection of constraint to the quantitative arena. While it is not immediately evident from the foregoing discussion, it is also the case that the models of content analysis usually presented in standards books on the subject (such as Holsti, 1969; Krippendorff, 1980; Rosengren, 1981) would, if classified along the Goetz-LeCompte continuum, tend to fall toward the deductive-verificatory-enumerative-objective pole; typological analysis, enumerative systems, and standardized observational protocols are terms and concepts that fit their style rather well. Thus naturalistic data processing may be guided by but should not be constrained by the conventional modes of content analysis; while there is much commonality there are also many crucial differences.

THE CONSTANT COMPARATIVE METHOD

The section that follows is based almost exclusively on the description of the constant comparative method provided by Glaser and Strauss (1967). However, the reader should keep two caveats in mind in pursuing this material, as well as the original reference, should he or she decide to refer directly to it. First, it should be noted that Glaser and Strauss do not address themselves to working within the naturalistic paradigm; indeed, they argue (p. 3) that a major purpose of theory in the field, sociology, is "to enable prediction and explanation of behavior," a purpose with which the naturalist probably would not agree. There is no reason to suppose that these authors were even aware of the existence of a competitive paradigm; they surely viewed themselves as working within the mainstream of sociological inquiry except on one dimension: the source of theory.

Second, the reader should be aware that Glaser and Strauss are describing, in the constant comparative method, a means for deriving (grounding) theory, not simply a means for processing data. They indicate that they will

> describe in four stages the constant comparative method: (1) comparing incidents applicable to each category, (2) integrating categories and their properties, (3) delimiting the theory, and (4) writing the theory. Although this method of generating theory is a continuously growing process—each stage after a time is transformed into the next—earlier stages do remain in operation simultaneously throughout the analysis and each provides continuous development to its successive stage until the analysis is terminated. (p. 105)

Since our interest is not particularly in theory development at this point, we shall truncate these steps by limiting ourselves to their data processing aspects. We may note in passing our enthusiastic endorsement of the notion of a "continuously developing process" in which each stage provides guidance for the next throughout the inquiry.

We now consider the Glaser-Strauss stages individually:

(1) Comparing incidents applicable to each category. Glaser and Strauss launch into an explanation of this stage with only the briefest attention to the question of the *source* of the categories into which "incidents" may be classified for comparison. They indicate that the categories "emerge." But this casual statement is an enormous underestimate of the effort, ingenuity, and creativity that are involved. Spradley (1979), in his discussion of "domain analysis" is more helpful, suggesting that domains—categories—may be names for things, cover terms (whose elements or taxons are "included terms"), and semantic relationships. The latter is a particularly difficult set to identify; Spradley (1979, p. 111) indicates that in his own work he has found it useful to look systematically for certain semantic domains of the following sort:

- strict inclusion—X is a kind of Y.
- spatial—X is a place in Y, X is a part of Y.
- cause-effect—X is a result of Y, X is a cause of Y.
- rationale—X is a reason for doing Y.
- location for action—X is a place for doing Y.
- function—X is used for Y.
- means-end—X is a way to do Y.
- sequence—X is a step (stage) in Y.
- attribution—X is an attribute (characteristic) of Y.

While we may take some issue with the "cause-effect" domain, preferring, say, a "mutual shaping" domain (x is shaped by Y and vice versa), this list is a very useful one to review should the inquirer fail to produce an adequate category (domain) list intuitively. It is also useful as a check on an intuitively derived set.

However the categories may be derived, it is clear that as a first step Glaser and Strauss would have us assign "incidents" (units?) to them, initially on a "feels right" or "looks right" basis. The investigator should not fail to draw on his or her tacit knowledge in making these judgments; errors made as a result of using such knowledge are correctable on successive review, but incidents recognized tacitly, once eliminated, are virtually impossible to recapture.

Glaser and Strauss suggest that coding of incidents may be done in any way that suits the investigator; they specifically mention marginal notes or entries on index cards. Today we would include direct entry on a computer. Glaser and Strauss are unclear about how such notes and/or cards become classified into categories; we shall be more explicit about a process later.

The first rule of the constant comparative method is that "while coding an incident for a category, compare it with the previous incidents in the same and different groups coded in the same category" (Glaser & Strauss, 1967, p. 106). The analyst need not have an explicit reason that he or she can state propositionally to justify assigning an incident to a category, but it is incumbent that the analyst engage in making comparisons, for, as Glaser and Strauss (1967, p. 106) put it:

> This constant comparison of the incidents very soon starts to generate theoretical properties of the category. The analyst starts thinking in terms of the full range of types or continua of the category, its dimensions, the conditions under which it is pronounced or minimized, its major consequences, its relation to other categories, and its other properties.

Glaser and Strauss further indicate that as a result of this thought process the analyst will discover that he or she has developed two kinds of categories: those that he or she has constructed him- or herself and those that have emerged as categories used by the respondents—their local language and cultural covering terms. They comment:

> As his theory develops, the analyst will notice that the concepts abstracted from the substantive situation will tend to be current labels in use for the actual processes and behaviors that are to be explained, while the concepts constructed by the analyst will tend to be the explanations.

Thus the process of constant comparison stimulates thought that leads to both descriptive and explanatory categories.

After a time—brief, according to Glaser and Strauss—the analyst will find conflicts in his or her thinking. The fact that the category is only incompletely and imperfectly defined will cause thinking to stray and make the task of assigning subsequent incidents difficult. At this point, "the second rule of the constant comparative method is: *stop coding and write a memo on your ideas"* (Glaser & Strauss, 1967, p. 107). The analyst is urged to spend as much time as may be necessary to get the ideas down, in order to "tap [their] initial freshness" and to "relieve the conflict." That is, the writing of memos has both cognitive and cathartic uses.

The aim of the memo writing is, primarily, to uncover the *properties* of the category. Knowledge of properties makes it possible to write a *rule* for the assignment of incidents to categories that will eventually replace tacit judgments of "look-alikeness" or "feel-alikeness" with propositional rule-guided judgments. Initial memos will probably not accomplish that goal; however, multiple memos written about a category will provide a kind of "developmental history" and, when taken as a set, provide a comprehensive, useful, and universally applicable definition of it. Glaser and Strauss point out that when working as a member of an inquiry team an analyst may wish to discuss these memos with one or more teammates, as an aid to clarification and possible extension. We may add that the same function can be served by a peer debriefer, whose own records of this interaction provide valuable input for the auditing activity that may be undertaken later in the interest of demonstrating trustworthiness.

(2) Integrating categories and their properties. This second of the stages described by Glaser and Strauss begins subtly—with a shift from comparing incidents with other incidents classified into the same category to comparing incidents to the primitive versions of the rules (properties) describing the category. That is, the comparison shifts from a more or less intuitive "look-alikeness" or "feel-alikeness" judgment to a judgment of whether a new incident exhibits the category properties that have been tentatively identified. The process not only becomes more rule-oriented but at the same time tests the properties; if new incidents fail to exhibit some of the properties, perhaps they ought not to be used to define the category, perhaps a subcategory is needed, or perhaps the category needs to be redefined. It is this dynamic working back and forth that gives the analyst confidence that he or she is converging on some stable and meaningful category set. The test is two-edged, exposing both incident and category to searching criticism.

This process of making category properties explicit not only facilitates the task of rule definition but also enables the investigator to begin on the task of category integration. Relationships become more evident and the category set becomes more coherent—more than a mere taxonomy within which to classify data. It begins to take on the attributes of an explanatory theory, or at least (and more to the point for the naturalist) a particular construction of the situation at hand. Furthermore, if data collection and processing go on more or less simultaneously, later data collection efforts can be directed more specifically at fleshing out categories, filling in gaps in the larger taxonomy or category set, clearing up anomalies or conflicts, and extending the range of information that can be accommodated. Glaser and Strauss (1967, p. 109) comment:

> If the data are collected by theoretical sampling at the same time that they are analyzed (as we suggest should be done), then integration of the theory is more likely to emerge by itself. By joint collection and analysis, the sociologist is tapping to the fullest extent the in vivo patterns of integration in the data itself; questions guide the collection of data to fill in gaps and to extend the theory—and this is also an integrative strategy. Emergence of integration schemes also occur in analyses that are separate from data collection, but more contrivance may be necessary when the data run thin and no more can be collected.

Thus there is a distinct integrative advantage in combining collection and processing of data, for data can be collected for so long as is necessary to complete the integration task. If, in this quotation, the word "theory" is replaced by "construction," and "sociologist" by "naturalistic inquirer," the concepts will fit present purposes exactly.

(3) Delimiting the theory. Again, if we substitute "construction" for "theory," our purposes will be well served by the discussion that Glaser and Strauss mount on the topic of delimiting. These authors argue that as the task of theory (construction) development proceeds, the constant comparative method begins "to curb what could otherwise become an overwhelming task" (p. 110). Delimiting begins to occur at the level of the theory or construction, because fewer and fewer modifications will be required as more and more data are processed (particularly since the data collected last will be specifically aimed at facilitating closure under the requirements of purposive or theoretical sampling). The inquirer begins to realize both *parsimony* and *scope* in his or her formulation. Second, as delimiting occurs the original list of categories will be reducible in size because of improved articulation and integration; options need no longer be held open. At the same time the categories become *saturated,* that is, so well defined that there

is no point in adding further exemplars to them (unless of course one is committed to some enumeration strategy). Glaser and Strauss (1967, p. 113) conclude:

> The universe of data that the constant comparative method uses is based on the reduction of the theory and the delimitation and saturation of categories. Thus, the collected universe of data is first delimitated and then, if necessary, carefully extended by a return to data collection according to the requirements of theoretical sampling. Research resources are economized by this theoretical delimiting of the possible universe of data, since working within limits forces the analyst to spend his time and effort only on data relevant to his categories. In large field studies, with long lists of possibly useful categories and thousands of pages of notes embodying thousands of incidents, each of which could be encoded in a multitude of ways, theoretical criteria are very necessary for paring down an otherwise monstrous task to fit the available resources of personnel, time, and money. Without theoretical criteria, delimiting a universe of collected data, if done at all, can become very arbitrary and less likely to yield an integrated product; the analyst is also more likely to waste time on what may later prove to be irrelevant incidents and categories.

We need only add that the theoretical criteria emerge grounded in the data, and are not given a priori.

(4) Writing the theory. We reserve the discussion of writing the theory (or the construction) to the next chapter.

SOME OPERATIONAL REFINEMENTS

In this section we shall endeavor to be more explicit about the steps that might be followed in data processing activities. We shall discuss the relevant operations separately as tasks of unitizing, categorizing, filling in patterns, and member checks.

(1) Unitizing. The "incidents" referred to in the Glaser and Strauss discussion of the constant comparative method are not given much operational definition by them. But it is clear that whether these incidents arise intuitively or from some more elaborate algorithm such as that suggested by Spradley, what we are dealing with is *units* of information that will, sooner or later, serve as the basis for defining categories.

Some inquirers find this task absurdly easy. Judi Marshall (1981, pp. 396-397), for example, observes:

> It always amuses me when I read books on how to do content analysis that you have to decide on some sort of level of analysis—looking at a word, a sentence, or a section. But the units are really fairly obvious—you get chunks of meaning which come out of the data itself. If you read a side of transcript, there is something which comes out to you as, say, someone's attitude toward their job, or the feeling of powerlessness in relation to the people in the Union. These are chunks of meaning, and you don't have to look at individual sentences, or debate what the level of analysis is. Also the books say, "Arrive at the categories you will use." Well, I don't do that either, but let the categories build up all the time as I put things together that *go* together. I think this is partly about how much anxiety and uncertainty you're willing to tolerate for how long; I think the more you can, the better the analysis works out.

Most inquirers will not be as cavalier as Marshall, without doubt, but *in principle* the task is little more complicated than she makes out. For us, what is taken as a unit should have two characteristics. First, it should be heuristic, that is, aimed at some understanding or some action that the inquirer needs to have or to take. Unless it is heuristic it is useless, however intrinsically interesting. Second, it must be the smallest piece of information about something that can stand by itself, that is, it must be interpretable in the absence of any additional information other than a broad understanding of the context in which the inquiry is carried out. Such a unit may be a simple factual sentence, for example:

> Respondent indicates that she spends about ten hours weekly traveling from school to school in her role as itinerant teacher.

It may be as much as a paragraph, for example:

> Respondent believes that there are essentially three reasons that itinerant teachers are not accepted as "members of the family" in the school in which they serve:
>
> (1) because they are excused from the normal routines that characterize teachers' lives, such as lunchroom or playground supervision or club sponsorship;

(2) because they are seen as "experts" whose utilization by a regular teacher implies an inability of that teacher to solve his or her own problems (a kind of incompetence); and

(3) because they carry a kind of stigma that attaches itself to the students whom they serve.

These units are found within observational and interview notes, documents and records, notations about unobtrusive informational residues or nonverbal cues, and the like. Having located a unit, the analyst enters it onto an index card (or it may be directly entered into a computer). The information should be noted in such a way that it will be comprehensible to some person other than the inquirer (for example, a teammate or an inquiry auditor). During this unitizing phase of data processing, the analyst should err on the side of overinclusion. It is easier to reject what later appears to be irrelevant material than to recapture information suddenly realized to be relevant but discarded earlier.

Each index card should be coded (preferably on the back, where it is not immediately evident to a reader) in multiple ways that may be useful for the particular inquiry. These codes may include the following:

- A designation for the particular *source* (interview notes, annual report, etc.) from which the unit is drawn. It will facilitate later review if the page and paragraph at which the unit appears are also included. So, for example, the designation 23-14B might indicate interview respondent number 23 (notes should not contain information about names, in the interest of anonymity), p. 14, paragraph B of interview notes.
- A designation for the *type* of respondent (because later it may be important to know whether the cards categorized together represent the same or different types of persons); for example, ET for elementary teacher, S for superintendent, P for parent.
- A designation for the *site* (schoolroom, building, town, etc.) when multiple sites are included.
- A designation for the particular data collection *episode* during which the unit was collected, for example, SV-3 for site visit 3, PI-6 for Panel Interview 6, and the like.

In any particular study it is likely that thousands of index cards will accrue representing the raw field data. The inquirer is likely to become discouraged when confronted with the task of abstracting that much information onto cards. But the tendency to label material as irrelevant just to avoid having to deal with it should be stoutly resisted. Time spent at this stage, however laborious, will be amply rewarded later. Moreover, if the inquirer is following the injunctions of naturalistic inquiry, data processing will begin with the first set of such cards produced. Later stages will produce fewer and fewer cards as the study becomes more and more focused; thus the task does diminish after a time. Carelessness at this stage will certainly result in a study less useful and insightful than it might have been, for everything else depends upon the quality of effort invested in this unitizing task.

(2) Categorizing. The essential tasks of categorizing are to bring together into provisional categories those cards that apparently relate to the same content; to devise rules that describe category properties and that can, ultimately, be used to justify the inclusion of each card that remains assigned to the category as well as to provide a basis for later tests of replicability; and to render the category set internally consistent. Note that the category set that emerges cannot be described as *the* set; all that can reasonably be required of the analyst is that he or she produce *a* set that provides a "reasonable" construction of the data. "Reasonable" is most easily defined as a judgment that might be made subsequently by an auditor reviewing the process.

The guiding method is the method of constant comparison, as described earlier. Operationally, the following steps are involved:

(1) Given the pile of cards that has resulted from the unitizing process, and that will be more or less haphazardly arranged, select the first card from the pile, read it, and note its contents. This first card represents the first entry in the first yet-to-be-named category. Place it to one side.

(2) Select the second card, read it, and note its contents. Make a determination on tacit or intuitive grounds whether this second card is a "look-alike" or "feel-alike" with Card 1, that is, whether its contents are "essentially" similar. If so, place the second card with the first and proceed to the third card; if not, the second card represents the first entry in the second yet-to-be-named category.

(3) Continue on with successive cards. For each card decide whether it is a "look/feel-alike" of cards that have already been placed in some provisional category or whether it represents a new category. Proceed accordingly.

(4) After some cards have been processed the analyst may feel that a new card neither fits any of the provisionally established categories

nor seems to form a new category. Other cards may now also be recognized as possibly irrelevant to the developing set. These cards should be placed into a miscellaneous pile; they should *not* be discarded at this point, but should be retained for later review.

As the process continues in this fashion, new categories will emerge rapidly at first, but the rate of emergence will diminish sharply after some fifty to sixty cards have been processed. At this point certain of the "look/feel-alike" categories will have accumulated a substantial number of cards, say, six to eight, and the analyst may begin to feel pressed to start on the memo-writing task leading to the delineation of category properties and devising of a covering rule. Proceed:

(5) Take up cards that have accumulated in such critical-size categories. Make an effort to put into a propositional statement the properties that seem to characterize the residue of cards. Combine these properties into a rule for inclusion. Write the provisional rule on another index card and place it immediately adjacent to the category. Give the category a name or title that catches as well as possible the "essence" of the rule, to make it easier in later sorting to note quickly the content of each category. When the rule has been provisionally established, review each of the cards in the category to be sure that their inclusion can be justified on the basis of the rule. Some cards may be discarded into the miscellaneous pile, or form the nucleus for a new category. In some cases this review will lead to an immediate revision of the rule itself, to accommodate the included cards in a more satisfactory way. The analyst should be on the watch for anomalies, conflicts, or other inadequacies that require attention.

(6) Continue with steps 3 and 4 above, and with step 5 as other categories approach critical size, until the cards have been exhausted. Whenever a card is now assigned to a category for which a provisional rule has been devised, the card should be included or excluded *not* on the basis of its "look/feel-alike" quality but on the basis of its fit to the rule. Anomalies, conflicts, and other inadequacies may become evident as this step proceeds, and must be dealt with as indicated in step 5. If such problems are dealt with by rule revision, cards assigned to the category on the basis of the earlier rule formation must be reviewed to be certain that they still "belong."

(7) When the pile of unit cards has been exhausted, the entire category set should be reviewed. First, attention should be given to the cards assigned to the "miscellaneous" pile. Now that the full category set is apparent it may be the case that cards labeled as

miscellaneous during early stages of the categorizing process may be seen to fit in somewhere after all. Some cards may be judged to be clearly irrelevant and may be discarded. Others may remain unresolved, no clear-cut decison about them apparently possible. As a rule of thumb, these unassignable (but not discardable) cards ought not to exceed more than 5 to 7 percent of the total; a percentage in excess of that figure probably signals a serious deficiency in the category set.

Second, the categories themselves should be reviewed for overlap. The set is inadequate if there are ambiguities about how any particular card might have been categorized. Some unit cards may have been prepared inappropriately in the first place, bearing dual content. In such cases the cards should be rewritten onto two cards so that un-ambiguous assignments can be made. Categorization can be ac-complished most cleanly when the categories are defined in such a way that they are internally as homogeneous as possible and externally as heterogeneous as possible. The analyst should check for that characteristic.

Third, the set of categories should be examined for possible rela-tionships among categories. It is possible that certain categories may be subsumable under others; that some categories are unwieldy and should be further subdivided; and/or that some categories are *miss-ing,* a fact made evident by the logic of the category system (or some subportion of it) as a whole. For example, if the category system has a subset of cards dealing with various aspects of affording parents of handicapped children due process in developing IEPs (individual educa-tional programs), it would be immediately evident, say, if no cards were included that described the appeal process to which aggrieved parents might have recourse. Further, other categories may be in-complete, showing sufficient presence to have been included but not sufficient to be definitively established. Missing, incomplete, or other-wise unsatisfactory categories should be earmarked for follow-up as part of the continuous data collection/processing sequence.

(8) Categories that require it may be pursued in subsequent data collection efforts through the use of several available strategies. Guba (1978, p. 59) describes these as follows (note the relationship of these categories to induction, deduction, and abduction, respectively):

> *(1) Extension:* The inquirer begins with a known item or items of in-formation and builds on them. He uses these items as bases for other questions or as guides in his examination of documents. Amoeba-like, he inches his way from the known to the unknown.

(2) *Bridging:* The inquirer begins with several known, but apparently disconnected, items of information. The term "disconnected" simply means that their relationships are not understood. That they *are* relationships is a premise of high probability because the items have been placed into the same category. The [inquirer] now uses these two points of reference for further inquiry in an effort to identify the connections and understand them.

(3) *Surfacing:* As the inquirer becomes more and more familiar with the area, he is able to propose new information that ought to be found in the field and then to verify its existence. This process of surfacing is similar to the familiar process of hypothesis formation, or to the process of suggesting new categories, once a subject of known categories has been identified, because the logic of the situation "demands" them.

(9) At the end, the inquirer will need to have recourse to rules that will guide a "stop collecting and processing" decision. There are four criteria to inform such a "stop" decision (Guba, 1978): *exhaustion of sources* (although sources may be recycled and tapped multiple times); *saturation of categories* (continuing data collection produces tiny increments of new information in comparison to the effort expended to get them); *emergence of regularities*—a sense of "integration" (although care must be exercised to avoid a false conclusion occasioned by regularities occurring at a more simplistic level than the inquirer should accept); and *overextension*—the sense that new information being unearthed is very far removed from the core of any of the viable categories that have emerged (and does not contribute usefully to the emergence of additional viable categories).

(10) Finally, the analyst should review the entire category set once again as a guarantee that nothing has been overlooked.

The steps that have been outlined above are those that would be applied by each data collector/analyst to the data that he or she has collected individually. At the end of this process (or at convenient intermediate points, as, for example, immediately following step 7 above) the individual inquirer may wish to relate his or her work to that of other members of the inquiry team, should there be any (as is usually the case). The following steps may be followed in engaging in *team* as opposed to *individual* categorizing. We assume that each inquirer has first processed his or her own data as described under "unitizing" and "categorizing" above, at least through step 7 of the categorizing process.

(1) The team should assemble in a room furnished with sufficiently large tables so that each team member may be able to place all category cards, together with their title and rule cards, on the table before him or her.

(2) A member of the team is designated as the leader for purposes of this activity. The leader is seated at a table considerably larger than the others; eventually the leader's table will have to accommodate all the cards contributed by every team member.

(3) The leader selects a prominent category from among his or her own set, reads the title and the defining rule aloud, and inquires whether any other team member has a similar category. Usually such categories exist, although the precise titles and rules may vary.

(4) Each team member with a corresponding category announces his or her title and rule for that category. The team discusses the feasibility of combining the several offered categories, devising a title and a rule for the emergent category on the spot. Team member cards (including the leader's) that fit this new formulation are placed into the new category, after careful review for fit to the rule. Cards that no longer fit are placed into a team miscellaneous pile for later review.

(5) The process continues until all leader categories are exhausted, whereupon members still having unexamined categories assume the leader role in order. Only after all members' categories are exhausted is the process terminated.

(6) The team as a whole continues with step 7 as outlined for the individual analyst above. The purpose, here as there, is to deal with the "miscellaneous" pile, to review the categories themselves for adequacy, and to examine the category set for relationships. Steps 8 through 10 above may now be carried out by team members operating from the team framework rather than an individual framework; this decision is optional.

It might be noted, finally, that the conclusion of the categorization process, whether done by individual analysts or by the inquiry team as a whole, provides a useful opportunity to apply a major trustworthiness technique: the member check. If the issue is whether the analyst (or team) has successfully produced a reconstruction of the respondents' constructions, the best way to determine that is to take the reconstruction back to the respondents for their examination and reaction. Sufficient care taken at this point bodes well for the overall satisfactory outcome of the inquiry, as it might be judged, for example, by an external auditor.

COMPUTER-ASSISTED
DATA PROCESSING

While the existence of electronic computers has virtually revolutionalized quantitative data analysis, its impact on qualitative data analysis, which is at the heart of the naturalistic data processing problem, has been much more modest. Indeed, it seems safe to assert that, as Drass (1980) has noted, computers have been able to be adapted only to the mechanical and not the interpretative phases of data analysis. The mechanical phase is prior to the interpretative, and involves a

> set of operations that retrieve, modify, or transform data. All analytic procedures must include these operations for it is through these activities that data are structured and presented for interpretation. Although these activities may vary in terms of the specific operations they perform (e.g., counting codes vs. attaching codes), they share in common the fact that they are *non-interpretive* in nature, i.e., *they function only to modify or retrieve data rather than to interpret or make sense out of the data.* (Drass, 1980, p. 334; latter emphasis added)

Interpretation is still in the hands of the analyst, even when using a program such as LIPSQUAL, which Drass describes and recommends. He notes that "LIPSQUAL *aids* the interpretive phase of data analysis only to the extent that the interpretive phase relies upon the mechanical phase for the presentation of data" (p. 337).

It would, however, be inappropriate to conclude that the computer cannot be of substantial assistance, even if only with the mechanical phase. Sr. Margaret O'Brien (1982), in an extensive analysis carried out for her qualifying paper in the educational inquiry methodology doctoral program at Indiana University, has identified and described a variety of techniques that may be useful. She suggests that there are two major categories of language data processing programs, which she identifies as *text management* and *text-analytic* methods. Text management methods deal with "editing, formatting, and sorting" that "transform raw textual material into a format and order that is conducive to subsequent analysis" (O'Brien, 1982, p. 3). Examples can be found in Hockey (1980), Gilbert (1980), Oakman (1980), and Ross (1979). Text-analytic methods "assist the researcher in the examination of the underlying structure of the language corpus for the purpose of making inferences about it" (p. 3). The implications of the word "assist" should not be lost on the reader; the programs do not draw inferences, but simply arrange or display the material in ways that aid the inquirer to make interpretations. As O'Brien (1982, pp. 4-5) notes, these methods are found at four levels: univariate, bivariate, multivariate, and parsing:

> The *univariate methods* of the computerized text analysis abstract subsets of data using single words as the unit of analysis. The univariate methods include *frequency counts, concordances, indices,* and *simple retrievals.* The *bivariate methods* of level two make use of the computer's Boolean logic capacity to search and retrieve from the main corpus subsets which include simultaneous occurrences of two character strings. The *bivariate methods* include collocation techniques and complex retrievals. The *multivariate methods* of level three utilize the Boolean logic and matrix manipulation capacity of the computer to describe the relationships among clusters of data. The third level methods include cluster analysis, factor analysis and multidimensional scaling. The *parsing techniques* of level four either strip the message of unessential information and write the stripped-down message in propositional form, or they rewrite the sentences in parsed formats, that is according to their syntactical relationships. The major parsing methods are agent-action-object methods, semantic network methods and augmented transition network methods.

Some useful discussion and/or examples can be found in the following references: for *bivariate methods:* Allen (1977), Dillon and Federhart (1982), Geffrey et al. (1973), Moskovich and Kaplan (1979), and Reed and Schoenfelder (1979); for *multivariate methods:* Bierschenk (1977), Finney et al. (1977), Frey and Raming (1977), Hartsough and Laffal (1970), Margolis and Elifson (1979), and Needham (1965); for *parsing techniques:* Ross (1979) and Tennant (1981).

It seems clear from the above discussion that while substantial inroads have been made in the task of adapting computers to qualitative data analysis, much remains to be done. No way yet exists that permits the analyst to utilize the computer in ways that would take context into account—a critical shortcoming from the naturalist's point of view. Further, as in the use of any prior existing technique, the selection of a technique de facto places its own constraints even on the mechanical phase of analysis and, by that fact, indirectly on the interpretative phase. O'Brien's own conclusions about what needs to be done to make computers more useful indicate that "it would be necessary to: (1) develop education-based dictionaries with appropriate sets of equivalent words [a task that O'Brien is undertaking in her dissertation]; (2) develop a stronger theoretical base for the bivariate and multivariate methods; and (3) conduct more studies comparing computer results to human results'' (p. 80). The latter is of course crucial.

SOME CAVEATS

It must be clear to the reader that the art of naturalistic data processing is far from well developed. Miles (1979, p. 591) has described qualitative data as ''an attractive nuisance,'' commenting:

> Qualitative data tend to overload the researcher badly at almost every point: the sheer range of phenomena to be observed, the recorded volume of the notes, the time required for write-up, coding, and analysis can all become overwhelming. But the most serious and central difficulty in the use of qualitative data is that methods of analysis are not well formulated. For quantitative data, there are clear conventions the researcher can use. But the analyst faced with a bank of qualitative data has very few guidelines for protection against self-delusion, let alone the presentation of ''unreliable'' or ''invalid'' conclusions to scientific or policy-making audiences. How can we be sure that an ''earthy,'' ''undeniable,'' ''serendipitous'' finding is not, in fact, wrong?

Adams (1981) and Sadler (1981) go to some lengths to point out the constraints or limitations that the naturalistic data processor might encounter. Sadler is especially articulate on this matter, suggesting 13 such:

- *Data overload:* ''an informational bottleneck . . . which places severe limitations on the amount of data able to be received, processed, and remembered by the human mind'' (p. 27).
- *First impressions:* persistence on the first stimuli received (''anchoring'') so that later revision is resisted; the *order* of information is thus important.
- *Availability of information:* information that is difficult to unearth or retrieve receives less attention than that which is easier.
- *Positive and negative instances:* a tendency to ignore information that conflicts with already-held hypotheses and to emphasize that which confirms them.
- *Internal consistent, redundancy, and novelty of information:* a tendency to discount more extreme (novel, unusual) information; what is novel may be seen as unimportant.
- *Uneven reliability of information:* a tendency to ignore the fact that some sources are more credible than others, to persevere with an earlier

hypothesis even if all of the sources of information that were used to devise the hypothesis are finally found to be noncredible.

- *Missing information:* a tendency to devalue something for which some information may be missing or incomplete.
- *Revision of a tentative hypothesis, evaluation, or diagnosis:* reacting to new information either conservatively or by overreacting (overcompensation).
- *Base-rate proportion:* a tendency to assume some average base rate when no actual base-rate data are available, or to suppress concrete base-rate information in favor of clinical information.
- *Sampling considerations:* a tendency to be "less sensitive to the absolute size of the sample than to the ratio of sample size to population" (p. 30).
- *Confidence in judgment:* a tendency "to have an almost unshakeable confidence in the correctness of their decisions, even in the face of considerable relevant, contrary evidence" (p. 30).
- *Co-occurrences and correlation:* a tendency to interpret observed co-occurrences as evidence of a strong correlation.
- *Consistency in judgments:* a tendency for repeated evaluations of the same data to be different.

While many of Sadler's points are of rather less import under the naturalistic paradigm than under the conventional, there is little doubt that his caveats are generally meaningful and should be kept in mind in all data processing activity.

Numbers of authors, perhaps because of their insensitivity to the matter of *paradigm* rather than *technique* differences, place the onus for improvement of data processing squarely at the level of method. Firestone and Dawson (1982, p. 1), for example, assert that "perhaps the major stumbling block to further use of qualitative methods is the underdevelopment of data analytic techniques." Huberman and Miles (1982, p. 4) assert that

> over the past seven or eight years, both of us have found ourselves contending with many of these shortcomings of qualitative research methodology, most notably the lack of general procedural canons or specific decision rules for analyzing and verifying data.

In their paper, Huberman and Miles describe a variety of techniques that they have found useful in their own broad-scaled work, discussing aspects of both data reduction ("carving up, aggregating and partitioning [data] according to some decision rules"; pp. 6-7) and data displays. Especially interesting is the latter section, in which they deal with such techniques as matrices (including progressive matrices), figures, profiles, organizational charts, flowcharts, event charts, and networks. Naturalistic data analysts are well advised to be conversant with these approaches, although they should be constantly aware that in perusing sources such as Huberman and Miles they are reading scholars still substantially committed to the conventional paradigm. Nevertheless, there is much to be learned from their presentation. For example, cross-site analysis leading to generalization is one of Huberman and Miles's major interests. A more extensive treatment may be found in their recent book, *Qualitative Data Analysis: A Sourcebook of New Methods* (Miles & Huberman, 1984).

13

Case Reporting, Member Checking, and Auditing

> Circumstances alter cases.
> *("Sam Slick," aka Thomas Chandler Haliburton)*

> The guarantee of objectivity in human science is the participation in the *dialogue* between the investigator and the investigated, in which reciprocal interaction occurs.
> *(Mary Hesse, 1980)*

> The prime purpose of the audit is to enhance the value of information already prepared and supplied by the auditee.
> *(J. A. Edds, 1980)*

In this chapter we shall describe the three major events that terminate the naturalistic inquiry: development of the case report, carrying out the comprehensive member check, and commissioning and facilitating the external audit.

DEVELOPING THE CASE REPORT

Why Report in the Case Study Mode?

That there is no agreement among persons working in nonstandard paradigms about reporting techniques can be taken as axiomatic. For example, Lofland (1974, p. 109), after analyzing a variety of what he terms "qualitative field research reports," concludes:

> The analyzed reports are alike in their data collection methods and in their employment of qualitative materials, but despite these similarities, they display remarkable diversity. Qualitative field workers seem to practice democratic pluralism—or chaos and anarchy, depending upon your moral persuasion.

We shall propose that for naturalistic inquirers, the reporting mode of choice is the *case study,* and shall describe its development in some detail. The rationale supporting this proposal is simply, first, that such a report format is most useful in achieving what we believe to be the two major purposes of reporting (raising understanding and maintaining continuity) and, second, that the case format has certain characteristics that are especially advantageous to the naturalistic inquirer.

With respect to the first point, we believe that the ultimate purpose of any report is to improve the reader's level of understanding of whatever the report deals with, whether some research finding, evaluative judgment, or policy formulation. Case studies, as Stake (1978) reminds us, achieve this purpose best because "they may be epistemologically in harmony with the reader's experience," because they permit the reader to build on his or her own tacit knowledge in ways that foster empathy and assess intentionality, because they enable the reader to achieve personal understandings in the form of "naturalistic generalizations,"[1] and because they enable detailed probing of an instance in question rather than mere surface description of a multitude of cases.

Further, the case study is a fitting capstone to the *continuous* reporting process that characterizes naturalistic inquiry—the culmination and codification of myriad formal and informal reports that have gone before. Every summarizing statement at the end of an interview to which a respondent is asked to react, every debriefing held with respondents at the end of some phase of information collection, every orientation session held with individuals and groups that may become participants, every formal and informal report (quarterly, milestone, and the like), every press release about the ongoing inquiry, virtually everything that the inquirer says or does during the inquiry becomes an occasion for informing respondents and the audiences from which they are drawn. Further, the principle of negotiated outcomes (see Chapter 8) requires not only that the agreement of respondents be solicited at the *end* of the inquiry (as it should be; see the following section on comprehensive member checks) but whenever possible *throughout* the inquiry, not only for the sake of establishing credibility, but to assure that one is on safe ground in unfolding the next step of the emergent design. Whether or not such continuous reporting has been effectively carried out may be best assessed by the "Principle of No Surprise," namely, that when the culminating case report is released no one will be surprised by its contents, since all content aspects will have been reviewed multiple times with the respondents. The case study is, in our judgment, the best means for summarizing all of the data that have previously been tested and displaying them for that final review.

With respect to the second point, that is, the advantages of the case study reporting mode for the naturalistic inquirer, we believe the following points should be mentioned:

- *The case study is the primary vehicle for emic inquiry.* We have noted (Chapter 1) the fact that naturalistic inquiry is directed toward the emic posture while the positivist paradigm is directed toward the etic, that is, that the naturalistic inquirer tends toward a reconstruction of the *respondents' constructions* (emic) while positivistic inquirers tend toward a construction that they bring to the inquiry a priori (etic). The conventional, technical inquiry report seems to be well suited to the latter, but there can be little doubt that the case report is best suited to the former.
- *The case study builds on the reader's tacit knowledge,* presenting a holistic and lifelike description that is like those that the readers normally encounter in their experiencing of the world, rather than being mere symbolic abstractions of such. Readers thus receive a measure of *vicarious* experience; were they to be magically set down in the context of the inquiry they would have a feeling of *déjà vu.*
- *The case study is an effective vehicle for demonstrating the interplay between inquirer and respondents.* Both data collection and analysis, on the one hand, and interpreting and reporting, on the other, are heavily influenced by this interplay, in accordance with the second axiom (inquirer-respondent interdependence). The nature and impact of this interaction can be judged from a case report to a far better extent than from a technical report (the conventional style of which serves to obfuscate this relationship). The reader has an opportunity to judge the extent of *bias* of the inquirer, whether for or against the respondents and their society or culture.
- *The case study provides the reader an opportunity to probe for internal consistency.* This characteristic does not refer simply to stylistic consistency or factual consistency (although those may be included), but, more important, to trustworthiness. While Campbell (jointly with Stanley, 1963) originally rejected the case study as a viable inquiry mode, by 1975 he began to have second thoughts, suggesting that the case study might have many degrees of freedom (rather than only one, as he had originally thought) because each new item of information provided another point of leverage from which to test interpretations. It is this sense of internal consistency that is most crucial.
- *The case study provides the "thick description" so necessary for judgments of transferability.* We see from Axiom 3 that judgments of transferability depend upon a sufficient knowledge base for *both* sending and receiving contexts. It is the responsibility of the inquirer to pro-

vide a sufficient base to permit a person contemplating application in another receiving setting to make the needed comparisons of similarity.

• *The case study provides a grounded assessment of context.* If phenomena not only take their meaning from but actually depend for their existence on their contexts, it is essential that the reader receive an adequate grasp of what that context is like. The case study represents an unparalleled means for communicating contextual information that is grounded in the particular setting that was studied.

Now while the majority of this section will be devoted to the case study, it should be evident that the case study *by itself* is probably *not* a sufficient account of what was done. If naturalistic inquiry is particularly suspect on the grounds of "soft" or "sloppy" methodology (an allegation we vigorously deny) then it is especially important that the methodology of the inquiry be communicated as well. The case study is not an especially appropriate vehicle for this task; while the case study is meant for the *consumer* of the inquiry, reports on methodology are more typically directed at the inquirer's *peers and critics.* Hence we suggest that a methodological report be developed that may be either *appended* to the case or issued as a *separate volume,* particularly if the inquiry encompasses more than one case (for example, Skrtic, Guba, & Knowlton, 1985; Stake & Easley, 1978). Since such technical reports are well understood and commonly used, no further explication will be provided in this chapter; the reader should be aware, however, that *such an accompanying technical report is a sine qua non.*

Some Overall Considerations in Developing a Case Study Report

Just what is a case study? While the literature is replete with references to case studies and with examples of case study reports, there seems to be little agreement about what a case study is. Definitions that are preferred range from such simplistic statements as "a slice of life" or a "depth examination of an instance" to such more formal statements as Denny's (1978) "intensive or complete examination of a facet, an issue, or perhaps the events of a geographic setting over time." We note in our earlier book that

many different forms of writing have been labeled "case studies," as the following list suggests: individuals (developmental histories, etiologies of psychopathologies); agencies or organizations (social work agencies, banks, university departments); societies (nude beaches, community influentials); cultures (Trobriand Islanders, Potlatch Indians);

movements (Yippies, Zen Buddhists); events (freshman orientations, presidential inaugurations); incidents (strikes, nuclear accidents); methodologies (an instance of use of critical path analysis; an application of geocode analysis); programs (Comprehensive Employment Training Act—CETA, Head Start); projects (development of a new curriculum, a national study of schools, colleges, and departments of education). The range of information that has been included within a case study has varied from a few test scores for an individual to volumes of demographic, social, industrial, and cultural information for an entire society. (Guba & Lincoln, 1981, p. 371)

There is no simple taxomomy within which various kinds of case studies might be classified. In *Effective Evaluation,* we note:

- *Case studies may be written with different purposes in mind,* including to *chronicle* (to record temporally and sequentially, as in a history), to *render* (as in a description or to provide vicarious experience), to *teach* (as instructional material for students such as the Harvard Law School case studies, especially when the materials are open-ended), and to *test* (to use the case as a trial for certain theories and hypotheses). A given case may serve multiple purposes.
- *Case studies may be written at different analytic levels,* including a *merely factual* level, an *interpretative* level, and an *evaluative* (judgmental) level; each level presupposes the former.
- *Case studies will, depending on purpose and level, demand different actions from the inquirer/writer,* ranging, for example, from simple recording for a factual chronicle to the weighting of complex alternatives for the evaluative test.
- *Case studies will, depending on purpose and level, result in different products,* from a simple register for a factual chronicle to elaborated judgments for the evaluative test.

Given the above terms, it seems likely that the naturalistic inquirer will always wish to chronicle and render at the factual level, to engage in interpretation for research, and, in the case of evaluation and/or policy analysis, to engage in evaluation.

What is in a case study report? Obviously the content of a case study report depends on its purpose, its level, and its audience, and a multiplicity of more particular factors, but for purposes of *inquiry* reports, we suggest that those elements that are included in Table 13.1 are minimal. We have divided the table into two broad categories: substantive considerations and methodological considerations. The former will be placed into the case study itself, while the latter are properly placed in a methodological appendix or in a separate technical volume to accompany the case.

The substantive case report should contain the following:

- An explication of the problem, evaluand, or policy option that is the occasion for the study; see Chapter 9 for a discussion of those terms.
- A thorough description of the context or setting within which the inquiry took place and with which the inquiry was concerned. This is one of the two items that make up the bulk of the "thick description" for which we have repeatedly called.
- A thorough description of the transactions or processes observed in that context that are relevant to the problem, evaluand, or policy option. This is the other item involved most closely in thick description.
- A discussion of the saliencies that are identified at the site; that is, those elements identified as important that are studied in depth.
- A discussion of outcomes of the inquiry, which may most usefully be thought of as the "lessons to be learned" from the study. The reader should carefully note that these lessons are *not* generalizations but "working hypotheses" that relate to an understanding of the site.

The methodological appendix or companion volume should contain the following:

- A thorough description of the credentials of the investigator(s). If the human investigator(s) are also to serve as the major instruments of the study, the reader is entitled to the same order of information about them as one might provide in a conventional report about paper-and-pencil or brass instruments. Certainly the kind of training and experience

TABLE 13.1   Content of the Case Study Report

Aspects	Intention	Implementation	Modification
Substantive Considerations			
Problem, evaluand, or policy option			
Context or setting			
Transactions			
Saliencies			
Outcomes (Lessons)			
Methodological Considerations			
Investigator(s)			
Methods			
Trustworthiness steps			

should be covered, and statements about the investigators' predispositions (for example, to the naturalistic paradigm) and biases toward the problem or setting should be explicated insofar as the investigators have the insight to do so.

• A thorough description of the methods that were employed, including the nature of the finally unfolded design.

• A thorough description of the measures that were taken to increase the probability of a trustworthy study and to assess that trustworthiness at various places in the study, particularly, of course, at the end via member check and audit.

Table 13.1 also suggests that these five substantive and three methodological considerations should be assessed at several different times during the study. There is, first, the level of intention: What were the expectations of the study team with respect to each of these eight aspects? For example, how was the problem (or evaluand or policy option) initially formulated as the study was being projected? What were the investigators' assumptions, going in, about what the context or setting would be like? What were the expected transactions? What saliencies were anticipated? What did the team think could be learned? What kinds of investigator experience, training, and skills were projected as needed? What methods were planned? What trustworthiness steps were projected? We may note that the recording of this information *prior to any substantial acquaintance with the site* provides a reader a baseline of expectations, illustrates the investigators' biases, and also provides a way of estimating the openness of the investigators to the situation; if the later case reports reflects only those things that were expected in the first place, we may confidently assert that the investigators were *not* open to actual context or events.

Second, these eight factors should be reassessed at the time that the study is initially implemented. It is unlikely that expectations will be exactly borne out; the problem (or evaluand or policy option) will be found to be just a bit out of kilter; the context and transactions somewhat different than had been imagined; the saliencies perhaps more complex and more voluminous; the outcomes not entirely predictable. At the methodological level, the investigator team that is finally assembled may differ in important ways (training, experience, biases) from that originally envisioned; the methods projected may not be entirely appropriate or feasible; the trustworthiness techniques may not be applicable in every instance.

Finally, the eight aspects should be reassessed continuously as the project moves through time. Methods and trustworthiness steps will change with the developing design. The investigator becomes a better instrument because of experience gained along the way. The problem (or evaluand or policy option) becomes somewhat redefined, or perhaps altered substantially. The context and transactions take on a different hue, sometimes because of the presence of the inquiry team (in accordance with Axiom 2). Saliencies come to be viewed differently by both investigators and respondents as information and insights grow. The prudent inquirer will plan both for regular reviews and for exploiting serendipitous opportunities to review.

Who should write the case study report? The writing of a case study report is in many ways more demanding than the writing of a conventional technical report such as a journal article, a report to a funding agency, a monograph, or a book. Many adjectives can be found to describe the task: frustrating, grinding, taxing, convoluted—but also artistic, creative, exciting, and gratifying. The person who can manage all of the tasks in good humor, while avoiding both schizophrenia and cardiac arrest, cannot be found easily. Only a paragon of the sort described by the Boy Scout oath would do. Yet it is possible to say something about what such a person should be like.

First, he or she ought to possess above-average writing skills. Writing a case study is more like writing a novel than a journal article. The plot line of a case should be exciting and should unfold in skillful ways. Foreshadowing techniques must be well used. Intricate relationships must be made clear. Someone who does not have considerable skill in creative writing will not make a good case study reporter.

Second, the person ought to be someone able to subject his or her work repeatedly to searching criticism—from teammates as well as from respondents—as the case is honed into its final form. The object of the game is not only to produce a novelesque story, but one that is credible to others who are acquainted with the facts of the case, either because they helped to gather those facts or because they are native to the context. Once the case writer has committed him- or herself to paper, he or she becomes ego-invested in what was said, feeling a natural inclination to defend his or her own interpretation as *the* interpretation. The writer who can accept criticism and use it to develop a better case is rare.

Finally, the person ought to be someone who is intimately familiar with the case—certainly someone who was an active participant in gathering and processing the data and preferably someone in a leadership position in the inquiry. The tacit knowledge such a person will have developed will be of immeasurable utility in organizing the report so that it makes sense and relates the several items of information in most meaningful ways.

What conventions might the case writer keep in mind at the outset? It is useful for the case study writer to begin on the writing task with certain guiding conventions in mind:

(1) The writing should be informal. The task of the writer is largely emic, that is, to portray the world of the site in terms of the constructions that respondents use, seeing the world "through their eyes," as it were, and expressing their constructions in their own natural language. The writing should also be sufficiently detailed so that if a reader of the case were suddenly to be transported to the site, he or she would experience a feeling of *déjà vu*. Nothing of significance that might be encountered ought to be omitted.

(2) The writing should not be interpretative or evaluative except in those sections explicitly intended for such purposes. Another way to say this is that the writer's attempt to portray the *constructions* of respondents ought not to be confused with his or her own *re*constructions. Of course interpretations or evaluations offered by respondents are data, but the reader should not be placed in the position of wondering whether those interpretations or evaluations are the writer's or the respondents'. In case of doubt, signal the difference, for example, placing in italics or otherwise marking off the writer's interpretations or evaluations when they appear in presumably factual sections of the report.

(3) The writer should err on the side of overinclusion in the first draft of the report. Some case study writers recommend that the first draft be a "data dump," a draft in which all of the data, even those of presumably marginal relevance, are included. One reason for this advice is that specific inclusion-exclusion criteria are virtually impossible to formulate in advance; until the writer has seen at least a first draft he or she is not competent to make a solid relevance judgment. Indeed, the first draft is likely to be a surprise to the writer, who will not have imagined it in just that way when the writing began. It is of course easy to eliminate later those materials found to be irrelevant or immaterial, when judged in the light of the full case.

(4) The writer should scrupulously honor promises of confidentiality and anonymity. Every effort should be made to alter the circumstances of a case sufficiently to protect those who have been promised confidentiality or anonymity. This criterion is, unfortunately, double-edged. Relatively simple changes may suffice to cloak an individual or a site from an external audience; for example, name changes, changes in compass direction, omission of information that, while not

crucial to the case, would give away the site because of its idiosyncratic nature. The task of maintaining confidentiality or anonymity is much more difficult, however, when the audience consists of persons familiar with the local situation, for example, other respondents. Keeping the identity of a teacher who passes negative judgments about his or her principal from that principal may be an almost impossible task; the very nature of the complaint or the way that it is phrased may reveal identity to the cognoscenti.

(5) The writer should maintain an audit trail. The audit is a major trustworthiness technique, but auditability depends on the keeping of records in such a way (Chapter 11) that an auditor can later connect assertions in the report with the raw data on which they are presumably based.

(6) The writer should have a firm termination date in mind for the case. This is not the date by which the case report will have been completed, but the date beyond which events reported and interpreted in the case study will no longer be changed. Because earlier drafts of the case are subjected to a number of reviews, including the critical comprehensive member check to be discussed later in this chapter, new developments will have occurred before finalization that may substantially alter the case were they to be included. Efforts to up-date the report continuously soon result in an infinite regress. The writer is advised to decide early what the "official" termination date will be; later events may, if deemed of sufficient importance, be touched on in an "epilogue," but should not be the occasion for undertaking yet another revision of the case itself.

Operational Steps in Case Writing

A large proportion of the time that will finally be required to complete the case study must be devoted simply to getting organized to do it. The more time and energy that are devoted to this preliminary task, the more easily the writing will go.

The first organizational task that must be carried out is indexing the data materials so that they can be recovered quickly as needed. A major portion of this task will have been completed through the processing of data; the categories that evolve permit subsuming virtually all of the relevant cards, provide an overall framework for assessing the available data, and provide an easy means for accessing the original data on which the cards are based. The latter feature is important both to guide the later auditing process and to enable the writer quickly to find any datum and check the context in which it emerged, should that be necessary.

Insofar as certain key documents will have been included in the data processing, cards will also exist for these data sources. Numbers of documents probably will not have been analyzed as data but may still be useful, for example, personnel directories, covering state legislation, newsletters, or press releases. Indexes to such materials may be prepared in much the same way that an index is developed for a book; quick skimming and noting of key terms, names, and concepts is sufficient to produce a working guide. Of course, what is taken to be relevant depends heavily upon the tacit knowledge of the indexer, who, if not the case writer him- or herself, ought to be someone well acquainted with the site.

A second organizational task is the development of a provisional outline for the case. This outline is prepared in the framework of the very preliminary concept of the case that has been more or less intuitively developed by the writer—a decision, as it were, about what the story line will be. It is to be expected that this outline will undergo dramatic revision as the writing proceeds; nevertheless, it is important that it be prepared if for no other reason than to make certain that all of the available information will find a place somewhere in the report (the idea of the "data dump"). There is time enough later to reorganize and streamline this outline as may become appropriate. The outline should also account for each of the major categories of Table 13.1.

The third organizational task is to cross-reference the indexed material to the provisional outline. This task, while arduous and boring, must nevertheless receive great care, for the writer will later depend upon this cross-referencing to find materials from which to write. Since the case outline is likely to be a fairly detailed document, not easily kept in mind, it is suggested that a "short form" working outline be prepared that contains only the major categories of the original and so can more easily be retained in the mind of the writer. For quick visual reference it should be displayed in large type and posted near the work station. The writer then reviews all indexed materials, asking him- or herself *for each item* where that piece of information might fit into the outline. When the broad category has been identified from the outline abstract, the writer turns to the more detailed outline to decide just where to place it. It is possible that an item may appear to fit in more than one place. The writer should record on the *case outline* the identifying number (or other designation that may be used) from the materials index. Later, when the writer comes to this point in the outline in writing, he or she will immediately be referred to the items of information that are relevant.

The writer is now ready to begin the actual writing. The outline is systematically followed (although the writer should not hestitate to add, delete, or rearrange as his or her sense of what the case report should look like develops). This part of the case development is likely to be the most arduous of all, taxing in the extreme because of its humdrum quality. Anyone who has ever written a dissertation or an inquiry report is aware of the fact that the interest and motivation of the writer peaks long before the task is complete; after that it becomes a simple question of whether the writer's energy will outlast the demands made on it. The material loses all of its novelty and the task becomes less challenging than oppressive. Yet it is at just this point that the quality of the case will be made or broken; the writer dare not give in to his or her impulse to "get it over with."

A major task that accompanies the writing is the maintenance of an audit trail. The writer should report no "fact" without noting its source, make no assertion without supportive data. It is our suggestion that the author maintain a separate index that is accessed in serial order as the writing progresses. For example, the first fact requiring documentation that appears in the report is noted by placing the number 1 in the right-hand margin near the line or lines in which the item appears. In an index placed as an appendix to the report, the reader should be able to find, listed opposite number 1, references to cards and/or documents that report the fact or support the allegation. For example, we may have a notation such as the following for, say, fact or assertion number *56:*

56.   C22.5, M6, OE4.2.

This code might inform a reader or auditor that this fact or assertion is based on materials found in Card Category 22.5, on p. 6 of a document previously coded "M" (for example, an operating manual), and in a folder of fugitive documents, p. 2 of item 4 (OE for "odds and ends"!). We should note in passing that, following on the procedures we recommended for index card development in the previous chapter, each of the cards would contain further references that would lead an interested party back to raw interview or observational notes (or other sources). Both cards and field notes are of course kept anonymously.

Several other problems will be confronted by the case writer as the case develops. There is the question of how the case should be related to existing literature in the field. Should the case contain references to such literature, either by way of providing a base from which the case proceeds (which is usual in conventional inquiry) or as a source of critique for the case (or of the literature from the case)? It would be an unusual problem indeed (or evaluand or policy option) for which some related literature could not be found. If there are themes in the literature that should be dealt with in the case, should they not be inserted somewhere? And if the literature is to be critiqued via the case, should not the case writer know in what sense, so as to be sure to include materials that would make such a critique possible? In conventional inquiry this consideration poses no problem, but in naturalistic inquiry, in which theory and hypotheses (if any) are expected to be grounded in the case, a preoccupation with existing literature may introduce an unwanted bias. On the other hand, ignorance of the literature may lead the writer to make inclusion-exclusion decisions in ways that make later comparison of case to literature impossible. It is suggested that one member of the investigative team be given the special responsibility of becoming knowledgeable about the literature, and that this person provide to the case study writer (as well as to other team members) global summaries of the most important conclusions made or questions raised therein, to serve as a guideline for inclusion-exclusion decisions, both for data collection *and* reporting.

Difficulties in protecting anonymity and confidentiality will continue to plague the writer. There may be instances in which it might be argued that such protection is not a right of the respondents, as in, for example, evaluation of a major public project. Stake (1982), in his meta-evaluation of the AIR-conducted evaluation of the federally supported Cities-in-Schools Project, suggests in a footnote:

> Most of my colleagues would anonymize as many people, programs, and places as they could. Exposure regularly leads to undervaluing. To an important extent, personalistic detail such as I have provided is demeaning. I regret that. My model is not the journalistic exposé. Nevertheless, I have rejected anonymization because it limits reader opportunity to combine new information with that already held. And here, where millions in public money were spent for a small program, and three-quarters of a million more for the evaluation, arguments for privacy seem unpersuasive.

But studies that do not directly serve the public's right to know, and especially those in which confidentiality and anonymity were promised as part of the process of soliciting consent, it is the writer's obligation to be as protective as possible of the rights of respondent individuals and organizations.

It is of course not possible to *guarantee* confidentiality and anonymity. As an *internal* audience, local readers of a case are invested with too much tacit information to make it possible to "hide" the true identity of people and places from them. Furthermore, locals will be called upon to provide member checks of the case itself; if the case is altered too much in the interest of protection it may thereby become insufficiently credible to the checkers, who can no longer recognize their local circumstances. Clearly a balance must be struck. One possible strategy is to present the case rather straightforwardly to member checkers, having first solicited from them assurances that they will not discuss the case with anyone not privy to the member-check process. When the case is cast into its final form, more dramatic changes can be made for the sake of a more general readership.

Nor is it possible to guarantee confidentiality and anonymity with an *external audience*. The circumstances of a case, even when well disguised, almost certainly will provide clues to the reader determined to ferret out the identity of the site. Anyone reasonably familiar with the context of any case can, although not without considerable effort, pinpoint with accuracy where the site must be—and who its major actors are. For example, in the previously mentioned case studies of rural cooperatives providing services to handicapped youngsters under the provisions of P.L. 94-142 (Skrtic et al., in press), knowledge of variations in covering state laws, of organizational patterns of state departments of education, of incidence of various handicapping conditions throughout the United States, and other similar factors that cannot be disguised in the cases make identification possible. In that study, another factor leading to exposure asserted itself: The pride that some of the site directors took in their local operations led them to *want* to be identified!

Clearly the case writer will need to balance many factors that relate to confidentiality and anonymity. The virtual impossibility of writing a foolproof report should be humbling to the inquirer who glibly promises protection without appreciating the full implications of that promise. But the fact that the task is in the final analysis impossible should not deter the writer from making every effort to hide true identities; while the *determined* reader may ultimately win out, the large body of readers will not be so determined. From them the writer can keep secrets, given a willingness to exercise a bit of ingenuity.

Reviews and Revisions

When the first draft of the case is completed, the writer should solicit reactions to it from a number of perspectives. First, reviews should be mounted by other members of the inquiry team, including not only those who may actually have visited the site, but all others knowledgeable about the overall study as well. While the competence of these two subgroups varies with respect to the matters to which the review should attend, both will have useful contributions to make. At least the following matters should receive close attention:

(1) Is the case an adequate representation of what the site is like? Clearly those who have actually visited it will be in the best position to make such a judgment. Tacit residue of experiences there will be as important to this decision as will more propositionally stateable recollections. If the case report does not "feel right" to those knowledgeable about the site, some revision is called for. The nature of that revision can be delineated in careful discussion between the writer and the dissenters.

(2) Are there errors of fact or interpretation? Different team members may be in possession of conflicting information or may make different interpretations of even the same information. Perhaps a simple mistake was made, if the error is one of fact. A careful check of data sources is usually sufficient to remedy the latter problem. But if an error in interpretation is claimed, discussion is called for between writer and dissenters. If the problem cannot be adjudicated through such discussion, it may be necessary to gather further information, possibly through correspondence or by telephone. The draft should not be considered in final form until all such disagreements among team members about interpretation have been resolved.

(3) Are there important omissions in the draft? Even when the writer sees the first draft as a "data dump," it is likely that inclusion-exclusion decisions will have led to certain omissions that other team members see as undesirable. Some things may simply have been overlooked. Or it may be the case that seeing the draft stimulates the memories of other team members who now recall data that for one reason or another had not been preserved in the data processing. When it appears that there have been such omissions, the task becomes one of editing in the desired additional material.

(4) Have team or writer interpretations been erroneously portrayed as interpretations proffered by respondents? We earlier noted the desirability of not interpolating inquirer interpretations into the case study except in those sections in which such interpretations are obviously intended, as, for example, the "lessons to be learned." Nevertheless, the writer may have through ignorance or oversight inserted

such interpretations elsewhere. If challenged on such a point it is up to the writer to demonstrate that the interpretation in question was derived from respondent input; inability to do so is automatically a reason for rewriting.

(5) Have confidentiality and anonymity been adequately protected? We have already reviewed the difficulties that the case writer will encounter in attempting to provide maximum protection. In view of that fact it is prudent to have other team members review the case to make certain that all reasonable effort has been expended. Such a review may assume legal importance should any respondent ever claim that his or her rights were not respected; while the team cannot be expected to *guarantee* confidentiality and anonymity it can reasonably be expected to exercise *all reasonable precautions* in that direction.

(6) Are "hot" issues included that could just as well be left out? It is inevitable in a case of any complexity that issues will emerge that are politically or socially "hot," bearing, for example, on minority rights or fiscal stewardship. The case writer may well experience a surge of righteous indignation, putting on the mantle of the investigative reporter intent on exposing the blatant dereliction involved. But tilting at windmills is *not* a prime purpose of writing cases; unless the issue has immediate relevance to the case, so that the case would be seriously compromised without including it, it is better left out. The review should be aimed, among other things, at identifying such useless sallies and eliminating them. Of course that may be easier said than done, if the writer should prove to be a committed Don Quixote in disguise.

There is one form of "hot" issue that may require action, and that is one in which the public's right to know outweighs the rights of one or more respondents to privacy. Information of this sort is often not directly relevant to the case, but it may be crucial in other ways. Consider, for example, that an interviewer may inadvertently be told, perhaps in an aside in an interview, that the football coach in a certain high school is a homosexual who is making serious efforts to convert the boys on the team to his own lifestyle. Does the interviewer have an obligation to reveal this information in some way? Perhaps so, but the case report will rarely be the proper means for that revelation. Information of this sort that the writer has inadvertently included should be striken.

A second review, in addition to that conducted by the team members themselves, is a substantive review conducted by persons knowledgeable about the cognitive area or discipline with which the case deals. For example, the rural special education project (Skrtic et al., 1985) submitted cases for review to members of the department of special education in the university that housed the study, to be certain that there were no errors of fact or interpretation that such substantive experts would recognize. Of course, most of the team members were, in this case, specialists in special education themselves, so the need for an external substantive review was minimal. But an external review is nevertheless always desirable, along the lines of the principle that "two heads are better than one."

A third review, which may be conducted by the inquiry team itself and/or by an outside group, is directed at the organization and style of the case report. It is useful in this review to employ the figment of the "ignorant but sophisticated reader," that is, a reader who is ignorant of the particular area with which the case deals but who is otherwise a sophisticated consumer of inquiry reports. Will a reader of such qualification find it easy to consume *this* report? Is it well organized? Is the writing as free from jargon as possible? Has the writer provided as many helps to the reader as might be useful—subheads, introductory and summary sections, good transitions, logical sequence, and so on? If the first and second reviews described above are substantive, this third review is formal. Its importance should not be underestimated. Editors of journals, monograph series, and books well know that poor organization and style have killed more writing than have inadequate facts and erroneous interpretations.

When these reviews have been completed, the original writer undertakes a revision of the case. While it will not be possible to incorporate all of the suggestions that have been made, the writer is obligated to take all of them seriously and to make every effort to honor them. When the redraft has been completed, it should again be submitted for critique, although perhaps via a more streamlined process, as, for example, by asking reviewers to comment only on those sections that have been changed. Several revisions may take place before everyone is satisfied (within the bounds of practicality) that the team as a whole can and should stand behind the case report. It is then time to submit it for its comprehensive member check.

CARRYING OUT A
COMPREHENSIVE MEMBER CHECK

While both formal and informal member checks will have been carried out throughout the project, the completion of the draft case provides a final opportunity to test the credibility of the inquiry report as a whole with respondents at the case site(s). The purpose of this comprehensive check is not only to test for factual and interpretative accuracy but also to provide evidence of credibility—the trustworthiness criterion analogous to internal validity in conventional studies. The comprehensive member check is thus of critical importance to the inquirers, the respondents, *and* the consumers of the inquiry report.

Such a member check must be carried out at each site covered by a case. Of course, if one case covers multiple sites (a practice we do not recommend because of the crucial importance of context) it may be possible to hold just one member check attended by appropriate representatives from the several sites. A number of steps are involved in the checking process:

(1) Selecting the review panel. Several considerations enter into this selection process. First, the panel should be representative of as many of the stakeholding groups involved as possible, so that the adequacy of the inquirer's *re*constructions can be tested against the constructions held by those several groups. In the special education case already cited (Skrtic et al., 1985) it was deemed important to draw panel members representing cooperative central staff, itinerant teachers, other special education teachers, regular teachers, principals, superintendents, parents, and board members.

Second, the review panel should be about equally divided among persons who acted as respondents in the study and counterpart individuals who have not had previous contact with the investigators. The first group is able to attest that the information in the report reflects adequately what was provided to the field team, while the second brings the perspective of an unbiased and naive group to the assessment. Splitting panel members among experienced and naive respondents has another advantage in that the inquiry team, knowledgeable about the characteristics and experience of the former, can select persons who can make a maximal contribution, while a local gatekeeper (for example, the cooperative director in the special education study) can select the latter group in ways that he or she regards as "protective" from the local point of view. A better-balanced panel results.

Third, members of the review panel should be selected to be representative of as many local settings as possible (a point different from saying that they should represent different stakeholding groups). If different school systems are involved, for example, or different buildings, or different civic groups, or different service agencies, and so on, the members should be identifiable with as many such settings as possible.

Fourth, it is desirable to select the review panel to represent as many different perspectives as possible. Since the inquiry team can select its half of the panel before the local gatekeeper selects the remaining half, the gatekeeper can be asked to nominate persons whose point of view (regardless of the stakeholding group or setting involved) is *as different as possible* from those espoused by the inquiry team's already-identified nominees.

Finally, it is important to pay some attention to the period of tenure of each nominee. Some minimum length of service is necessary before one can have reasonable confidence in the opinions that panel members might proffer. It is probably desirable to represent as large a range of service periods as possible, but no person should be named who has not spent at least a year in the studied context.

The question may arise whether the review panel members should be compensated for their service, since it is a not inconsiderable period of time to which they are being asked to commit. In general, direct payment should be avoided, since the availability of a stipend may draw persons much more interested in receiving the money than in rendering the service. In cases in which funds are necessary to secure the release of members from their regular work-place obligations in order to participate in the committee's activities (as might be true, for example, if teachers are to participate, since substitutes must be hired to replace them), payment should be made to the releasing agency rather than directly to the individual. Travel expenses that are incurred should of course be reimbursed directly.

Nominees may be contacted either by the inquiry team or a local liaison to secure their consent to participate. It is useful to have two nominees for each slot on the panel since some refusals will undoubtedly occur.

(2) Preparing and delivering the information packet. Those persons selected to be members of the review panel must receive copies of the case to be critiqued as well as certain accompanying instructional materials and operational forms.

First, the packet must include a copy of the case, as refined through the final interview review. The case may be less protective of anonymity and confidentiality than the final, public version will be. That fact should be noted in the cover letter, and assurances given that further disguising will take place before publication. The case may also be incomplete here and there, as the writer discovers that some essential information is still lacking. Such incomplete aspects should be called to the reviewers' attention, both in the cover letter and, when appropriate, in interpolated "boxed-off" sections in the draft itself. Reviewers are expected to provide additional information as they are in a position to do so.

Second, the packet should contain appropriate consent forms to be signed by the reviewer and returned at the time of the review panel meeting. The consent form should briefly remind the reviewer of the intent and scope of the study. The task of the panel to review the draft for factual and interpretative accuracy should be pointed out. Reasonable assurances regarding anonymity should be given, paralleling those suggested for the participant's consent form (see Chapter 10). Signing the consent form binds the reviewer to maintain secrecy concerning the particulars included in the draft and the discussion by the review panel in executive session. A separate sign-off space may be provided in which the reviewer may (need not) give consent to have his or her review comments quoted.

Third, the packet should include a number of blank comment sheets, providing the reviewer an easy means to summarize and index comments. This sheet may be as simple as a two-column page in which a slim left-hand column is used to note the page and line numbers to which the comment refers, and the right-hand column is used to record the comment. The reviewer may use these sheets to guide his or her input during the committee meeting, and/or may hand them to the team members at the time of the review for their subsequent use. Reviewers should also be given the option, in the cover letter, to make their comments verbally only, or to provide them to the inquiry team anonymously in correspondence or by telephone.

Fourth, the packet should contain a cover letter, which, in addition to the items alluded to above, provides information about the time and place of the day-long panel meeting as well as any other logistical information (for instance, the process for reimbursing travel expenses). The meeting place should be located as centrally as possible.

The informational packet should be delivered to the panel members *at least two weeks* prior to the formal meeting of that group. In many instances it may be easiest to deliver all of the packets to some central gatekeeper (in the special education project, this person was the cooperative director) who agrees to distribute them to the various members (possibly by some internal routing mechanism that requires no postage). If necessary, however, the packets may be sent directly to the committee members by mail or other delivery service.

(3) Holding the review meeting. The review panel is asked to assemble on the day of the meeting at the earliest time consistent with

travel requirements. Since the agenda will be very crowded it is wise to arrange for as much time as possible, an objective considerably aided if lunch can be catered. A typical agenda for this meeting might take the following form:

(1) Introduction of participants.
(2) A brief reminder of the purpose and nature of the study being reviewed.
(3) An overview of the inquiry methodology employed (especially important since the review committee members are not likely to be well versed in naturalistic approaches). This overview should include a description of member checking as a trustworthiness measure. The panel's role in this regard should be explained.
(4) An orientation to the review process:
    (a) Three levels of feedback are to be entertained, in order: a *judgment of overall credibility* (if the case study is not found to be credible, overall, there is little point in pursuing the remainder of the agenda); *statements about major concerns or issues* that have occurred to the reviewers—most likely these will have been recorded on the comment sheets provided and can be treated systematically on a page-page basis; and *statements about factual or interpretative errors* that the reviewers have detected—these too may already have been recorded on the comment sheets. Reviewers are reminded that should they wish to provide feedback anonymously they are free to do so using mail, or any other feasible means.
    (b) Three levels of agreement will be entertained: *complete consensus* on some judgment, whether positive or negative; *split consensus,* in which some subgroup maintains one judgment while another subgroup maintains a different judgment, possibly but not necessarily in conflict; and *majority consensus* with a strong *minority dissent.* These three situations are intended to accommodate instances in which the review committee agrees, is seriously divided, or is confronted by a militant minority. Dual reports or minority reports are admissable in the latter instances.
    (c) Special attention will be given to concerns about confidentiality and anonymity toward the close of the session. The reviewers are again reminded that further disguising will take place before the case is publicly released.
(5) Movement through the agenda as outlined above, covering as many points as possible before the agreed-upon adjournment time.
(6) Adjournment, with collection of comments from those who wish to turn them in. Protocol demands statements of thanks, preferably followed up later with letters of appreciation.

One other observation needs to be made with respect to the review panel meeting. Certain persons from whom member checking should be sought should be excluded from the formal meeting for one of two reasons. First, certain persons have status so much different from those of other panelists (for example, school district superintendents, board members, service directors, and the like) that their presence might overwhelm other participants, who might remain silent or defer to these more authoritative opinion makers. Second, certain key persons might be unable to attend, for example, because of emergencies or inability to be absent from duties for a day-long period. These persons may be contacted on an individual basis in an interviewlike situation, but solicited for essentially the same responses as the other panelists. Additional time on site will be needed for these add-on interviews, but that time may also profitably be used to collect additional information that had been found to be lacking when the case was being written.

The site visit that includes the final member check is the last visit the inquiry team will pay; protocol demands a final debriefing session such as those that ended other site visits. Again, this final debriefing is usefully followed by letters of appreciation to all concerned.

(4) Considering inputs from the member-check process. It is quite likely that the member-check process will highlight the need for further revisions and extensions. New information needed to complete earlier unfinished sections should be added. Factual errors should be corrected. But ascribed errors of interpretation are not so easily disposed of. The inquiry team cannot assume that the checkers are right and the team wrong when interpretations are called into question. It is quite possible that local reactions are precipitated by myths, fronts, or self-delusions (Douglas, 1976). On the other hand, the team is under obligation to consider all such imputations seriously, remembering especially the tendency of inquirers to persist in believing that their own interpretations are somehow more valid and objective than those of involved parties. In the final analysis, the team must use its own best judgment, but care must be taken lest that judgment is too cavalierly rendered. In all circumstances, the case study is now cast into final form, possibly with an epilogue that updates the material without requiring systematic changes in the case itself. The team is now ready for a final audit.

COMMISSIONING AND FACILITATING
THE EXTERNAL AUDIT

The use of an external auditor for purposes of establishing levels of dependability and confirmability (and, as an option, secondary assessment of the level of credibility) has been described in detail in Chapter 11. Both the elements needed for an audit trail, and the actual steps to be carried out by the auditor, are described in tables prepared by Halpern (1983) and included in this volume as Appendices A and B. Here we are concerned primarily with the logistics rather than the process of the audit. It is assumed that the inquiry team will have compiled the audit trail that is an essential prerequisite of the audit process.

The first task that the inquirer must undertake is that of identifying a potential auditor and securing that person's tentative agreement to serve. As we noted in Chapter 11, the auditor must possess some special characteristics: a high level of methodological sophistication (particularly in relation to the techniques of naturalistic inquiry), minimal substantive knowledge about the subject matter of the study, personal disinterest, recognized integrity, and, preferably, experience as an auditor. Since the auditing concept is relatively new, it will probably be some time before the latter qualification will come to be routinely possible to fulfill. We have also noted that the auditor should be someone who is an approximate peer of the inquiry team leader, so as neither to dominate or be dominated by that person. At this point in time the inquiry team will probably identify such a person either through personal knowledge or on the nomination of some other knowledgeable party; one can hope that in years to come lists of qualified auditors will be available, just as now one can easily find a qualified physician or plumber through the use of nothing more complicated than the Yellow Pages!

We have also seen that there are some trade-offs between selecting an auditor early on in the study or at its termination point. Auditors selected early can be of formative assistance (for example, in defining what should be included in the audit trail), but their early involvement may also imply their early cooptation. Auditors selected at the termination point may be less involved and fairer, but may also suffer from a paucity of information about the project that cannot easily be made up. Nevertheless, that choice remains open.

When an auditor has been identified, agreements must be reached on a tentative basis about that person's involvement. We say tentative because early steps in the Halpern algorithm call for certain assessments of auditability to be made; it is only at Halpern's step 7 that a binding contract is negotiated. Until that time the auditor and auditee both retain the option of withdrawal should serious impediments arise. Nevertheless, arrangements will need to be concluded both at this tentative point and at a later point about the extent of involvement expected; consideration will have to be given to such mundane matters as fees and reimbursement of expenses. Experience would indicate that if the auditor is not retained until the project is terminated, a total of ten days for both tentative and firm portions of service is probably sufficient. Travel expenses will include transportation to and from the study headquarters and perhaps four or five days of meals and lodging.

If we follow the case of the terminally engaged auditor, the initial service will probably be rendered at the auditor's home base for several days and on site for several more days. If the auditor is not familiar with the Halpern algorithm, background materials must be provided and the auditor must have some time to become familiar with them. In addition, existing case reports, technical reports, and other relevant documents such as the study proposal, contract with the funding agency (if any), planning memos, and other similar information should be made available for prior study. The auditor is then brought to the project site for the actual auditing work.

Once on site, it will be useful to follow an agenda somewhat as follows:

- The auditor should be given another overview of the project as a whole and provided the opportunity to ask clarifying questions.
- The Halpern algorithm should be reviewed so that both auditor and auditee are in agreement on what the process entails.
- The auditor should be familiarized with all the audit trail materials that exist, including all field notes, all documents, all unitized and categorized data (in the form of index cards), all theoretical notes (methodological and personal journals, and the like), the cases and accompanying technical reports, drafts of research literature syntheses, the audit mechanism used in the case itself (marginal numbers, appended indexes), and any other materials believed to be relevant. These items should be laid out in easily accessible form with proper labels to simplify accessing. The auditor should take whatever time is needed to become familiar with what is available, but not necessarily with every detail of information included therein.
- The auditor proceeds with steps 1-6 as outlined by Halpern. The members of the inquiry team remain available during this time to assist in any manner the auditor requires.
- The auditor and auditee complete step 7. If the two agree that the audit should continue, an appropriate contract consistent with Halpern's recommendations is struck. If the auditor demurs, the process must be recycled with another auditor or abandoned.
- Assuming agreement, the auditor completes the remaining steps of the Halpern algorithm. On completion, the auditor may well return to home base to construct the "letter of attestation" that must be furnished (see Chapter 11 for a recommended outline).

- On receipt of the letter of attestation, should the auditee disagree with the findings, negotiations may take place that may lead to report revisions, changes in the findings, or an agreement to continue to disagree.
- The letter of attestation is appended to the case report as evidence that an audit has taken place. If there remains a disagreement between auditor and auditee, the latter is entitled to affix a counterstatement laying out his or her position.

FINALE

When the three terminating steps—developing a case report, subjecting it to a comprehensive member check, and commissioning and facilitating an external audit—have been completed, the study is ready for public release. These steps are arduous and frustrating; the inquiry team must at last commit itself to its reconstructions and interpretations (remembering that these are always site-specific) and then submit itself to the searching criticism of its own membership, of a review committee on site, and of an external auditor standing in for the eventual readership. It seems safe to say that conventional inquiry rarely if ever exposes itself so completely. Those who doubt the trustworthiness of a well-conducted naturalistic study can have but little acquaintance with these taxing steps. On the other hand, the naturalist can rest secure in the knowledge that all has been done that can be to make the study trustworthy.

NOTE

1. But see the section in Chapter 5 that takes exception to the concept of naturalistic generalization as proposed by Stake.

Appendix A

APPENDIX A Audit Trail Categories, File Types, and Evidence

Audit Trail Classification	File Types	Evidence
(1) Raw data	(A) electronically recorded materials 　(1) videotapes (and transcripts) 　(2) audiotapes (and transcripts) 　(3) Stenomask recordings (and specimen records and chronologs) (B) field notes 　(1) interview records 　(2) observational records (C) unobtrusive measures 　(1) public documents 　(2) private records 　(3) physical traces (D) survey results	(a) dialogue; social interactions (and tapes) (b) descriptions of phenomena, events, feelings of and by respondents (c) descriptions of events, characteristics of environment, and behaviors of respondents by inquirer (d) photographs (e) records; flow of operations; test scores (f) completed surveys (g) expert testimony
(2) Data reduction and analysis	(A) writeups of field notes 　(1) descriptions (B) summaries 　(1) condensed notes 　　(a) events 　　(b) behaviors 　(2) units of information 　　(a) themes 　　(b) behaviors 　　(c) ideas 　　(d) concerns 　(3) quantitative summaries (C) theoretical notes 　(1) working hypotheses 　(2) concepts 　(3) hunches	(a) summarized transcripts (b) category cards (index cards) with referent index; lists of units of information (c) tally sheets; computer analyses

(3) Data reconstruction and synthesis

    (A) categorical structure
        (1) themes
        (2) definitions
        (3) relationships
            (a) hierarchies of concepts and categories
            (b) explanations of concepts

    (B) findings and conclusions
        (1) interpretations
        (2) inferences
            (a) explanations of hierarchies and structure

    (C) final report
        (1) connections to existing literature
        (2) integration of concepts, relationships, and interpretations
            (a) completed and published documents

(4) Process notes

    (A) methodological notes
        (1) procedures
        (2) decisions
        (3) strategies
        (4) rationale
            (a) daily activities
            (b) decision-making rules and procedures
            (c) sampling techniques
            (d) descriptions of emerging design
            (e) explication of analytic strategy
            (f) instrument development

    (B) trustworthiness notes
        (1) credibility
        (2) dependability
        (3) confirmability
            (a) peer debriefing interactions
            (b) member checks, interactions, and calculations
            (c) triangulation reactions
            (d) prolonged engagement and role
            (e) process for selection of auditor, peer debriefer, and member checker

    (C) audit trail notes
        (1) substance of trail
        (2) structure of trail
            (a) indexes
            (b) dates
            (c) cross-references
            (d) linkages

(continued)

APPENDIX A   Continued

Audit Trail Classification	File Types	Evidence
(5) Intentions and disposition	(A) proposal (1) goals, objectives, and inquiry questions (2) intended methodology (3) relevant literature (4) information on current theory (B) personal notes (1) reflexive notes (2) motivations (C) expectations (1) predictions (2) intentions	(a) written document (b) bibliography (a) self-evaluation and criticism (b) theoretical preferences (c) methodological preferences (d) doubts
(6) Instrument development	(A) pilot/preliminary schedules of questions (B) observation formats (C) surveys	(a) rough drafts (b) final product (c) feedback notes

© 1983, Edward S. Halpern. Reproduced by permission.

APPENDIX B   A Procedure for Auditing Naturalistic Inquiries

Events	Auditee Tasks	Auditor Tasks	Guiding Questions for Auditor Diagnosis and Report Entries	Referent Audit Trail Categories
Pre-Entry Phase				
(1) Contact by auditee	(A) initiate contact (B) determine need for audit (C) prepare audit trail for review	(A) determine need for audit		
(2) Orientation to the study	(A) explain record-keeping system	(A) become familiar with audit trail (B) become familiar with content		4.C./5.A.
(3) Discuss audit alternatives	Decision to continue with audit unconditionally, conditionally, with a new auditor, or abandon audit (A) revise audit trail as necessary			
Auditability Phase				
(4) Familiarity with study	(A) arrange logistics for auditor (B) remain available for consultation	(A) identify research questions/problems		5.A.1.
		(B) identify methodological choices		5.A.2./4.A.
		(1) perspective/paradigm		5.A.C./4.A.
		(2) techniques		5.A.2./4.A.
		(3) rationale		5.A.C./4.A.4.
		(C) identify theoretical framework		
		(D) identify findings and conclusions		3.B.
		(1) recognize structure of categories		3.A.

(continued)

385

Events	Auditee Tasks	Auditor Tasks	Guiding Questions for Auditor Diagnosis and Report Entries	Referent Audit Trail Categories
(5) Familiarity with audit trail		(A) identify audit trail components		4.C.1.
		(B) determine audit trail structure		4.C.2.
		(C) identify type I linkages (linkages between audit trail components).		4.C.
(6) Determine auditability	—	(A) determine completeness of audit	*Completeness* (are the following available?	
			(1) raw data	1.A.B.C.D.
			(2) data reduction and analysis	2.A.B.C.
			(3) data reconstruction and synthesis	3.A.B.C.
			(4) process notes	4.A.B.C.
			(5) intentions and dispositions	5.A.B.C.
			(6) instrument development	6.A.B.C.
	—	(B) determine comprehensibility	*Comprehensibility*	
			(1) does the derivation of each audit trail component make sense?	4.A..C./5.A.2.
			(2) is the audit trail self-explanatory?	4.A..C.
			(3) does the audit trail explain the inquiry?	4.A..C.
	—	(C) determine utility	*Utility*	
			(1) are the dates of the materials recorded?	
			(2) are materials cross-referenced?	4.C.
			(3) are materials indexed?	4.C.
			(4) are there explanations as to where each component can be found and how it was used?	
			(5) do materials show how auditee chose to collect data?	4.A./5.A.
			(6) do materials show what and from whom auditee sampled?	4.A./5.A.
			(7) do materials show how data were organized?	1.A.B.C./2.A.B.C./ 4.C.
			(8) do materials illustrate the emerging theory?	2.C./3.A.B.

(D) establish linkages

Linkages
(1) are type II linkages obvious (audit trail component linked to methodological choices)?
(2) are there gaps?

Discuss auditability
(A) revise audit trail as necessary
(B) decide whether to proceed

(A) make recommendations as necessary
(B) decide whether to proceed

Decision to continue with contract

Formal Agreement Phase
(7) Negotiate contract

(1) establish time line
(2) determine goals
(3) specify roles
(4) arrange logistics
(5) determine product outcomes
(6) determine format
(7) identify renegotiation criteria

Trustworthiness Phase
(8) Assess confirmability

(a) Assess whether findings are grounded in data

(A) sample findings
(B) identify audit trail components linked to each finding
(C) verify the linkage/connection

(1) is there isomorphism across linkages—e.g., from raw data to analyzed data to synthesized data

1./2./3./4.A.3.

(2) does the relative weighting given to categories reflect the data?

1.A..B..C/3A.

(continued)

Events	Auditee Tasks	Auditor Tasks	Guiding Questions for Auditor Diagnosis and Report Entries	Referent Audit Trail Categories
(b) Assess whether inferences are logical	—	(A) identify analytic strategy(ies)	(1) has an appropriate analytic technique been selected?	1.A.B.C./2.C./4.A.3.,4.
		(B) assess match between strategy and data	(2) has the analytic technique been applied properly?	2.B./4.A.3./4.B.1./5.B.1.
		(C) assess application of strategy	(3) has a compatible unit of analysis been selected?	1./2.B.2./3.B.1., 3.C.1./4.A.3.
		(D) assess accuracy of the descriptions of phenomena and concepts	(4) do category labels accurately describe the concepts?	2.B./2.C./3.A.
			(5) do examples clearly explain categories? do category labels reflect examples?	1.A.B.C./2.B.1./3.A.B.C.
			(6) do examples fairly represent the data?	1./2.C./3.
		(E) determine whether inferences are faulty or logical.	(7) are there illogical or unsubstantiated interpretations of the data?	1./2.B.2./3.B.1./4.A.3./5.B.1.
			(8) are alternative inferences possible (alternative explanations, permutations)?	1./2.B.2.C./3.B./4.A.3.,4./4.B./5.B.2..C.
			(9) are there unexplained phenomena (unused data)?	1./2.C.1./3.A.,B/4.A.2.,4.B.
(c) Assess utility of category structure	—	(A) assess clarity of categorical/conceptual structure	(1) is there evidence of category overlap?	2.C./3.A.,C.2.
			(2) is there an unintended mixture of levels of analysis?	2.B.2./3.A./4.A.3.
			(3) is there an unclear method of analysis?	4.A.3.
		(B) assess explanatory power of category structure	(4) have an optimal set of categories been extracted?	1.A.B.C./2.C.1./3.A.,B.
			(5) do categories reflect the emerging working hypotheses?	2.C.1./3.A.
			(6) do categories match the theory?	3.A.,C.1./5.A.3.,4.
			(7) do categories represent an exhaustive use of the data? support saturation?	1./2.B.,C./3.A., C.2./4.A.2.,B.3.
		(C) assess fit between categories, definitions, and examples	(8) do categories describe phenomena at the same level?	2.B.2./3.A.1.
			(9) are categories mutually exclusive?	3.A./4./B.3.

			Code
(d) Assess degree and incidence of inquirer bias	(A) Assess incidence of undisciplined subjectivity	(1) is there an imposition of inquirer's own terminology in the data?	1.B.1./2.A./3.C.2/5.C.1.
		(2) is the generation of a concept limited by the theoretical position?	3.B./5.A.,B.,C.
		(3) is there a sufficient description of the inquirer's tacit processes?	4.B./5.B.
(e) Assess accommodation strategies	(A) assess the design and implementation of confirmability efforts, and integration of the outcomes	(1) are there sufficient efforts to ensure confirmability?	4.A.,B.3/5.A.2.
		(2) does the inquirer account for negative evidence?	2.C./3.A.3./4.B.
		(3) does inquirer accommodate negative examples?	2.C./3.A.3./4.B.
(9) Assess dependability			
(a) Assess appropriateness of inquiry decisions and methodological shifts	(A) identify inquiry decision	(1) is there evidence of purposive or theoretical sampling?	2.C./4.A.2.,3.
	(B) identify working hypotheses	(2) is there support for purposive/theoretical decisions?	2.C./4.A.4.
	(C) locate audit trail entries describing inquiry processes, decisions, and rationale	(3) is there evidence of a systematic process for changing the instrumentation?	4.A./5.B.1./5.A.B.C.
	(D) locate support for decisions	(4) is there support for altering techniques?	2.C./4.A.,B.2.
(b) Assess degree and incidence of inquirer bias	(A) identify decisions and rationale to bound the inquiry	(1) is there evidence of early closure?	2.C./4.A.2.,4./5.B.,C.1.,C.2.
		(2) are there unitized, uncategorized data?	2.B.2.,C./3.A.
		(3) is there insufficient or conflicting evidence disproving claim of saturation?	1.A.B.C./2.B./3.A.B.

(continued)

APPENDIX B Continued

Events	Auditee Tasks	Auditor Tasks	Guiding Questions for Auditor Diagnosis and Report Entries	Referent Audit Trail Categories
			(4) are there unexplored areas that appear in the field notes?	1.B./2.B.2./3.A.
			(5) is there unnecessarily strict adherence to an interview schedule?	1.B.1./2.C.1.,3./ 4.A.2.,3./6.A.
			(6) was the study discontinued to meet a deadline?	4.A.2./5.A.1.B.,C.
			(7) was the focus influenced by a sponsoring agency?	4.A./5.A.B.
			(8) is there a sufficient search for negative cases?	1.B./2.C./3.B./4.A.
		(B) identify instances that suggest cooptation	(1) are there shifts in feelings of empathy?	2.B.2./3.A.B./ 5.B.C.
			(2) is there an identification with figure(s) of authority in the setting?	4.A.2.,4./5.A.1.B.
			(3) is there unused, conflicting evidence?	2.B.,C.3./3.B.
			(4) is there unexplained neglect of potential leads?	1.B./4.A./5.B.
		(C) identify whether premature judgments	(1) is there an overemphasis of personal notes in the analysis?	2.A.B.C./4.A.3./ 5.B.
	—		(2) is there an overuse of personal notes when making methodological choices?	4.A.2.,3.,4.
			(3) is there sufficient support to substantiate findings?	1.B./2.B./3.A.B./ 4.B.2.
	—	(D) assess whether there is a Pygmalion effect	(1) is there an unfounded convergence of personal and field notes?	1.B./2.C./5.B.
			(2) does the documentation lack a rationale for decisions?	4.A.2.,3.,4.

390

		Code
	(3) is there an unsubstantiated rationale for theoretical assumptions?	2.C.1./5.A.B.C.
	(4) is there a smooth convergence of preliminary questions and categories of outcomes?	2.B./1.A./5.A.1./6.A.B.C.
(E) assess whether there is a Hawthorne effect	(1) is there an unexplained similarity in language between respondents and the initial theoretical positions?	1.B./5.A.B.C./6.A.B.C.
(F) determine whether the inquirer is biased through naivete		5.B.1..2.
(G) determine appropriateness of sampling decisions	(1) has a homogeneous sample been selected?	2.C./4.A.
	(2) is there a relationship between working hypotheses and selection of sources?	2.C./4.A..B.
(H) identify the prevalence of triangulation	(1) is there an unbalanced reliance on one method?	4.A..B.1./5.A.1.
	(2) is there a connection between working hypotheses and selection of sources?	2.C./4.A..B.1.
(A) identify major design decisions	(1) are there sufficient efforts to ensure dependability?	4.B.2.
(B) evaluate the rationale for design decisions	(2) is there evidence of sufficient purposive/responsive flexibility?	2.C./4.A..B.2./5.B.
(c) Assess the overall design and implementation of efforts, and integration of the outcomes for dependability		

(continued)

APPENDIX B Continued

Events	Auditee Tasks	Auditor Tasks	Guiding Questions for Auditor Diagnosis and Report Entries	Referent Audit Trail Categories
(10) Review credibility				
(a) Assess the design and implementation of the strategies, and the integration of the outcomes	—	(A) look for evidence of triangulation	(1) is there evidence of triangulation?	3.B./4.A.1../B.1./5.A.2.
		(B) look for evidence of peer debriefing	(2) is there evidence of member checking?	4.B.
		(C) look for evidence of member checks	(3) is there evidence of preliminary validations (ongoing member checks)?	4.B./5.B.
			(4) is there evidence of peer debriefing?	4.B.
			(5) are the raw data isomorphic with phenomena under investigation?	1./4.B./6.A.
(b) Assess corroboration between descriptions of methodological choices, data sources, findings, and audit trail.	—		(1) is there evidence of responsive flexibility?	4.A.2../4.B./5.B.1../C.1.
Closure Phase				
(11) Feedback and renegotiation	(A) assess accuracy of auditor claims	(A) present findings		
	(B) assess adherence/fulfillment to contract/agreement	(B) discuss discrepancies and determine nature of closure		
(12) Complete agreement		(A) write final report		

©1983, Edward S. Halpern. Reproduced by permission

References

Abel, Reuben. (1976). *Man is the measure*. New York: Free Press.

Adams, Kay A. (1981). *The keen-edged feather: Intuitive analysis and reporting in qualitative analysis*. Paper presented at the annual meeting of the American Educational Research Association, Los Angeles.

Ad Hoc Committee on Ethical Standards in Psychological Research. (1982). *Ethical principles in the conduct of research with human participants*. Washington, DC: American Psychological Association.

Allen, Shure. (1977). Text-based lexicography and algorithmic text analysis. *Association for Literary and Linguistic Computing Bulletin, 5*, 126-131.

Allport, Gordon W. (1942). *The use of personal documents in psychological science*. Bulletin 49. New York: Social Science Research Council.

Anderson, D., & Benjaminson, P. (1976). *Investigative reporting*. Bloomington: Indiana University Press.

Argyris, Chris. (1980). *Inner contradictions of rigorous research*. New York: Academic.

Babchuk, Nicholas. (1961). The role of the researcher as participant observer and participant-as-observer in the field situation. *Human Organization, 21*, 225-228.

Back, Kurt W. (1956). The well-informed informant. *Human Organization, 14*, 30-33.

Bahm, A. J. (1971). Science is not value-free. *Policy Sciences, 2*, 391-396.

Bain, Robert K. (1950). The researcher's role: A case study. *Human Organization, 9*, 23-38.

Bakan, David. (1972, March). Psychology can *now* kick the science habit. *Psychology Today, 11*, 26-28, 87-88.

Barnes, John. (1979). *Who should know what? Social science privacy and ethics*. Harmondsworth, England: Penguin.

Bartlett, F. C. (1937). Psychological methods and anthropological problems. *Africa, 9*, 401-420.

Barton, L., & Walker, S. (1978). Sociology of education at the crossroads. *Educational Review, 30*, 269-283.

Beals, Ralph L. (1957). Native terms and anthropological methods. *American Anthropologist, 57*, 716-717.

Beauchamp, Tom L., Faden, Ruth R., Wallace, R. Jay, & Walters, Leroy. (Eds.). (1982). *Ethical issues in social science research*. Baltimore: Johns Hopkins University Press.

Berger, P. L., & Luckman, T. (1973). *The social construction of reality*. London: Penguin.

Berkowitz, Leonard, & Donnerstein, Edward. (1982). External validity is more than skin deep. *American Psychologist, 37*, 245-257.

Bermant, Geoffrey, Kelman, H. C., & Warwick, D. P. (Eds.). (1978). *The ethics of social intervention*. New York: Halsted.

Bhikko, Sunno. (1975). An Interview with Achaan Chaa. *Loka: A Journal of the Naropa Institute, 1*, 121-125.

Bierschenk, Bernhard. (1977). A computer-based content analysis of interview texts: Numeric description and multivariate analysis. *Didakometry, 53* (Malmo School of Education).

Bilmes, J. (1975). Misinformation in verbal accounts: Some fundamental considerations. *Man, 10,* 60-71.

Birdwhistell, R. L. (1970). *Kinesics and context: Essays on body-motion communication.* Philadelphia: University of Pennsylvania Press.

Blanshard, Brant. (1962). *Reason and analysis.* LaSalle, IL: Open Court.

Bogdan, R. (1972). *Participant observation in organization settings.* Syracuse, NY: Syracuse University Press.

Bogdan, R., & Biklen, S. K. (1982). *Qualitative research for education.* Boston: Allyn & Bacon.

Bogdan, R., & Taylor, S. J. (1975). *Introduction to qualitative research methods.* New York: John Wiley.

Bogdan, Robert, Taylor, Steven, DeGrandpre, Berhard, & Haynes, Sandra. (1974). Let them eat programs: Attendants' perspectives and programming on wards in state schools. *Journal of Health and Social Behavior, 15,* 142-151.

Bok, Sisella. (1978). *Lying: Moral choice in public and private life.* New York: Random House.

Bok, Sissela. (1982). *Secrets: On the ethics of concealment and revelation.* New York: Pantheon.

Boruch, Robert F., & Cecil, Joe S. (1979). *Assuring the confidentiality of social research data.* Philadephia: University of Pennsylvania Press.

Boruch, R. F., & Cecil, J. S. (Eds.). (1983). *Solutions to ethical and legal problems in social research.* New York: Academic.

Bower, R. T., & de Gasparis, P. (1978). *Ethics in social research: Protecting the interests of human subjects.* New York: Praeger.

Brand, Myles. (1979). Causality. In Peter D. Asquith & Henry E. Kyburg, Jr. (Eds.), *Current research in the philosophy of science: Proceedings of the Philosophy of Science Association.* (pp. 252-281). Ann Arbor, MI: Edwards Brothers.

Braybrooke, David, & Lindblom, Charles E. (1963). *A strategy of decision.* New York: Free Press.

Brewer, Marilynn B., & Collins, Barry E. (Eds.). (1981). *Scientific inquiry and the social sciences* (a volume in honor of Donald T. Campbell). San Francisco: Jossey-Bass.

Bronfenbrenner, Urie. (1977). Toward an experimental ecology of human development. *American Psychologist, 32,* 513-531.

Bulmer, Martin. (1980). The impact of ethical concerns upon sociological research. *Sociology: The Journal of the British Sociological Association, 14,* 125-130.

Bulmer, Martin, (1983). The methodology of *The Taxi Dance Hall:* An early account of Chicago ethnography from the 1920s. *Urban Life, 12,* 95-120.

Burgess, Ernest W., (1945a). Sociological research methods. *American Journal of Sociology, 50,* 474-482.

Burgess, Ernest W. (1945b). Research methods in sociology. In G. Curvitch & W. Moore, *Twentieth century sociology,* (pp. 20-41). New York: Philosophical Library.

Cabresi, Guido, & Bobbitt, Philip. (1978). *Tragic choices.* New York: W. W. Norton.

Campbell, Donald T. (1957). Factors relevant to the validity of experiments in social settings. *Psychological Bulletin, 54,* 297-312.

Campbell, Donald T. (1975). "Degrees of freedom" and the case study. *Comparative Political Studies, 8,* 178-193.

Campbell, Donald T., & Stanley, Julian C. (1963). Experimental and quasi-experimental designs for research on teaching. In N. L. Gage (Ed.), *Handbook of research on teaching*. Chicago: Rand McNally. (Also published as *Experimental and Quasi-Experimental Designs for Research*. Chicago: Rand McNally, 1966).

Carley, Michael. (1980). *Rational techniques in policy analysis*. London: Heinemann Educational Books.

Caro, Francis G. (Ed.). (1971). *Readings in evaluative research*. New York: Russell Sage Foundation.

The case of a missing molecule. (1983, January 10). *Newsweek*, p. 55.

Castañeda, Carlos. (1974). *Tales of power*. New York. Simon & Schuster.

Castañeda, Carlos. (1977). *The second ring of power*. New York: Simon & Schuster.

Caulkins, Douglas. (1984). *Narrative conventions in West European ethnography*. Paper presented at the Mellon Faculty Development Seminar, University of Kansas, Lawrence.

Cazden, Courtney B. (1980). What we don't know about teaching the language arts. *Phi Delta Kappan, 61,* 595-596.

Cesara, Manda.(1982). *Reflections of a woman anthropologist*. London: Academic.

Clark, David, Astuto, Terry, & Kuh, George. (1983, April). *Strength of coupling in the organization and operation of colleges and universities*. Paper presented at the annual meeting of the American Educational Research Association, Montreal, Canada.

Clarke, Gerald. (1982, November 2). Yorktown: If the British had won . . . *Time*, pp. 56-60.

Colvard, Richard. (1967). Interaction and identification in reporting field research: A critical reconsideration of protective procedures. In Gideon Sjoberg (Ed.), *Ethics, politics and social research* (pp. 319-358). Cambridge, MA: Schenkman.

Controlled drinkers sue Sobells. (1983, September). *APA Monitor*, p. 3.

Cook, P. H. (1951). Methods of field research. *Australian Journal of Psychology, 3,* 84-98.

Cook, Thomas D., & Campbell, Donald T. (1979). *Quasi-experimentation: Design and analysis issues for field settings*. Chicago: Rand McNally.

Corsaro, William. (1980). *Something old and something new: The importance of prior ethnography in the collection and analysis of audio-visual data*. Unpublished manuscript, Indiana University.

Crano, William D. (1981). Triangulation and cross-cultural research. In Marilyn B. Brewer & Barry E. Collins (Eds.), *Scientific inquiry and the social sciences*. San Francisco: Jossey-Bass.

Cressey, D. R. (1953). *Other people's money: A study in the social psychology of embezzlement*. New York: Free Press.

Cronbach, Lee J. (1975). Beyond the two disciplines of scientific psychology. *American Psychologist, 30,* 116-127.

Cronbach, Lee J. (1982). *Designing evaluations of educational and social programs*. San Francisco: Jossey-Bass.

Cronbach, Lee J., & Suppes, Patrick. (1969). *Research for tomorrow's schools: Disciplined inquiry in education*. New York: Macmillan.

Denny, Terry. (1978, May). *Storytelling and educational understanding*. Paper presented at the national meeting of the International Reading Association, Houston.

Denzin, Norman K. (1978). *Sociological methods*. New York: McGraw-Hill.

Dexter, Lewis A. (1956). Role relationships and conceptions of neutrality in interviewing. *American Journal of Sociology, 62,* 153-157.

Dexter, Lewis A. (1970). *Elite and specialized interviewing*. Evanston, IL: Northwestern University Press.

Dickson, Paul. (1982). *Words*. New York: Delacorte.

Diener, E., & Crandall, R. (1978). *Ethics in social and behavioral research*. Chicago: University of Chicago Press.

Diesing, P. (1972). *Patterns of discovery in the social sciences*. London: Routledge & Kegan Paul.

Dillon, Martin, & Federhart, Peggy. (1982). The use of discriminant analysis to select content-bearing words. *Journal of the American Society for Information Science, 33*, 245-253.

Dobbert, Marion Lundy. (1982). *Ethnographic research: Theory and application for modern schools and societies*. New York: Praeger.

Donner, Florinda. (1982). *Shabono*. New York: Delacorte.

Douglas, Jack D. (1976). *Investigative social research*. Beverly Hills, CA: Sage.

Drass, Kriss Anthony. (1980). A computer program for the analysis of qualitative data. *Urban Life, 9*, 332-353.

Dror, Yehezkel. (1981). *Ventures in policy sciences*. New York: American Elsevier.

Duval, S., Duval, V. H., & Neely, R. (1979). Self-focus, felt responsibility, and helping behavior. *Journal of Personality and Social Psychology, 37*, 1769-1778.

Earman, John. (1976). Causation: A matter of life and death. *Journal of Philosophy, 73*, 5-25.

Eaton, Joseph W., & Weil, R. J. (1951). Social processes of professional teamwork. *American Sociological Review, 16*, 707-713.

Edds, J. A. (1980). *Management auditing: Concepts and practice*. Dubuque, IA: Kendall/Hunt.

Eisenstein, Zillah R. (Ed.). (1979). *Capitalistic patriarchy and the case for socialist feminism*. New York: Monthly Review Press.

Eisner, Elliot W. (1975). The perceptive eye: Toward the reformulation of educational evaluation. *Occasional Papers of the Stanford Evaluation Consortium*. Stanford, CA: Stanford University. (mimeo)

Eisner, Elliot. (1979). *The educational imagination*. New York: Macmillan.

Eisner, Elliot. (1983). Anastasia might still be alive, but the monarchy is dead. *Educational Researcher, 12*, 13-14, 23-24.

Eisner, Elliot. (1984). Can educational research inform educational practice? *Phi Delta Kappan, 65*, 447-452.

Elden, Max. (1981). Sharing the research work: Participative research and its role demands. In Peter Reason & John Rowan (Eds.), *Human inquiry: A sourcebook of new paradigm research*. New York: John Wiley.

Emery, Stewart. (1978). *Actualizations: You don't have to rehearse to be yourself*. Garden City, NY: Doubleday.

Ennis, Robert H. (1973). On causality. *Educational Researcher, 2*, 4-11.

Esterson, A. (1972). *The leaves of spring: A study in the dialectics of madness*. Harmondsworth, England: Penguin.

The expulsion of Steven Mosher. (1983, September). *Anthropology Newsletter*, pp. 2, 5ff.

Farley, J., & Geison, G. (1974). Science, politics, and spontaneous generation in nineteenth-century France: The Pasteur-Pouchet debate. *Bulletin of the History of Medicine, 48*, 161.

Fast, J. (1970). *Body language*. New York: M. Evans.

Fetterman, David. (1981). Protocol and publication: An ethical obligation (a reply to Ray Rist). *Anthropology and Education Quarterly, 12*, 82-85.

Fetterman, David M. (Ed.). (1984). *Ethnography in educational evaluation.* Beverly Hills, CA: Sage.

Feyerabend, P. K. (1975). *Against method.* London: Verso.

Filstead, J. W. (Ed.). (1972). *Qualitative methodology: Firsthand involvement with the social world.* Chicago: Markham.

Finney, Joseph C., et al. (1977). MMPI alcoholism scales: Factor structure and factor analysis. *Quarterly Journal of Studies on Alcohol, 38,* 1055-1060.

Firestone, William, & Dawson, Judith. (1982). *Approaches to qualitative data analysis: Intuitive, procedural, and intersubjective.* Paper presented at the annual meeting of the American Educational Research Association, New York.

Fischer, Frank. (1983). Ethical discourse in public administration. *Administration & Society, 15,* 5-42.

Fleck, Ludwig. (1979). *Genesis and development of a scientific fact.* Chicago: University of Chicago Press.

Ford, Julienne. (1975). *Paradigms and fairy tales* (2 vols.). London: Routledge & Kegan Paul.

Frasher, James M., & Frasher, Ramona. (1979, August). *To what do we attribute the exclusion of attribution?* Paper presented at the National Conference of Professors of Educational Administration, Edmonton, Alberta.

Freeman, Derek. (1983). *Margaret Mead and Samoa: The making and unmaking of an anthropological myth.* Cambridge, MA: Harvard University Press.

Frey, David, & Raming, Henry. (1977). Primary factors in American counseling. *Psychotherapy: Theory, Research, and Practice, 14,* 273-285.

Geer, Blanche. (1964). First days in the field. In Phillip E. Hammong (Ed.), *Sociologists at work* (pp. 322-344). New York: Basic Books.

Geertz, Clifford. (1973). Thick description: Toward an interpretive theory of culture. In Clifford Geertz (Ed.), *The interpretation of cultures.* New York: Basic Books.

Geffrey, Annie, et al. (1973). Lexicometric analysis of cooccurrences. In A. J. Aiken, R. W. Bailey, & H. Smith (Eds.), *The computer and literary studies.* Edinburgh: Edinburgh University Press.

Gephart, William J., Ingle, Robert B., and Saretsky, Gary. (1973). *Similarities and differences in the research and evaluation processes.* Bloomington, IN: Phi Delta Kappa.

Getzels, J. W., & Guba, E. G. (1956). Social behavior and the administrative process. *School Review, 64,* 423-441.

Gilbert, Leon. (1980). Computer-aided indexes and concordances to early German: A critical study. *Association for Literary and Linguistic Computing Bulletin, 8,* 249-262.

Glaser, Barney G., & Strauss, Anselm L. (1967). *The discovery of grounded theory.* Chicago: Aldine.

Glass, Gene V (1975). A paradox about the excellence of schools and the people in them. *Educational Researcher, 4,* 9-13.

Gödel, Kurt. (1962). *On formally undecideable propositions.* New York: Basic Books.

Goetz, Judith P., & LeCompte, Margaret D. (1981). Ethnographic research and the problem of data reduction. *Anthropology and Education Quarterly, 12,* 51-70.

Gold, Raymond L. (1958). Roles in sociological field observations. *Social Forces, 36,* 217-223. (Reprinted in McCall, G. J., & Simmons, J. L. (Eds.), *Issues in participant observation: A text and reader.* Reading, MA: Addison-Wesley, 1969.)

Gorden, R. L. (1980). *Interviewing: Strategy, techniques, and tactics* (rev. ed.). Homewood, IL: Dorsey.

Green, Judith, & Wallet, Cynthia. (1981). *Ethnography and language in educational settings.* Norwood, NJ: Ablex.

Griffith, Thomas. (1981, April 27). Stuck with labels. *Time.*

Guba, Egon G. (1978). *Toward a methodology of naturalistic inquiry in educational evaluation. Monograph 8.* Los Angeles: UCLA Center for the Study of Evaluation.

Guba, Egon G. (1981a). Criteria for assessing the trustworthiness of naturalistic inquiries. *Educational Communication and Technology Journal, 29,* 75-92.

Guba, Egon G. (1981b). Investigative journalism. In Nick L. Smith (Ed.), *New techniques for evaluation* (pp. 167-262). Beverly Hills, CA: Sage.

Guba, Egon G. (1984). The effects of definitions of policy on the nature and outcomes of policy analysis. *Educational Leadership, 42,* 63-70.

Guba, Egon G., & Lincoln, Yvonna S. (1980). The distinction between merit and worth in evaluation. *Educational Evaluation and Policy Analysis, 2,* 61-71.

Guba, Egon G., & Lincoln, Yvonna S. (1981). *Effective evaluation.* San Francisco: Jossey-Bass.

Guba, Egon G., & Lincoln, Yvonna S. (1982a). Epistemological and methodological bases of naturalistic inquiry. *Educational Communication and Technology Journal, 30,* 233-252.

Guba, Egon G., & Lincoln, Yvonna S. (1982b). The place of values in needs assessment. *Educational Evaluation and Policy Analysis, 4,* 311-320.

Gulliksen, Harold. (1950). *Theory of mental tests.* New York: John Wiley.

Hall, E. T. (1959). *The silent language.* Garden City, NY: Doubleday.

Hall, E. T. (1966). *The hidden dimension.* Garden City, NY: Doubleday.

Hall, E. T. (1976). *Beyond culture.* Garden City, NY: Doubleday.

Halpern, Edward S. (1983). *Auditing naturalistic inquiries: The development and application of a model.* Unpublished doctoral dissertation, Indiana University.

Hamilton, David. (1976). *A science of the singular.* Workshop Paper on Case-Study Research, CIRCE, University of Illinois, Urbana. (mimeo)

Hamilton, David. (1979, June). *Some more on fieldwork, natural languages, and naturalistic generalisation.* Discussion paper, University of Glasgow. (mimeo)

Hammond, Robert L. (1973). Evaluation at the local level. In Blaine R. Worthen and James R. Sanders (Eds.), *Educational evaluation: Theory and practice.* Worthington, OH: Jones.

Hansen, J. F. (1979). *Sociocultural perspectives on human learning: An introduction to educational anthropology.* Englewood Cliffs, NJ: Prentice-Hall.

Haring, Douglas G. (1954). Comment on field techniques in ethnography, illustrated by a survey in the Ryuku islands. *Southwestern Journal of Anthropology, 10,* 255-267.

Harper, R. G., Wiens, A. N., & Matarazzo, J. (1978). *Non-verbal communication: The state of the art.* New York: John Wiley.

Harre, Rom. (1981). The positivist-empiricist approach and its alternative. In Peter Reason & John Rowan (Eds.), *Human inquiry: A sourcebook of new paradigm research.* New York: John Wiley.

Harsanyi, Zsolt, & Hutton, Richard. (1981). *Genetic prophecy: Beyond the double helix.* New York: Rawson, Wade.

Hart, David K. (1983). The honorable bureaucrat among the Philistines: A reply to "Ethical discourse in public administration." *Administration & Society, 15,* 43-48.

Hartsough, Ross, & Laffal, Julius. (1970). Content analysis and scientific writing. *Journal of General Psychology, 83,* 193-206.

Heisenberg, Werner. (1958). *Physics and philosophy.* New York: Harper & Row.

Helms, Lelia B. (1981). Policy analysis in education: The case for incrementalism. *The Executive Review, 1,* 6.

Hempel, C. (1964). *Aspects of scientific explanation.* New York: Free Press.

Heron, John. (1981). Philosophical basis for a new paradigm. In Peter Reason & John Rowan (Eds.), *Human inquiry: A sourcebook of new paradigm research.* New York: John Wiley.

Hesse, Mary. (1980). *Revolutions and reconstructions in the philosophy of science.* Bloomington: Indiana University Press.

Hetherington, Joal. (1981). When in doubt, don't. *Kansas Alumni Magazine,* pp. 17-24.

Hinkle, Roscoe C., Jr., & Hinkle, Gisela J. (1954). *The development of modern sociology.* New York: Random House.

Hirschman, Albert O. (1970). *Exit, voice and loyalty: Responses to decline in firms, organizations and states.* Cambridge, MA: Harvard University Press.

Hite, Shere. (1976). *The Hite report.* New York: Macmillan.

Hite, Shere. (1981). *The Hite report on male sexuality.* New York: Alfred A. Knopf.

Hockey, Susan M. (1980). *A guide to computer applications in the humanities.* Baltimore: Johns Hopkins University Press.

Hoffer, Eric. (1951). *The true believer.* New York: Harper & Row.

Hofstadter, Douglas R. (1979). *Gödel, Escher, Bach.* New York: Basic Books.

Hofstadter, Douglas R., & Dennett, Daniel C. (Eds.), (1981). *The mind's I.* New York: Basic Books.

Holsti, O. R. (1969). *Content analysis for the social sciences and humanities.* Reading, MA: Addison-Wesley.

Homans, G. A. (1978). What kind of a myth is the myth of value free social science? *Social Science Quarterly, 58,* 530-541.

House, Peter W. (1982). *The art of public policy analysis.* Beverly Hills, CA: Sage.

Huberman, A. Michael, & Miles, Matthew B. (1982). *Drawing valid meaning from qualitative data: Some techniques of data reduction and display.* Paper presented at the annual meeting of the American Educational Research Association, New York.

Hufbauer, K. G. (1971). *The formation of the German chemical community.* Unpublished doctoral dissertation, University of California, Berkeley.

Humphreys, Laud. (1975). *Tearoom trade: Impersonal sex in public places.* Chicago: Aldine.

In Search of a Perfect G. (1982, September 13). *Time,* p. 102.

Jackson, Philip W. (1968). *Life in classrooms.* New York: Holt, Rinehart & Winston.

Jacobs, G. (Ed.). (1977). *The participant observer.* New York: Braziller.

Jenkins, W. I. (1978). *Policy analysis: A political and organizational perspective.* New York: St. Martin's.

Johnson, J. M. (1975). *Doing field research.* New York: Free Press.

Johnson, Jack M. (1973). *The social construction of official information.* Unpublished doctoral dissertation, University of California, San Diego.

Jones, Edward E., Kanouse, David E., Kelly, Harold H., Nisbett, Richard E., Valins, Stuart, & Weiner, Bernard. (1972). *Attribution: Perceiving the causes of behavior.* Morristown, NJ: General Learning.

Kaplan, Abraham. (1964). *The conduct of inquiry.* San Francisco: Chandler.

Keller, Evelyn Fox. (1983). Feminism as an analytic tool for the study of science. *Academe, 69,* 15-22.

Kelly, G. A. (1955). *The psychology of personal constructs* (2 vols.). New York: W. W. Norton.

Kelly, G. A. (1969a) Ontological acceleration. In B. Maher (Ed.), *Clinical psychology and personality: The selected papers of George Kelly.* New York: John Wiley.

Kelly, G. A. (1969b). Language of hypothesis. In B. Maher (Ed.), *Clinical psychology and personality: The selected papers of George Kelly.* New York: John Wiley.

Kelman, H. C. (1968). *A time to speak: On human values and social research.* San Francisco: Jossey-Bass.

Kerlinger, Fred N. (1973). *Foundations of behavioral research* (2nd ed.). New York: Holt, Rinehart & Winston.

Kidder, Louise H. (1981). Qualitative research and quasi-experimental frameworks. In Marilynn B. Brewer & Barry E. Collins (Eds.), *Scientific inquiry and the social sciences.* San Francisco: Jossey-Bass.

Kim, Jaegwon. (1973). Causes and counterfactuals. *Journal of Philosophy, 70,* 570-572.

Kimmel, Allan J. (Ed.). (1981). *Ethics of human subject research.* San Francisco: Jossey-Bass.

Kolaja, Jiri. (1956). Contribution to the theory of participant observation. *Social Forces, 35,* 159-163.

Krathwohl, David R. (1980). The myth of value-free evaluation. *Educational Evaluation and Policy Analysis, 2,* 37-45.

Krippendorff, Klaus. (1980). *Content analysis.* Beverly Hills, CA: Sage.

Kuhn, Thomas S. (1970). *The structure of scientific revolutions* (2nd ed., enlarged). Chicago: University of Chicago Press.

Kuhn, Thomas S. (1974). Second thoughts on paradigms. In F. Suppe (Ed.), *The structure of scientific theories* (pp. 459-517). Urbana: University of Illinois Press.

La Barre, Weston. (1980). *Culture in context: Selected writings of Weston La Barre.* Durham, NC: Duke University Press.

Ladas, Alice K., Whipple, Beverly, & Perry, John D. (1982). *The G Spot.* New York: Holt, Rinehart & Winston.

Lasswell, Harold D. (1971). *A pre-view of policy sciences.* New York: American Elsevier.

Lather, Patricia A. (1983). *Feminism, teacher education and curricular change: Counter-hegemony and the possibility for oppositional schooling.* Unpublished doctoral dissertation, Indiana University.

Lazersfeld, Paul F., & Rosenberg, Morris. (Eds.). (1955). *The language of social research.* New York: Free Press.

LeCompte, M. D., & Goetz, J. P. (1982). Problems of reliability and validity in ethnographic research. *Review of Educational Research, 52,* 31-60.

Levine, Harold G., Gallimore, Ronald, Weisner, Thomas S., & Turner, Jim L. (1980). Teaching participant-observation methods: A skills-building approach. *Anthropology and Education Quarterly, 11,* 38-54.

Levine, Robert E. (1981). Knowledge and fallibility in anthropological field research. In Marilynn B. Brewer & Barry E. Collins (Eds.), *Scientific inquiry and the social sciences.* San Francisco: Jossey-Bass.

Lewis, C. I. (1971). *An analysis of knowledge and valuation.* LaSalle, IL: Open Court.

Life Library of Photography. (1972). *Frontiers of photography*. New York: Time-Life Books.

Lincoln, Yvonna S. (1981). *Strategies for insuring the dependability (reliability) of naturalistic studies*. Paper presented at the joint annual meeting of the Evaluation Network and the Evaluation Research Society, Austin, Texas.

Lincoln, Yvonna S., & Guba, Egon G. (1981). *Do evaulators wear grass skirts? "Going native" and ethnocentrism as problems in utilization*. Paper presented at the joint annual meeting of the Evaluation Network and the Evaluation Research Society, Austin, Texas.

Lipsky, Michael. (1980) *Street level bureaucracy*. New York: Russell Sage.

Lofland, John. (1974). Styles of reporting qualitative field research. *American Sociologist, 9,* 101-111.

Lombard, G.F.F. (1950). Self-awareness and scientific method. *Science, 112,* 289-293.

Longstreet, W. S. (1978). *Aspects of ethnicity*. New York: Columbia University Press.

Lucas, W. (1974a). *The case survey and alternative methods for research aggregation*. Santa Monica, CA: Rand Corporation.

Lucas, W. (1974b). *The case survey method: Aggregating case experience*. Santa Monica, CA: Rand Corporation.

Lutz, Frank. (1982). Tightening up loose coupling in organizations of higher education. *Administrative Science Quarterly, 27,* 653-669.

Mackie, J. L. (1974). *The cement of the universe: A study of causation*. Oxford: Clarendon.

Magoon, A. Jon. (1977). Constructivist approaches in educational research. *Review of Educational Research, 47,* 651-693.

Manica, Peter T., & Secord, Paul F. (1983). Implications for psychology of the new philosophy of science. *American Psychologist, 38,* 399-413.

Mann, John (1972). The outcomes of evaluative research. In Carol H. Weiss (Ed.), *Evaluating action programs*. Boston: Allyn & Bacon.

Marceil, Joseph C. (1977). Implicit dimensions of idiography and nomothesis: A reformulation. *American Psychologist, 32,* 1046-1055.

Margolis, Robert D., & Elifson, Kirk W. (1979). A topology of religious experience. *Journal for the Scientific Study of Religion, 18,* 61-67.

Marshall, Judi. (1981). Making sense as a personal process. In Peter Reason and John Rowan (Eds.), *Human inquiry: A sourcebook of new paradigm research*. New York: John Wiley.

Massarik, Fred. (1981). The interviewing process re-examined. In Peter Reason & John Rowan (Eds.), *Human inquiry: A sourcebook of new paradigm research*. New York: John Wiley.

McCall, G. J., & Simmons, J. L. (Eds.). (1969). *Issues in participant observation: A text and reader*. Reading: MA: Addison-Wesley.

McCann, H. Gilman. (1978). *Chemistry transformed: The paradigmatic shift from phlogiston to oxygen*. Norwood, NJ: Ablex.

McGrath, Ellie. (1983, March 14). Battle in the scholarly world. *Time*, p. 72.

McGrath, Joseph E. (Ed.). (1981). Judgment calls: An unorthodox view of the research process. [Special issue] *American Behavioral Scientist, 25*(2).

McGrath, J. E., Martin, J., & Kulka, R. A. (1981). Some quasi-rules for making judgment calls in research. *American Behavioral Scientist, 25,* 221-225.

Mead, Margaret. (1933). More comprehensive field methods. *American Anthropologist, 35,* 1-15.

Mead, Margaret. (1971). *Coming of age in Samoa.* New York: William Morrow.

Mehrabian, A. (1972). *Nonverbal communication.* Chicago: Aldine.

Michotte, A. (1963). *The perception of causality.* London: Methuen.

Miles, Matthew B. (1979). Qualitative data as an attractive nuisance: The problem of analysis. *Administrative Science Quarterly, 24,* 590-601.

Miles, Matthew B., & Huberman, A. Michael. (1984). *Qualitative data analysis: A sourcebook of new methods.* Beverly Hills, CA: Sage.

Mill, John Stuart (1906). *A system of logic.* London: Longman. (Original work published 1843).

Miller, S. M. (1952). The participant observer and "over-rapport." *American Sociological Review, 17,* 97-99.

Milosz, Czeslaw. (1982). *Visions from San Francisco Bay.* New York: Farrar Strauss Giroux.

Mitroff, I. I., & Kilmann, R. H. (1978). *Methodological approaches to social science.* San Francisco: Jossey-Bass.

Moore, R. (1966). *Niels Bohr: The man, his science, and the world they changed.* New York: Knopf.

Morgan, Gareth. (Ed) (1983a). *Beyond method: Strategies for social research.* Beverly Hills, CA: Sage.

Morgan, Gareth. (1983b). The significance of assumptions. In Gareth Morgan (Ed.), *Beyond method: Strategies for social research.* Beverly Hills, CA: Sage.

Morgan, Gareth, & Smircich, Linda. (1980). The case for qualitative research. *Academy of Management Review, 5,* 491-500.

Morris, Roberta A., Sales, Bruce D., & Berman, John J. (1981). Research and the Freedom of Information Act. *American Psychologist, 36,* 819-826.

Moskovich, Wolf, & Kaplan, Ruth. (1979). Distributive statistical techniques in linguistic and literary research. In D. E. Ager, F. E. Knowles, & J. Smith (Eds.), *Advances in computer-aided literary and linguistic research: Proceedings of the Fifth International Symposium in Literary and Linguistic Research.* Birmingham, England: AMLC.

Moustakas, Clark. (1981). Heuristic research. In Peter Reason & John Rowan (Eds.), *Human inquiry: A sourcebook of new paradigm research.* New York: John Wiley.

Murphy, J. T. (1980). *Getting the facts: A fieldwork guide for evaluators and policy analysts.* Santa Monica, CA: Goodyear.

Nagel, Stuart. (Ed.). (1980). *Improving policy analysis.* Beverly Hills, CA: Sage.

Needham, R. M. (1965). Applications of the theory of clumps. *Journal of Mechanical Translation, 8,* 113-127.

Nejelski, P. (Ed.). (1976). *Social research in conflict with law and ethics.* Cambridge, MA: Ballinger.

Nelson, Michael. (1979, September). What's wrong with policy analysis. *Washington Monthly,* pp. 53-59.

Nurmi, Hannu. (1974). Causality and complexity: Some problems of causal analysis in the social sciences. *Annales Universitatis Turkensis, Ser. B.* (Turku, Finland).

Oakman, Robert L. (1980). *Computer methods for literary research.* Columbia: University of South Carolina Press.

O'Brien, Sr. Margaret. (1982, December). *Language data processing methods and their relevance to educational research: An explication, exemplification, and evaluation.* Educational Inquiry qualifying paper, Indiana University.

Oleson, Virginia L., & Whittaker, Elvi Waik. (1967). Role-making in participant observation: Processes in the researcher-actor relationship. *Human Organization, 26,* 273-281.

Ortony, Andrew. (Ed.). (1979). *Metaphor and thought.* Cambridge: Cambridge University Press.

Palmer, Vivien M. (1928). *Field studies in sociology: A student's manual.* Chicago: University of Chicago Press.

Parlett, M., & Hamilton, D. (1972). *Evaluation as illumination: A new approach to the study of innovatory programs.* Occasional Paper 9. Edinburgh: Center for Research in the Educational Sciences, University of Edinburgh.

Patton, Michael Quinn. (1978). *Utilization-focused evaluation.* Beverly Hills, CA: Sage.

Patton, Michael Quinn. (1980). *Qualitative evaluation methods.* Beverly Hills, CA: Sage.

Patton, Michael Quinn. (1981). *Creative evaluation.* Beverly Hills, CA: Sage.

Patton, Michael Quinn. (1982). *Practical evaluation.* Beverly Hills, CA: Sage.

Paul, Benjamin D. (1953). Interview technique and field relationships. In A. L. Broeber (Ed.), *Anthropology today.* Chicago: University of Chicago Press.

Pearsall, Marion. (1965). Participant observation as role and method in behavioral research. *Nursing Research, 14,* 37-42.

Pelto, Pertti. (1970). *Anthropological research: The structure of inquiry.* New York: Harper & Row.

Pelto, P. J., & Pelto, G. H. (1978). *Anthropological research: The structure of inquiry* (2nd Ed.). Cambridge: Cambridge University Press.

Perrow, Charles (1981, Winter). Distintegrating social sciences. *NYU Education Quarterly,* pp. 2-9.

Phillips, D. C. (1981). Toward an evaluation of the experiment in educational contexts. *Educational Researcher, 10,* 13-20.

Phillips, D. C. (1983). After the wake: postpositivistic educational thought. *Educational Researcher, 12,* 4-12.

Pollie, Robert. (1983). Brother, can you paradigm? *Science, 6,* 76-77.

Pope, Maureen L. (1982). Personal construction of formal knowledge. *Interchange, 13,* 3-14.

Pope, M. L., & Shaw, M.L.G. (1981). *Personal construct psychology and education.* London: Academic.

Popham, W. James. (1975). *Educational evaluation.* Englewood Cliffs, NJ: Prentice-Hall.

Popper, Karl R. (1959). *The logic of scientific discovery.* New York: Basic Books.

Powdermaker, Hortense. (1967) *Stranger and friend: The way of an anthropologist.* New York: W. W. Norton.

Provus, Malcolm. (1971). *Discrepancy evaluation.* Berkeley, CA: McCutchan.

Quine, W. V. (1953). *From a logical point of view.* Cambridge, MA: Harvard University Press.

Reason, Peter. (1981). *Patterns of discovery in the social sciences,* by Paul Diesing: An appreciation. In Peter Reason & John Rowan (Eds.), *Human inquiry: A sourcebook of new paradigm research.* New York: John Wiley.

Reason, Peter, & Rowan, John (Eds.). (1981). *Human inquiry: A sourcebook of new paradigm research.* New York: John Wiley.

Reed, Alan, & Schoenfelder, J. Laurie. (1979). CLOC, a general purpose concordance and collocation generator. In D. E. Ager, F. E. Knowles, & J. Smith (Eds.), *Ad-*

vances in computer-aided literary and linguistic research: Proceedings of the Fifth International Symposium on Computers in Literary and Linguistic Research. Birmingham, England: AMLC.

Reese, W. L. (1980). *Dictionary of philosophy and religion.* Atlantic Highlands, NJ: Humanities.

Reinharz, Shulamit. (1979). *On becoming a social scientist.* San Francisco: Jossey-Bass.

Reinharz, Shulamit. (1981). Implementing new paradigm research: A model for training and practice. In Peter Reason & John Rowan (Eds.), *Human inquiry: A sourcebook of new paradigm research.* New York: John Wiley.

Reinharz, Shulamit. (1983a). Experiential analysis; A contribution to feminist research. In Gloria Bowles & Renate Duelli Klein (Eds.), *Theories of women's studies.* London: Routledge & Kegan Paul.

Reinharz, Shulamit. (1983b). Feminist research methodology groups: Origins, forms, functions. In Vivian Patraka, and Louise A. Tilly (Eds.), *Feminist re-visions: What has been and might be.* Ann Arbor: University of Michigan, Women's Studies Program.

Reinharz, Shulamit, Bombyk, Marti, & Wright, Janet. (1983). Methodological issues in feminist research. *Women's Studies International Forum, 6,* 437-454.

Reiss, Albert J., Jr. (1959). The sociological study of communities. *Rural Sociology, 24,* 118-130.

Reynolds, D. (1980/1981). The naturalistic method of educational and social research. *Interchange, 11,* 77-89.

Richards, Audrey I. (1939). The development of field work methods in social anthropology. In F. C. Bartlett et al., *The study of society* (pp. 272-316). London: Kegan Paul.

Richardson, Stephen A. (1952). Training in field relations skills. *Journal of Social Issues, 8,* 43-50.

Ripley, Randall B., & Franklin, Grace A. (Eds.). (1975). *Policy-making in the federal executive branch.* New York: Free Press.

Rist, Ray. (1981). Shadow versus substance: A reply to David Fetterman. *Anthropology and Education Quarterly, 12,* 81-82.

Rosenblatt, Roger. (1983, February 21). The Commission report: The law of the mind. *Time,* p. 39.

Rosengren, Karl E. (Ed.). (1981). *Advances in content analysis.* Beverly Hills, CA: Sage.

Ross, D. (1979) Beyond the concordance: Algorithms for description of English clauses and phrases. In D. E. Ager, F. E. Knowles, and J. Smith (Eds.), *Advances in computer-aided literary and linguistic research: Proceedings of the Fifth International Symposium on Computers in Literary and Linguistic Research.* Birmingham, England: AMLC.

Rowan, John. (1981). A dialectical paradigm for research. In Peter Reason & John Rowan (Eds.), *Human inquiry: A sourcebook of new paradigm research.* New York: John Wiley.

Ruebhausen, Oscar M., & Brim, Orville G., Jr. (1966). *Privacy and behavioral research.* Washington, DC: Office of Education, U.S. Department of Health, Education and Welfare. (Reprinted from the *Columbia Law Review,* 1965, *65,* 1184.)

Russell, Bertrand. (1913). On the notion of cause. *Proceedings of the Aristotelian Society, 12* and *13,* 1-26.

Ryan, Mary P. (1979). Femininity and capitalism in antebellum America. In Zillah R. Eisenstein (Ed.), *Capitalistic patriarchy and the case for socialist feminism.* New York: Monthly Review Press.

Sadler, D. Royce. (1981). Intuitive data processing as a potential source of bias in educational evaluations. *Educational Evaluation and Policy Analysis, 3,* 25-31.

Scheffler, I. (1967). *Science and subjectivity.* Indianapolis: Bobbs-Merrill.

Schneider, David M. (1983). The coming of a sage to Samoa. *Natural History, 6,* 4-10.

Schofield, R. E. (1964). Joseph Priestley, the theory of oxidation, and the nature of matter. *Journal of the History of Ideas, 25,* 285-294.

Schofield, R. E. (1970). *Mechanism and materialism: British natural philosophy in an age of reason.* Princeton, NJ: Princeton University Press.

Schon, D. A. (1979). Generative metaphor: a perspective on problem-setting in social policy. In A. Ortony (Ed.), *Metaphor and thought.* Cambridge: Cambridge University Press.

Schulman, Paul R. (1975). Non-incremental policy-making: Notes toward an alternative paradigm. *American Political Science Review, 69,* 354-370.

Schultz, Alfred. (1970). *On phenomenology and social relations.* Chicago: University of Chicago Press.

Schutz. A. (1967). *The phenomenology of the social world.* Evanston, IL: Northwestern University Press.

Schwandt, Thomas A. (1980). *Some consequences of the value-free claim for the conduct of inquiry.* Unpublished qualifying paper, Inquiry Methodology, School of Education, Indiana University.

Schwartz, Morris S., & Schwartz, Charlotte, G. (1955). Problems in participant observation. *American Journal of Sociology, 60,* 343-354.

Schwartz, Peter, & Ogilvy, James. (1979). *The emergent paradigm: Changing patterns of thought and belief.* Analytical Report 7, Values and Lifestyles Program. Menlo Park, CA: SRI International.

Schwartz, Peter, & Ogilvy, James (1980, June). *The emergent paradigm: Toward an aesthetics of life.* Paper presented at the ESOMAR meeting, Barcelona, Spain.

Scott, W. Richard. (1963). Field work in a formal organization: Some dilemmas in the role of observer. *Human Organization, 22,* 162-168.

Scriven, Michael. (1971). Objectivity and subjectivity in educational research. In L. G. Thomas (Ed.), *Philosophical redirection of educational research* (71st Yearbook of the National Society for the Study of Education, Part 1). Chicago: University of Chicago Press.

Scriven, Michael. (1973). Goal-free evaluation. In Ernest R. House (Ed.), *School evaluation: The politics and process.* Berkeley, CA: McCutchan.

Sechrest, Lee. (Ed.). (1979). *Unobtrusive measurement today.* San Francisco: Jossey-Bass.

Sells, Saul B. & Travers, R.M.W. (1945). Observational methods of research. *Review of Educational Research, 40,* 394-407.

Shapiro, Letty Ann. (1982). *How undergraduate students study in college: An emergent inquiry.* Unpublished doctoral dissertation, Indiana University.

Shenker, Israel. (1981). After 340 years, Galileo may beat the Inquisition. *Smithsonian, 12,* 90-96.

Sheppard, R. Z. (1981, October 19). The way to treat a lady. *Time,* p. 101.

Shulman, Lee S. (1981). Disciplines of inquiry in education: An overview. *Educational Researcher, 10,* 5-12.

Skagestad, Peter. (1981). Hypothetical realism. In Marilynn B. Brewer & Barry E. Collins (Eds.), *Scientific inquiry and the social sciences.* San Francisco: Jossey-Bass.

Skrtic, Thomas, Guba, Egon G., & Knowlton, H. Earle. (1985). *Interorganizational special education programming in rural areas: Technical report on the multisite naturalistic field study.* Washington, DC: National Institute of Education.

Smith, Louis M. (1979). An evolving logic of participant observation, educational ethnography, and other case studies. *Review of Research in Education, 6,* 316-77.

Smith, Mary Lee. (1981). Naturalistic research. *Personnel and Guidance Journal, 59,* 585-589.

Smith, Nick L. (Ed.). (1983). *Dimensions of moral and ethical problems in evaluation.* Paper and Report Series, No. 92, Research on Evaluation Program. Portland, OR: Northwest Regional Educational Laboratory.

Spradley, J. P. (1979). *The ethnographic interview.* New York: Holt, Rinehart & Winston.

Spradley, J. P. (1980). *Participation observation.* New York: Holt, Rinehart & Winston.

Stake, Robert E. (1967). The countenance of educational evaluation. *Teachers College Record, 68,* 523-540.

Stake, Robert E. (Ed.). (1975). *Evaluating the arts in education: A responsive approach.* Columbus, OH: Merrill.

Stake, Robert. (1977). Some alternative presumptions. *Evaluation News,* (3), 18-19. (no volume number listed).

Stake, Robert E. (1978). The case-study method in social inquiry. *Educational Researcher, 7,* 5-8.

Stake, Robert E. (1980, April). *Generalizations.* Paper presented at the annual meeting of the American Educational Research Association, Boston.

Stake, Robert E. (1982, December). *The meta-evaluation case study of Cities in Schools.* Unpublished manuscript in draft form.

Stake, R. E., & Easley, J. A., Jr. (Eds.). (1978). *Case studies in science education.* Urbana: University of Illinois, Center for Instructional Research and Curriculum Evaluation.

Stavrianos, Bertha K. (1950). Research methods in cultural anthropology in relation to scientific criteria. *Psychological Review, 57,* 334-344.

Stokey, Edith, & Zeckhauser, Richard. (1978). *A primer for policy analysis.* New York: W. W. Norton.

Strouse, Jean. (1981, October 19). Mrs. Trilling on Mrs. Harris. *Newsweek,* p. 101.

Stufflebeam, Daniel L., Foley, Walter J., Gephart, William J., Guba, Egon G., Hammond, Robert L., Merriman, Howard O., and Provus, Malcolm. (1971). *Educational evaluation and decision-making.* Itasca, IL: Peacock.

Suchman, Edward A. (1967). *Evaluative research.* New York: Russell Sage Foundation.

Tannahill, Reay. (1980). *Sex in history.* New York: Stein & Day.

Taylor, Gordon Rattray. (1983). *The great evolution mystery.* New York: Harper & Row.

Tennant, Harry. (1981). *Natural language processing.* New York: Petrocelli.

Tranel, Daniel D. (1981). A lesson from the physicists. *Personnel and Guidance Journal, 59,* 425-429.

Travers, Robert M.W. (1980). Letter to the editor. *Educational Researcher, 10,* 32.

Trice, H. M. (1956). Outsider's role in field study. *Sociology and Social Research, 41,* 27-32.

Tyler, Ralph W. (1949). *Syllabus for Education 360.* Chicago: University of Chicago Press.

Ukeles, Jacob B. (1974). Policy analysis: Myth or reality? *Public Administration Review, 37,* 223-228.

Van Maanen, John. (1982). *Varieties of qualitative research.* Beverly Hills, CA: Sage.

Vidich, Arthur J. (1955). Participant observation and the collection and interpretation of data. *American Journal of Sociology, 60,* 354-360.

Warner, Edwin. (1981, April 6). Trouble on the team. *Time,* pp. 8-11.

Wax, Rosalie H. (1952). Reciprocity as a field technique. *Human Organization, 11,* 34-37.

Wax, Rosalie. (1971). *Doing fieldwork: Warnings and advice.* Chicago: University of Chicago Press.

Webb, E. J., Campbell, D. T., Schwartz, R. D., & Sechrest, L. (1966). *Unobtrusive measures.* Chicago: Rand McNally.

Webb, E., Campbell, D., Schwartz, R., Sechrest, L., & Grove, J. B. (1981). *Nonreactive measures in the social sciences.* Boston: Houghton Mifflin.

Weber, Max. (1947). *The theory of social and economic organization* (T. Parsons, Ed.; A. Henderson & T. Parsons, Trans.). New York: Free Press.

Weick, Karl E. (1976). Educational organizations as loosely coupled systems. *Administrative Science Quarterly, 21,* 1-19.

Weinberg, Martin S., & Williams, Colin J. (1972). Fieldwork among deviants: Social relations with subjects and others. In Jack Douglas (Ed.), *Research on deviance* (pp. 165-186). New York: Random House.

Weiss, Carol H. (1980). Knowledge creep and decision accretion. *Knowledge: Creation, Diffusion, Utilization, 1,* 381-404.

When doctors play God: The ethics of life and death decisions. (1981, August 31). *Newsweek,* pp. 48-54.

Why Haig quit: Contexting it. (1982, July 5). *Newsweek,* p. 24.

Wicker, Tom. (1981, April 5). Haig's down, but not out yet. *Herald-Times* (Bloomington, IN).

Wiemann, John M. (Ed.). (1983). *Nonverbal interaction.* Beverly Hills, CA: Sage.

Wildavsky, Aaron. (1979). *Speaking truth to power: The art and craft of policy analysis.* Boston: Little, Brown.

Wiles, David K. (1981). The logic of y = f(×) in the study of educational politics. *Educational Evaluation and Policy Analysis, 3,* 67-73.

Will, George. (1983, July 24). Lawrence, Kansas. *Journal World,* p. 5a.

Willems, Edwin P., & Raush, Harold L. (1969). *Naturalistic viewpoints in psychological research.* New York: Holt, Rinehart & Winston.

Williams, P. N. (1978). *Investigative reporting and editing.* Englewood Cliffs, NJ: Prentice-Hall.

Wimsatt, William C. (1981). Robustness, reliability, and overdetermination. In Marilynn B. Brewer & Barry E. Collins (Eds.), *Scientific inquiry and the social sciences.* San Francisco: Jossey-Bass.

Winkler, Karen J. (1980, January 14). A question of historical malpractice. *Chronicle of Higher education,* pp. 2-3.

Wolcott, Harry F. (Ed.). (1981, Fall). Teaching fieldwork to educational researchers: A symposium [Special issue]. *Anthropology and Education Quarterly, 14.*

Wolcott, H. F. (1973). *The man in the principal's office: An ethnography.* New York: Holt, Rinehart & Winston.

Wolf, Fred Alan. (1981). *Taking the quantum leap.* San Francisco: Harper & Row.

Wolf, Robert, & Tymitz, Barbara. (1976-1977). Ethnography and reading: Matching inquiry mode to process. *Reading Research Quarterly, 12,* 5-11.

Wolfgang, A. (1977). The silent language in the multicultural classroom. *Theory into Practice, 16,* 145-152.

Wulff, K. W. (Ed.). (1979). *Regulation of scientific inquiry: Societal concerns with research*. Boulder, CO: Westview.

Young, Frank W., & Young, Ruth C. (1961). Key informant reliability in rural Mexican villages. *Human Organization, 20,* 141-148.

Young, M.F.D. (1971). *Knowledge and control: New directions for the sociology of education*. London: Macmillan.

Zelditch, Morris, Jr. (1962). Some methodological problems of field studies. *American Journal of Sociology, 67,* 566-576.

Zigarmi, D., & Zigarmi, P. (1978, March). *The psychological stresses of ethnographic research*. Paper presented at the annual meeting of the American Educational Research Assocation, Toronto.

Zukav, Gary. (1979). *The dancing Wu-Li masters*. New York: Bantam.

Index

412   NATURALISTIC INQUIRY

About the Authors

Yvonna S. Lincoln is Associate Professor of Education at the University of Kansas. She holds the baccalaureate degree in history and sociology from Michigan State University (1967), the master's degree in history from the University of Illinois (1970), and the doctorate in higher education, organizational theory, and program evaluation from Indiana University (1977). She has served on the faculty of Stephens College, taught at Indiana University, and been a member of the Kansas faculty for seven years. A sociological field study of the outmigration of high school youth from economically depressed rural areas of the northern peninsula of Michigan early in her career, coupled with her later extensive work in history and historiography, made her uncomfortable with conventional research and evaluation tools as she encountered these during her doctoral work. At the same time, she began to realize that field methods as utilized by sociologists were firmly based on the same epistemological and methodological assumptions as the scientific method. She felt a strong need to search out approaches in which the reality of field research as she had experienced it could be made to match the assumptions of the guiding inquiry paradigm. Ongoing experience with a number of evaluation contracts reinforced that need. Shortly after the completion of her doctoral work she began an active collaboration with Egon Guba, whose own interets in this area had begun to jell, which resulted in an earlier book (*Effective Evaluation: Improving the Usefulness of Evaluation Through Naturalistic Approaches;* Jossey-Bass, 1981), in the present volume, and in a forthcoming volume (*Organizational Theory and Inquiry: The Paradigm Revolution;* Sage) for which she is the editor and major contributor and Guba a chapter author. She and Dr. Guba have jointly and individually written numerous other papers related to naturalistic inquiry as an emergent paradigm (see references).

Egon G. Guba is Professor of Education at Indiana University, Bloomington. He holds the baccalaureate degree in mathematics and physics from Valparaiso University (1947), the master's degree in statistics and measurement from the University of Kansas (1950), and the doctorate in quantitative inquiry from the University of Chicago (1952). He has served on the faculties of Valparaiso University, the University of Chicago, the University of Kansas City, the Ohio State University (where he directed the Bureau of Educational Research and Service for five years), and Indiana University (where he was Associate Dean for Academic Affairs of the School of Education for six years). His interest in naturalistic inquiry was initially stirred by the experience of directing the field evaluation of Project Discovery, jointly sponsored by Encyclopedia Brittanica

Films and the Bell and Howell Corporation. The study was intended to determine how teachers in four field sites would adapt to and utilize hundreds of thousands of dollars worth of films and filmstrips (and accompanying projection and room-darkening equipment) placed in their own buildings and instantaneously accessible. It was soon apparent that normal methodological approaches would not be useful to this end and field techniques were substituted. Stimulated by this experience, Guba began to question the applicability of conventional methods not only to evaluation but to other forms of disciplined inquiry as well. At the same time, encounters with Yvonna Lincoln, who raised disturbing questions about evaluation methods, fueled his own growing skepticism. His at first almost tacit questioning became more formalized in the summer of 1977, when, as a visiting scholar at the Center for the Study of Evaluation at UCLA, he developed a monograph on the applicability of naturalistic methods to evaluation. Since then he has devoted himself to the further explication of naturalistic inquiry, with the results that have already been noted above.

Egon Guba and Yvonna Lincoln enjoy a domestic as well as a professional partnership, practicing a commuting marriage between their respective home bases in Bloomington, Indiana, and Lawrence, Kansas.

AGAINST LIBERATION